Download Worksheets on Nolo.com

You can download the worksheets in this book at:

 www.nolo.com/back-of-book/MT.html

We'll also post updates whenever there's an important change to the law affecting this book—as well as articles and other related materials.

More Resources
from Nolo.com

 Legal Forms, Books, & Software
Hundreds of do-it-yourself products—all written in plain English, approved, and updated by our in-house legal editors.

 Legal Articles
Get informed with thousands of free articles on everyday legal topics. Our articles are accurate, up to date, and reader friendly.

 Find a Lawyer
Want to talk to a lawyer? Use Nolo to find a lawyer who can help you with your case.

NOLO
LAW for ALL

NOLO

The Trusted Name

(but don't take our word for it)

"In Nolo you can trust."

THE NEW YORK TIMES

"Nolo is always there in a jam as the nation's premier publisher of do-it-yourself legal books."

NEWSWEEK

"Nolo publications . . . guide people simply through the how, when, where and why of the law."

THE WASHINGTON POST

"[Nolo's] . . . material is developed by experienced attorneys who have a knack for making complicated material accessible."

LIBRARY JOURNAL

"When it comes to self-help legal stuff, nobody does a better job than Nolo . . ."

USA TODAY

"The most prominent U.S. publisher of self-help legal aids."

TIME MAGAZINE

"Nolo is a pioneer in both consumer and business self-help books and software."

LOS ANGELES TIMES

17th Edition

Solve Your Money Troubles

Attorneys Amy Loftsgordon and Cara O'Neill

SEVENTEENTH EDITION	JULY 2019
Editor	AMY LOFTSGORDON
Book Design	TERRI HEARSH
Cover Design	SUSAN PUTNEY
Proofreading	SUSAN CARLSON GREENE
Index	VICTORIA BAKER
Printing	BANG PRINTING

ISSN 2163-0348 (print)
ISSN 2325-4947 (online)

978-1-4133-2647-5 (pbk)
978-1-4133-2648-2 (ebook)

This book covers only United States law, unless it specifically states otherwise.

Please note

We believe accurate, plain-English legal information should help you solve many of your own legal problems. But this text is not a substitute for personalized advice from a knowledgeable lawyer. If you want the help of a trained professional—and we'll always point out situations in which we think that's a good idea—consult an attorney licensed to practice in your state.

About the Authors

Amy Loftsgordon is a legal editor and writer at Nolo, focusing on foreclosure, debt management, and personal finance. She edits a number of Nolo books and is the coauthor of *The Foreclosure Survival Guide* and *Credit Repair*. Before joining Nolo, Amy worked in the areas of foreclosure and debt collections for over 15 years. She has drafted foreclosure-related training programs and loan servicing compliance procedures, as well as written training manuals for collection operations. Amy was also instrumental in preparing expert reports used in lawsuits against banks and servicers accused of mishandling collection, preforeclosure, loss mitigation, foreclosure, and REO processes.

Amy received a B.A. from the University of Southern California and a law degree from the University of Denver Sturm College of Law. She is licensed to practice law in Colorado.

Cara O'Neill is a bankruptcy and litigation attorney in Northern California and a legal editor and writer with Nolo. Before joining Nolo, she practiced in the area of criminal and civil litigation, and bankruptcy. She also served as an administrative law judge, and taught law courses as an adjunct professor. In 1994, she received her law degree from the University of the Pacific, McGeorge School, graduating Order of the Barristers—an honor society recognizing excellence in courtroom advocacy. Cara has edited, authored, and coauthored several Nolo books, including *How to File for Chapter 7 Bankruptcy*, *Chapter 13 Bankruptcy*, *The New Bankruptcy*, and *Credit Repair*.

Acknowledgments

Many thanks to the previous co-authors of *Money Troubles*, John Lamb and Margaret Reiter, for their many years of consumer and debt experience. And a special thank you to Lina Guillen, Nolo's family law expert, who updated Chapters 2 and 12 of this edition.

—The Nolo Editorial Staff

Table of Contents

Your Legal Companion to Solving Your Money Troubles

If you have debt problems, you are not alone. Millions of honest, hardworking people have trouble paying their debts.

Before and during the recession of 2008, consumer debt rose steadily. Subsequently, consumers became more frugal and lenders implemented stricter standards. As the economy recovered, creditors began loosening their lending standards. Now, people are once again borrowing money and accruing debt, sometimes more than is manageable.

But there is good news. By knowing your legal rights and asserting them, you can free yourself of bill collectors and give yourself a fresh financial start. Often, it's easier than you think to affirmatively deal with your debt problems. Debtors who assert themselves might get more time to pay, get a lower interest rate, have late fees dropped, settle debts for less than the full amount, and even reestablish credit.

Solve Your Money Troubles can help you take charge. This book does the following things.

Tells you how recent changes in the law can help you. *Solve Your Money Troubles* explains how laws and regulations provide more protections and benefits to consumers. By knowing your rights under these laws and regulations, you can better avoid abusive credit practices, take advantage of consumer benefits, and manage student loan debt.

Shows you how to protect your legal rights. For example, *Solve Your Money Troubles* explains in detail how to respond to a lawsuit, wage attachment, car repossession, foreclosure proceeding, or property lien.

Helps you understand your debts. If you know how the law categorizes different kinds of debts, you'll know what kinds of collection efforts you can expect from different creditors and which negotiating strategies you can try with them.

Shows you effective alternatives to bankruptcy. Bankruptcy is the right tool for many people to deal with their debt problems, but it's not for everyone. *Solve Your Money Troubles* shows you the steps you can take to avoid bankruptcy when appropriate.

Gives you practical tips and information. *Solve Your Money Troubles* contains sample letters and statements that you can use to:

- get debt collectors off your back
- ask a creditor for more time to pay, or
- ask a creditor to lower the amount of a bill.

Solve Your Money Troubles also refers you to places to lodge a complaint or ask for information and contains charts of state laws summarizing consumer laws, debt collection laws, credit reporting agency regulations, and more.

Helps you evaluate your individual debt situation. *Solve Your Money Troubles* includes several online worksheets to help you figure out how much you earn, how much you owe, how much you spend, and what you own.

With these worksheets, you can prioritize your debts, determine whether you are judgment proof, and decide what approach to take: Do nothing, negotiate with your creditors, get outside help negotiating, or possibly file for bankruptcy.

Get Legal Updates and More at Nolo.com

You can find the online companion page to this book at:

www.nolo.com/back-of-book/MT.html

There you will find the worksheets referenced throughout the book, important updates to the law, legal information not contained in the book, podcasts, links to online articles on debt, credit, and bankruptcy, links to helpful calculators regarding credit cards and loans, and more.

How Much Do You Owe?

To successfully plan your strategies with your creditors, you need to come to terms with your total amount of debt. You might find this uncomfortable, but most credit counselors will tell you that people tend to overestimate their debt burdens.

You'll start by comparing what you bring in each month with what you owe on your monthly expenses (such as food, housing, and utilities) and your other debts (for example, student loan payments).

However, having a ballpark idea of the amount of your income and debt burden is not enough to tackle your debt problem. Getting precise numbers is a crucial part of the process, so you won't want to skip it. This process will help you prioritize your debts and help you decide which strategies to use to solve your money troubles.

To figure out how much you earn and how much you owe, follow the instructions on the next pages and use the online worksheets. If you are married or have jointly incurred most of your debts with someone, fill out the worksheets together.

You'll find the worksheets mentioned throughout this book on the online companion page at:

www.nolo.com/back-of-book/MT.html

Warning Signs of Debt Trouble

If you have panic attacks when you try to figure out your total debt burden, you'll feel better if you skip this chapter and come back to it when you are better able to confront the information. Before doing that, however, ask yourself the following questions. If you answer "yes" to any one of them, you are probably in—or headed for—serious debt trouble:

- Are your credit cards charged to the maximum?
- Do you use one credit card to pay another?
- Are you making only minimum payments on your credit cards while continuing to incur charges?
- Do you skip paying certain bills each month?
- Have creditors closed any accounts on you?
- Have you taken out a debt consolidation loan? Are you considering doing so?
- Have you borrowed money or used your credit cards to pay for groceries, utilities, or other necessities (for reasons other than convenience or to get perks on a credit card)?
- Have you bounced any checks?
- Are debt collectors calling and writing you?

How Much Do You Earn?

Start by figuring out how much you earn each month. You'll need a calculator and your pay stubs to complete the first online worksheet—Worksheet 1. You'll enter your monthly income from each source. If you are paid more often than monthly, use the instructions on Worksheet 1 to convert your pay to a monthly amount. If you have income that doesn't fit into one of these categories, list it as "other."

How Much Do You Owe?

On Worksheet 2, you list your debts. Gather the documents that show payments on all your debts, the total amount owed on each debt, and any amount past due, including any interest or fees that have been added. Be as thorough and complete as possible. Once complete, Worksheet 2 will tell you exactly how much you should be paying each month to remain current on your debts, as well as how far behind you are. Here's how to fill it out.

Column 1: Debts and other monthly living expenses. In Column 1, enter the type of debt. Don't enter a debt more than once. So, for example, if you already deducted from your income in Worksheet 1 a debt that is paid out of your paycheck, such as child support, don't deduct that same debt again here.

If you are married, you may not be certain which debts are yours and which belong to your spouse. If your marriage is intact and

you're having mutual financial problems, enter all your debts in Column 1. If, however, you are separated or recently divorced, or are married but having financial problems of your own, see Chapter 2 for help on figuring out which debts you are obligated to pay. If you generally share expenses and maintain a household with someone else, consider combining your income and paying all of your debts with joint funds, regardless of who actually incurred the debt. Enter both partners' debts in Column 1.

Column 2: Outstanding balance. In Column 2, enter the entire outstanding balance on the debt. For example, if you borrowed $150,000 for a mortgage and still owe $125,000, enter $125,000. Your latest account statement might list the entire outstanding balance. If not, the creditor's automated telephone system or online account information might provide the information you need. If you can't get the balance and you prefer not to talk to the creditor, use your best guess for now.

Columns 3 and 4: Monthly payment and total past due amount. In Columns 3 and 4, enter the amount you currently owe on the debt. If the lender has not established set monthly payments—for example, for a doctor's bill—enter the entire amount of the debt in Column 4 and leave Column 3 blank. If the debt is one for which you make regular monthly payments—such as your car loan or mortgage—enter the amount of the monthly payment in Column 3 and the full amount you are behind (monthly payment multiplied by the number of missed months, plus any fees or charges that have been added, like over-limit fees or late payment charges) in Column 4.

For credit card, department store, and similar debts, enter the monthly minimum payment in Column 3 and your entire balance in Column 4. But keep in mind that eventually you should make more than the minimum payment on your credit cards. (Chapter 10 discusses the danger of making only minimum payments each month.)

Column 5: Is the debt secured? In Column 5, indicate whether the debt is secured or unsecured. A secured debt is one for which a specific item of property (called "collateral" or "security") guarantees payment. The most common type of secured debt occurs when you sign a credit agreement (sometimes called a security agreement) that allows the creditor to take a particular item of property under certain specified conditions—without suing you first. Examples of conditions that might allow the creditor to take your property include your failure to make a payment, your failure to maintain insurance on the property, or your failure to comply with the payment agreement in some other way. Typically, you sign a credit agreement giving the creditor a security interest in your property when you finance a car purchase, get a mortgage, get a second, third, or additional loan on your home, or buy an appliance or a piece of furniture with store credit.

A creditor might also be able to secure its debt without your agreement by filing a lien against your property. This can happen in two circumstances. First, the creditor can file a lien if the law specifically allows for it. An example is a mechanic's lien— the law specifically states that a worker or material supplier can file a lien against your real property if you or the contractor fail to pay them. Second, a creditor can file a lien against your property if it has sued you and obtained a judgment against you. This is called a judgment lien.

Unsecured debts are typically bank credit card debt; bills owed for utilities, medical, or legal services; student loans; and spousal or child support.

Secured property is usually something very important, like your car or house. Because such property can be taken quickly, without the delay of a lawsuit, secured debts are usually a high priority for you to pay.

Specify the collateral the creditor is entitled to take if you default on the debt. (After you have read more about whether a debt is secured or not in Chapter 4, you can come back and review Column 5 to see if you need to make any changes.)

Column 6: What priority is the debt? Leave Column 6 blank until you read Chapter 4. It will help you prioritize the debts.

Add it up. When you've entered all your debts in the worksheet, total up Columns 2, 3, and 4. Column 2 represents the total balance of all your debts, even though some of it may not be due now; Column 3 represents the amount you are obligated to pay each month; and Column 4 shows the amount you would have to come up with to get current on all your debts.

RELATED TOPIC

Don't forget your other expenses. None of us have monthly expenses consisting entirely of loan or credit payments. We also have to pay rent and buy groceries, pay for movies and restaurants, buy clothing and household goods, and so on. These other expenses are covered in Chapter 3, and now might be a good time to review that information. By listing your non-debt-payment expenditures, you will get a more complete picture of your finances to help you determine how much you have left to repay debts.

If You're Married, Divorced, or Separated

Single people who have never been legally married owe their debts and own their property as individuals. No fuss, no muss. Marriage, domestic partnership, or a civil union, however, makes things more complicated. If one of these relationships has been part of your life, this chapter helps you understand:

- what debts you owe individually
- what debts you owe jointly with your current or former spouse or partner
- what property you own individually
- what property you own jointly with your current or former spouse or partner, and
- when your property may be taken for each type of debt.

Each state has its own rules on marital property ownership, but the most important factor is whether you live in a community property or an equitable distribution state. This largely determines who owes and owns what in the marriage.

Keep in mind that while this chapter explains general legal principles, every state has its own set of laws, and many exceptions exist. It's important to verify the rules in your particular state.

Community Property States

Alaska *	Louisiana	Tennessee**
Arizona	Nevada	Texas
California	New Mexico	Washington
Idaho	South Dakota	Wisconsin

* If spouses agree in writing

** If spouses set up a valid community property trust

Community Property States

The basic idea of community property is that in most situations a husband and wife act as a "community," acquiring property and incurring debts as a unit.

Who Owes What Debts?

If you live in a community property state (listed above), which spouse owes which debts depends on when the debts were incurred and whether you are still married, separated, or divorced.

Debts Incurred While You're Single

All debts someone incurs before the marriage or after the marriage is dissolved are owed only by that person.

EXAMPLE: Oliver owes $3,000 for a computer he bought before he married Caitlin. Only Oliver is responsible for that debt.

Debts Incurred During Marriage and Before Permanent Separation

In community property states, most debts incurred during the marriage and before a permanent separation are joint debts for which both spouses are liable. This is true even if only one spouse is a party to the debt—for example, because only that spouse signed the paperwork. There is an exception to this rule: If the creditor wasn't aware the spouse was married and was looking only to the spouse who incurred the debt for payment, it's possible that the creditor might be limited to collecting from the contracting spouse only.

EXAMPLE: On a credit application for a kayak purchase, Daniel claims to be unmarried and does not include his spouse's income or job. Daniel's spouse might not be liable to pay for the kayak if Daniel defaults.

Typically, the couple's community property is liable only for debts incurred for the benefit of the community, but this is not always true. For example, if a spouse owes a separate income tax debt, community property might be taken to pay this debt. The nonobligated spouse may be entitled to reimbursement of his or her share of community assets used to pay these kinds of debts.

Debts Incurred During Marriage but After Permanent Separation

For debts incurred during the marriage but after the spouses have permanently separated, the following rules apply: If the debt was incurred for necessities of life for either spouse or their children, then both spouses are responsible for paying it. If both parties agree to a purchase, or the purchase is necessary to maintain a jointly owned asset (for example, to repair a leaky roof in the home they own together), then both are liable. If one spouse incurs a debt for that spouse's benefit only (a vacation, for example), only that spouse owes the debt.

EXAMPLE 1: After permanently separating from her husband, Paula uses her credit line at Home Depot to fix the roof of the family home that they own together. Because everyone in the family benefits from the repaired roof, Paula's husband would also be liable for repayment of the debt.

EXAMPLE 2: Megan, a married woman, uses her separate credit card to charge a trip to the Bahamas that she is taking with her lover. Ira, the spouse who stayed at home, would not be liable for the debt because it does not benefit him and the creditor was not expecting to look to his assets for repayment.

Who Owns What Property?

If you live in a community property state, property is owned jointly or separately, depending on:

- when you got the property
- whether you were married, separated, or divorced at the time you got it
- how you got the property—for example, whether it was a gift or an inheritance, purchased with separate property, or purchased with joint property
- how you hold title to the property— for example, if title to your house is in both your and your spouse's names, it is community property (if separate property is used to pay down the mortgage or make repairs, however, a mixture of community and separate property results)
- whether you and your spouse entered into a written premarital agreement that changes the property law rules that would otherwise apply
- whether you or your spouse "transmuted" (changed) the character of the property in a written agreement, and

- whether community or separate funds were used to acquire the property and whether the two funds were "commingled" (mixed together).

When the form of ownership is not stated in writing and the asset was purchased with commingled funds, then the asset is considered to be entirely community property unless one of you can clearly trace and identify your separate contribution.

Property Acquired Before Marriage or After Divorce

All property owned by a spouse prior to marriage or acquired after the marriage is dissolved by a final court judgment is that spouse's separate property, unless its nature is "transmuted" in writing or community funds are used to finance or improve the property, in which case it may become partly community.

EXAMPLE: Gillian, a single woman, owns stock worth $10,000. She marries Otis; they stay married for four years and then separate and later divorce. At that time, the stock has appreciated in value to $25,000. Because Gillian came into the marriage with the stock and held it in her name alone, it is all her separate property.

Property Acquired During Marriage and Before Permanent Separation

All property acquired by one or both spouses during the marriage and before a permanent separation is community property, unless either of the following is true:

- The spouse acquired the property as a gift or an inheritance.
- The property was clearly paid for with funds that were the separate property of one spouse, and only that spouse's name appears on the account, deed, title, or ownership papers.

EXAMPLE 1: Andy and Portia get married while they are still in school. Andy graduates and starts a business that generates a large income. Both the business and the income are community property, because they were acquired during the marriage.

EXAMPLE 2: Courtney and David marry in a community property state. Shortly afterward, Courtney learns that she has inherited $50,000 from her grandmother. This is Courtney's separate property.

EXAMPLE 3: David's brother gives him an expensive bass-fishing boat. This is a gift, so it is David's separate property even though he's married when he acquires it.

EXAMPLE 4: Before getting married, Mohammed owned a valuable coin collection. After his marriage, Mohammed sells the collection and buys the equipment necessary to start a radio station. The equipment is Mohammed's separate property because it was purchased with money from the sale of his separate property assets.

Property Acquired After Permanent Separation

All property acquired by a spouse during the marriage but after a permanent separation is separate property.

EXAMPLE: Ella wins the lottery after she and Alex permanently separate. If Alex and Ella divorce and then get back together, the lottery winnings would still be Ella's separate property.

What Property Is Liable for Payment of Debts?

If you live in a community property state, which property is liable for payment of which debts depends on two factors: whether the property is separate or community property, and whether the debt is an individual debt of one spouse or a joint debt of both spouses.

Separate Property

The separate property of a spouse is liable for that spouse's individual debts (debts incurred solely for his or her benefit). The separate property of one spouse is also liable for all joint debts. However, it is not liable for the other spouse's individual debts (debts incurred solely for his or her benefit).

EXAMPLE 1: Bradley and Grace are married and live in a community property state. Each came into the marriage with a sizable inherited trust fund. Each trust fund is separate property of the spouse who owns it, because the trust funds were received through inheritance and acquired prior to the marriage. Bradley's trust fund is liable for his premarital debts, and Grace's trust estate is liable for her premarital debts. But neither trust is liable for the other spouse's premarital debts.

EXAMPLE 2: Shortly after they are married, Bradley and Grace buy a business. The business fails and they become delinquent on the note. The holder of the note can go after both trusts, even though they are separate property, because the debt was jointly incurred.

Community Property

Community property is liable for all joint debts (debts incurred for the benefit of the community). In addition, one spouse's share of community property is liable for that spouse's separate debts.

EXAMPLE 1: Andrew and Stephanie marry in a community property state and buy a home. Because they bought the home during the marriage, it is community property. Without telling Stephanie, and using his separate credit history, Andrew signs a promissory note for $100,000 to buy a new Tesla Model S, which he parks at his office. Several months later, Andrew can't make the payments, and the holder of the note comes calling. The creditor can go after Andrew's separate property and can also assert a claim against half of the home's value, which is Andrew's share of the community property.

EXAMPLE 2: Andrew and Stephanie had permanently separated when Andrew bought the Tesla Model S. This would make no difference, because Andrew's share of the community property home is still liable for Andrew's separate debts.

Equitable Distribution States

In equitable distribution states (all states except the community property states listed above), the family courts apply an equitable distribution method to property and debt division. Instead of requiring a 50/50 split, courts determine property division based on what is fair and equitable under the circumstances of the case.

Who Owes What Debts?

If you live in an equitable distribution state, who owes what debts depends on when the debt was incurred and, in some instances, what the debt was for.

Debts Incurred Before Marriage or After Divorce

All debts incurred by a spouse before the marriage begins or after it has ended are that spouse's individual debts.

EXAMPLE: Tyler owes $2,000 on a smart home surveillance system he purchased before he married Lauren. The $2,000 is Tyler's separate debt, and only he is responsible for it.

Debts Incurred During Marriage

All debts incurred by the spouses jointly during the marriage are joint debts. All debts incurred by one spouse during the marriage and before permanent separation are usually separately owed by that spouse unless any of the following is true:

- The creditor looked to both spouses for repayment or considered both spouses' credit information.
- The debt was incurred for family necessities, such as food, clothing, or shelter.
- The debt was incurred for medical purposes (in some, but not all, of equitable distribution states).

EXAMPLE 1: On a credit application for the purchase of a kayak, Kinayah does not include her spouse's income or job. Kinayah's spouse, Rachel, would not be liable to pay for the kayak if Kinayah defaulted.

EXAMPLE 2: Goldie uses her personal credit card to pay for her husband's emergency room visit. In about half the states, this would be a joint debt; in the other half, only Goldie would be liable for the debt.

Debts Incurred After Permanent Separation

An individual is generally liable for debts incurred after permanent separation, unless the debt was incurred for family necessities.

EXAMPLE: After Dewevai and Sam permanently separate, Sam borrows $1,000 to pay their child's school tuition. Because this is a family necessity, both Dewevai and Sam are liable for the debt.

Who Owns What Property?

In equitable distribution states, how property is owned before, during, and after marriage is governed by when the property was acquired, whether the property was paid for with joint or separate funds, and how title is held.

Property Acquired Before Marriage or After Divorce

All property one spouse owned before marriage, acquired during marriage by gift or inheritance, or acquired after divorce is that spouse's separate property.

EXAMPLE: When Sarah and Josh got married, Sarah owned five pairs of Louboutin heels, and Josh owned an expensive craft beer-making kit. The shoes are Sarah's separate property, and the home brewery is the separate property of Josh.

A spouse's separate property remains separate unless it's "commingled" (mixed together) with marital property or the other spouse's separate property. If this happens, that separate property might become partly marital property, completely marital property, or even the other spouse's separate property, all depending on what can be proved by tracing back where the property came from and how it became commingled.

Property Acquired During Marriage

Because state laws differ, you will need to consult an attorney or do some legal research to learn about the marital property laws of your state (see Chapter 18). Generally speaking, in the District of Columbia and a large majority of states, property and earnings accumulated during marriage are marital (joint) property and are subject to division and equitable distribution in a divorce proceeding. Equitable distribution means a court will divide the property equally—or in a way the court believes is fair—but not necessarily a 50/50 split.

In some equitable distribution states, the rules for property ownership during marriage, whether or not the spouses are permanently separated, are as follows:

- All property acquired by a spouse during marriage that has a title document in that spouse's name only (such as a deed or an investment account) is that spouse's individual property.

  EXAMPLE: After Ashley and Carlos marry, they buy a house and put the house in the name of Carlos only. The house is the separate property of Carlos, but Ashley might be able to claim an interest in the home's equity.

- All nontitled property acquired by a spouse during marriage with that spouse's separate funds is that spouse's separate property.

  EXAMPLE: Cherish, who is married to Scott, uses her personal savings account to buy a computer. Cherish owns the computer as her separate property.

- All property acquired by the spouses jointly, or acquired by one spouse from joint funds, is joint property (unless title is taken in the name of one spouse only).

  EXAMPLE: Cherish and Scott use their joint savings account to buy matching kitchen appliances. Appliances don't come with title documents, so Cherish and Scott own them jointly.

What Property Is Liable for Debts?

If you live in an equitable distribution state, which spousal property is liable for which debts depends on whether the property is separately or jointly owned; whether separately owned property was used to pay for necessities; and, in some states, whether joint property is titled "tenancy by the entirety."

Separate Property

A spouse's separate property is generally liable for that spouse's separate debts. It is also liable for the other spouse's separate debts if they were incurred for necessities.

EXAMPLE 1: Ralph and Ryan, a married couple, live in a home that Ralph owns in his name only. A bank sues Ryan for payment of a $5,000 loan he took out to pay for a vacation to Italy. Because this is Ryan's separate debt and the house is Ralph's separate property, the bank can't use the equity in the house to collect Ryan's separate debt.

EXAMPLE 2: Instead of a vacation, Ryan uses the loan to repair the roof on the house. Because the debt is for a necessity benefiting Ralph as well as Ryan, Ralph's separate property, including the house, is liable for the debt.

Joint Property

With one major exception, a couple's jointly owned property is liable for the separate debts of each spouse as well as for their joint debts.

Joint Property Held as Tenancy by the Entirety

The exception is this: In a number of equitable distribution states, a married couple can hold property jointly in the form of "tenancy by the entirety." In many of these states, the creditor of either spouse cannot reach property held as "tenancy by the entirety" unless the debt is a joint debt.

EXAMPLE 1: Kai and Irina, a married couple, own a home in Wyoming in both their names as "tenants by the entirety." Kai runs up a large balance on his personal credit card. Even though the home is jointly owned, the credit card company has no recourse against it because of the way title is held.

EXAMPLE 2: Same case, but the home is held in both names as joint tenants. Here, Kai's creditor could proceed against the home as jointly owned property.

Rules for Domestic Partnerships and Civil Unions

Although same-sex marriage is now legal across the United States, several states continue to offer same-sex couples the option of entering into civil unions or domestic partnerships which extend many of the rights and obligations of marriage—including those that apply to debts and property ownership. Currently, Colorado, Hawaii, Illinois, and New Jersey offer civil unions. California, Washington D.C.,

Maine, Nevada, Oregon, Washington, and Wisconsin offer domestic partnerships (or limited forms of domestic partnership).

Civil union and domestic partnership laws in the 11 states that offer them attempt to treat registered same-sex couples as married for purposes of state law, but the specific rights and benefits for these relationships vary somewhat, depending on where you live. If you have registered and live in one of these states, you and your partner are subject to your state's rules for married couples, including community or equitable distribution property rules. But if you're registered and living in a state that does not recognize your civil union or domestic partnership, you might not receive the same rights as married couples under your state's laws. If you have questions about your property rights or are worried about liability for your partner's debts, you should consult with a local lawyer to learn about your state's laws and how they apply to your situation.

For more information, see *A Legal Guide for Lesbian & Gay Couples*, by Emily Doskow and Frederick Hertz (Nolo).

Create a Budget and Control Spending

Creating a budget is an extremely important step when it comes to controlling your spending. You'll review all of your income sources, living expenses, debts, and savings to figure out the best way to spend your money—and where you can cut back. While it might not be an especially fun task, this process will allow you to come up with a plan to distribute the money that you do have.

If you'd rather not create a budget yourself, contact a nonprofit debt counseling agency. These organizations primarily help people negotiate with creditors, but they can also help you set up a budget for free or for a nominal fee. (See Chapter 18 for information on finding a reliable debt counselor.)

Figure Out Where Your Money Goes

Before creating a budget that limits how much you spend, take some time to figure out exactly how much money you spend now. To do this, use online Worksheet 5: Daily Expenses.

Here's how to use the form:

1. Make eight copies of the form or reproduce the contents of the form on your phone, tablet, or computer, whichever you're most likely to use from day to day so you can record your expenditures for two months.

It's important to track expenses for a couple of months to make sure your budget isn't based on a week or two of unusually high or low expenses. If you are married or live with someone with whom you share expenses, you should each record your expenditures.

2. Select a Sunday to begin recording your expenses.
3. Record that Sunday's date in the blank at the top of one copy of the form.
4. Carry that week's form with you at all times.
5. Record every expense you pay by cash or cash equivalent. "Cash equivalent" means check, ATM or debit card, or automatic bank withdrawal. Be sure to include bank fees. Also, don't forget savings and investments, such as deposits into savings accounts, certificates of deposit, or money market accounts, or purchases of investments such as stocks or bonds.

Don't record expenses you charge on a credit card. Your goal is to get a picture of where your cash goes, and you won't actually pay off a credit card purchase right away. When you make a payment on a credit card bill, that's when you should list the items your payment covered as an expense on your sheet. If you don't pay the entire bill each month, list older items you charged that total a little less than the amount of your payment, and attribute the rest of your payment to interest.

EXAMPLE: On Sunday night, you pay your bills for the week and make a $450 payment toward your $1,000 credit card bill. The $1,000 includes a $500 balance from the previous month, a $350 airline ticket, a few restaurant meals, and accrued interest. On your daily expenditures form for Sunday, list $450 in the second column. In the first column, identify corresponding expenses—for example, the plane ticket and one restaurant meal—and attribute some of it to interest. In this example, you have to look at your credit card statements from previous months.

6. At the end of the week, repeat this process with another copy of the form. Go back to Step 3.

7. Include expenses you pay once a month or so, such as $50 for your child's swim class, $10 for an office party gift, or a $20 donation to a local charity. Also include monthly payments such as your rent or mortgage; educational loans; credit card payments; car payments; insurance payments; utility, telephone and cell phones, Internet, and cable bills; and other similar expenses.

8. Once you've tracked expenses for eight weeks, list on any form under the category "Other Expenditures" seasonal, annual, semiannual, or quarterly expenses you incur but did not pay during your two-month recording period. The most common are property taxes, car registration fees, magazine subscriptions, tax preparation fees, and insurance payments. But there are others. For example, if you are recording expenses in the winter months, don't forget summer expenses such as camp fees for your children or pool maintenance. Similarly, if you do this exercise in the summer, be sure to account for your annual holiday gift expenses. Think broadly and be thorough.

Be tough-minded—if you omit any money, your picture of how much you spend, and your budget, will be inaccurate.

At the end of two months, review Worksheet 5. Are you surprised at the dollar total or at the number of items you purchased? Are you impulsively spending your money, or do you tend to consistently spend it on the same types of things?

Make a Spending Plan

After you've kept track of your expenses for two months and have figured out your income (from Chapter 1, using Worksheet 1), you're ready to create a spending plan, or budget. Your twin goals in making a spending plan are to give you control over how you spend your money so you can use it for the things you have decided you really need and want, rather than overspending on impulse buys, and to start saving money—an essential part of getting your finances under control and eventually rebuilding your credit.

To make and use a monthly budget, follow these steps:

1. Make several copies of Worksheet 6: Monthly Budget. (Keep in mind that you don't have to use a paper version of this form. For some people, it will be easier to use a spreadsheet on a smartphone, tablet, or laptop.) Making a budget you can live with is a process of trial and error, and you may have to draft a few plans before you get it right.

2. Get out Worksheet 1: Monthly Income (from Chapter 1) and Worksheet 5: Daily Expenses.

3. Review the expenses listed on Worksheet 6. As you'll see, they are divided into common categories, such as home expenses, food, and transportation. If you don't have any expenses in a particular category, you can cross it out or simply leave it blank. If you have a type of expense that isn't listed on the form, add that category to a blank line.

4. In the first column (labeled "Projected"), list your average actual monthly expenses in each category. Calculate these amounts by adding together your actual expenses for the two months you tracked, then dividing the total by two. If you have seasonal, annual, or quarterly expenses, include a monthly amount for those as well. For example, if you pay $3,600 in property taxes for the year, you should list a projected expense of $300 a month ($3,600 ÷ 12) in this category.

5. Add up all of your projected monthly expenses and enter the total on the line marked "Total Expenses" at the bottom of the "Projected" column.

6. Enter your projected monthly income (from Worksheet 1) below your projected total expenses.

7. Compare your projected income to your projected expenses. If you are spending more than you earn, you'll either have to earn more or spend less to make ends meet. Unless you're anticipating a big raise, planning to take on a second job, or selling valuable assets, you'll probably have to lower your expenses. Review each category to look for ways to cut costs. Rather than trying to cut out an entire expense, look for expenses you can reduce slightly without depriving yourself of items or services you really need. For example, you might be willing to forgo one trip to a restaurant per month, subscribe to a less expensive cable package, or spend less on clothing. (See Chapter 5 for ways to cut expenses.)

8. Return to your budget and enter the adjustments you came up with. When you're finished, add up these new figures and come up with a new total expense amount. If it's less than your income, your budget is complete. If not, go back and try to find other places to cut back.

9. Label the remaining columns with the months of the year. Unless you prepared your budget on the first of the

month, start with next month. During the course of the month, keep track of and update your expenses in each category.

10. At the end of the month, total up how much you spent. How did you do? Are you close to your projected figures? If not, go back and try to make some changes to keep the numbers in balance.

Check your figures periodically to help you keep track of how you're doing. Don't think of your budget as etched in stone. If you do, and you spend more on an item than you've budgeted, you'll only find yourself frustrated. Use your budget as a guide. If you constantly overspend in one area, don't berate yourself: Instead, change the projected amount for that category and find another place to cut. Keep in mind that a budget is just a tool to help you recognize what you can afford and where your money is going.

Are You a Compulsive Spender?

Habitual overspending can be just as hard to overcome as excessive gambling or drinking. If you think you may be a compulsive spender, you'll need to get a handle on your spending habits.

Debtors Anonymous, a 12-step support program similar to Alcoholics Anonymous, has programs nationwide. You can also attend meetings over the phone or online. For local meetings and other information, visit www.debtorsanonymous.org or call 800-421-2383.

Create Good Spending Habits and Avoid Financial Pitfalls

There are no magic rules that will solve everyone's financial troubles. But the following suggestions should help you stay out of financial hot water. If you have a family, everyone will have to participate—no one person can do all the work alone. So, make sure your spouse or partner and children understand that the family is having financial difficulties and agree together to take the steps that will lead to recovery including:

- **Create a realistic budget and stick to it.** This means periodically checking it and readjusting your figures and spending habits.
- **Don't impulse buy.** When you see something in a store or online you hadn't planned to buy, don't purchase it immediately. Take time to think it over. It's unlikely you'll end up buying it.
- **Avoid sales.** Buying a $500 item on sale for $400 isn't a $100 savings if you didn't need the item to begin with. It's spending $400 unnecessarily.
- **Get medical insurance.** Even a stopgap policy with a large deductible can help if a medical crisis comes up. You can't avoid medical emergencies, but living without medical insurance is an invitation to financial ruin.
- **Charge items only if you can afford to pay for them now.** If you don't currently have the cash, don't charge based on future income—sometimes future income doesn't materialize. If you must charge, a good rule of thumb is not to

charge anything that won't exist when the statement arrives (such as meals, groceries, or movie tickets).

- **Live without credit for a while.** Credit counselors often advise paying cash to cut your spending. Even if you don't spend less, you will likely still save by not having the cost of carrying a balance on the cards.

- **Avoid large rent or house payments.** Obligate yourself only for what you can now afford, and increase your mortgage payments only as your income increases. If you are married and both working, keep the payments low enough that you can handle them even if one of you loses his or her job. Consider refinancing your house if your payments are unwieldy and you can qualify for a lower interest rate. Another possibility is to ask your mortgage lender to modify your existing loan to make the payments more affordable. (See Chapter 8 for information on refinancing and other strategies for dealing with high mortgage payments.)

- **Avoid cosigning or guaranteeing a loan for someone.** Your signature obligates you as if you were the primary borrower. You can't be sure that the other person will pay.

- **Avoid joint obligations with people who have questionable spending habits—** even a spouse or partner. If you incur a joint debt, you're probably liable for it all if the other person defaults.

- **Don't make high-risk investments.** Opt for certificates of deposit, money market funds, and government bonds over speculative real estate, penny stocks, and junk bonds.

Prioritizing Your Debts

Some debts are more important than others. This chapter helps you to prioritize your debts so that you can decide which ones are essential to pay and which you might ignore for a while.

Often, creditors with low-priority debts will be pushing hardest for repayment. But paying the noisiest creditors might not be in your best interest. Instead, base your decision about which debts to pay first on the consequences of not paying a debt. If they are severe, paying the debt is essential. If they aren't, payment is a lower priority. It follows that repayment of secured debts is almost always a top priority, because if you don't pay, you stand to lose valuable property and still could be liable for paying the debt.

If You're Considering Bankruptcy

If you're thinking about filing for bankruptcy, read Chapter 15 before you make any payments on your debts. It doesn't make sense to pay debts you will eventually erase (discharge) in bankruptcy. Also, some payments made during the 90 days before filing for bankruptcy— or one year for payments that benefit a relative or business associate—might be canceled and the funds returned to the bankruptcy court.

Secured and Unsecured Debts

Legally, debts fall into two primary categories: secured or unsecured. Before you can prioritize your debt, you need to understand the difference, because the consequences of not paying a secured debt differ tremendously from those of not paying an unsecured debt.

Secured Debts

A secured debt means that a specific item of property, sometimes called "collateral" or "security" guarantees payment of the debt. The most common type of secured debt is one that you voluntarily enter into with a creditor when you make a credit agreement. It's usually referred to in the credit agreement as a "security interest." If you don't pay, most states let the creditor take the property without first suing you and getting a court judgment. And, the creditor might not even have to give you notice before taking the property. If you've ever had a car repossessed when you failed to make a loan payment, you already know how secured debts work. Some examples of these follow.

Mortgages or home equity loans. The real estate is security for the loan. If you don't pay, the lender can foreclose on the property, even if you used the money for something besides your home.

Loans for cars or other vehicles, for which the vehicle is the security. If you fail to pay, the lender can repossess the vehicle.

Store charges with a security agreement— for example, when you buy furniture or a major appliance using a store credit card. If you don't pay back the loan, the seller can take the property. Most store purchases, however, are unsecured, and even on the secured ones, you don't have to let the creditor into your home to get the property; so, practically speaking, you are unlikely to lose this kind of secured property, if it is inside your home.

Personal loans from finance companies. Your personal property, such as furniture or electronics equipment, may be pledged as security. Federal law lets certain creditors use household goods (for example, appliances, a television, kitchenware, a wedding ring, or personal effects) as collateral only if you're buying the goods with the money you're borrowing or the creditor takes possession of the goods when it makes the loan. (16 C.F.R. §§ 444.1, 444.2.)

A creditor might also be able to secure its debt without your agreement by filing a lien against your property. This can happen in certain circumstances where a law specifically allows for it. It can also happen when a creditor files a lien against your property after it has sued you and obtained a judgment against you. Here are some examples:

- **Lawsuit judgments against you.** If someone sues you and wins a money judgment, a judicial lien can be placed on your real estate (or in many states, on other property as well). The creditor could foreclose and force the sale of the property, but that's uncommon

because it's so expensive. Instead, the creditor usually waits until you sell the property, when the lien gets paid off.

- **Liens created by law.** For example, someone who works on your house and doesn't get paid can place a lien on your home, without going to court. This is called a mechanic's or materialman's lien. In some states, a homeowners' association can do this if you don't pay your association dues. Although these creditors might be able to foreclose (force a sale and get paid from the proceeds), usually they wait to get paid until you sell the property.
- **Tax liens.** Federal, state, and local governments can place liens on your property if you owe delinquent taxes.

Unsecured Debts

An unsecured debt is one that is not secured by collateral. For example, when you charge clothing on your credit card, the clothes aren't collateral for your repayment. So if you don't pay, the bank that issued the credit card has only one option if you don't pay voluntarily: to sue you and try to collect what it's owed.

Most debts are unsecured, including:

- credit card purchases or cash advances
- gasoline and department store card charges, unless the agreement you signed to open the account contained a security agreement
- loans from friends and relatives

- student loans
- alimony and child support
- medical, dental, legal, or other bills for professional services
- rent
- utility bills
- church or synagogue dues, and
- union dues.

Take a look back at Worksheet 2, Column 5 now and see if you need to make any changes to mark whether the debt is secured or not, and, if secured, to note the security. You might need to review the documents you signed when you got the credit to see if they say anything about a security interest in any property. To learn more about credit contracts and understanding loan terms, read Chapter 10.

High-Priority Debts

If you could face serious, even life-threatening, consequences as a result of letting a debt slide, it's a high-priority debt. Usually the most important debts are those secured by collateral that you want to keep, such as your house. However, an unsecured debt might also be essential.

Even if you don't hear from these creditors, don't assume they won't collect their debts. Because secured collectors have such a powerful weapon (they can seize the collateral if you stop making payments), they don't need to hound you the way that collectors with lower-priority debts do.

EXAMPLE: Josh is taking an experimental heart medication for which his health insurance only pays 50%. His outstanding bill to his pharmacist is currently $350. This is an unsecured debt, but if he doesn't pay it, he won't be able to get the prescription refilled there. Because he has a poor credit history, he probably couldn't get credit elsewhere. Unless Josh can find other assistance, such as subsidized prescription benefits, this is a high-priority debt.

Other high-priority debts are described below.

Rent. Payments for a place to live are obviously essential. Many people get into serious debt problems because they fail to stay current on their rent. Unless you know you are going to move and have a new place to live, make paying your rent a top priority. If necessary, ask your landlord for a temporary rent reduction. Explain your financial problems and when you'll be able to resume making full payments. Other alternatives include moving into a less-expensive unit owned by the landlord or doing repairs or providing services in return for reduced rent. In any of these cases, be sure you get written confirmation of your agreement from your landlord. (See Chapter 6 for a sample letter confirming an agreement with a landlord.)

Mortgage. Home mortgages and equity loans or lines of credit are secured by your home. If you can't pay, you could lose your home in foreclosure. If you're a homeowner in financial trouble, consider looking for a roommate to help with the mortgage. You might be able to negotiate reduced payments or qualify for a mortgage reduction. (See Chapter 8 for information about working something out with your mortgage lender.) Although the usual rule is to treat your secured debts, especially the loan on your home, as top priority, that is not always the best option. Be sure to consider your alternatives: Sell the house and use the proceeds to pay your creditors and rent a place to live; try to arrange a short sale if your home is worth less than the loans on it; try to get the lender to accept a deed in lieu of foreclosure; or stop making mortgage payments during the period of time it takes the creditor to complete the foreclosure process. (See Chapter 8 for more information about how to deal with mortgage or equity loan payments you can't afford or to learn about foreclosure.)

 CAUTION

Carefully consider the pros and cons before you sell your house. Your house might be worth more in six months or a year than it is today. Selling it could deprive you of an asset that could make you money over time and lock you out of the housing market once you are back on your feet. On the other hand, if you bought your house with little or nothing down, you have no equity in it, and your mortgage payment is growing (perhaps due to an adjustable interest rate), it might not make sense to try to keep the house. Before you decide, see Chapter 6 and Chapter 8 for alternatives to consider if you are behind on your mortgage or an equity loan.

Utility bills. Being without gas, electricity, heating oil, water, or a telephone is dangerous. You might not have to pay parts of your telephone bill to keep basic phone service (see Chapter 3). For ways to reduce your utility bills, see Chapter 5.

Child support. Your children might be depending on this money to meet their basic needs. Not paying can also land you in jail. If you really cannot pay the required child support, and your income has dropped sharply, you can ask the court to reduce your obligation. (See Chapter 12.)

Car payments. If you need your car to keep your job, make the payments. If you don't, consider selling it to avoid repossession, which will inevitably occur if you fall behind on the payments. You might be able to use the money to buy a cheaper car. If you sell the vehicle, but the sales amount falls short of what you owe your lender, in most cases, you will have to make up any difference. If you don't sell the vehicle and it's repossessed, the lender will sell it at a fraction of its value, and the difference you owe will probably be even bigger. (See Chapter 7 for more information.)

If you lease your car, you can't just sell it. Instead, you must call the leasing company and arrange to end the lease early. You will have to pay any past-due payments and an early termination penalty (which can be large), but at least you will be out from under the monthly lease payments.

Don't even consider transferring the car to someone who promises to make the monthly payments for you. Such a transfer almost certainly will violate your purchase contract or lease and probably is illegal. And if the business or person who takes the car doesn't make the payments, you'll be responsible for the resulting default on the loan, which will become part of your credit record.

In deciding whether to hold onto the car, consider the amount of your monthly insurance payment, which you'll have to keep current if you keep the car. Lenders usually consider failure to maintain insurance to be an event of default, which can lead to repossession. Also, the lender can obtain insurance to protect its interest in the car, which usually is very expensive, and hold you responsible for the premiums.

Other secured loans. Secured debts, you'll recall, are linked to specific items of property such as a house or car. In addition, debts on boats, RVs, and expensive electronic gear are likely to be secured. This means that the property (called collateral or security) guarantees payment of the debt. If you don't repay the debt, most states let the creditor take the property without first suing you and getting a court judgment. If you don't care if the property is taken, don't worry too much about missing a payment or two. If the property is something you cannot live without, however, and you think the creditor will take it, you'll need to keep that debt current. Or try to work out a compromise with the creditor. (See Chapter 6.) Remember: If you bought the boat, RV, or home theater system using your equity line or a second

mortgage, missing a payment is just like missing a mortgage payment—you could wind up losing your house.

Unpaid taxes. If the IRS is about to take your paycheck, bank account, house, or other property, negotiate to set up a repayment plan immediately. You have the right to an installment agreement if all of the following are true:

- You owe $10,000 or less.
- You've paid your income tax and filed returns on time for the past five years.
- You haven't entered into an installment agreement with the IRS during that period.
- The IRS determines that you can't pay the full amount of tax you owe when it's due.
- You agree to pay the full amount within three years. (See IRS Form 9465-FS, *Installment Agreement Request*, available at www.irs.gov.)

Even if the amount you owe exceeds $10,000, or it will take you more than three years to pay, or you've defaulted on an agreement with the IRS in the past, the taxman might still be willing to negotiate a payment plan if you can convince the agency that you'll stick with it (although you might have to pay a fee, along with interest and penalties). If you owe less than $50,000, you can file an online application to set up an installment plan. (For tips on negotiating a compromise for taxes owed, see Chapter 6, "Income Taxes.")

RESOURCE

More information on tax negotiation. The best resource available to help you deal with the IRS is *Stand Up to the IRS*, by Erica Pless and Frederick W. Daily (Nolo).

Medium-Priority Debts

Some debts fall into a middle ground. Not paying them won't cause dire consequences in your personal life but could prove painful nonetheless. In deciding whether to pay these debts, consider your relationship with the creditor—is this person a friend, valued family member, someone you depend on? You'll naturally want to honor those debts if you can. Also, consider whether the creditor has begun collection efforts. You might be tempted to ignore a creditor who has contacted you for the first time but will want to deal with the one who is about to get a judgment against you. On the other hand, it might be easier to negotiate terms of payment earlier in the process. And you might be able to reduce some of these priority debts. (See Chapter 6.)

Here are some types of debts that might be of medium priority for many people. But depending on your particular situation, some of these might be high or low priority for you.

Car insurance. In some states, you can lose your driver's license if you drive without insurance. Also, lenders that finance car sales usually consider failing to maintain insurance to be a default. That can lead either to a lender's buying insurance that is often much more expensive than what you could find and charging you for it, or repossessing your vehicle. Getting car insurance after you let your insurance lapse will also probably cost more than keeping your existing insurance current. For ways to lower the cost of your car insurance, see Chapter 5, "Reducing Insurance Policy Premiums."

Medical insurance. Especially if you are under a physician's care, you'll want to continue making payments on your medical insurance.

If you have medical insurance through work and you lose your job, you'll probably be able to keep your insurance coverage for at least 18 months and, in some cases, 36 months (extended coverage like this is referred to as "COBRA"), but you will have to pay the whole premium plus 2% to compensate your ex-employer for continuing to handle the coverage.

For details about COBRA, go to the Department of Labor's website at www.dol.gov (run a search for "COBRA" and follow the link).

Or you can sign up for health insurance coverage under the Affordable Care Act.

In a few situations, such as losing your job-based coverage, getting married, or having a baby, you might qualify for a special enrollment period. (If you qualify for a special enrollment period, you can enroll in the program outside the annual open enrollment period. For details, go to www.healthcare.gov.)

Homeowners' insurance. If you don't keep up your homeowners' insurance, your lender could treat this as a default on the loan and start foreclosure. More likely, however, the lender will just buy insurance, sometimes at a much higher cost than your current insurance, and charge you that additional amount as part of your mortgage payment.

Car payments for a car that is not essential for your job. If not having a car is extremely inconvenient, making car payments might make sense.

Items your children need. Paying for a tutor for your child might not seem essential, but if the alternative is to have your child grow up unable to read, you probably want to keep paying for the help. Or, look for a free tutor through your child's school or local community center.

Court judgments. A creditor who wins a court judgment can collect it by taking a portion of your wages or other property. If a judgment creditor is about to grab some of your pay, paying this creditor might be essential even if the original debt wasn't.

Federal student loans. Although federal and federally backed student loans are unsecured, those debts might merit higher priority in certain circumstances. For example, a defaulted student loan can keep you from getting a new student loan or grant to go back to school. Also, student loan collectors have special rights that are not available to the average unsecured creditor. For example, the IRS can intercept your income tax refund to collect a defaulted student loan.

Agencies that guarantee student loans and the Department of Education can garnish up to 15% of your disposable income (see Chapter 11). Finally, student loans are very difficult to discharge in bankruptcy. Don't confuse federal or federally backed student loans (for example, FFEL, PLUS, Direct, and Stafford) with private student loans. Private student loans are not offered or backed by the federal government. Private student loans generally don't have the special collection rights that federal or federally backed student loans have, but private loans are just as difficult to discharge in bankruptcy. (See Chapter 11 for ways to reduce your monthly student loan payments or even eliminate them altogether.)

Low-Priority Debts

A low-priority debt is one with no immediate or devastating effects if you fail to pay. Paying these debts is a desirable goal, but not essential.

Credit cards. In most cases, credit card debt fits into the low-priority category. True, the consequences of not paying credit card debt have increased significantly in recent years, and if you're on the edge financially, the effects of not paying could be devastating. But in general, if you don't pay your credit card bill, the worst that will happen before the creditor sues you is that you will lose your credit privileges. If you need a credit card, for example, to charge an upcoming medical operation or to rent a car on a business trip, keep—and pay the minimum on—one card, and put that card on your high-priority list.

If you don't make your minimum credit card payments on time, the card issuer might increase your interest rate and fees on the card. Some credit card companies will raise your rate on their card if you fail to pay *another* creditor. (To learn more, see Chapter 10.)

If, after prioritizing your debts, you decide that paying off your entire credit card bill is a realistic goal, making minimum payments should be a short-term remedy only. You'll have to pay more than the minimum if you want to make a dent in the debt. (See Chapter 10 for more on the dangers of making only minimum payments.)

Department store and gasoline charges. If you don't pay these bills, you'll probably lose your credit privileges for those cards. If the debt is large enough, you might be sued. If the creditor took a security interest in personal property you bought using the credit card (this is unusual), the creditor might try to repossess the property, although vehicles are usually the only things creditors bother to repossess. Keep in mind that even if the creditor wants to take property that is inside your home, you do not have to let the creditor into your home.

Loans from friends and relatives. You might feel a moral obligation to pay, but these creditors should be the most understanding with you.

Online streaming services and subscriptions. These debts are never essential.

Legal, medical, and accounting bills. These debts are rarely high priority. A medical bill might be, however, if you are still receiving necessary treatment from the provider to whom you owe money.

Other unsecured loans. Remember, an unsecured loan is not tied to any item of property. The creditor cannot take your property. If you refuse to pay, the creditor can collect from you only by suing you and obtaining a court judgment. These unsecured debts are rarely, if ever, essential to pay first. Keep in mind, however, that a court judgment turns an otherwise low-priority, unsecured debt into a high-priority one. A creditor can collect on a court judgment by taking a portion of your wages or other property. (See Chapter 13.)

Review Your Worksheets

Take a look back at Column 6 in Worksheet 2. Mark with a "1" each of the high-priority debts. Mark the medium-priority debts with a "2" and the low-priority debts with a "3." Add up the monthly payments for the items with high priority. At the end of each month, do you have enough to pay everything with high priority? If you don't, read it over. Change the least important debts you marked with a 1 to medium priority, and keep changing debts until you can pay each month what is high priority. If you can pay everything with high priority, add up the items with medium priority. If you can't pay both the high priority and medium priority, you might need to change some medium-priority items to low priority. Remember: Some things must go. You can't afford to pay for everything you'd like to. This doesn't mean you're a bad person. It just means you need to buckle down and tighten up your finances for a while.

Don't get discouraged if you can't meet what you think are your medium or even just your high priorities. Chapter 6 will help you negotiate with your creditors so you might be able to reduce your payments or debts. Chapter 5 will help you figure out ways to reduce your expenses or find more money to pay your debts. If you do manage to reduce your payments or debts, or gain increased money to pay them, remember to go back to change your worksheets to reflect your current income and debts.

TIP

Stick to your plan. If you decide to stop paying some lower-priority debts, temporarily or permanently, don't deviate from your plan just because creditors are breathing down your neck. If you give in to creditors that are trying to collect low-priority debts, you might not have enough money to pay your essential debts. For example, if you pay a few dollars on an old hardware store bill just because its collector is the loudest or most persistent, you might face eviction or have your heat turned off because you don't have enough money left to pay the rent or utility bill.

Finding Money to Pay Your Debts

You might be considering several methods of raising cash to pay your debts. Before doing so, ask yourself if bankruptcy is a realistic option for you. (Chapter 14 can help you make this decision.) If it is, raising cash to pay debts you will ultimately erase in bankruptcy is a waste of your time and already-stretched resources. On the other hand, if you can raise the cash to pay off your debts with a reasonable amount of effort, avoiding bankruptcy is preferable. Whatever you do, it's a good idea to find ways to cut your expenses or get the benefits for which you are eligible.

Cutting expenses is probably the best place to start. Then consider ways to raise cash—since this might involve paying fees and costs, make sure the benefit outweighs the cost. You should also review benefits for which you might qualify to make your money go farther. Along the way, avoid options that sound tempting, but might end up digging you into a deeper financial hole. We discuss all of these strategies in this chapter.

Cut Your Expenses

An excellent way to increase your cash flow is to cut expenses. This might also help in negotiating with creditors—your efforts to live more frugally demonstrate how serious you are about getting your finances under control. To that end, keep a list of the changes you make.

There are many ways to cut expenses—some require bigger sacrifices than others. We start with those that require little sacrifice,

and then move on to cuts that might require greater sacrifice or financial reshuffling.

A few things to keep in mind:

- When deciding if a small change will help, calculate the savings over a year, not just over a week or month.
- Consider what you need to make you happy. According to studies of happiness, experiences (not purchases) are what make most people happy (assuming you've got your basic needs met). And often, the anticipation of a purchase provides more pleasure than the purchase itself.

 RELATED TOPIC

Servicemembers can cut expenses and more. Members of the armed services, reservists, and their dependents can reduce payments on credit obtained before active duty and stop collection efforts while on active duty. (See Chapter 6 for details.)

Cutting Expenses That You Don't Need

You can probably cut hundreds to thousands of dollars from your spending each year in ways that won't reduce your standard of living. Here are some ways to cut without feeling the bite.

Reducing Insurance Policy Premiums

You can often lower insurance costs by hundreds of dollars by reducing the amount of your coverage or increasing your deductibles. Just make sure you can afford the deductible if you do need to make a claim. You can often get better rates if you get car and homeowner's insurance from the same company. When shopping for better rates, see if your state department of insurance publishes rate comparisons. (You can find state insurance department websites from the National Association of Insurance Commissioners at www.naic.org.) Remember, some insurance is simply not worth the cost, so you might decide to get rid of it altogether (credit insurance or some kinds of expensive life insurance, for example).

Car insurance. Get the minimum coverage required by your state (check your state's DMV for these numbers) and opt for a high deductible. The longer you're with a carrier, the lower your rate is likely to be. But it still might be worth shopping around. If you find a better rate, ask your current carrier to match it.

Homeowners' insurance. It is harder to reduce homeowners' insurance because the lender won't want your home to be underinsured. But sometimes insurers insist on more insurance than is necessary. If you suspect this is the case, speak with your insurance agent and lender, and contact your state insurance agency for information on state requirements. You can also save money by choosing a higher deductible.

Medical insurance. Sometimes you can lower your monthly premium payment by agreeing to a higher deductible or a less expensive plan. But watch out for plans that are so bare-bones that they might fail you if you get a serious illness.

 TIP

The Affordable Care Act may help you save money. This law currently requires medical insurers to allow parents to cover their children until age 26, prevents insurance companies from denying coverage when you become ill, and eliminates annual and lifetime caps on coverage, among other things.

Life insurance. If you have a life insurance policy with a cash value, you usually can apply that money toward your premium payments. Or, reduce insurance premium payments by converting a whole or universal life policy (relatively high premiums and a cash value buildup) into a term policy (low premiums with no cash value). If you don't have any dependents, you don't need life insurance—get rid of it.

Private mortgage insurance. If you have at least 20% equity in your home, cancel your private mortgage insurance (PMI). PMI is meant to protect the lender if you put down less than 20% when you buy a home. But lenders rarely cancel the policy after you reach 20% equity.

A federal law applying to most mortgages obtained after July 29, 1999 requires lenders to automatically cancel PMI on the date the borrower's equity is expected to reach 22%, based on the original value of the property and the original schedule of payments (so it does not matter if the value of the property dropped). You must be current on payments. It also allows buyers with good payment histories to request cancellation of the PMI based on the original value, when either the original schedule of payments or actual payments (the borrower gets to choose) reaches 20%. For this early cancellation of the insurance, the lender might also require the borrower to show the value of the property is not less than the original value and certify there are no second mortgages on the property. Loans designated as "high risk" when made are not eligible for termination until the percentage reaches 23%. If the law doesn't apply to you, you can still contact your lender and request cancellation. Most will do so once the equity reaches 20%. Some states also have laws regulating PMI.

Other insurance and extended warranties. If you have credit insurance, accident insurance, extended warranties on goods you've bought, or other odd policies and can cancel them and get a substantial refund, do so. These types of insurance and warranties are seldom worth the cost.

Reducing Property Taxes

Have your home reassessed to lower your property taxes. Check with your local assessor's or similar office to learn how to do this.

Reducing Student Loan Payments

A variety of lower-cost payment plans based on your ability to pay are available to reduce your student loan payments. (See Chapter 11 for details.)

Reducing Utility Bills

Conserve gas, water, and electricity in your home. You can usually get a free energy audit from your local utility company.

Reducing Your Transportation Costs

Improve your gas mileage by tuning up your car, checking the air in the tires, and driving less. Try to carpool, work at home (telecommute), ride your bicycle, take the bus or train, and combine trips.

Reducing Recurring Bills

Carefully review your regular monthly bills for any charges you don't recognize and services you don't want (such as voice mail, call waiting, credit card protection plans, or a variety of so-called membership services).

Reducing Purchase Prices by Bargaining

According to *Consumer Reports* magazine, only about a quarter of people surveyed had tried bargaining when making purchases. Those who did haggle on such things as clothing, credit card fees, cellphone bills, furniture, electronics, and even medical services were successful. A great place to practice haggling is at a local farmers' market, especially toward the end of the day.

Reducing Other Expenses

The suggestions below require more sacrifice. These reductions might affect your lifestyle, but in some instances you might decide that the change is for the better. Where and how you cut will depend on your income, debt level, and standard of living.

If you have a large income but also high expenses and enormous debt, you might be able to cut expenses significantly if you:

- Take the children out of private schools.
- Move to a smaller house.

- Reduce the number of vehicles you own.
- Switch to less costly cars.
- Put off expensive vacations.
- Stop buying clothes or lavish gifts.
- Eat at home instead of going out.

If your savings from the steps above are not enough to deal with your debt, or you never spent money on private schools and fancy cars to begin with, here are some more modest suggestions for cutting expenses and making your income go further:

- Shrink food costs by clipping coupons, buying sale items, buying in bulk, and shopping at discount outlets.
- Discontinue cable, or at least the premium channels.
- Look for less expensive ways to spend time with family and friends. Take walks, do charity work, use public parks.
- Buy store brands. Most rank as well as name brands.
- Reduce your phone bill, especially your cellphone bill. Use Wi-Fi when you can, cut your phone insurance, and get rid of features you don't use (like enhanced voicemail). Look into saving money by switching plans within your carrier, or changing carriers. If you do change, avoid buying a new phone or entering into a one- or two-year contract with a large early-termination penalty. Consider getting a prepaid cellphone or pay-as-you-go service.
- Carry your lunch to work; eat breakfast and dinner at home.
- Put off major purchases unless they're absolutely necessary. If you must buy a vehicle, an appliance, or furniture, try to get it secondhand.
- Give experience gifts instead of buying gifts. For example, give a "Get Out of Dishwashing Free" card or a gift certificate for your gardening services.

For more suggestions, visit www.consumer reports.org, www.bankrate.com, or other websites.

Increase Your Income

The first and most obvious way to raise more money is to earn money. We're willing to bet that this has already occurred to you, if you're working now. There are a number of ways to earn more money:

- Increase the hours you work (for many people this means getting a second job or starting a business on the side).
- Increase the amount you earn in the time you work (this might mean switching jobs).
- Have every person in your family work who is capable of working, even students.
- Make sure your investments are giving you the best possible return.

Consider these options, but be sensible. Any of these strategies could backfire. Taking a second job or having your spouse go back to work could mean you're suddenly paying a lot for babysitters, fast food, transportation, dry cleaning, and additional income taxes, with precious little net benefit to your overall situation. Most new businesses fail and many require additional debt to get off the ground. Nor will it help to work yourself into a nervous breakdown or invest in speculative schemes.

Keep in mind that you need cash on hand to pay your living expenses and essential debts (such as housing and transportation). Prioritizing your needs, becoming more conservative about expenses, and searching for any benefits you might qualify for could show faster results that will get you through the rough times and set you on a good course for the future.

Get Some of Your Tax Refund Early

Many people have much more money withheld from their paychecks than they will need to pay their income taxes for the year. By adjusting the withholding to better match your income, you can get more money in each paycheck to help you keep current or catch up on bills each month, instead of having to wait until the end of the year to get a refund. Ask your employer for a new IRS W-4 form or get the form from the IRS website at www.irs.gov. Complete it by following the instructions or by getting help from a tax adviser.

The goal is to adjust your withholding so you can keep more of your income but still not owe any taxes at the end of the year. If you are afraid of withholding too little and then owing a large tax payment or penalty in April, use the IRS's withholding calculator to assist you in determining the correct withholding amount. Go to the IRS's website at www.irs.gov and search for "withholding calculator." If your income is regular, the IRS form should do a good job of estimating the correct withholding amount. Even if you do owe more taxes at the end of the year, you can usually pay this amount over time. (See Chapter 6 for more information on this.) You most likely won't have to pay a penalty, unless your underpayment is way out of line. If you have any doubts, get help from a tax adviser.

Once you return the form to your employer, you should start seeing more money with your next paycheck. (If your income increases, don't forget to readjust your W-4 withholding to match.)

Get Your Tax Refund Fast

Sometimes, getting a tax refund quickly will help you through a crisis, especially if the IRS owes you a lot.

If you're getting a refund, file your tax return early. You can file your return electronically and have your refund deposited directly into your account. But it's a bad idea to get a tax refund anticipation loan in the meantime; see "Avoid Tax Refund Anticipation Loans and Checks," below. See under "Other Free or Subsidized Government Services" for free tax preparation services available.

You should, however, be aware that as of 2017, if you claim the Earned Income Tax Credit or Additional Child Tax Credit on your tax return, the earliest that the IRS will issue your refund is February 15.

CAUTION

Student loan debtors: Don't count your dollars before they're hatched. If you are expecting a large tax refund—and you've defaulted on a student loan—don't count on seeing the money. Intercepting tax refunds is the method most frequently used by the government to collect outstanding student loan dollars. Yearly, the federal government pockets more than a billion dollars by grabbing tax refunds (without having to get a judgment first) from defaulted student loan borrowers. And if you legitimately owe the money, stopping a tax refund intercept is very difficult. For more information on student loan collections, see Chapter 11.

Sell a Major Asset

You can raise cash and keep associated costs to a minimum by selling a major asset, such as a car or, as a last resort, your house. This might be a good idea if you can no longer afford your house or car payments—or if you happen to have a second house or car you can do without.

Don't automatically decide to sell property. Try to be realistic about how much you can get for it and whether it's worthwhile to sell. For example, you might be better off keeping a useful car that's now worth less than its remaining loan balance. And remember, if you lease your car, you must return it to the lessor; you can't just sell it. If you decide to sell, you will net the most money if you own the property free and clear, although you should plan to pay income or capital gains taxes that could be due on the sale, and other expenses from the proceeds of the sale.

It is usually possible to sell property that you haven't finished paying off. You will almost always do better selling the property yourself rather than waiting to get cash back from a foreclosure or repossession sale. Those sales are not usually carried out in a way to get the best prices; they usually do not result in much, if any, money being left for you. (You might also get a better price if you don't have to sell in a hurry.) With the proceeds of the sale, you'll have to pay off the lender(s) and any secured creditors to whom you pledged the asset as collateral. And you'll have to pay off any liens placed on the property by your creditors. You can use what's left to help pay your other debts. Even if nothing is left, getting rid of large monthly payments could help you afford your other bills. (See Chapter 8 for information on selling your home if you owe more than it's worth.)

TIP
Help selling your car. For tips on selling your car yourself, check out the *Car Talk* website at www.cartalk.com.

CAUTION
Don't forget possible tax consequences. If you are selling stocks, real estate, or anything else that is valuable that has increased (or decreased) in value, or on which you might owe capital gains or some other transaction tax, consult a tax professional *before* the sale. Sometimes a sale can be legally structured to obtain a favorable tax result. Other times, you might find out that the tax consequences of selling are so unpleasant that you would be better off doing something different, such as using the asset as collateral for a loan or choosing another asset to sell.

Sell Smaller Items

Even if you're not a packrat, you probably own things you never use or don't need any more. Thanks to the Internet, it has never been easier to get rid of property you have no use for. All kinds of property can be sold on eBay (www.ebay.com) and similar auction websites. These sites are proof of the old maxim, "One man's trash is another man's treasure." They provide an instant audience of millions of potential buyers of practically anything.

With any luck, you'll connect with someone who collects obscure items in your clutter. Baseball cards and comic books have been collected for years, but there are also collectors of dolls, ashtrays, electronic equipment, musical instruments, "retro" furniture, old dishes, china, and antiques of any kind. A good way to figure out what an item is worth is to search eBay for similar items and see what buyers are bidding for them.

In addition to auction sites, some retailers (including Amazon.com) let you sell used books and other items to other customers. Or try online community classified ads, like Craigslist. You might not get much money for each individual book or item, but if you have several dozen or some hundreds to sell, it can provide some badly needed cash.

 CAUTION

It can cost money to sell things. When you sell online, it's up to you to pack up the sold item and pay for shipping. Make sure you're getting enough for the item to make a profit after the costs of shipping. Also, *beware*

of scams. Reputable websites like Amazon and eBay are generally careful to collect the money from the buyer, but if you sell directly to an online buyer, you could ship your stuff and never get any money back.

Or the buyer could pay with a bogus check for more than the amount of the sale and ask you to return the difference. Check out the Internet Crime Complaint Center at www.IC3.gov for Internet crime prevention tips.

You don't have to know how to use a computer to get rid of your belongings. There are always the traditional low-tech ways to sell:

- Advertise in the newspaper.
- Have a yard sale (be sure to ask about a local permit).
- Take a load to the flea market.
- Take vintage or expensive clothing to a resale shop.
- Take books (and perhaps musical recordings, depending on the reseller) to a used book store.
- Take good jewelry to a jeweler who sells "estate jewelry."

Before you go to a reseller, have a ballpark idea of what your things are worth and a realistic idea of what condition they're in. That way, you'll be a better negotiator, you won't get cheated, and you won't insist on an unrealistically high price that results in no sale.

A consignment shop is another option, but make sure that it's reputable and well established in your community. Consignment shops usually keep 35% to 50% of what they can sell an item for and give you the rest.

Before doing business with a shop, check with your local Better Business Bureau to see if complaints have been lodged against it or go to www.bbb.org. If there are complaints, that's a warning. Unfortunately, the absence of complaints doesn't necessarily mean you can trust that shop. A business can change names or defraud a lot of people before complaints catch up to it.

If you decide to use a particular shop, ask how they insure items in their store in case of fire, theft, or other loss and review contract terms. If the store assures you the items are insured, ask for a copy of the insurance policy. If the store won't provide that, get a receipt for the item you leave and have them write on it that the item is insured in full.

TIP

You may collect more money if you sell it yourself. Why? At a shop, resale items in good condition are often priced at about 70% of what they would bring if they were new. A shop has overhead, and it needs to make a profit— typically, by charging almost double what it pays for an item. At most, the shop will offer you about a third of what the item would sell for new. If you invest some time in a yard sale or flea market, you could likely sell it for more.

Withdraw Money From a Tax-Deferred Account

If you have an IRA, a 401(k), or another tax-deferred retirement account, you can get cash to pay off debts by withdrawing money before retirement. But if you do so, you'll probably have to pay a penalty and taxes. Or, with a 403(b), 457, or 401(k) plan, you might be able to borrow money from it (instead of withdrawing it).

There are some hardship exceptions that allow you to withdraw money early from some retirement plans without having to pay the penalty, for example, if you become disabled, or have very high medical expenses. For details, see the following IRS publications at www.irs.gov: Publication 590-B (for IRAs) and Publication 575 and IRS Topic 558 (for 401(k)s, 403(b)s, and 457s).

Different plans have different require-ments for borrowing and withdrawing money. Withdrawing money early from a tax-deferred account is expensive. Generally, any money that you take out of your 403(b), 457, or 401(k) plan before you reach age 59½ is treated as an early distribution on which you'll owe penalties and income taxes.

Instead of withdrawing money, you can usually borrow up to half of your vested account balance, but not more than $50,000. Then you pay the money back, with interest, over five years. If you can't pay the money back within five years (or immediately, if you leave your job), your "loan" will be treated like an early withdrawal and you'll pay both an early distribution tax penalty and income tax.

There are serious disadvantages to both options. You should only consider these if you have other substantial retirement funds or you are truly desperate. Also, consult your tax adviser before you do anything. Always look to raise money from nonretirement resources first.

RESOURCE

Need more information on retirement accounts? If you are considering withdrawing or borrowing money from your retirement account to pay off debts, get a copy of *IRAs, 401(k)s & Other Retirement Plans: Strategies for Taking Your Money Out*, by Twila Slesnick and John C. Suttle (Nolo).

Apply for Government and Agency Help

When you find yourself having money troubles, don't overlook official help. Despite a decline in available social services in recent years, the government still provides something of a "social safety net" to help people with temporary money problems.

Earned Income Tax Credit

If you qualify for an Earned Income Tax Credit (EITC), you can get a lump sum of cash from the federal government when you file an income tax return. The credit is given to low- and moderate-income workers. For the 2018 tax year, the tax credit (the equivalent of cash back to you) ranges from $519 to $6,431, depending on your income and family size. For example, a married couple filing jointly with three children earning less than $54,884 might qualify for the maximum credit of $6,431. To see if you are eligible, go to the IRS website (www.irs.gov), hover over "Credits & Deductions," and then select "Earned Income Tax Credit (EITC)." The only way to get the credit is to file a tax return, and claim the credit on the return. So, even if you aren't required to file a return, you should consider filing one anyway. As of 2017, if you claim the EITC on your tax return, the earliest that the IRS will issue your refund is the 15th of February.

Unemployment Insurance Benefits

You might be eligible to apply for unemployment benefits if any of the following occurs:

- You are fired for any reason, other than for gross misconduct.
- You quit your job for an extremely good job-related reason.
- You are laid off.

Check online for the phone number of the closest unemployment office. For a link to the unemployment insurance website in your state, see the Department of Labor's employment and training information website at http://ows.doleta.gov/unemploy. For an online calculator, try your state's website or its employment department. Be sure to ask your state agency these questions:

- How much is my benefit amount? (It will depend on how much you earned at work.)
- How long can I collect benefits? (This is usually 26 weeks, but some states offer more. To see how many weeks of unemployment are available in your state, go to the Center on Budget and Policy Priorities website at www.cbpp.org and search for "How Many Weeks of Unemployment Compensation Are Available?")

- If I start working again before then, will my benefits be reduced? (You may be able to increase your income, up to a point, without losing all of your benefits.)

Unemployment programs typically require a fair amount of paperwork. You are expected to look for work while you are collecting benefits, and you might have to report in writing on your search.

Health Insurance Benefits

You might qualify for health insurance coverage or financial help to pay health costs from the following government programs:

- Medicaid is a joint federal and state program that provides health and medical coverage to low-income people. Benefits vary from state to state. Medicaid could cover things that Medicare generally does not, such as long-term care. Visit www.healthcare.gov for help in determining if you qualify for Medicaid.
- The Medicare Savings Programs provide financial help with Medicare expenses for senior citizens with limited incomes and resources. You can get information from www.medicare.gov or call 800-633-4227, 877-486-2048 (TTY).
- Your state's Children's Health Insurance Program (CHIP) might provide coverage for your children. Call 877-543-7669 or go to www.insurekidsnow.gov.
- Under the Affordable Care Act, you might qualify for a subsidy if you don't have insurance through work and can't afford the full cost of a private plan. Visit www.healthcare.gov for more information.

Human Service Agencies

Contact other agencies to find out if you qualify for food stamps, general assistance, veterans' benefits, workers' compensation, Social Security, or disability benefits.

Look into the following:

- Supplemental Security Income (SSI) provides cash assistance to persons who are at least 65 years old, or people of any age who are blind or disabled, who have limited incomes and few resources. In most states, people eligible for SSI are automatically enrolled in Medicaid.
- The Supplemental Nutrition Assistance Program (SNAP) (formerly called the Food Stamp program) provides monthly assistance to low-income persons to purchase food at grocery stores. To locate your local SNAP office and to find out about other food and nutrition programs for which you might qualify, go to www.fns.usda.gov.

Human service agencies in each state administer several federal benefit programs for persons with low incomes, including Medicaid, Medicare Savings Programs, and SNAP. These agencies go by various names depending on the state, such as department of social services, human services, or public aid. You can get an application for SNAP at the local Social Security Administration (SSA) office; this office can also help families applying for SSI to fill out the application. You can find the nearest Social Security office by going to www.ssa.gov and clicking on "Contact Us" and then "Find an Office" or by calling 800-772-1213 or TTY at 800-325-0778.

Other Free or Subsidized Government Services

Many government agencies offer free or discounted services that can save you money. Some are offered through private companies, rather than directly through an agency. It pays to check what is available for you.

Reduced Utility Charges

Many utility companies offer reduced rates and payment plans to elderly and low-income people. In addition, the federal Low Income Home Energy Assistance Program (LIHEAP), which is state run, helps low-income customers pay their utility bills. Don't assume you won't qualify as low income. To find out if you qualify and where to apply, call your utility company and ask; contact the National Energy Assistance Referral (NEAR) project at 866-674-6327 or www.ncat.org/low-income-energy-assistance; or contact your state's LIHEAP office for assistance. You can find that office on the LIHEAP website at www.acf.hhs.gov/ocs/liheap-state-and-territory-contact-listing. If you qualify, you'll be able to get future bills reduced—and you might be able to spread out payments on past bills.

Free Tax Preparation

About 70% of Americans qualify to have their income tax returns prepared for free, but most don't take advantage of any of these three free programs:

- **Volunteer Income Tax Assistance Program (VITA).** You qualify for the VITA if your income for the year was below $55,000 (for a 2018 tax return). VITA, which is staffed by trained and tested volunteers, offers tax preparation services at community and neighborhood centers, libraries, schools, shopping malls, military bases, and other locations across the country. Most offer free electronic filing, which means you will usually get your refund within one to two weeks. For more information go to www.irs.gov/individuals and search for "VITA." To find a VITA location near you, call 800-906-9887 or use the online VITA locator tool on the IRS website.

- **AARP's Tax Counseling for the Elderly (TCE).** Free income tax preparation is also available to persons 60 years of age or older under the Tax Counseling for the Elderly (TCE) program. Call 888-227-7669 for information about a location near you. AARP operates many of the tax preparation sites for seniors under the name Tax-Aide. It provides tax return preparation for low- and moderate-income seniors, including electronic filing, which means you will usually get your refund within one to two weeks. To locate a Tax-Aide office, go to www.aarp.org and search for "Tax-Aide," or call 888-227-7669.

- **Other free tax services.** Even if your adjusted gross income is as high as $66,000 (for 2018 filing), you probably qualify for a free service to help you prepare and file your taxes online, including electronic filing, which means you will probably get your tax refund within one to two weeks. However, watch out. The free online filing is provided by private companies and they will likely try to sell you additional services. (To find out more, go to www.irs.gov and search for "Free File.")

Free Home Weatherization

The federal Weatherization Assistance Program provides assistance for low- and moderate-income families to improve the energy efficiency of their homes. By taking advantage of these programs to weatherize your home, you can reduce your utility bills and possibly increase the property value of your home.

To find out what services are available, start with the U.S. Department of Energy's website at https://www.energy.gov/eere/wipo/where-apply-weatherization-assistance to find a link to the program in your state. (Go to the "Contact Your State Weatherization Administrator" link.) Assistance with paying your home energy bills is also available through the U.S. Department of Health and Human Services LIHEAP program. To see if you qualify, call 866-674-6327 or send an email to energyassistance@ncat.org.

 RESOURCE

More information on benefits. BenefitsCheckup, sponsored by the National Council on Aging, is a free online service (www.benefitscheckup.org). You anonymously fill out a questionnaire, and the website finds public benefits programs you might be eligible for and tells you how to apply. These programs might pay for some of the costs of prescription drugs, health care, utilities, and other essential

items or services. Nolo also publishes a variety of products that deal specifically with applying for several kinds of benefits:

- *Nolo's Guide to Social Security Disability: Getting & Keeping Your Benefits*, by David A. Morton III, MD
- *Social Security, Medicare & Government Pensions: Get the Most Out of Your Retirement & Medical Benefits*, by Joseph L. Matthews, and
- *Long-Term Care: How to Plan & Pay For It*, by Joseph L. Matthews.

Private Agencies

There might be a host of nonprofit associations available to help you out. In some cases, it helps if you are a member of a fraternal organization or an ethnic or religious group, a native son or daughter, and so on. You can get to the right organizations by using your phone book, surfing the Internet, or calling friends, your local senior center, or local churches.

Consider a Home Equity Loan

Many banks, savings and loans, credit unions, and other lenders offer home equity loans, also called second mortgages, and home equity lines of credit also called HELOCs. Traditionally, lenders who make home equity loans establish how much you can borrow by starting with a percentage of the market value of your house—usually between 50% and 80%—and deducting what you still owe on it. The lender will also consider your credit history, income, and other expenses in deciding whether—and how much—to lend you.

EXAMPLE: Winnie's house is worth $200,000, and she owes $120,000 on her first mortgage. A bank has offered her a home equity loan at 75%, that is, for $30,000. The lender figures it like this: 75% x $200,000 = $150,000; $150,000 − $120,000 = $30,000.

Be careful that you don't simply max out your credit cards again after you use your home equity to pay down your debts. Many borrowers wind up deeper in debt—this time with a large equity line to repay as well.

There are two basic kinds of home equity loans:

- **Closed-end loan.** You borrow a fixed amount of money and repay it in equal monthly installments for a set period (a home equity loan).
- **Line of credit.** You borrow as you need the money, drawing against the amount granted when you opened the account (a home equity line of credit, also called a HELOC).

It may sound attractive to take out a home equity loan at a relatively low interest rate to pay off a high-interest credit card balance. This is a bad idea. As discussed earlier, if you don't pay back your credit card debt, you might get sued. But if you don't pay back a home equity loan, you could lose your house. So, don't use the proceeds of a home equity loan to pay off unsecured debts such as a credit card balance—doing so effectively turns unsecured debt into secured debt and puts your house at risk.

Home equity loans have other disadvantages, including:

- Some home equity loans are sold by predatory lenders at very high rates. Predatory lenders target people in financial trouble or with past credit problems. Avoid any lender who tells you to falsify information on a loan application or pressures you into applying for more money than you need or monthly payments you cannot afford. Predatory lenders may also change information on the typed version of your loan application from the information you gave to make your income look higher. Check carefully any documents, including any loan application you are asked to sign. Making your income look higher is a recipe for getting a loan you cannot afford. If you can't afford the loan, you may be setting yourself up to lose your home and destroy your credit rating.
- The same kind of predatory tactics involved in refinancing a mortgage also happen in equity loan transactions. For example, lenders might increase the interest rate or fees on the final loan documents after enticing you with what sound like very low rates. For suggestions on how to handle these and other predatory tactics, see "Refinancing" in Chapter 8.
- Some home equity loans are "interest-only" loans; your monthly payments pay only the interest on the loan and do not reduce the principal amount that you borrowed. You could make payments for years and still owe the full amount you borrowed.

- Teaser rates might make a home equity loan look more attractive than it is. Equity loans often have variable interest rates that rise or fall with a particular interest rate index (these are sometimes referred to as adjustable rate mortgages or ARMs). But often, the rate for the first six months to three years is much lower. Once the initial period ends, the rate automatically jumps up to the regular variable rate, which can make your loan payments much higher. Many people have been caught in this trap, when loans they took out in the past couple of years suddenly cost a lot more every month, and they were unable to refinance to lower their payments. If you're considering an equity loan, make sure you know the teaser rate, the regular rate, when the regular rate kicks in, and how much your payments will likely be then.

- You are obligating yourself to make another monthly or periodic payment. If you are unable to pay, you may have to sell your house or, even worse, face the possibility of the lender's foreclosing. *Before you take out a home equity loan, be sure you can make the monthly payment, both initially and after any teaser rate resets.*

- While interest may be tax deductible (it isn't always), it may be high. Your tax deduction doesn't save you the full amount of interest you pay; instead, it allows you to subtract that interest from your income when you calculate your income tax. So your true savings from taking an interest deduction are only a fraction of the interest you pay out in the first place. Check Bankrate.com for current rates (www.bankrate.com).

- With a home equity loan, the interest payments are not deductible if you use the money for a purpose other than to buy, build, or improve your home. Before 2018, you could deduct the interest on up to $100,000 in home equity loans ($50,000 if you used married-filing-separate status). You could use the money for any purpose—like to to pay off credit cards or help pay for your child's college education—and still get the deduction. The Tax Cuts and Jobs Act, however, eliminated this deduction for 2018 through 2025. The interest you pay on a home equity loan used to purchase, build, or improve your main or second home remains deductible. The loan must be secured by your main home or a second home, can't exceed the cost of the home, and the amount you can deduct is limited. Ask a tax professional if you have questions about deductibility.

- You might have to pay an assortment of up-front fees for an appraisal, credit report, title insurance, and points. These fees can cost thousands of dollars. In addition, for giving you an equity line of credit, many lenders charge a yearly fee of $50 to $75 or so.

- You must pay what you still owe on the equity loan, plus what you owe on the mortgage, when you sell your house.

TIP

Review home equity loan disclosures.
Before you agree to a home equity loan, review all of the lender disclosures, particularly the APR, finance charge, and amount financed. Get an itemization of the expenses included in the amount financed. With these numbers, you can better compare costs. If you are getting a closed-end loan, well before the date scheduled to sign the loan documents, ask the lender if there are changes to the good-faith estimate. If there are, get the new disclosures. (See Chapter 11 for more on what to look for in credit contracts.) Finally, go to the CFPB's website (at www.consumerfinance.gov/learnmore) and search for "Adjustable Rate Mortgages" to learn about equity loans and "Home Equity Lines of Credit" to learn about equity lines of credit.

Canceling a Home Equity Loan

Under the federal Truth in Lending Act, you have the right to cancel a home equity loan or second mortgage until midnight of the third business day (excluding Sundays and federal holidays *but including Saturdays*) after you sign the contract or are given the loan disclosures, whichever is later. You must be given notice of your right to cancel and two copies of a cancellation form when you sign the contract.

Use the Equity in Your Home If You Are 62 or Older

A variety of plans are designed to help older homeowners make use of the accumulated value (equity) in their homes without requiring them to move, give up title to the property, or make payments on a loan. The most common types of plans are called reverse mortgages and deferral loans for property tax and home repair.

These plans can raise a senior citizen's standard of living and help an older person maintain independence by providing cash for everyday living expenses, home maintenance, or in-home care. But they're not for everybody. Reverse mortgages can be very expensive and a real trap for seniors.

Reverse Mortgages

Reverse mortgages are loans that homeowners age 62 or older can take out against the equity in their home. A reverse mortgage provides cash advances to the owner and requires no repayment until the end of the loan term or when the home is sold. To determine the amount it will lend to you, a reverse mortgage lender usually considers your age, equity in your home, and current interest rates. With a reverse mortgage, because you make no payments, the interest accumulates, and the amount you owe increases over the length of the loan, instead of decreasing. And reverse mortgages cost money: closing costs, loan origination fees, accrued interest, and, in most cases, an additional charge to offset the lender's risk that you could default on the loan. All in all, a reverse mortgage costs more than a regular mortgage and comes with many risks. It should usually be a last resort.

HECM Reverse Mortgages

Almost all reverse mortgages today are part of the Federal Housing Administration's Home Equity Conversion Mortgage (HECM, pronounced "heck-em"). These federally insured loans are available through an FHA approved lender.

If you have a HECM reverse mortgage, you don't have to repay the loan until you stop living in the home or fail to comply with the contract terms. You're required to pay property taxes and insurance and maintain the home in good repair. Before making a HECM loan, lenders must complete a financial assessment and determine whether the homeowner can afford the tax and insurance payments. If a homeowner doesn't have the necessary funds, the lender will establish a set-aside account to pay these expenses (the set-aside amount will reduce the money available to the borrower). FHA is considering a rule that would require proof of the borrower's ability to cover the cost of utilities, as well.

Through 2019, you can borrow up to $726,525, depending on the value of your home, the current interest rate, and the age of the youngest borrower or eligible non-borrowing spouse. You can choose among several payment options from the HECM loan. Most are in the form of open-ended loans with adjustable interest rates.

Term option. Fixed monthly cash advances are made for a specific time.

Tenure option. Fixed monthly cash advances are made for as long as you live in your home.

Line of credit. You use the money only as you need it, until you have used up the line of credit.

Combination. You can also get a combination of monthly payments and a line of credit.

Fixed rate. Lenders also offer fixed-rate HECM loans, but you must take out all of the loan proceeds at the beginning and you can only access the amount permitted under first-year disbursement limits. The remaining loan amount is forfeited. (As of October 1, 2013, the amount you can get in the first year of a HECM is capped. Your lender first calculates how much you can borrow in total by looking at your age, the interest rate, and the value of your home. The total amount is called the "initial principal limit." In general, you can take out up to 60% of your initial principal limit in the first year, unless there are other mandatory obligations, such as paying off an existing mortgage. If so, you can take out enough to pay off the existing mortgage plus 10%.) These loans are very expensive and risky. They usually have a higher interest rate than other reverse mortgages, and you pay interest on the whole loan amount for the entire length of the loan. Since you have to receive all of the funds in one lump sum, you might have to pay interest on a large sum of money and could potentially use up what's left of your home equity. You generally cannot borrow as much with this type of reverse mortgage as with a line of credit or monthly payout option because you can't draw any more funds after the loan closes.

Whatever loan type you choose, you can change to a different payment option for a small fee, as long as there is still money left in your loan (which won't be the case if you have a fixed-rate loan).

The HECM mortgages are "federally insured. This means:

- After you move out of your home, if the lender cannot collect the full amount of the loan from the sale of the home or foreclosure, the government will pay the lender the difference.
- If the lender stops making payments it owes you, the government will make those payments to you.
- There are some rules to protect you. For example, if sale of the property after you move out is not enough to pay the loan, the lender cannot collect more from you or your heirs.
- You are required to receive counseling before you get a HECM reverse mortgage. Counseling agencies usually charge a fee for their services. Unfortunately, because counselors are sometimes paid out of the loan proceeds, they have a financial interest in encouraging you to get a loan, even if it is not in your best interest.

Other Reverse Mortgages

Reverse mortgages that are not insured by the FHA are known as proprietary reverse mortgages. They are also often called "jumbo reverse mortgages" because they're only available to those with high-value homes. This type of reverse mortgage is uncommon and all but disappeared after the housing crash—but they're making a comeback. A few private mortgage lenders now offer jumbo reverse mortgages, typically with a maximum loan amount of several million dollars and interest rates at around 6 to 8%. There is really no good reason to choose this expensive and risky type of uninsured loan unless you have a huge amount of equity in your home that you cannot borrow against under the HECM program.

Some states also offer very-low-cost government-sponsored reverse mortgages that are available only for specific purposes. (See "Deferral Payment Loans," below.)

Pros and Cons of Reverse Mortgages

There are pros and cons to reverse mortgages. In general, a reverse mortgage works best for older people with a lot of equity in their homes.

But before you sign up, consider these disadvantages:

- Once you borrow against your equity with a reverse mortgage, there's no turning back. This equity will not be available to you unless you pay off the loan.
- The costs of a reverse mortgage can be very high, and some mortgages have unfair terms.
- A reverse mortgage might also restrict your freedom. The entire reverse mortgage comes due if you are no longer living in your home. An extended stay away from your home, such as a long trip, a visit to your children, or a stay in an assisted-living

facility (for HECM loans, the absence must be more than a year) can be considered evidence that you are no longer living in the home, especially if you haven't properly secured it in your absence and, therefore, that your entire loan must be paid off immediately.

- Elderly homeowners who put their reverse mortgage in the name of just the older spouse (because the younger spouse is not yet 62) might find that when the older spouse dies, the lender declares the whole loan due. The younger spouse is suddenly left without a home. However, if you took out a HECM in just the name of the older spouse on or after August 4, 2014, the younger nonborrowing spouse can remain in the home after the older spouse dies and the loan repayment will be deferred—so long as you meet certain criteria. For example, the borrower and nonborrower must be married at the time the loan closes, among other things. Similar protections are now available to the nonborrowing spouse for HECMs taken out before August 4, 2014, as long as specific conditions are met. So, while HECMs are now safer for nonborrowing spouses, keep in mind you must meet all eligibility requirements to stay in the home. Talk to a reverse mortgage specialist to get detailed information about the nonborrowing spouse rules.
- Some unscrupulous lenders offer products that sound like reverse mortgages, but are really conventional loans. Others sell reverse mortgages that lend more money than you need, or that have very high costs or unfair terms. Some unscrupulous individuals offer to refer senior homeowners to lenders that provide reverse mortgages, in exchange for a percentage of the loans. Information on reverse mortgages is free from the U.S. Department of Housing and Urban Development.
- A reverse mortgage makes it difficult to leave your home to your heirs after you die, because your estate has to pay the loan back—and, usually, the house is sold to cover the debt.
- Because you don't make payments, the amount of money owed increases over the life of the loan. While you retain title to your home, you must pay the property taxes, insurance, and the costs of keeping up the property.
- A reverse mortgage (or annuity payments funded by a lump sum reverse mortgage) might affect your ability to receive need-based government benefits, such as Supplemental Security Income (SSI). Although loan advances from a reverse mortgage are not considered "income," they could increase your amount of "liquid assets" above limits set by government benefit programs.

Annuities and Reverse Mortgages

The lender or a third party might suggest that you purchase an annuity in conjunction with a reverse mortgage. An annuity is an insurance product financed out of the home's equity, which provides monthly payments to the borrower beginning immediately or some years later.

Do not buy an annuity. It ties up the money from the reverse mortgage for an extended period, imposes additional transaction costs, imposes substantial penalties for early withdrawal, and might not benefit elderly homeowners (who might not live to see their first annuity payment, if there is a delay of several years). Indeed, the federal government and California prohibit lenders from requiring a homeowner to purchase an annuity as a condition of obtaining a reverse mortgage.

More Information

You can get free information on reverse mortgages from the following organizations:

- the U.S. Department of Housing and Urban Development (HUD). Call them at 800-225-5342, TTY at 800-877-8339, or visit their website, www.hud.gov, and search for "reverse mortgages."
- AARP (formerly the American Association of Retired Persons). Call 888-687-2277 or visit its website, www.aarp.org and search for "reverse mortgages."
- The CFPB has a variety of information about the pros and cons of reverse mortgages. Go to www.consumerfinance.gov and search for "reverse mortgages."

Be careful of people who come to speak at senior centers about reverse mortgages unless they come from a government agency. Often insurance agents or loan brokers offering predatory-type loans use "free" talks at senior centers to drum up business.

Deferral Payment Loans

Deferral payment loans are need-based loans used for a special purpose: to make property tax payments or to pay for home repairs. The cost of these loans is very low, and repayment is deferred as long as you live in your home. Deferral payment loans are generally available through state or local government agencies. If you qualify, these programs are a much better option than getting a reverse mortgage.

There are two types of deferral payment loans:

- **Property tax deferral loans.** Many states provide vouchers to approved applicants to pay their property taxes, or allow taxes to be delayed until the home is sold. Contact your tax assessor to see if such a program is available in your county.
- **Home repair deferral loans.** These are loans for home repairs at no or very low interest.

Borrow the Money

If you have good credit and have hit a temporary rough patch, you might be able to get an unsecured personal loan from a bank or credit union. (This means that you sign loan papers and make regular payments but give them no collateral.) Another potential source for a loan is a community development bank or loan fund that makes loans in distressed communities not served by other lenders. (Your local bank may have a program like this or know who offers them locally.) For more about community banks and to locate one near you, go to http://ncif.org.

But before you borrow money from an institution, ask yourself:

- Can you pay back the money?
- Can you find a loan on better terms?

Some people are lucky enough to have friends or relatives who can and will help out. Before asking your college roommate, Uncle Paul, or someone similar for help, consider the following:

- Can the lender really afford to help you?
- Do you want to owe this person money? If the loan comes with emotional strings attached, be sure you can handle the situation before taking the money.
- Will the loan help you out, or will it just delay the inevitable (most likely, filing for bankruptcy)? Don't borrow money to make payments on debts you will eventually discharge in bankruptcy.
- Will you have to repay the loan now, or will the lender let you wait until you're back on your feet? If you have to make payments now, you're just adding another monthly payment to your already unmanageable pile of debts.
- If the loan is from your parents, can you treat it as part of your eventual inheritance? If so, you won't ever have to repay it. If your siblings get angry that you are getting some of your parents' money, be sure they understand that your inheritance will be reduced accordingly.

RESOURCE

Resources for personal loans. *101 Law Forms for Personal Use,* (Nolo), includes customizable promissory notes for lending money between family members. Nolo's website at www.nolo.com also sells forms online that you can use to create and print your own promissory note.

CAUTION

One word of warning: If a friend or relative lends you money at a below-market interest rate or gives you cash as a gift, that person might have to pay gift taxes. For 2019, gifts of more than $15,000 per person per year are subject to gift taxes. And the definition of "gift" includes a break on interest (although because the amount of the "gift" is the break on interest per year, not the amount loaned, most loans won't incur gift taxes on the principal amount borrowed).

What to Avoid When You Need Money

Making wise financial decisions when the bills are piling up is not easy. But, even if you feel desperate, don't jump at every opportunity to get cash fast. If you make a bad choice, you'll just get yourself deeper into debt. Here are some of the options that you should avoid.

Avoid Consolidation Loans

Some bank subsidiaries and consumer finance companies lend money in the form of consolidation loans. Finance companies make secured consolidation loans, usually requiring that you pledge your house or car as security. These loans are just like second mortgages or secured vehicle loans.

The amount of interest you could be charged on a secured consolidation loan can vary greatly, from about 7% to more than 36%, depending on your credit rating and the security. Those offering consolidation loans are often unwilling to provide you with interest rate information until you fill out an application, making it difficult to comparison shop. If you are considering a consolidation loan, tell the lender that even if you provide answers to their questions, you do not want to have an application submitted until you get information about the interest rate.

If you default on the loan, the finance company can foreclose on your home or take your car or other property.

TIP
You might be able to cancel the loan. If the consolidation loan is secured by your principal residence, you can cancel it for up to three business days after you sign the loan papers.

Finance companies and similar lenders also make unsecured consolidation loans—that is, they lend you some money without requiring that you pledge any property as a guarantee that you'll pay. But the interest on these loans often reaches 36% or more. They also charge all kinds of fees or require you to purchase insurance, often bringing the effective interest rate closer to 50%.

If you still want to take out a consolidation loan, you are better off borrowing from a bank or credit union than a finance company. Many finance companies engage in illegal or borderline collection practices if you default and are not as willing as banks and credit unions to negotiate if you have trouble paying. And loans from finance companies can be viewed negatively by potential creditors who see them in your credit file.

CAUTION
Be careful when pledging your home. Think carefully about whether you want to convert unsecured debts (for example, credit card debt) into debt that's secured by your home. If you can't make the payments on the secured debt, you could lose your home.

TIP
A good alternative to debt consolidators. A safer and less-expensive alternative is to find a reputable credit counseling agency. See Chapter 18 for more information.

Avoid Tax Refund Anticipation Loans and Checks

Although getting a tax refund fast is often a good way to get quick cash, you should avoid a refund anticipation loan (RAL) or refund anticipation check (RAC). A RAL—or "tax refund advance"—is a type of loan borrowed from a nonbank lender. It's based on the borrower's anticipated tax refund. The IRS and federal regulators have cracked down on these kinds of loans, so predatory RALs with sky-high interest rates and excessive fees have mostly disappeared from the market. While RALs still exist, most are no-fee loans, though some do charge interest and certain limited fees (like credit-check and application fees). Because the lender won't make much money from a RAL, you usually also have to pay for a tax preparation service to get this kind of loan. That service might be expensive. If you're considering getting a RAL, be sure to consider all associated costs.

A refund anticipation check (RAC)—also called a "refund transfer"—is used to deliver tax refunds and to pay for tax preparation services. A tax preparer will offer a RAC to people who can't afford to pay tax preparation fees up front. With a RAC, the IRS deposits the refund into a temporary bank account.

The tax preparation fee (and other costs) get deducted. The consumer receives the remaining amount. (Some companies put the balance on a prepaid card, which might charge fees. To learn about the disadvantages of using prepaid cards, see Chapter 17.)

A RAC is usually very costly. For instance, if the cost of the service is $35 in addition to the $350 tax preparation fee, the APR would be 174%. Extra fees, such as "document processing" fees, "application" fees, or "technology" fees ranging from $25 to several hundred dollars, can increase the cost of a RAC even more.

RALs and RACs also pose some risks. You must repay such a loan even if your refund is denied, is less than expected, or is frozen. If you can't repay the loan, the lender might assign the debt to a collection agency. The unpaid debt will appear on your credit report.

There are other ways to get your tax refund quickly without paying the high fees charged in refund anticipation checks and loans.

In most cases, you can file your return electronically and get the money within a week or two at most (by having the refund deposited directly into your bank account, for example).

Keep in mind, though, that as of 2017, if you claim the Earned Income Tax Credit (EITC) or Additional Child Tax Credit on your tax return, the IRS will not issue your refund until after the 15th of February. Also, don't forget the free alternatives to paying for tax preparation services. Low- and moderate-income taxpayers can get help from the Volunteer Income Tax Assistance (VITA) program, AARP's Tax-Aide, and the online Freefile. (See "Free Tax Preparation" above.) Some free tax preparation programs can also help you open a bank account into which your refund can be directly deposited.

For more information on how to get a refund sooner see "Get Your Tax Refund Fast," above. For answers to other tax questions, contact the IRS at 800-829-1040 (voice) or 800-829-4059 (TTY), or visit its website at www.irs.gov. If you haven't already adjusted your tax withholding to give you more money each payday instead of having to wait for the tax refund, see above, "Get Some of Your Tax Refund Early."

Avoid Pawnshops

Visiting a pawnshop should be one of the last ways you consider raising cash. At a pawnshop, you leave your property, such as jewelry, electronic and photography equipment, or musical instruments. In return, the pawnbroker typically lends you approximately 25% to 60% of the item's resale value. The average amount of a pawnshop loan is about $75 to $100.

You are given a short time, typically a few months, to repay the loan and are charged fees and interest, often at an exorbitant rate. Although you borrow money for only a few months, paying an average of 10% a month interest means that you are paying an annual interest rate of 120%. Interest rates could vary from 12% to 240%, depending on whether state law restricts rates pawnshops can charge. You might also be charged storage costs and insurance fees.

If you default on your loan to a pawnshop, the property you left at the shop to obtain the loan becomes the property of the pawnbroker. You are usually given some time, typically 30 to 60 days, to pay your debt and get your property back; if you don't, the pawnbroker can sell it. In some states, if the sale brings in money in excess of what you owe on the loan, storage fees, and sales costs, you're entitled to the surplus. But don't count on getting anything.

Avoid Car Title Loans

A bank or another financial institution might agree to make a secured loan against the value of your car, called a "car title loan," "auto title pawn," or "car equity loan." You keep and drive the car, but the lender keeps the title as security for repayment of the loan, as well as a copy of your keys. These loans are dangerous, because missing even one payment can mean

losing your car, even if the car is worth far more than the amount you owe. In fact, in 2016, the Consumer Financial Protection Bureau (CFPB) released a report showing that one out of every five borrowers who takes out a car title loan loses the car to repossession. Lenders might also ask you to use your home, as well as your car, as collateral. This means that if you miss any payments, you risk losing your house as well as the car. These loans can come with a steep interest rate because your car is considered a used car and its value rapidly decreases. For example, according to the Consumer Federation of America, you might pay $63 to $181 for a one-month $500 title loan. Monthly finance charges of 25% (300% annual interest) are common.

The U.S. military classifies car title loans as predatory loans. The Military Lending Act prohibits lenders from making car title loans to servicemembers who are on active duty for at least a month (and their dependents).

Avoid Payday Loans

The payday loan industry is growing fast. In some states, these loans are illegal. Some lenders call these "advance loans." Think twice before you get one of these loans.

A payday loan works like this: Either you give the lender a check and get back an amount of money less than the face value of the check, or you sign an agreement giving the lender the right to withdraw money either from your bank account or from a prepaid card to which money, like wages, is regularly added. For example, if you give the lender a postdated check for $300, it might give you

$250 in cash and keep the remaining $50 as its fee. The lender holds the check for a few weeks (often until your payday). At this time, you must pay the lender the face value of the check ($300), usually by allowing it to cash the check. If you can't make the check good, the lender requires you to pay another fee ($50 in this example). At this point, you owe the lender $350 (the $250 borrowed plus the first $50 fee, plus a new fee of $50). The cost is the same if you give the lender the right to access your bank account or a prepaid card instead of a check. The money you borrow (minus the lender's fee) is deposited directly to your account or card and the payday lender withdraws the payment when due. If you need another loan that week, the lender charges an additional fee, and so on. Many people who can't make the original check good get into a "treadmill of debt" because they must keep writing new checks or allow additional withdrawals from their accounts to cover the fees that have accumulated, in addition to paying off the amounts borrowed. According to the CFPB, almost 70% of payday loan borrowers take out a second loan within a month. One in five new borrowers takes out ten or more consecutive payday loans, each time adding on additional fees and interest to the balance owed. The annual percentage rate on even one payday loan is astronomical, ranging from 200% to 500% or more. The CFPB is working on developing a law that would require a lender to determine whether a borrower can afford to repay a payday loan. (See "The CFPB Payday Rule: When Will It Go Into Effect?" below.)

The CFPB Payday Rule: When Will It Go Into Effect?

In 2017, the CFPB issued a new rule called the "Payday Rule." This rule, once in effect, would require payday lenders to conduct a "full-payment test" to determine upfront whether a borrower could afford to repay a loan without rolling it over. (This requirement is also known as the "ability-to-pay" test.)

The Payday Rule also includes a "debit attempt cutoff" for certain payday loans. Under the rule, after two unsuccessful attempts to debit a borrower's account, the lender can't try to take money out of the account again unless the borrower provides a new authorization. And, the lender has to give written notice before attempting to debit an account at an irregular interval or amount.

The Payday Rule was supposed to go into effect in early 2018, but the CFPB delayed the effective date and announced it would reconsider the rule—in particular, the ability-to-pay requirement—sometime in 2019.

Consumer advocates who support the Payday Rule say that tough laws are needed to rein in payday lenders, which usually target low-income borrowers. But opponents say that it unfairly hinders the payday loan industry, which serves millions of customers who often don't have access to more traditional banking products. Whether the rule will be implemented in its current form, if at all, is still up in the air at the time of writing.

The U.S. military classifies payday loans as predatory loans. Federal rules limit to 36% the annual percentage rate that lenders can charge servicemembers who are on duty for more than 30 days (or their dependents) in extensions of consumer credit, including payday loans. This means, for example, that a payday lender cannot charge a servicemember more than $1.38 in interest on a $100 loan for two weeks. To calculate the amount of interest on the loan, take the annual interest rate and divide it by 365 days. Multiply that number by the length of the loan (the number of days), and then multiply by the amount you're borrowing. Payday lenders are not permitted to roll over loans to military personnel or their dependents either.

Scams That Target Military Personnel

Companies that offer payday loans, refund anticipation loans, auto title (auto pawn) loans, and rent-to-own arrangements, as well as used car dealers that emphasize in-house financing, cluster around military bases and advertise inside bases in official-looking military newspapers.

As explained above, federal law regulates refund anticipation loans, car title loans, payday loans, and other types of loans to active duty personnel. The Servicemembers Civil Relief Act provides additional protections, as explained in more detail above and in Chapter 6.

Some states also have laws aimed at curbing payday loan abuses, including laws limiting interest rates to 36% or less.

However, Internet-based payday lenders that conduct online transactions across state lines often claim that they don't have to comply with state laws and licensing requirements. In response, some courts have upheld a state's right to regulate out-of-state, Internet-based lenders that make loans to that state's residents, even when the lender does not have a physical presence in the state.

Even in states with laws regulating payday lenders, you should still beware of payday lenders affiliated with Native American tribes. Generally, Native American tribes cannot be sued in state court. Some payday lenders offering loans over the Internet associate themselves with a tribe, claiming state laws do not apply to them based on sovereign immunity rather than the Internet-nature of the loan. These lenders offer very-high-cost payday loans and do not comply with state consumer protection laws. Other online lenders operate their businesses from overseas, which makes it difficult, if not impossible, to enforce state laws.

A payday loan is a very expensive way to borrow money.

Avoid Payday Lender Prepaid Cards

Some payday lenders offer "prepaid" cards, which means the payday loan is deposited directly to a debit card. You can use the debit card to purchase groceries, clothing, or other items. To get the loan, you must agree to have your future income directly deposited to the card, and you must give the lender advance permission to withdraw money on your payday to repay the loan. This type of prepaid card is often subject to high overdraft fees and unexpected charges, such as a fee for a making a successful payday loan payment.

Avoid "Easy Solutions" to Debt Problems

Watch out for television, radio, Internet, or direct mail ads that claim easy solutions to debt problems. Sometimes, you can't tell exactly what these companies are offering.

Ads for Consolidation Loans

Some could turn out to be ads for expensive consolidation loans you should avoid, often with high interest rates, hidden fees, and security clauses that put property you already own at risk. (See "Avoid Consolidation Loans," above.)

Ads for Unlicensed Bankruptcy Assistance

Others could be unlicensed people claiming they can eliminate your debts through bankruptcy; often, these services file incorrectly or don't follow through, which makes it harder for you to get bankruptcy relief if you need it.

Ads for Debt Relief Services

Many of the ads that promise to get you out of debt are for debt relief services. Some offer debt management or credit counseling services. These companies claim they can arrange a plan to pay back your creditors, often with reductions in interest rates or other favorable terms so you can afford repayment. Debt settlement companies (also called debt pooling or prorating services) claim they can greatly reduce your debts, often by 50% or more. They operate by negotiating with your unsecured creditors to get them to accept a reduced lump sum or fewer payments to pay off your debt. They usually ask or require you to make regular payments into an account with a bank from which they collect their fee and pay the creditor when enough money has accumulated. Debt negotiation companies claim they can get creditors to reduce your regular payments, but do not necessarily create an overall plan like credit counselors do.

In recent years, the debt relief service business has boomed. The Federal Trade Commission and state attorneys general have sued hundreds of these companies for misleading consumers about what the companies can accomplish or how much their fees really are and for violating consumer protection laws or specific state laws governing debt relief services. The IRS has ended the nonprofit status of a number of so-called nonprofit credit counseling companies that were making profits, either directly or through affiliates.

No matter what they call their services, these companies generally produce poor results and charge very high fees and interest rates. They siphon off your limited resources in fees and charges, pay only a few (if any) creditors, and jeopardize much of your property. What's more, many do not deal with your secured debts, which often are (or should be) your highest priority for repayment. These companies often induce people to devote precious resources to paying unsecured debts when folks should be using that money to pay secured debts.

These companies claim that they can negotiate with creditors on your behalf, promising substantially reduced payments and an end to collection calls from creditors. They charge hefty fees for this service, which most consumers can do on their own. Instead of helping you obtain relief and work your way out of debt, the debt negotiator might leave you with even more negative information in your credit report and being sued by collectors. In extreme cases, companies reportedly have used consumers' money to pay the company's operating expenses instead of paying the consumers' creditors. Even if the company provides the services promised, you're better off using the money you would spend on the high fee to make payments to your creditors.

Almost all states regulate debt relief companies, and some states prohibit debt settlement companies from doing business. These state laws usually don't apply to lawyers and merchant-owned associations claiming to help debtors.

The Federal Trade Commission Telemarketing Sales Rule offers some limited protection against abusive for-profit debt relief companies. The rule only applies to for-profit companies, services related to unsecured debts, and services rendered after the debt relief

company calls you or you call in response to an ad, not if the company communicates with you through the Internet or the mail.

Before you have to pay any money, the rules require debt relief service companies to disclose:

- the total cost of the service, along with any significant restrictions, limitations, or conditions regarding the service
- all terms and conditions of the return policy (or a statement informing you that there is a no-refund policy)
- when the debt relief service provider will make a settlement offer to each of the creditors
- how much money (or the percentage of each outstanding debt) that you must save before the company makes a settlement offer to creditors
- the possible consequences of not making timely payments (for example, your credit will likely be adversely affected), and
- your rights regarding a dedicated account if the debt relief company requires you to set aside funds in an account. (16 C.F.R. § 310.3.)

Most important, the rules prohibit a company from collecting fees from you (or your account) until it has obtained an agreement to reduce at least one debt and you have made at least one payment on that agreement. (16 C.F.R. § 310.4.) The rules also place guidelines on fee amounts.

If you need help negotiating with creditors or debt collectors, see Chapter 18 for how to choose a legitimate credit counseling agency.

Negotiating With Your Creditors

This chapter will help you negotiate with your creditors on debts you can't pay fully. You should consider this strategy for essential debts, such as your house and utilities. Once you've stabilized your financial situation, you might also want to try to work out a deal with creditors for nonessential debts that you believe you can afford to keep up. If a creditor has turned your debt over to a debt collector, see Chapter 9, which provides information on negotiating with debt collectors. Your negotiation strategies and the governing laws will likely be different when dealing with a debt collector, than when dealing with original creditors.

When you're going through tough times, creditors might be willing to work with you, realizing that they are better off getting something now, rather than less or nothing later. Unsecured creditors like credit card companies, for example, might be willing to take less to pay off your delinquent debt because they know you can probably wipe out all or most of that debt in bankruptcy. But don't forget that unsecured debt is usually your lowest priority. More important is to negotiate with those holding secured loans on your house and car.

But tread cautiously. The creditor is likely to ask you to do something in exchange, such as getting a cosigner (who will be liable for the debt if you don't pay, even if you erase the debt in bankruptcy), waiving the statute of limitations (the number of years the lender has to sue you if you stop making payments—see Chapter 14), paying higher interest, paying for a longer period, or giving a security interest in your house or car. Agreeing to terms like these could ultimately make your situation worse. If you're asked to sign a document you don't understand or have concerns about, don't sign. First, consult with a credit counselor or lawyer.

SKIP AHEAD

Don't negotiate if you're going to file for bankruptcy. If you will probably file for bankruptcy soon, contacting your creditors is the last thing you should do. It's better to figure out first whether bankruptcy is your best option, and if so, which debts will be wiped out by bankruptcy. Then, work at managing the debts that won't be wiped out when you do your bankruptcy planning. There's no point in paying anything on debts just before you file if they will be wiped out by bankruptcy. Additionally, you could find yourself owing taxes that you wouldn't otherwise need to pay. You can learn more in the upcoming section, "Beware of the IRS If You Settle a Debt."

Prepare a Negotiating Plan

Before you begin negotiating, you should devise a negotiation plan—that is, figure out what you want and how you might get it. This will help you focus on what's most important and resist creditors or debt collectors that try to get you to pay them when it is in your best interest to use your limited funds elsewhere.

To come up with a plan, you'll have to:

- prepare a budget (Chapter 3 walks you through the steps to do this)
- figure out how much money you have to put towards debts
- decide which creditors get paid first (see Chapter 4), and
- determine your goals for each debt.

Communicate With Your Creditors

The first step toward working out a deal with your creditor is to keep the lines of communication open. As soon as it becomes apparent that you're going to have trouble paying your bills, call your creditors and find out what they're willing to do to help a customer in financial distress. In many cases, a creditor will agree to provide some relief to individuals without the means to pay. For instance, a creditor might be willing to reduce a payment amount, extend time to pay, drop late fees, or make some other adjustment.

You should be aware that negotiating down your balance isn't as simple as it has been in the past. Since the 2008 recession, creditors have become less willing to accept a customer's claim of financial distress. Now many refuse to provide any accommodation without first receiving proof of an inability to pay. For instance, don't be surprised if you're asked to complete an application form, or to provide financial documentation, such as paycheck stubs and bank statements.

Before you agree to do so, you'll want to seriously consider whether the potential savings is worth turning over otherwise private information to your creditor. You should assume that your creditor will use your employment and banking information to collect against you in the future (more in Chapter 13).

Also, some creditors won't negotiate down a debt balance until you're several months behind on payments—if at all. In that case, it's likely that you'll have more success after your creditor turns the account over to a debt collector (plan on that taking three to six months).

Even though many creditors won't be willing to reduce your balance, it's still in your best interest to reach out. You won't know your options until you ask.

Once you start negotiating, don't give up if the creditor doesn't accept your first offer. Be persistent. If you're still unable to pay as time goes on, the creditor might be more willing to consider your offer.

In the meantime, keep a written log of your negotiation efforts for each debt. Record how much you owe; the date, time, and substance of each conversation; and the person with whom you communicate. It's best to confirm any offer you make in writing and be sure to keep a copy.

Although writing a letter requesting an accommodation isn't as effective as it might have once been, some people aren't comfortable calling creditors. In that case, we've included a sample letter you can use to contact a creditor, as well as a letter you can modify when it's time to confirm your agreement in writing.

Sample Letter to Creditors

August 19, 20xx

Collections Department
Big Bank of Bismarck
37 Charles Street
Bismarck, ND 77777

Re: Krystal and Sergio Grange Account 411-900-LOAN

To Whom It May Concern:

On June 5, 20xx, your bank granted us a three-year $13,300 personal loan. Our agreement requires us to pay you $325 per month, and we have diligently made those payments since July 1, 20xx.

We now, however, face several emergencies. Sergio had a heart attack last April and has been out of work ever since. His doctors don't believe that he'll be able to work until November. Also, Krystal's company laid her off last week. She will receive unemployment and is looking for work. Unfortunately, many industries in our town have closed down, and jobs are few.

Currently, we cannot pay you more than $120 a month. We expect to resume the full $325-per-month payments this November when Sergio returns to work. We ask that you accept $120 a month until then, and add the missed payment amounts to the end of our loan.

Thank you for your understanding and help.

Sincerely,

Krystal Grange
Sergio Grange

Krystal and Sergio Grange
701-555-8388
cc: Leonard O'Brien, President, Big Bank of Bismarck

Sample Letter to Creditor Confirming Agreement
to Reduce Payments Temporarily

August 22, 20xx

Jillian Brown
Collections Department
Big Bank of Bismarck
37 Charles Street
Bismarck, ND 77777

Re: Krystal and Sergio Grange Account 411-900-LOAN

Dear Ms. Brown:

This letter confirms our oral agreement on August 21, 20xx.

On June 5, 20xx, your bank granted us a three-year $13,300 personal loan. Our original agreement requires us to pay you $325 per month, and we have diligently made those payments since July 1, 20xx.

As we explained in our conversation with you, we now, however, face several emergencies. Sergio had a heart attack last April and has been out of work ever since. His doctors don't believe that he'll be able to work again until sometime in November. Also, Krystal's company laid her off last week. She will receive unemployment and is looking for work. Unfortunately, though, many industries in our town have closed down, and jobs are few.

We explained that we cannot pay you more than $120 a month right now, and that we expect to resume the full $325-per-month payments in November. You agreed to accept our $120 a month as a satisfactory monthly payment until then, not charge us any late fees even though we are paying a reduced amount, and to add the missed payments to the end of our loan. We understand that that will extend our loan payments of $325 for four months, through October 5, 20xx, with the remaining balance of $120 due on November 5, 20xx. If this is not your understanding, please contact me at once.

Thank you for your understanding and help.

Sincerely,

Krystal Grange
Sergio Grange

Krystal and Sergio Grange
701-555-8388
cc: Leonard O'Brien, President, Big Bank of Bismarck

TIP

Find the person with authority.
When you call a creditor's customer service department, work your way up the chain until you find someone who can make a decision on your proposal. Follow up a phone conversation with a confirming letter, stating whom you talked to and what agreement you reached. Keep a copy of your letter. See the samples above.

Tips for Negotiating With Creditors

The following tips will help you in your negotiations.

Identify your bottom line. If you owe a doctor $1,100 but can't pay more than $600 on the debt over six months, don't agree to pay more.

Try to identify the creditor's bottom line. If a bank offers to waive two months' interest if you pay the principal on your car loan, that might mean that the bank will waive three or four months of interest. It might be worth pushing a bit harder.

Bill collectors lie a lot. If they think you can pay $100, they might vow that $100 is the lowest amount they can accept. Being skeptical makes sense..

Explain your financial problems. Be bleak, but never lie.

Offer a lump sum to pay off the debt. In tough economic times, creditors may settle for a lot less if you can pay in a lump sum. If a creditor will settle for 30% to 70% of the total debt if you pay in a lump sum, but will insist on 100% if you pay over time, try to get the money to pay the reduced amount

and settle the matter. Ask that the unpaid debt and negative information in your credit file associated with the debt be removed from your credit file in exchange for the settlement. Creditors might not agree, but if they do, be sure to get written confirmation that the debt will be considered as paid in full when you pay the agreed amount, and that the creditor will submit either an Automated Credit Dispute Verification (ACDV) form or an Automated Universal Data (AUD) form (standard forms creditors use to report to credit reporting agencies) deleting the "account/tradeline" from your credit report. You can learn more about e-OSCAR, the online reporting system, at www.e-oscar.org.

Offer a payment plan to reduce your payments and the total you owe. If you can't pay a lump sum to settle the debt, but the creditor agrees to put you on a new schedule for repaying the debt, consider asking the creditor to "re-age" your account, which makes the current month the first repayment month and stops showing late payments in your credit report. Sometimes, a creditor won't re-age an account until you make two or three monthly payments first. But think carefully before asking a creditor to re-age the account, especially if it's been reported as delinquent for some time. Re-aging means that the account will appear on your credit report for seven years after the repayment date, rather than seven years after the earlier delinquency date. Some consumer advocates argue that re-aging an account is a bad idea for this reason. On the other hand, some debt management plans favor re-aging because the account appears as current on the credit report. You'll have to decide what is best for you. (See Chapters 9, "How to Handle Time-Barred or "Zombie" Debts" and 16 for details on credit repair.)

Don't split the difference. If you offer a low amount to settle a debt and the creditor proposes that you split the difference between the creditor's higher demand and your offer, you might want to treat the split-the-difference number as a new top and propose an amount between that and your original offer.

Consider mentioning bankruptcy. If bankruptcy is an option you are considering, you might want to mention that your other option is to file for bankruptcy if the creditor refuses to make concessions. You might find that an unreasonable creditor is willing to compromise.

But think carefully before doing this. In most cases, a "mentioned bankruptcy" notation will immediately be added to your account file with that creditor. If you incur any additional debt after that date—even with a different creditor—you could have a difficult time eliminating that debt in bankruptcy if you do eventually file. The creditor will argue that once you mentioned bankruptcy, you had no intention of repaying your bills and that all debts you incurred after that date should not be wiped out (taking on debt with no intention of repaying it is a type of fraud). Depending on the circumstances, a bankruptcy judge might agree.

If you don't feel comfortable negotiating —for example, you hate bargaining at flea markets and would rather sell your used car to a dealer than find a buyer yourself—ask a friend or relative to negotiate on your behalf.

As long as your negotiator will keep to your bottom line, it will be hard for the creditor to shame or guilt the negotiator into agreeing to pay a higher amount. Some creditors are reluctant to negotiate with anyone other than you or your lawyer. If need be, prepare a power of attorney giving your negotiator the right to handle your debts on your behalf.

Rent Payments

Depending on the market conditions, it might not hurt to ask your landlord to reduce your monthly rent. If the landlord knows it will be difficult to rerent your place, the landlord might agree to accept a partial payment now and the rest later, or might temporarily lower your rent, rather than evict you. The landlord might further agree to let you pay a little bit each month to make up any back rent you owe. Of course, if rents are skyrocketing, as they are in some areas of the country, this probably won't be a good strategy.

If your landlord agrees to a rent reduction or lets you make up past-due payments, send the landlord a letter confirming the arrangement by certified mail, return receipt requested. (See sample letter, below.) Be sure to keep a copy for yourself. Once the understanding is written down, the landlord will have a hard time evicting you for not paying the rent, as long as you make the payments under your new agreement.

If you decide to move but have months remaining on a lease, your landlord might try to sue you for the remaining months' rent. Legally, however, in most states, the landlord must use reasonable efforts to

Sample Letter to Landlord

September 22, 20xx

Frank O'Neill
1556 North Lakefront
Minneapolis, MN 67890

Dear Frank:

Thanks for being so understanding about my being laid off. This letter is to confirm the telephone conversation we had yesterday.

My lease requires that I pay rent of $750 per month. You agreed to reduce my rent to $600 per month, beginning October 1, and lasting until I find another job, but not to exceed three months. That is, even if I haven't found a new job, my rent will go back to $750 per month on January 1. If this is not your understanding, please contact me at once.

Thank you again for your understanding and help. As I mentioned on the phone, I hope to have another job shortly, and I am following all leads in order to secure employment.

Sincerely,

Abigail Landsberg

Abigail Landsberg

try to rent the place to minimize the loss. If the landlord can't rerent it despite making reasonable efforts, you will be on the hook for the balance of the rent. If you advanced one or two months' rent or paid a cleaning or security deposit when you moved in, the landlord should put that money not reasonably needed for cleaning or repair toward any rent you owe.

Mortgage Payments

We cover mortgage payments in Chapter 8. Federal government programs have been set up to encourage lenders to help homeowners refinance; modify their mortgages; negotiate short sales (sales for less than the amount of the loan); or perhaps turn over the property to the lender (deed in lieu).

Utility and Telephone Bills

If you miss one month's utility bill—including a bill for heating oil or gas deliveries—you probably won't hear from the company, unless you have a poor payment history. If you ignore a few past-due notices, however, the company will threaten to cut off your service. Call the company before the threats become dire. Most utility companies will let you get two or three months behind as long as you tell them when you'll be able to make up what you owe. If your service has been shut off, the company will most likely require you to make a security deposit before it reconnects you. The deposit rates following disconnects are regulated in some states and a utility company might be required to offer you a payment plan. But beware of prepaid plans. (See Chapter 7, "Loss of Utility Service," for more information.) You might want to call a Legal Aid or Legal Services office (see Chapter 18) to learn about your state's law.

Special Protections for Active Servicemembers

The Servicemembers Civil Relief Act or SCRA (50 U.S.C. §§ 3901–4043) gives servicemembers on active duty for 30 days or more, including reservists and members of the National Guard called up for active duty, and, in most cases, their dependents, some special rights. Most do not happen automatically, however, so it is up to you to assert these rights. These rights include:

- Real estate foreclosure proceedings can be stayed (stopped) and the terms of a servicemember's mortgage can be adjusted during active duty and the months following. A court may also establish your equity in the property and require you be paid that amount on foreclosure.

- Civil court proceedings can be delayed up to 90 days or more while you are on active duty, and for 90 days afterward. Even if a creditor has a judgment, you may be able to delay efforts to enforce it. Courts also can fashion a more equitable remedy in eviction cases.

- A servicemember may terminate a lease on a vehicle if he or she leased it before entering military service and then went on active duty for 180 days or more. A servicemember who signs a lease while on active duty and who is later reassigned outside the continental United States or reassigned elsewhere from a U.S. possession outside the continental United States, or who is sent on temporary duty for 180 days or longer, also can terminate a vehicle lease. The lessor cannot charge an early termination penalty, but can charge for excess mileage and wear and tear.

- A servicemember may terminate a lease on a home or an office if he or she signed the lease before entering military service and then went on active duty. A servicemember also can terminate a lease signed when he or she was on active duty if the servicemember is reassigned or deployed for 90 days or more.

- The interest rate on credit cards, mortgages, bank loans, federal student Direct Loans, guaranteed student loans under FFEL (see Chapter 11), vehicle financing, and the like is reduced to 6% annually for the entire time the servicemember is on active duty. Payments must be reduced accordingly. This reduction applies only to obligations incurred by the servicemember, or the member and spouse jointly, before the member went on active duty. The creditor must forgive any interest that exceeds 6% for the entire time of active duty.

- A creditor's right to rescind or terminate a servicemember's installment contract for the purchase or lease of real or personal property (including vehicles) due to a breach of the contract's terms (including defaulting on payments) is limited if the first payment was made before the servicemember went on active duty and the breach happened before or during active duty. Additionally, the property cannot be repossessed without a court order.

- Servicemembers have protections against default judgments being entered against them in civil actions.

Special Protections for Active Servicemembers (continued)

- The military has classified tax refund anticipation loans (RALs), auto title loans (if the creditor takes the vehicle's title as security and the loan is for 181 days or less, but not used to buy a car), and payday loans as predatory loans and limits the annual percentage rate on these loans to 36% for active duty servicemembers or their dependents. This means, for example, that now a payday lender cannot charge a servicemember more than $1.38 in interest on a $100 loan for two weeks. If you were charged a higher rate on a RAL, auto title loan, or payday loan, you should be able to get the rate reduced to 36%. Because a higher rate is a violation of law, you may be able to get the lender to agree to make things right by reducing the cost to below 36% or to eliminate all charges entirely.
- Student loans can be deferred while on active duty (see Chapter 11).

Servicemembers who want to take advantage of these rights must follow specified steps and procedures, and there are exceptions and limitations. For more information, go to the CFPB's website at www.consumerfinance. gov (under the "Get Assistance" tab, click on "Servicemembers and Veterans"), do an Internet search for U.S. Armed Forces Legal Assistance, or contact your military legal assistance lawyer.

Some consumers fall behind on energy bills during periods when they use a lot of energy and incur high bills (winter in the north, for example). Many energy utilities offer programs that average your periods of high and low usage and allow you to pay a uniform monthly payment all year long. And you might be able to get a reprieve from paying the bill which can give you time to explore ways to reduce your bill for the long term.

RELATED TOPIC

Review ways to cut utility expenses. Before you begin negotiating with the utility company, review the ways you can cut your utility expenses in Chapter 5, and learn about possible limits on the utility company's ability to cut off your services in Chapter 7 ("Loss of Utility Service").

Car Payments

Your options for handling car payments depend on whether you are buying or leasing your vehicle.

Purchase Payments

If you expect you'll have trouble making your car payments for several months, your best bet is to sell the car, pay off the lender, and use whatever is left to either pay your other debts or buy a reliable used car.

If you want to hold onto your car and you miss a payment, immediately call the lender and speak to someone in the customer service or collections department. Don't delay. Cars are more quickly repossessed than any other type of property. The creditor doesn't have to get a court judgment before seizing the car. (See Chapter 7.) And cars lose value fast—the creditor who has to auction one off wants the largest possible return.

On the other hand, some creditors may not be eager to repossess your vehicle. According to one industry consultant, creditors lose thousands of dollars per car repossession.

Negotiate Your Phone Bill

Of all utility bills, the phone bill is often the most difficult to understand. Charges may be posted by at least three separate companies: your local carrier, long distance carrier, and Internet service provider. You might also have special features billed to you, such as call waiting or voice mail.

The part of your bill for local service is a higher priority bill than the charges for other services. Also, check to see if you have been paying for services you did not order. If you have, you may be able to negotiate not only to have them removed from future bills, but also to get money back for prior unauthorized charges.

You may also be able to reduce the cost of phone service by eliminating unneeded phones or services or using a prepaid cell phone plan. For tips on how to reduce phone costs, see Chapter 5.

Figure out which of these possible options may be most useful to you and then try to negotiate the change:

- **Extension of time to pay.** If you present a convincing argument that your situation is temporary, the lender might grant you an extension, meaning the delinquent payment can be paid at the end of your loan period. The lender probably won't grant an extension unless you've made at least six payments. Also, most lenders charge a fee for granting an extension and don't grant more than one a year. Fees for extending car loans vary tremendously. Some lenders charge a flat fee, such as $25. Others charge a percentage (usually 1%) of the outstanding balance. Others charge one month's worth of interest.
- **Different payment due date.** Ask if the lender will change your monthly payment date so that it corresponds better to when you receive your income. Some lenders that agree to this might also waive late fees or reduce the interest charged, which would lower your payment amount.
- **Rewritten loan with lower payments.** The lender may offer to rewrite the loan to reduce the monthly payments. This means, however, that you'll have to pay for a longer period and you'll have to pay more total interest. Make sure that getting a lower monthly payment doesn't require you to take out a larger total loan. Try to avoid loans that have a prepayment penalty or that include interest calculated in any way other than the simple interest method.

The bottom line is that most car lenders would prefer to be paid rather than repossess your car. Reaching out to your lender about your options should be worth the effort.

Lease Payments

If you can't afford your automobile lease payments and want to cancel your lease, look carefully at the provisions in your contract describing what happens if you default and how you can terminate the lease early. Many of these provisions include claims that you'll owe a very large sum of money or complex formulas that are difficult to understand. Ending a lease early is expensive—you can expect the early termination fee to be hefty. But if the fee seems way out of line, you might be able to get the lessor to agree to a reduction.

Look in your lease agreement for the explanation of how the early termination fee is calculated. Ask the lessor to confirm exactly how much you will have to pay to terminate the lease early in your particular circumstances.

Many (but not all) car leases must comply with the federal Consumer Leasing Act (CLA). The CLA requires that early termination fees be reasonable and that the explanation be clear and conspicuous (the CLA also requires lease contracts to contain other disclosures). If you think the early termination fee is not reasonable or the explanation of how it's calculated is not clear, use that in your negotiation. If you are not sure if your lease is covered by the CLA, want help determining if the amount is reasonable, or just want help negotiating with the car lease company, contact a local consumer attorney.

Secured Loan Payments

If a personal loan or store agreement is secured—for example, you borrowed money to purchase a refrigerator or couch and you pledged it as security for your repayment—the lender may threaten to send a truck to pick up the property if you don't make reasonable payments.

But few lenders take personal property other than vehicles. The resale value of used property is low. The lender is not in the used furniture business and doesn't want your dining room table or stereo. Almost always, the lender values the debt—even if it is hard to collect—more than the property. Also, the lender can't get into your house to get the property without a court order or your permission. Few lenders ever go to the expense of getting a court order. This means you have the upper hand in the negotiation.

The lender may extend your loan or rewrite it to reduce the monthly payments. The lender might even be willing to reduce the amount owed to the current value of the property. Be prepared to discuss your financial situation.

Can you give back the collateral and call it even? If you don't need or want the collateral, you can offer to give it back to the creditor or collection agency. They don't have to take it, however, and probably won't if the item has substantially decreased in value or is hard to sell.

Even if the creditor or collection agency takes the property back, in most states, you'll be liable for the difference between what you owe and what the creditor can sell the property for. This difference is called a deficiency and, as explained in Chapter 7, is often reason enough to avoid having property repossessed.

If you can no longer afford to keep the property, your best strategy in many cases is to offer to give it back in exchange for a written agreement waiving any deficiency. See the sample letter, below. If the creditor refuses, you may be better off trying to sell the item yourself and using the proceeds to pay your debts.

Exemptions won't help you. Chapters 14 and 15 cover exempt property—the property your creditors, including debt collectors, can't take, even if you file for bankruptcy or get sued. There's one major exception to exempt property: collateral for a secured debt. So, for example, if you received a loan to buy a car, most likely you signed a document agreeing that the car would be security for the loan. You can't keep a creditor from repossessing the collateral even if it would otherwise be exempt.

Insurance Payments

Your medical, homeowners', and auto insurance payments may be essential debts. At the same time, your life or disability insurance payments probably aren't, unless you or other members of your family are ill.

Most policies have a grace period—which means you will still be covered by your insurance for a few days or weeks, even if you don't pay your premium on time. If you think you might be late with a payment, check with your insurer or read your policy to find out the length of your grace period.

Ordinarily, you won't be able to negotiate reduced premium payments or extend payments over a long time unless you reduce the insurance coverage or increase the deductibles. If you can't pay for the whole year at once, you may be able to pay for just six months, or even monthly—but you'll probably pay a bit more overall. (To learn about ways to reduce the cost of insurance, see Chapter 5.) You can also do some comparison shopping. Contact your insurance agent to ask for a better price.

If your insurance policy—life or otherwise—has lapsed, and your financial picture is improving, many insurance companies will let you reinstate your policy if you pay up what you owe within a certain number of days after the premium payment first became due. You may also have to pay interest on your back premiums. After that period, the company will probably make you reapply for coverage. If your risk factors have increased since you originally took out the insurance—for example, you took out auto insurance two years ago and have since had a car accident and a moving violation, and your insurance just lapsed—you may be denied coverage or offered coverage only at a higher rate.

Medical, Legal, and Other Service Bills

Critics of hospital billing argue that the vast majority of hospital bills contain overcharges, particularly if you are uninsured. Before assuming that your bill is correct, review it carefully and be sure that you understand and agree with every charge. With hospital

Sample Letter Offering to Give Back Secured Property in Exchange for a Written Agreement Waiving Deficiency

April 18, 20xx
Collections Department
The Computer Store
5151 South Olvera Place
Santa Fe, NM 70804
Re: Martina Smith
Account No. 1294-444-38RD (computer)

To Whom It May Concern:

I've received your notice indicating that my account is overdue.

I would like to pay my bill, but I have lost my job and have not been able to find another one over the last four months.

I do not know when I will be able to resume payments on the computer I purchased. I have already paid about half of what I owe, and the computer is still in good condition. I am willing to return it to you, if you agree not to charge me any more for it and to waive any deficiency. If you agree, please sign below and return a signed copy of this letter to me. When I have received your signed copy, I will call to arrange for you to pick up the computer.

Thank you for your consideration in this matter. If you wish to speak to me, please feel free to call me at my home at 505-555-9333.

Sincerely,

Martina Smith

Martina Smith

The Computer Store agrees in exchange for receiving the computer and the payments already made on account number 1294-444-38RD to waive any deficiency balance on this account.

Name: _____

Title: _____

Date: _____

Signature: _____

bills and lawyers' bills, in particular, ask for specific itemization if the bill gives only broad categories. And if the bill is filled with indecipherable codes, ask someone in the billing office to explain what every code means.

Once you understand what each charge is, look for mistakes, such as duplicate charges, charges based on operating room use for longer than you were there, daily charges for days you were not hospitalized, and charges for procedures or medications you either did not receive or that are billed for more expensive ones than those you did receive. Many doctors, dentists, lawyers, and accountants will accept partial payments, reduce their total bills, drop interest or late fees, and delay sending bills to collection agencies if you communicate how difficult your financial problems are and try to get their sympathy. Some doctors, especially, won't spend too much effort in collecting the outstanding bills of longtime patients who suddenly find themselves unable to pay.

If your insurance will eventually cover all or most of your medical bill, but the medical provider is pursuing you because the insurer hasn't paid yet, gather together evidence of:

- your submission of the bill to your insurance company, and
- your insurance company's coverage for the specific medical care you received.

Armed with this information, call the doctor or hospital's collections department and ask for an appointment. At the meeting, provide the collector with copies of your documentation and plead with the person to cease collection efforts against you. Let the collections representative know that your medical condition may worsen if the stress of the collection calls and letters doesn't stop (if this is, in fact, true). If you get nowhere with the collections representative, make an appointment to see the department supervisor. Also, if the bill is from a hospital, see if the facility has an ombudsman or patient's advocate. Such a person works to help resolve disputes between patients and the hospital. But remember: If you haven't yet paid the amount of any deductible, you still owe it. The insurance company won't pay it, and the doctor or hospital will continue to come after you.

Be leery if you're asked to use a credit card for medical bills. Some credit card companies are trying to get doctors and dentists to offer you a choice of paying cash or paying with a credit card. You're better off owing the doctor directly instead of putting your medical charges on a credit card. You have more negotiating leverage with the doctor than with a large credit card company.

Child Support and Alimony Payments

No matter how difficult your financial situation, you won't be relieved of your duty to pay court-ordered child support unless you take affirmative steps to legally reduce your support obligation. Because a court ordered you to pay, only a court can order a change in the amount you must pay. Thus, when your income drops, immediately file the necessary paperwork (usually called a motion, a petition, or an order to show cause) with the court, asking that your future child support payments be reduced, at least temporarily. Alimony is different because the court doesn't always retain the power to change that type of support, the way it does with child support. If you must pay alimony, it's likely that your final divorce judgment or settlement agreement defines when that obligation ends. If it doesn't say that losing your job or income is a reason for support to end or change, then generally, you're stuck paying until the obligation is done.

The court cannot retroactively reduce child support. The court can set up a payment schedule for you to get current, but if you miss payments before you ask for a reduction, the court can't erase your debt. (See Chapter 12 for information on reducing child support or alimony.)

Income Taxes

If you cannot pay the IRS taxes you owe, the IRS will encourage you to charge the extra amount on your credit card. This may be a bad idea, because the interest on your credit card will probably be a lot higher than the interest and penalties the IRS will charge if you reach an agreement with it.

Remember, if you owe the IRS up to $10,000 and you have not been in tax trouble recently, you are entitled to an installment agreement to pay your taxes. (See Chapter 4, "Unpaid taxes," and IRS Form 9465-FS.) If you don't meet these criteria, you may still be able to negotiate an installment agreement, but the IRS gets to decide whether to give you one.

If you cannot afford an installment agreement, you can make an "offer in compromise." This means that you make a lump sum offer to the IRS to settle what you owe. The IRS will accept an offer in compromise in only three situations:

- There's a doubt that the assessed tax is correct.
- You may not have the ability to pay the full amount owed.
- You could pay the full amount, but doing so would cause you economic hardship.

You must also meet all of the following:

- You have filed all required federal tax returns before you apply for a compromise.
- You are not in bankruptcy. (If you are in bankruptcy, any compromise would need to be negotiated in connection with the bankruptcy.)
- Unless you qualify for low-income certification, when you apply, you must pay an application fee (currently $186) and a payment equal to either your first proposed payment (if you propose periodic payments) or 20% of your offer amount (if you propose a cash or lump sum offer).
- You submit required financial information.

(See IRS Form 656-B and the *Offer in Compromise* booklet (available at www.irs.gov), for additional information.)

Finally, you may be able to eliminate, reduce, or spread out your IRS debt by filing for bankruptcy. (Bankruptcy is covered in Chapter 14.)

RESOURCE

For a complete discussion of your options with the IRS, see *Stand Up to the IRS,* by Erica Pless and Frederick W. Daily (Nolo).

Student Loan Payments

There are lots of options available for repaying federal student loans and federally guaranteed student loans. In some cases, you may even be able to cancel your debt altogether. If you have private student loans, however, your options are more limited. We cover your options for dealing with student loan debt in Chapter 11.

Credit Card Payments

If you don't have enough money to keep current on all your debts, remember that credit card debt is usually not a top priority for repayment because most credit cards are unsecured. (But keep in mind that you'll likely have to take steps to take care of it at some point—especially if you owe a large balance. Creditor lawsuits are covered in Chapter 13.) However, if you have a secured credit card, especially if it is secured by your home, you should treat it like other important secured debts.

TIP

How the CARD Act can help. When negotiating with your credit card company, it helps to know what the company can and cannot do. The federal CARD Act places limits on interest rate increases in certain situations and provides other protections to consumers. To learn about the CARD Act, see Chapter 17.

If You Want to Keep Your Credit Card

Credit card companies are no longer making the huge reductions in interest rates, monthly payments, or balances owed as they were during the recession of 2008. But because companies want to keep customers, you may still be able to negotiate better terms if you want to keep your card.

Call your credit card company and ask for an interest rate reduction (which will also lower your payments), elimination of fees you have been charged for late payments or over-the-limit charges, smaller monthly minimum payments (if you need that for a short time), or even a reduction in the balance you owe. Before you call, visit websites like www.bankrate.com to get information about what rates your current credit card company is offering new customers and what rates are available from other companies. Use this information when you negotiate.

If You Want to Settle the Debt or Get Rid of the Card

You may be able to settle your credit card debt for a third to half of what you owe. Credit card companies will ordinarily not offer such a deal until you are several months late. Usually, the company will require you to pay the settled upon amount in one payment or several payments. If you are already struggling with debt, it might be difficult to get a lump sum large enough to settle.

Alternatively, if you can't pay anything on your credit card and have decided that keeping the card isn't essential, one option is to stop making payments. Of course, there will be negative consequences. You may lose your credit privileges. You may be sued, but that will take some time. Your credit report will make you look like a riskier borrower, so other creditors will likely not offer you the best interest rates on new credit, if they offer you credit at all. And, of course, missed payments will bring down your credit score. However, the hit to your credit may be less severe than if you lose your home or car.

Charge Card Payments

If you can't pay a charge card bill—such as some American Express cards—you must approach the creditor differently. Charge cards are much less common than credit cards. With most charge cards, you are required to pay off the entire balance when your bill arrives. If you don't, you'll owe a late fee. If you don't pay the amount due for two billing periods in a row, you'll typically have to pay a heftier late fee of around $35 or a percentage of the past due amount (typically around 2 to 3%), whichever is greater. Also, the creditor can cancel the card once you default. Some charge cards give you the option to pay a bill off over time. If you choose to do this, you'll accrue interest on any charges you pay over time and face a penalty APR if you don't keep up with the minimum payment amounts. If your card company doesn't offer payments over time, call and ask that you be given a monthly repayment plan for paying off the bill. Offer to pay only what you can afford. The company usually doesn't report this arrangement to credit reporting agencies if you pay the monthly amount you agreed to.

Reducing Your Minimum Payments

If you can't make even the minimum payments on all your cards, and you haven't been able to get the companies to make substantial reductions in the balances, you could try to negotiate temporary reductions in the minimum payments (or interest rate, which will reduce the minimum payment somewhat) on as many cards as you can. Using the Nolo credit card repayment calculator (at www.nolo.com), you can be realistic in figuring out how long it would take you to pay off one card with the extra money saved from reduced minimum payments on the other cards. Then, propose that period for a temporary reduction in minimum payments to the other credit card companies.

 CAUTION

It's rarely a good plan to make only the minimum payment. Negotiating a temporary minimum payment reduction should be just that—a temporary strategy that you use to help pay off your balances. It's almost never a good idea to make only the minimum payment on your cards. To learn more, see Chapter 17.

Getting Help

If you are unsuccessful in negotiating lower interest payments, a lower balance, or reductions in fees or interest on your own or feel that you could use some help, try contacting a nonprofit credit counseling agency. (See Chapter 18 for information on choosing a credit counseling agency.)

In addition, your credit card statement will include a toll-free number where you can get contacts for three (if available) credit counseling agencies serving your area. Because contacts can only be provided for agencies approved by the U.S. Chapter 13 Trustee, you have some hope that the agencies will be legitimate. Even so, you should check out carefully any agencies you contact, as it often takes a while for a government office to find out that a company is engaging in fraudulent or abusive business practices.

 RELATED TOPIC

Send a letter confirming your agreement. Once you've had an initial discussion with a creditor, you should write to confirm the agreement you reached. Ask the creditor to agree to either remove negative information about the debt from your credit report or to re-age the debt—to start it over, so your initial repayment is shown as your first payment on the debt. This way, your account won't show any past late payments, although you may owe for a longer period of time. Before you decide whether to ask for the account to be re-aged, review "How to Handle Time-Barred or "Zombie" Debts" in Chapter 9, and "Statute of Limitations" in Chapter 13. There are some disadvantages to re-aging an account.

Negotiating When the Creditor Has a Judgment Against You

If you don't pay your debt, your creditor may sue you. Once it has a judgment against you, it also has an expanded arsenal of collection techniques. For example, a creditor can put a lien on your house, empty your bank accounts, or attach a portion of your wages. An otherwise nonessential debt can quickly become essential when it's turned into a judgment; so ideally, you'll avoid getting a judgment against you. But even if there is a judgment against you, you can still negotiate. Make an offer to the creditor, pointing out that it would save the creditor the trouble and expense of enforcing the judgment. Chapter 13 discusses what to do if you are sued.

Pay Off a Debt for Less Than the Full Amount

If you owe a creditor $750, you may be tempted to send a check for $450 and write on the check that "cashing this check constitutes payment in full." Almost all states have adopted laws that allow you to send partial payment as "payment in full," even if the creditor hasn't agreed to it, but only if the amount of the claim is uncertain, or you have a good-faith dispute over the amount of the claim and you're offering the check in good faith as full satisfaction of the claim. This is a way to resolve a disputed bill informally. It is not meant as a way to "pay pennies on the dollar" for a debt you know you owe.

If you dispute the amount owed but haven't reached an agreement with the creditor to pay less, write a letter with your check like the sample shown below.

California has two contradictory laws for settling a disputed debt by sending a check. The sample letter (below) that is for use "Outside of California" complies with the more recent California law (Cal. Com. Code §3311), which some courts have said trumps the older law. The advantage of using this letter: Creditors may be more likely to go along with your proposed settlement if they receive the check and letter at the same time. But if you want to be absolutely sure that your letters comply with whatever law a court ultimately upholds, use the two-step process outlined in the sample letters specifically for California.

If the creditor cashes a check you send as payment in full, which you've sent along with a letter like that shown below, by law you won't owe the creditor any more money. Nonetheless, the creditor might insist that you still owe money anyway. You may still get collection calls, and your credit report won't reflect that you've paid the debt. In this situation, even if you're in the right, you may have to get an attorney to enforce the law. For this reason, it's wise to try to write to the creditor asking for an agreement before you send any payment.

If you *don't* dispute the amount you owe and you want the creditor to accept less as payment in full but you haven't reached an agreement with the creditor for this arrangement, you can try sending a letter with a check for the lesser amount to satisfy the debt. Consider seeking an agreement with the creditor before sending any payment.

Don't Write Postdated Checks

Many aggressive debt collectors will try to pressure you into sending postdated checks: checks that bear a future date. Sending a postdated check is always a bad idea. If you don't have sufficient funds in your account when the collector cashes it, the check will bounce.

Although it's usually legal for creditors to accept postdated checks, they don't always wait to deposit them until the dates on the checks. And the bank is usually not liable if it cashes a check before the date on the check. There is an exception: If, in advance, you notify the bank of the check and date, the bank is not supposed to cash it early. However, the safest course is to not write a postdated check.

Instead of writing a postdated check, you might tell the creditor that you will personally deliver the check on the day you write it (assuming the creditor is local).

By contrast, it is illegal for professional debt collectors to accept checks postdated by more than five days, unless they notify you between three and ten days in advance of when they will deposit the checks. It's also illegal for a debt collector to deposit or threaten to deposit a check before the date stated on the check or to solicit a postdated check for the purpose of threatening or instituting criminal prosecution. (15 U.S.C. § 1692f.)

Sample Letter: Cashing Check Constitutes Payment in Full on Disputed Amount (Outside of California)

[In some states, you can send a letter like this to the person, office, or place designated by the creditor for communications regarding disputed debts—or to the proper collection agent if you are no longer dealing with the creditor company itself. Don't forget to write the statement at the end of this letter conspicuously on the check.

Be sure to check with an attorney in your state to find out if you can satisfy a disputed debt by sending a check for a lesser amount and, if so, what steps you should take to ensure that you comply with state law.]

January 5, 20xx
Herman's Rentals
345 Main Street
Anytown, NV

Attn: Customer Service
Name on account: Jason Butler
Invoice number: 456A

To Whom It May Concern:

Regarding the above-referenced invoice, I dispute the amount you claim that I owe you. For the past three months, I have received bills from you stating that I owe $300 for a three-day rental of your New-Finish-Now hardwood floor finisher. You will recall that I have spoken to you about this bill several times during the last three months.

As you will also recall, I rented the finisher on a Friday evening intending to return it on Sunday, for a total of two days' rental. When I came to your store on Sunday, it was closed and I could not return the finisher until Monday. None of Herman's employees told me that the store would be closed on Sunday. I believe that I owe you no more than $200, and it is obvious that there is a good-faith dispute over the amount of this bill.

In a good-faith effort to satisfy this debt, I have enclosed a check for $200 to cover the balance of the account. Cashing this check constitutes payment in full and releases all claims you may have related to this account.

Sincerely,

Jason Butler

Jason Butler
33 Shady Lane
Anytown, CA
123-456-7891
Enclosed: Check stating on front: "Cashing this check constitutes payment in full and releases all claims related to Invoice 456A, Jason Butler."

Sample Letter: Cashing Check Constitutes Payment in Full on Disputed Amount—First Letter (California)

[Send a letter like this to the person, office, or place designated by the creditor for communications regarding disputed debts—or to the proper collection agent if you are no longer dealing with the creditor company itself.]

January 5, 20xx
Herman's Rentals
345 Main Street
Anytown, CA

Attn: Customer Service
Name on account: Jason Butler
Invoice number: 456A
To Whom It May Concern:

Regarding the above-referenced invoice, I dispute the amount you claim that I owe you. For the past three months, I have received bills from you stating that I owe $300 for a three-day rental of your New-Finish-Now hardwood floor finisher. You will recall that I have spoken to you about this bill several times during the last three months.

As you will also recall, I rented the finisher on a Friday evening intending to return it on Sunday, for a total of two days' rental. When I came to your store on Sunday, it was closed and I could not return the finisher until Monday. None of Herman's employees told me that the store would be closed on Sunday. I believe that I owe you no more than $200, and it is obvious that there is a good-faith dispute over the amount of this bill.

In a good-faith effort to satisfy this debt, I will send you a check for $200 with a restrictive endorsement. If you cash that check, it will constitute an accord and satisfaction. In other words, you will receive from me a check that states, "Cashing this check constitutes payment in full and releases all claims you may have related to this account." If you cash that check, it will fully satisfy my obligation to you.

Sincerely,

Jason Butler

Jason Butler
33 Shady Lane
Anytown, CA
123-456-7891

Sample Letter: Cashing Check Constitutes Payment in Full
on Disputed Amount—Second Letter (California)

[Send this letter to the person, office, or place designated by the creditor for communications regarding disputed debts—or to the proper collection agent if you are no longer dealing with the creditor company itself. Wait a reasonable time before sending this letter (at least 15 days after you send the first letter), and indicate that amount of time. Don't forget to write the statement in quotations at the end of this letter conspicuously on the check.]

January 25, 20xx
Herman's Rentals
345 Main Street
Anytown, CA
Attn: Customer Service

Name on account: Jason Butler
Invoice number: 456A

To Whom It May Concern:

Fifteen days have passed since I sent you a letter dated January 5, 20xx, stating my intention to send you a check with a restrictive endorsement.

Enclosed is a check for $200 to cover the balance of my account. This check is tendered in accordance with my earlier letter. If you cash this check, you agree that my debt is satisfied in full and you release all claims you may have related to this account.

Sincerely,

Jason Butler

Jason Butler
33 Shady Lane
Anytown, CA
123-456-7891

Enclosed: Check stating on front: "This check is tendered in accordance with my letter of January 25, 20xx. Cashing this check releases all claims you may have related to Invoice Number 456A, Jason Butler, and constitutes payment in full."

Beware of the IRS If You Settle a Debt

If you settle a debt with a creditor, or the creditor writes off a debt you owe, you could wind up owing income tax on that money. Here's how: Creditors often write off debts after a set period of time—such as one, two, or three years after default. That means they cease collection efforts, declare the debt uncollectible, and report it to the IRS as lost income, so they can reduce their taxes. The same is true for negotiated reduction of a debt. The flip side of that is that the IRS thinks that you've gained income, because you don't have to pay the debt anymore. Debts subject to this law include money owed after a house foreclosure, after a property repossession, or on a credit card bill you don't pay.

Any bank, credit union, savings and loan, finance company, credit card company, other financial institution, or federal government agency that forgives or writes off $600 or more of the principal amount of a debt (the amount not attributable to interest or fees) must send you and the IRS a Form 1099-C at the end of the tax year. You must report the amount on this form as income when you file your tax return for the tax year in which your debt was settled or written off unless an exception applies.

Even if you don't get a Form 1099-C from a creditor, the creditor may very well have submitted one to the IRS. If you don't list the income on your tax return and the IRS has the information, it will send you a tax bill (or worse, an audit notice), which could end up costing you more in IRS interest and penalties in the long run.

Sample Letter: Cashing Check Constitutes a Release of All Claims When You Send Check for Less Than Full Amount Owed

[Send this letter to the person, office, or place designated by the creditor for communications regarding disputed debts, or to the proper collection agent if you are no longer dealing with the creditor company itself. Don't forget to write the statement in quotations at the end of this letter conspicuously on the check you enclose.]

June 1, 20xx

Attn: Customer Service
Name on account: Caroline Jones
Account number: 789B

To Whom It May Concern:

You have billed me a total of $400 on this account. I can pay only a total of $250 to satisfy this account in full. Enclosed is a check for $250 for the balance of my account. If you cash this check, you agree that my debt is satisfied in full and you release all claims you may have related to this account.

Sincerely,

Caroline Jones

Caroline Jones
890 First Street
Central City, MO
123-456-7890

Enclosed: Check stating on front:
"Cashing this check releases all claims that may be related to Account Number 789B (Caroline Jones) and constitutes payment in full."

Bad Checks

Writing a bad check when you know you don't have the money to cover it is a crime. You could face criminal prosecution, hefty bad-check processing fees (from the bank), and a lawsuit from the creditor to whom the check was written.

Some counties have diversion programs—classes for bad-check writers. If you choose to go, you must pay the tuition, make good on the bad checks you wrote, and pay an administrative fee.

If you get a notice to participate in a bad-check diversion program, read it carefully. Make sure the check actually fits within the "bad-check" crime definition. If you're not sure, contact the district attorney's office or consult with an attorney. You may be able to resolve the matter by paying what you owe to the person or company that got your bad check. (Get any agreement you reach in writing before you pay up.)

If you escape criminal prosecution, you'll still be charged a bad-check processing fee by your bank. Many banks charge more than $35 per overdraft.

In addition, the person to whom you wrote a bad check—or one where a stop payment was later ordered—can sue for damages unless you stopped payment because of a good-faith dispute. If the payee makes a written demand that you make good on the bad check, and you don't pay by the deadline (usually 30 days), the payee can sue you.

If you lose the lawsuit, you are likely to be ordered to pay:

- the face value of the check
- collection and mailing costs
- interest from the date of the check, and
- court and attorneys' fees.

In most states, additional damages can be awarded against you for writing a bad check. In many states, you must pay three times the amount of the check, with a cap of $500 or $1,000. In a few states, the additional damages are limited to a small amount ($50 or $100). If you plead financial hardship, the court may reduce the additional damages.

There are important exceptions to this rule. Even if you and the IRS got a Form 1099-C, you may not have to report the amount as income on your tax return if any of the following is true:

- A student loan was canceled because you worked in a profession and for an employer as promised when you took out the loan (see IRS Publication 4681).
- The canceled debt would have been deductible if you had paid it.

Stale Checks: How Long Will a Check Be Honored?

If you wrote a check several months ago, but the payee has not yet cashed it, can you add the balance back into your checkbook?

Perhaps, but not necessarily. A bank, savings and loan, or credit union is not required to honor a check presented for cashing more than six months after the check was written. Most banks do, however, unless the check has an express notation on it "not valid after six months" (called a "restrictive legend"). However, even with a restrictive legend on the check, your check still might get cashed. With electronic processing, banks normally cash checks without human review. Most bank account agreements say the bank does not have to honor a restrictive legend on a check.

What does this mean for you? If you wrote a check more than six months ago and the payee still hasn't cashed it, you can call your bank and put a stop payment on it. The debt, however, does not go away. Be prepared for the payee to try to collect, arguing that your stop payment was not in good faith. You should respond that you waited six months, and if a bank isn't obligated to honor a check that old, you shouldn't be, either.

A federal law called "Check 21" may make stale checks a thing of the past. This law allows banks to process electronic images of checks instead of the paper originals. One result is that checks can be processed much faster than before.

- You discharged the debt in a Chapter 11 bankruptcy (financial reorganization of an individual or business).
- The cancellation or write-off of the debt is intended as a gift (but this would be unusual).
- You were insolvent before the creditor agreed to settle or wrote off the debt.

Insolvency means that your debts exceed the value of your assets. Therefore, to figure out whether or not you are insolvent, you will have to total up your assets and your debts, including the debt that was settled or written off.

EXAMPLE 1: Your assets are worth $35,000, and your debts total $45,000. That means you are insolvent to the tune of $10,000. You settle a debt with a creditor who agrees to forgive $8,500. You do not have to report any of that money as income on your tax return, but you do have to file Form 982.

EXAMPLE 2: Your assets are worth $35,000 and your debts total $45,000. The creditor writes off a $14,000 debt. You must report $4,000 as income and file Form 982 for the $10,000 that is not counted as income.

If you calculate that your debts exceed the value of your assets (that is, you're insolvent), or if your debt was discharged in bankruptcy, you'll have to fill out and include IRS Form 982 with your tax return, which can be quite complicated. You can download the form from the IRS website at www.irs.gov, but you may need an accountant to complete it correctly.

What to Expect When You
Can't Pay Your Debts

This chapter discusses the consequences of not paying your debts. This is not usually a recommended strategy, but it's one many people follow—at least for a while. It also may be your only option for nonessential debts that you can't pay.

If you ignore your creditors long enough, they will probably take legal action to try to get either the money you owe, secured property you pledged to guarantee repayment, or other property. You may lose some property, including your bank accounts, your car, a portion of your wages—and possibly your house.

But it's not always as bad as you might think. Exemption laws generally protect essential property, such as your clothing, public benefits, household goods, and most of your wages. (See Chapter 16 for more information.) And most important, for all debts (except possibly child support), no matter how much you owe, you won't lose your liberty unless you do something foolish that infuriates a judge, such as deliberately disobeying an order or lying in court or in a court document.

After reading this chapter, you should know where you are most vulnerable—that is, where you are most likely to lose some property if you don't pay a debt. Review Column 6 of your Worksheet 2, which shows whether debts are top, medium, or low priority. If not paying a debt you've been thinking of as low priority means you'll probably lose something you really need, move that debt to the medium- or high-priority list and rethink your strategy.

 RELATED TOPIC

Special protection for military members. Active duty servicemembers get temporary protection from many of the creditor actions described in this chapter. For more information, see Chapter 6, "Special Protections for Active Servicemembers."

Eviction

If you don't have a legal reason for not paying your rent, your landlord can evict you. In many states, an eviction can take as long as a month or two. In other states, where the courts are not so busy or the laws favor landlords, the process can be as short as a couple of weeks. In every state, however, the landlord must begin by giving you a notice either to pay or get out, or in some states, to get out (without the option to pay). The notice gives you a few days (usually three to five) to get out, or in the states that allow it, to pay what you owe. In almost every state, if you do neither, the landlord must file a complaint (lawsuit) to evict you (and usually also to recover back rent owed). You then have a set number of days to file an answer (five is common), and then a week or two later the court holds a hearing.

Even if you ignore the lawsuit and the landlord gets a default judgment against you, the landlord must take that judgment to the local law enforcement officer. Many states require that you get a few days' to a week's advance notice of when the eviction is scheduled. If you're not out by the selected day, the sheriff or another law enforcement officer comes and physically removes you and your property. The length of this process varies from state to state, but it moves much faster than other types of lawsuits. And no matter where you live, a landlord can sue you for the back rent you owe.

If you've been evicted, it will be harder for you to rent a new place once you're back on your feet. Specialized credit reporting agencies, often called tenant-screening agencies, collect information from court records on eviction actions and report it to landlords when they check on prospective tenants. Most landlords consider being evicted, or even having an eviction action filed against you, a significant blot on your tenant history.

CAUTION

Find out the local rules. Landlord-tenant laws vary tremendously from state to state and even city to city. If paying your rent is a problem, get some help from a tenants' advocacy or other consumer group. Also, see *Every Tenant's Legal Guide* or *Renters' Rights*, both by Janet Portman and Marcia Stewart (Nolo), which suggest ways to deal with late rent and what happens in an eviction. If you think you have a defense to not paying your rent—for example, your living conditions are substandard—you can find out whether your state allows you to move out, withhold the rent, or repair the problem yourself and deduct the cost from the rent.

Repossession

A secured debt is one for which a specific item of property—called security or collateral—guarantees payment of the debt. If you don't pay a debt secured by personal property, the creditor has the right to take the property pledged as collateral for the loan. The creditor can't just walk into your house and take your couch, however. The creditor must have a court order or permission from someone in your household to enter your home.

Creditors who don't have a security interest in an item of property can't take it without approval of a judge or court clerk.

What Constitutes a Default?

Unless your contract says otherwise, if you miss even one payment, you have defaulted on your loan and, under most security agreements, the creditor is entitled to take the goods. If you make your payments but otherwise fail to comply with an important term of the security agreement, the creditor can also declare you in default and take the property. Sometimes lenders have the right to declare a secured debt in default, even if you're all paid up. Here are some examples:

- You sell the secured property.
- The security is destroyed or stolen, or its value substantially depreciates.
- You let required insurance lapse—some lenders require that you have collision and comprehensive insurance on motor vehicles, or that you buy credit life or credit disability insurance.

- You become insolvent (as defined by your lender).
- You refuse to let the creditor examine the collateral when requested.
- The creditor feels that the prospect of your paying is uncertain.

Be sure to read the security agreement's fine print carefully to see what is considered a default.

When You Have Defaulted

Whether a creditor has to notify you before it takes your property depends on what state you live in and on the terms of your original agreement with the creditor. Generally, unless the contract specifically says otherwise, the creditor must notify you that it has accelerated the debt and that the full contract amount is due. This warning can give you time to figure out a plan. However, in many contracts, you waive the right to receive advance notice. In some cases you can challenge these waiver clauses, but you will likely need the assistance of an attorney to do so.

Fortunately for consumers, many states require creditors to notify you of a "right to cure" the default. If you want to take advantage of the "right to cure," you must do so before the debt is accelerated and the property is repossessed. You get a certain period of time (usually a few weeks) to pay all missed payments and any late charges, get required insurance, or otherwise rectify the situation that caused the default. You will need to research your state law to see if you have a right to cure where you live. (See Chapter 18 for information on how to research your state law.)

A few states prohibit a creditor from repossessing property without first getting a court order. But even outside of these states, a creditor is unlikely to go ahead and take your property (except perhaps motor vehicles) unless you have defaulted in the past, have missed several payments, or are uncooperative, or if the creditor has learned something worrisome about your finances.

You can voluntarily return the collateral, but the creditor doesn't have to take it. And he or she probably won't if it's worth far less than you owe. If you want to give the property back, first call the creditor—ask to speak to someone in the collections department—and find out whether your entire debt will be canceled when the collateral is returned. If the creditor agrees to cancel the entire debt, get written confirmation. Also find out whether the creditor will refrain from reporting the default on your credit report. If the entire debt isn't canceled, there probably isn't much point in returning the item, as you'll be liable for the difference between what the collateral sells for and what you owe.

How Motor Vehicles Are Repossessed

The first property most lenders go after is a motor vehicle, especially if it's still pretty new. In a number of states, however, the lender must first send you notice of the default and give you the right to make up the payments, called a right to "cure," before repossessing your car.

A repossession company generally can't use force to get to your vehicle—repossessions must occur without any breach of the peace.

However, many common repossession tactics are not considered to breach the peace. For example, it's usually legal for a repossessor to hotwire a car. It's legal to use a duplicate key and take a car. Most courts have said it's legal to remove a car from a carport or an open garage (meaning the door is up). In some states, it's legal to take a car from a garage if the door is closed but unlocked, but a few cautious repossessors won't do this. It's generally illegal to break into a locked garage, even by using a duplicate key. But a repossessor might anyway, especially in parts of the country where the repossession won't be nullified and all the lender will be required to do is fix the lock.

The lender will supply the repossessor with your home and work addresses and any other useful information (such as where you attend school). Many vehicle purchase and lease agreements today authorize a lessor to use a vehicle's electronic locating device to locate the vehicle. A repossessor who finds the car in your driveway or on the street in front of your house, will usually wait until you're asleep or out, use a master key or hotwire it, and then drive away.

Although it might seem otherwise, the repossession company does not have unlimited power to take your car. In many states, if you or someone else (like a relative) objects at the time the repossessor tries to take your car, so that taking the car would breach the peace, he or she must stop. However, this doesn't mean you get to keep your car. The repossessor can try again another day or get a court order to take the car. Think carefully before you do this. If the company has to come back another

time or get a court order to take your car, this will increase its repo expenses. This means it will cost you more to get your car back or your debt will be larger after it's sold.

A word of warning—some consumers and agents attempting to repossess cars have reportedly been injured or killed, and children have been hauled away when the car was repossessed. Don't put yourself or others in danger just to keep your car. No car is worth an altercation that could escalate to physical harm.

How Other Property Is Taken or Repossessed

Few creditors try to take back personal property other than motor vehicles, for these reasons:

- The loan is often for only a few thousand dollars or less.
- The property may be worth far less than you owe.
- The repossessor will have a hard time getting into your house.

A few major department stores encourage debtors to return property. If the property is less than a year old, ask if they'll credit your account for 100% of what you owe if you return the property voluntarily. This means that your entire balance is wiped out, even if the property is worth less than the amount you owe.

If the lender hires repossessors to take back the property, you don't have to give it back or let them into your house unless a sheriff shows up with a court order telling you to do so. If, however, the property is sitting in the backyard—for example, a new gas barbecue and lawn furniture—it's generally fair game. But the repossessor can't use force to get into your house or to take your backyard furniture—for example, you can't be thrown out of a lawn chair. Some repossessors will jump a fence or even pick a lock, but most won't enter the premises unless they are invited or have a court order. Entering your house with a duplicate key when you are away to take your refrigerator or living room sofa is illegal.

As with car repossessions, if you or a member of your family ask the repossessor to leave your property, and the repossessor doesn't, this is generally considered to be a breach of the peace. So is using abusive language, a threat of violence, or violence. But lying or tricking you usually isn't a breach of the peace.

Can You Get Your Property Back?

You may be able to get your property back by reinstating the contract or redeeming the property.

Reinstatement

If your car or other property is taken, some states give you a short time during which you can get it back by reinstating the contract. Reinstatement means getting the property back and resuming the payments under the terms of the original agreement. In order to reinstate, you must fix the problem that caused the creditor to declare the default— for example, by paying all past-due payments and late fees, getting required insurance coverage, or paying unpaid fines or taxes— and pay the costs the lender has incurred in taking and storing the property, often several

hundred dollars. The right to reinstate is limited, however, and, depending on your state law, you probably can't get the property back if you:

- had the contract reinstated in the past
- lied on your credit application
- hid the property to avoid repossession, or
- didn't take care of the property and its value has substantially diminished.

Personal Belongings in Repossessed Vehicles

If the repossessor takes your motor vehicle, you're entitled to get back all your personal belongings inside of, but not attached to, the vehicle when it was repossessed. This means that you can get back your gym shorts, but not the $500 stereo system you installed. (You are entitled to a removable radio, however.) Also, make sure you look at your loan agreement. Some say that you must make that request within 24 hours of the repossession. Although such time limits may not hold up in court, it's safest to act quickly. Promptly contact the lender after your vehicle is repossessed and ask that your property be returned. Put the request in writing and list everything you left in the car. If the lender is uncooperative— which is unlikely—consider suing in small claims court.

Under state laws, ordinarily, the lender must give you notice of your right to reinstate the contract after repossession, even if the lender thinks you have given up the right. If the lender doesn't give you this notice, you may have the right to get the property back for nothing—but you will have to resume making payments on your loan. If you have been given notice and want to try to reinstate the contract, contact the lender as soon as possible to work out an agreement.

If you don't reinstate the contract within the time permitted by the agreement, the lender will send you a formal notice of its intent to sell the property.

Redemption

Every state allows you to redeem the property —to pay the entire balance to get the property back. To redeem property, you must pay not only the entire balance of the contract (instead of just the past amounts due), but also repossession and storage costs. You can redeem property within the time allowed, which is usually up to shortly before it is sold.

Redemption is rarely feasible. If you couldn't make payments in the first place, you probably can't come up with the entire balance due under the contract. Some people take out a home equity loan to get the money. This is dangerous: If you default on the home equity loan, you might end up losing your house instead of the personal property. Redemption might make sense if the property, such as your car, is essential to your livelihood and you can get someone to help you come up with the money to redeem it.

You might try to find a buyer for the car and ask the creditor to accept the offer, even if it is less than what you owe. You can agree you will still owe the difference (be sure the creditor is not padding the amount it claims

you owe). The creditor will probably not accept the offer, but it may help you show the creditor's sale did not comply with the law (see below).

Will You Still Owe the Lender? Deficiency Balances

If you don't reinstate or redeem the property by the deadline, it will be sold. If the proceeds don't cover the total of what you owe—and they almost never do—you could be liable for the balance, called a deficiency.

 SKIP AHEAD

If you're planning to file for bank-ruptcy, you probably don't have to worry about any deficiency. It will likely be wiped out in your bankruptcy case. (See Chapter 14.)

Although laws differ among states, generally, the lender must: send you a notice that the property will be sold; tell you whether it will be sold at a public sale or otherwise; and give you the time, date, and location of the public sale or the date after which it will be sold by another means. The notice must also tell you whether you are liable for any deficiency and must provide a phone number where you can find out how much you still owe. You are entitled to attend a public sale and bid. There are two kinds of sales: a public sale, which is open to anyone; or a private sale, to which the lender invites only certain people who it feels might be interested. Cars are frequently sold at private sales to which used car dealers and others who regularly buy repossessed cars are invited. If the notice doesn't give you the date and location of the sale, call the lender and find out.

The law requires that the lender conduct every aspect of the disposition of the vehicle in a "commercially reasonable" manner, but that may be interpreted differently in different courts. In fact, repossession sales are often attended only by used car dealers, who have a motive to keep the bids very low. This is one reason why most property sold at repossession sales brings in far less than the lender is owed. For instance, a car valued at $12,000 might sell for $5,000, and a refrigerator worth $800 might sell for $250. And even though you could have sold the item for much more, the sale usually will be considered "commercially reasonable." If you attend, you can bid (if you have the cash), but the dealers are apt to outbid you.

After the item is sold, the sale price is subtracted from what you owe the lender. Then, the cost of repossessing, storing, and selling the property is added to the difference. Very often, you are liable for that balance: the deficiency balance.

Here's one suggestion for avoiding a deficiency balance: If your property, especially a motor vehicle, is about to be repossessed, ask for a contract reinstatement just to get the vehicle back so you can sell it yourself. Even if you get $7,000 for a $9,000 car, it's better than the lender's repossessing it and selling it for $3,000. You can use the $7,000 to pay off your lender and will owe only $2,000 more, far less than the $6,000 you'd owe if the lender sold it through repossession.

Some lenders will forgive or write off the deficiency balance if you clearly have no assets. Where the amount forgiven is $600 or more, the lender will issue you a Form 1099-C or 1099-A, and the IRS will expect you to report the forgiven balance as income on your tax return. (See Chapter 6, "Beware of the IRS If You Settle a Debt.")

If the lender doesn't forgive or write off the balance, expect dunning letters and phone calls, probably from a debt collector.

As you can see in the following table, in half the states you won't be liable for a deficiency balance on the kinds of transactions indicated or if the amount still owing or that you originally paid is less than a few thousand dollars. (If your state is not listed, it does not place additional limits on deficiency balances after repossession.) Given the price of cars, you will almost always be liable for a deficiency if a motor vehicle is taken.

It is common for creditors to make mistakes in the repossession process. Most states bar creditors from collecting a deficiency balance if they fail to comply with notice requirements (such as notifying you of the right to cure or of the sale) or didn't sell the property in a commercially reasonable manner. If you think the creditor made a mistake, you must raise this defense at the time you are sued for the deficiency balance. Because these cases can be complex, it's a good idea to consult a lawyer.

If the creditor sues you, you should file an answer with the court. Your first line of defense is to review how your repossession was handled. You can argue that the creditor isn't

Are You Always Liable for Deficiency?

State	Statutes	When Deficiency Balances Prohibited
Alabama	Ala. Code § 5-19-13	If you paid $1,000 or less for the collateral
Arizona	Ariz. Rev. Stat. § 44-5501	If you paid $1,000 or less for the collateral
California	Cal. Civil Code § 1812.5; Cal. Health & Safety Code § 18038.7	If you bought goods on installment; on purchase-money mortgage for a mobile home, manufactured home, commercial coach, truck camper, or floating home (does not include loans not used to purchase the property, such as home equity loans or refinanced loans)
Colorado	Colo. Rev. Stat. § 5-5-103	If you paid $3,000 or less for the collateral
Connecticut	Conn. Gen. Stat. § 36a-785(f),(g)	If the fair market value of a car or boat is less than the amount owed, a creditor cannot collect a deficiency
Dist. of Col.	D.C. Code Ann. § 28-3812(e)	If you paid $2,000 or less for the collateral
Florida	Fla. Stat. Ann. § 516.31(3)	If unpaid balance at time of default is less than $2,000
Idaho	Idaho Code § 28-45-103	If you paid $1,000 or less for the collateral
Indiana	Ind. Code Ann. §§ 24-4.5-5-103, 24-4.5-1-106; 750 Ind. Admin. Code § 1-1-1	If you paid $4,000 or less for the collateral
Kansas	Kan. Stat. Ann. § 16a-5-103	If you paid $1,000 or less for the collateral
Louisiana	La. Rev. Stat. Ann. § 13:4108.2	If the seller does not get an appraisal before the sale, unless you have agreed in writing to a sale without an appraisal
Maine	Me. Rev. Stat. Ann. tit. 9-A § 5-103	If the amount you financed is $2,800 or less
Maryland	Md. Com. Law §§ 12-626, 12-115; 63 Md. Op. Atty. Gen. 92	If you paid $2,000 or less for the collateral or the contract does not provide right to collect deficiency
Massachusetts	Mass. Gen. Laws ch. 255, § 13J(e), ch. 255B, § 20B, ch. 255D, § 22	If unpaid balance at time of default is under $2,000 for motor vehicles and under $1,000 for other property
Minnesota	Minn. Stat. Ann. § 325G.22	If amount financed was $7,200 or less
Missouri	Mo. Rev. Stat. §§ 408.556, 365.145	If amount financed was $500 or less or the unpaid balance is $300 or less
Nebraska	Neb. Rev. Stat. § 45-1054	If the unpaid balance is $3,000 or less
Oklahoma	14A Okla. Stat. Ann. § 5-103	If you paid $5,100 or less for the collateral
South Carolina	S.C. Code Ann. § 37-5-103	If you paid $5,550 or less for the collateral
Utah	Utah Code Ann. § 70C-7-101	If you paid $3,000 or less for the collateral
Washington	Wash. Rev. Code Ann. § 60.10.030	For statutory personal property liens if you didn't agree to pay a deficiency balance when you entered the contract
West Virginia	W.Va. Code Ann. § 46A-2-119	If the unpaid balance is $1,000 or less
Wisconsin	Wis. Stat. § 425.209	If the unpaid balance is $1,000 or less
Wyoming	Wyo. Stat. Ann. § 40-14-503	If you paid $1,000 or less for the collateral

entitled to a deficiency if it didn't inform you about your right to cure the default or redeem the property (if you live in a state where you have these rights), didn't sell the item in a commercially reasonable manner, or didn't give you the date and location of the sale.

If you'd rather take the offensive, you can sue the lender for wrongful repossession. For large items, such as cars, you'll probably need a lawyer. But for smaller items, you can probably represent yourself in small claims court. (See Chapter 13 for more information.)

Tying Up Property Before a Lawsuit

There are two ways that a creditor can tie up your property before getting a court judgment: prejudgment attachment and *lis pendens*.

Prejudgment Attachment

Prejudgment attachment is a legal procedure that lets a creditor tie up property before obtaining a court judgment. It is the unsecured creditor's way of telling the world that the property covered by the attachment can be used to pay the creditor if it wins in court. (Secured creditors don't need to attach your property, because they can just repossess it if you don't pay. See "Repossession," above.)

Creditors may especially try to attach your property if you live out of state or have fled the state, or if the creditor believes you are about to spend, sell, or conceal your property.

In most states, a prejudgment attachment works like this: When the creditor is about to sue you, it prepares a document called a "writ of attachment," listing the property

you own that it believes you are hiding or about to sell, or that someone else is keeping for you. In some states, the creditor must file a bond in order to get a writ of attachment. The writ of attachment must be approved by a judge or court clerk. Writs are usually approved as long as there is no dispute that the property to be attached is yours. Then the creditor serves it on you and on everyone it thinks has some of your property. (Serving means providing a copy.) Usually, you must be delivered a copy by hand, but in some cases, the creditor can just mail it to you. The most common property to attach is a deposit account: savings, checking, money market, certificate of deposit, and the like.

Serving the writ freezes your property— the holder of your property can't let you sell it, give it away, or, in the case of deposit accounts, make withdrawals. You must be given the opportunity to have a prompt court hearing. This isn't the trial where you argue whether or not you owe the debt. This hearing pertains only to the attachment, and you'll want to argue that the attached property is exempt (see Chapter 15), you need the property to support yourself and your family, or the value of the property attached exceeds what you owe.

If you don't attend the hearing or you lose the hearing, the court will order that the attachment remain on your property pending the outcome of the lawsuit. You won't be able to withdraw or otherwise dispose of any of the attached property. You can get the attachment released by filing a bond for the amount of money you owe. But if you don't file a bond and the creditor wins the lawsuit, the judgment is almost certain to be paid out of the attached property. Prejudgment attachment is not available in some states (California, for example), if the claim is based on a consumer debt.

Lis Pendens

A *lis pendens* is similar to a prejudgment attachment because it prevents you from selling or mortgaging the property until the court rules on the lawsuit. It is different from a prejudgment attachment because a *lis pendens* can only be used if title to the particular property is the subject of a lawsuit, for example, if both you and your spouse in a divorce proceeding have a claim to ownership of the family home. The *lis pendens* is typically recorded with a county land or real estate records office so it provides notice to purchasers and creditors that the property is subject to a pending claim; so the title is not "clear."

Lawsuits

If you don't pay a debt, and the debt is not secured by particular property, the most likely consequence is that the creditor will sue you, unless the creditor thinks you are judgment proof or decides not to sue for other reasons. Being judgment proof means that you don't have any money or property that can legally be taken to pay the debt and aren't likely to get any soon. But because most court judgments last many years (up to 20 years in some states), and can often be renewed indefinitely, people who are broke may nevertheless be sued on the creditor's assumption that someday they'll come

into money or property. Similarly, very old people or people with terminal illness who are judgment proof may get sued by their creditors simply because the creditors know that it's easier to collect the debt at death (through the probate process) if they have a judgment than if they don't.

Being judgment proof doesn't mean that you have no money or property at all. It just means that if a creditor obtains a court judgment, you are allowed to keep all of your property because it is "exempt." Each state has declared certain items of property beyond the reach of creditors—these items are called exempt property. (Exempt property is covered in detail in Chapter 15.) Suffice it to say that if you receive no income except government benefits, such as Social Security or unemployment insurance, and have limited personal property and no real estate, you are probably judgment proof. There are a few important exceptions to this general rule. For example, most government agencies are permitted to collect debts owed to them by taking a percentage of certain federal benefits, such as Social Security.

If a creditor sues you in regular court (as opposed to small claims court) and you fight it, the lawsuit can take time—often several years—to run through the court system. If you don't oppose the lawsuit, or you let the court automatically enter a judgment against you (called a default judgment), the case could be over in 30 to 60 days.

If the creditor gets a judgment, it has a number of ways to enforce it. If you are working, the most common method is to garnish your wages, meaning that up to 25%

of your take-home pay is removed from your paycheck and sent to the creditor before you ever see it. The next most common method to collect a judgment is to seize your deposit accounts. Chapter 13 contains details on getting sued and defending against judgment collections.

Lawsuits Against Third Parties Who Hold Your Assets

If a third party holds property for you or owes you money, most states give creditors the right to sue those third parties to get your property or money. Sometimes that third party is a financial institution, such as a bank, savings and loan, or credit union, where you have a deposit account. It might be a landlord or utility company to whom you've made a security deposit. Or it could be a financial adviser, such as a stock broker, with whom you've deposited funds to invest on your behalf.

In a few states, a creditor can't pursue a third party until it has obtained a court judgment against you and tried to collect. In most states, however, the creditor can sue the third party even before winning a lawsuit against you. If that happens, you will have to be notified of the suit and allowed the opportunity to contest the debt.

Liens on Your Property

A lien is a notice attached to your property telling the world that a creditor claims you owe it some money. A lien is typically a public record. It is generally filed with a county records office (for real property) or with a state agency, such as the secretary of state (for cars, boats, office equipment, and the like). Liens on real estate are a common way for creditors to collect what they are owed. Liens on personal property, such as motor vehicles, are less frequently used but can be an effective way for someone to collect. To sell or refinance property, you must have clear title. A lien on your house, mobile home, car, or other property makes your title unclear. To clear up the title, you must pay off the lien. Creditors know that putting a lien on property is a cheap and almost guaranteed way of collecting what they are owed—sooner or later.

Generally, creditors have the right to have the property sold to pay off the lien, usually by way of a foreclosure sale. However, except for tax liens (see below), they rarely do so. This is because in most cases your mortgage was placed on the property before the liens and so must be paid off before any liens are paid. If the creditor forecloses on the lien, it has to keep up the payments on the mortgage or lose the property. Instead of forcing a foreclosure sale, creditors usually wait until the property is sold. Buyers often won't buy the property unless the title is clear, meaning it has no liens. So, the seller will use part of the purchase price to pay off the lien.

A creditor usually can place a lien on your real estate—and occasionally on personal property—after it sues you and wins a court judgment. But many creditors have a right to place a lien on your property without filing a lawsuit. Here are examples of other property liens:

- **Property tax liens.** Usually, a property tax lien takes priority over all other mortgages or liens on the property, even if the property tax lien was placed on the property later. If you do not pay your taxes, to protect its mortgage, the lender will usually pay the taxes and add that to your mortgage debt. If the taxes are not paid, the government can have your property sold to pay the property taxes. The government must follow whatever procedure the state prescribes, and you may have the opportunity to pay the taxes and costs and get your property back even after the "sale."

- **IRS liens.** If you fail to pay back taxes after receiving notices from the IRS, it may place a lien on all of your property, especially if you're unemployed, self-employed, or sporadically employed and the IRS would have trouble attaching your wages. Many creditors with property liens simply wait until the house is sold or refinanced to get paid. The IRS, however, doesn't like to wait and may force a sale if the amount you owe is substantial. For more information on dealing with IRS liens, see *Stand Up to the IRS*, by Frederick W. Daily (Nolo).

- **Child support liens.** If you owe a lot in child support or alimony, the recipient may put a lien on your real estate. The lien will stay until you pay the support you owe, until you sell or refinance your property, or until the recipient forces a lien sale, whichever happens first. (See Chapter 12.)

- **Mechanic's liens.** If a contractor works on your property or furnishes construction materials to be used on your property, and you don't pay up, the contractor can record a lien on your property called a mechanic's lien. In most states, the contractor must record the lien within one to six months of when the contractor wasn't paid. The contractor then must sue you to enforce the lien within about one year (the range generally varies from one month to six years, depending on the state). If the contractor wins the lawsuit, the contractor may be able to force the sale of your home.

- **Family law real property lien.** In a California marital action, a spouse may file a lien against his or her interest in community real estate to secure payment of attorneys' fees in the action. The lien affects only the filing spouse's interest in the property. (Cal. Fam. Code § 2033.)

Jail

Jailing someone for not paying a debt is prohibited in most instances. In a few situations, however, you could land behind bars.

You willfully violate a court order. This comes up most frequently when you fail to make court-ordered child support payments, the recipient requests a hearing before a judge, and the judge concludes that you could have paid but didn't. (See Chapter 12.) In a few states, a court can order you to make periodic payments on a debt. If you can pay some portion of the arrearage and arrange for ongoing payments, you can probably avoid jail—the judge would rather see the money paid than see you in jail not earning money. If you continue to refuse, though, you may be facing a jail term.

You refuse to pay income taxes. This is a crime, and if you're convicted you could go to jail.

You don't show up for a debtor's examination. If a creditor has a judgment against you, it can ask for court approval to conduct a debtor's examination—where you come to court and answer questions about your property and finances. (See Chapter 13.)

Bank Setoff

A bank setoff happens when a financial institution, such as a bank, savings and loan, or credit union, removes money from a deposit account—checking, savings, certificate of deposit, or money market account—to cover a payment you missed on a loan owed to that institution.

There are a few limitations on bank setoffs. For instance, most courts have said that banks cannot use setoffs to take income that is otherwise exempt under state or federal law (such as Social Security benefits, unemployment compensation, public assistance, or disability benefits) to cover another loan or credit the bank provided. But the bank can set off exempt money in your account to cover fees you owe from the *same* account (like overdraft fees). If you owe

fees on one account, open a separate account and have future exempt funds sent to that account. (See Chapter 15 for information on exempt property.) In addition, financial institutions cannot take money out of your account to cover missed consumer credit card payments owed to that institution, unless you previously authorized the bank to make withdrawals from your account. Be aware that most credit card contracts contain a term that allows for a setoff if you fall behind on your account. (15 U.S.C. § 1666h; Regulation Z of the Truth in Lending Act, 12 C.F.R. § 1026.12(d).)

Some states impose limits on bank setoffs as well. For example, with limited exceptions, California prohibits state-chartered savings and loan setoffs if the total balance of all your accounts with the financial institution is under $1,000. (California Financial Code § 6660(b).) And in Maryland, all bank setoffs for debts for the purchase of consumer goods are prohibited unless you have explicitly authorized the setoff or a court has ordered one. (Maryland Commercial Law § 15-702.)

Intercepting Your Tax Refund

If you are in default on student loan payments or behind in income taxes or child support, the agency trying to collect can request that the IRS intercept your federal income tax refund and apply the money to your debt.

Before the IRS takes your money, the agency must notify you and give you 60 days in which to present written evidence or have a hearing to show that any of the following is true:

- Your debt has been paid.
- The amount of the proposed intercept is more than you owe.
- The intercept is not legally enforceable.

If the intercept is for a student loan, you can make a written request to review the agency's file on your loan and the agency seeking the offset will consider other information, such as information showing you qualify to have your loan discharged because the school closed, falsely certified your eligibility, or failed to pay refunds owed because you left before completion of the course. (See Chapter 11.)

If you are married and the intercept is for child support from a previous relationship, your spouse can file a claim for his or her share of the refund. (See Chapter 12, "Your Income Tax Refund Could Be Intercepted," for information about how to file a claim.)

Tax refund intercepts are most common in the cases of defaulted student loans. Each year, for example, the federal government pockets hundreds of millions of dollars by grabbing tax refunds from hundreds of thousands of former students. (For more on student loan collections, including stopping or avoiding tax refund intercepts, see Chapter 11.)

If your tax refund is small, you will have less to lose from an intercept. See Chapter 5, "Get Some of Your Tax Refund Early," for suggestions on increasing the money you receive with your paycheck during the year, so your tax refund at the end of the year is smaller.

Loss of Insurance Coverage

If you miss payments on any insurance policy, your coverage will end. Most insurance policies have a grace period—which means you will still be covered for a few days or weeks, even if you don't pay your premium on time. The length of your grace period varies by type of insurance, state, and even with the particular insurer. Auto insurance often has grace periods as short as ten days. Health insurance often has a longer grace period—30 to 60 days. (Under the Affordable Care Act, those who receive federal subsidy assistance in the form of an advanced premium tax credit and who have paid at least one full month's premium within the benefit year get a three-month grace period.) If you think you might pay late, find out what your grace period is.

Even before your insurance lapses, if your lender required you to obtain the insurance as a condition of your loan, which is common on credit for automobile purchases, for example, you could face more than a canceled insurance policy. The lender could declare you in default of your loan and either repossess your personal property or foreclose on your house.

However, it is more likely that the lender will get an insurance policy for you and bill you or add the cost of the premiums to your debt. This is called "force-placed insurance." Often, lenders will require consumers to pay for coverage that is not actually required by the credit agreement, which can end up being very expensive. The lender may also fail to notify you before it gets this insurance and bills you for it. These types of practices may violate your state unfair and deceptive acts and practices statute.

In states that require you to have automobile insurance to drive or register a car, if your insurance lapses, you are violating the law if you continue to drive. Some insurers provide evidence of insurance (or cancellation of insurance) electronically to your state's motor vehicle department. The department can suspend your vehicle registration if it learns you no longer have insurance. You may have to pay a fee to get your car registered again, and you may be cited, fined, and even have your car towed if you are stopped while driving without insurance. If you get into an accident, you could also lose your driver's license.

Loss of Utility Service

If you miss payments on a utility or telephone bill, the company will try to cut off your service. State law and your state's public utilities agency or commission determines how long it takes to cut off your service, and what notices you must receive before that happens. Almost all states require the utility company to send you a notice before it turns off your electric or gas service for nonpayment. The time from notice to service shutoff varies from state to state, but five to ten days is typical. In some states you will receive a single written notice only. In others, the utility company must also call or visit before cutting off service.

Other state rules may prevent or delay the utility company from cutting off service in certain circumstances. For example, in most northern states, utility companies are not allowed to shut off heat-related utility services to residential customers during the winter months, during periods of extremely hot or cold temperatures, or during particularly bad weather. Many states limit when a utility company can shut off utilities for seriously ill, elderly, or disabled residents and, occasionally, for households with infants. In some states, these limits may only be available to low-income consumers. To learn about your state's rules, contact your utility service or go to https://liheapch.acf.hhs.gov and click on "Disconnect Policies" in the menu bar.

In order to reconnect service, you may have to pay overdue payments, a reconnection fee, and an additional deposit. For this reason, it's best to contact the utility company before service is cut to see if special circumstances can delay or prohibit cutoff, to determine if you qualify for programs that help people pay utility bills, or to try to negotiate a payment plan that you can afford. Many states require a utility company to offer a payment plan before cutting service. If the utility company won't help, contact your state public utility agency for assistance.

Be wary of "prepaid" or "pay as you go" service as a way to avoid shutoff. With prepaid service, you may not need to pay a deposit, but you pay in advance, and when your account runs out of money, your service can be cut, remotely, without notice. Such plans may charge additional fees, such as "transaction fees" every time you add money to your account. And they may not be governed by consumer protection laws like those that require advance notice before your utility service is cut.

 RELATED TOPIC

More help with utility bills. See Chapter 5, "Cut Your Expenses, Reducing Utility Charges," and "Free Home Weatherization," for programs that may reduce your utility payments. See Chapter 6, "Negotiating With Your Creditors" for tips on negotiation techniques and strategies.

Reducing Mortgage Payments and Dealing With Foreclosure

f you are having trouble keeping up with your mortgage payments, you are certainly not alone. And because of that, there are a variety of programs that can help if you are behind on your house payments or facing foreclosure. In this chapter, we'll walk through the foreclosure process, and then we'll look at strategies to deal with high mortgage payments and possible foreclosure.

Foreclosure

If you get behind on your mortgage or home equity loan payments, the lender has the right to foreclose—force a sale of your house—to recover what you owe. But mortgage lenders don't always foreclose, even if they have the right. Foreclosing can be expensive and time-consuming, and the house often sells for only a part of what is owed.

The Difference Between Judicial and Nonjudicial Foreclosure

The two most common types of foreclosure are judicial foreclosure and nonjudicial foreclosure. They are vastly different. A judicial foreclosure requires the creditor to file an action in court, which typically gives you up to a year or more before you have to part with your property. Nonjudicial foreclosures do not go through a court and often can be carried out within a three- to four-month period.

Why do some foreclosures go through court while others don't? It depends mostly on where you live. If you've defaulted on payments on a real estate loan that is secured by a deed of trust, the foreclosure process often occurs outside of court—that is, nonjudicially. On the other hand, if the foreclosure stems from a true mortgage or creditor's judgment against you in a lawsuit, the foreclosure probably will end up in court. (See "Mortgages and Deeds of Trust," below.)

Mortgages and Deeds of Trust

Some home loans are true mortgages. Others are secured by a deed of trust. Here's the difference:

- **Mortgage.** A loan in which you put up the title to real estate as security for the loan. If you don't pay back the debt on time, the lender can foreclose on the real estate and have it sold through a court proceeding to pay off the loan.
- **Deed of trust.** An alternative method of financing a real estate purchase. The deed of trust transfers the title to the property to a trustee, often a title company, who holds it as security for a loan. If you default on the loan, the trustee can sell the property at auction and pay the lender from the proceeds without going to court. In some states, the lender can choose whether it wants to use this process or the court process. Deeds of trust are often used in the West.

Even though mortgages and deeds of trust are different, except when it makes a legal difference, most people commonly refer to both as mortgages or home loans.

There are two other types of foreclosure that are used in only a handful of states: strict foreclosure and foreclosure by possession. In a strict foreclosure, the lender sues the borrower in court, as in a judicial foreclosure, but there is no sale afterwards. Once the court declares the borrower to be in default, the court transfers title to the property from the borrower directly to the lender. Strict foreclosure is used in only two states, Connecticut and Vermont.

Foreclosure by possession is allowed in Massachusetts, New Hampshire, and Rhode Island, but is rarely used. In this type of foreclosure, the lender enters and takes possession of the property without disturbing the peace.

Loan Servicers

The company that initiates the foreclosure is not necessarily the company that actually owns your home loan. Instead, it may be a loan "servicer." Many home loans are owned by many different investors. Typically, the servicer has a contract with the investors to represent them when dealing with the borrower. The servicer receives and processes your payments. Generally, you must deal with the servicer if you become late on your payments or a foreclosure process is started. Because the servicer represents the lender, for convenience, in this chapter we'll usually refer to both the servicer and the lender as the "lender," except when the distinction between the two is important.

Preforeclosure Protections and Required Notices

If your loan is secured by your principal residence, federal mortgage servicing rules require the servicer to contact you twice within the first 45 days after you miss a payment to give you information about how to get caught up and avoid foreclosure. (These options could include reducing the interest rate, deferring or forgiving principal, or extending the terms of the loan, for example.) The first attempt to contact you personally must be not later than 36 days after the payment was due. Then, within 45 days of the missed payment, the servicer must send you a letter about your options. The servicer must continue to take these steps while you remain delinquent. Also, the servicer must wait 120 days after you become delinquent before it can officially start the foreclosure.

Most mortgages and deeds of trust also require the servicer to send you a letter, called a breach letter, informing you that your loan is in default before starting a foreclosure.

Nonjudicial Foreclosure

The nonjudicial foreclosure process varies from state to state. Often the process will begin after the lender gives you some type of preforeclosure notice (such as a notice of intent to start a foreclosure) or satisfies any state outreach requirements (for example, attempting to contact you by phone). If you don't get caught up on the past-due amounts, the lender will then typically send you a formal notice telling you that your loan is in default. This notice, often called a notice of default, states that a foreclosure sale will take place unless you cure the default. State law might require the lender to send a separate notice of sale as well.

The method of delivery and type of notice you'll receive will depend on the state you're in. In some states, you'll only receive one notice, while in others you may receive two or three different types of notice. Lenders may be required to deliver notices by mail (first-class, registered, or certified mail), advertisement in a newspaper, posting in a public place, personal service, or any combination of the above.

Once a lender fulfills the statutory notice requirements, it can then sell the property. A lender is usually required to advertise the home for sale. The sale must be conducted in public and usually involves an auction procedure, but don't count on the auction bringing a market price. (See "The Sale," below.)

In order to challenge a nonjudicial foreclosure, you must file a lawsuit asking the court to stop the sale of your house. In most cases, you will need an attorney's assistance to do this. (See "Defenses to Foreclosure," below.)

Judicial Foreclosures

As with nonjudicial foreclosures, the process for judicial foreclosures varies from state to state. For example, some states require a preforeclosure notice that the lender give the borrower the opportunity to participate in foreclosure mediation (a process wherein you meet with the lender and a neutral third party to attempt to find a foreclosure alternative). To start a judicial foreclosure, the lender files a lawsuit against you in court. In all judicial foreclosures, you will receive a summons or another type of notice of the suit. The notice will explain your rights, including how much time you have to respond to the attached court papers. You have the right to challenge the legality of the foreclosure in court. See "Defenses to Foreclosure," below, and consult an attorney if you might have a reason to stop or delay foreclosure. If you don't respond to the papers or you lose in court, the court will issue a judgment to the lender, permitting it to hold a foreclosure sale.

Right to Cure Default

Some states have laws that give you the right to "cure" the payment default and "reinstate" the loan within a certain period of time before the foreclosure sale—that is, to pay all your missed payments, late fees, and other charges, keep your property, and continue with your regular monthly payments on the loan. If you live in a state that doesn't explicitly give you the right to stop the foreclosure sale by completing a reinstatement, check your mortgage contract. It might contain a provision that allows you to get caught up by a particular deadline. After the reinstatement period expires, you no longer have the right to reinstate the loan by bringing it current but must "redeem" it by paying off the entire balance.

Beware of Foreclosure Scams

Once the foreclosure process starts, in most states it becomes public record, so you are likely to be contacted by all sorts of people and companies offering help. Some may be legitimate; most won't be. Many unscrupulous people make money by taking advantage of people facing foreclosure.

Foreclosure scams rely on your desperation, lack of information, and faith in humanity ("No one would kick me when I'm down") or shared heritage, religion, or national origin ("Someone of my culture/religion wouldn't trick me"). Here are just few of the scams.

Phantom rescue. The scammer charges excessive fees for a few phone calls or a little paperwork that the homeowner could have done and for a promise of representation that never happens. The scammer abandons you when the period for reinstatement—which should have been used to get current on the loan, negotiate with the lender, or find effective assistance—runs out. The foreclosure then proceeds.

Bailout (also called sale/leaseback). The scammer tells you to surrender title to the house, with the promise that you can rent it and buy it back from the scammer later. You may be told that surrender of the title is necessary so that someone with better credit can get new financing to save the house. The terms of the buyback are so onerous that you can't buy the house back, and the rescuer pockets the equity. Alternatively, the scammer puts a new loan on the property, sucking all the equity out, then returns the property, with a much higher loan and payments you cannot possibly afford.

Bait and switch. Here, you don't realize that you are surrendering title to the house in exchange for the promised rescue. The scammer may trick you into surrendering title (perhaps when signing new loan documents), or may simply forge your signature on the deed. The scammer then keeps the house, refinances it for a higher amount, or sells it and keeps the profit.

Before agreeing to anything, read the fine print, and make sure you can truly afford the "fix." Also be wary of the following:

- high-rate loans to get you out of foreclosure
- "easy credit," low-cost loans regardless of credit history (these often have hidden costs)
- equity skimmers (folks who try to buy houses for a small fraction of their market value, often through misrepresentation, deceit, or intimidation) and
- foreclosure consultants (people who promise to help homeowners in foreclosure, charge high fees for little or no service, and then purchase the home at a fraction of its value).

If you need help, seek counseling through the Department of Housing and Urban Development (www.hud.gov, 800-569-4287, or (TTY) 800-877-8339), the Homeownership Preservation Foundation (www.995hope.org or 888-995-4673), or a reputable nonprofit organization such as the Consumer Credit Counseling Service (see Chapter 18).

Right of Redemption

Another way you can keep your home is by redeeming it—paying off the entire outstanding loan balance. No matter what state you live in, you have the right to redeem at any time before the foreclosure sale. Some states give you an additional period after the foreclosure sale to redeem by paying the total purchase price, plus interest and fees, to the foreclosure sale purchaser, or by paying off the total mortgage debt.

Usually, if you are in financial trouble, the only way to pay off the entire loan balance is to refinance the loan. Think carefully before doing so. You don't want to end up with another loan you can't afford. And, most people who are facing a foreclosure or who have gone through foreclosure will have a difficult time getting a new loan due to a poor credit score. (See below for more information on refinancing home loans.)

The Sale

Whether the foreclosure went through a court proceeding or is a nonjudicial foreclosure, before the actual sale, the lender (or trustee) is usually required to publish a notice of the sale in a newspaper in the county where your house is located. The notice includes information about the loan and the time and location of the sale; in most states, the sale must take place at least three to five weeks after the notice is published.

At the sale, the lender who foreclosed makes the first bid, sometimes for the amount owed, sometimes for less. If the house sells for more than you owe creditors who have a security interest in your house, you're entitled to the excess. But the foreclosing lender first gets to deduct the costs of foreclosing and selling, usually several thousand dollars. Don't expect to leave a foreclosure sale with money in your pocket.

In many states, particularly if the sale was after a court proceeding for foreclosure, the successful bidder doesn't actually get title to the house for a period of time, from several days to a year, known as the redemption period. During that period, you can "redeem" the property, by paying the successful bidder the amount of the winning bid plus interest and allowable costs or, in some cases, by paying off the total debt that you owed to the lender.

Defenses to Foreclosure

You may be able to delay or stop the foreclosure if you have legitimate, legal reasons for not paying the mortgage or trust deed or the lender has not properly followed state foreclosure procedures. If you think you might have a defense to foreclosure, contact a lawyer immediately. (See Chapter 18 for information on how to find a lawyer.)

Some possible defenses are described below.

Violations of the federal Truth in Lending Act. This law requires the lender to provide certain information about your loan before you sign the papers. If the lender failed to provide this information, you may be able to cancel the mortgage. This right to cancel applies only to loans *not* used to purchase your home. (See Chapter 3 for more on this law.)

Interest rates or loan terms that violate state or federal law. Although some states limit how much interest can be charged on a loan, for most financial institutions, those limits are preempted by federal law, so they do not apply. Federal law prohibits lenders from making deceptive or false representations about the loan. And for certain very expensive loans, federal law requires extra disclosures and prohibits some terms, like balloon payments. (See Chapter 11 for more on these expensive loans.)

Failure to follow foreclosure procedures. Each state requires lenders to follow specific procedures when foreclosing on a home. If the lender doesn't follow these rules (for example, by not giving proper notice of the foreclosure, failing to inform you of certain rights, or submitting faulty foreclosure paperwork to the court), you may be able to delay or stop the foreclosure.

Bankruptcy. Filing for bankruptcy automatically stops foreclosure proceedings, at least temporarily. (See Chapter 14 for more on bankruptcy.)

Watch Out for Deficiency Balances

A deficiency balance is the difference between what you owe the foreclosing lender and what the lender received at the sale. In many states, if the sale doesn't cover what you owe, the lender is entitled to a "deficiency judgement" for the difference. The lender often must attend a court hearing and present evidence of the value of the property to obtain the deficiency. Some states give consumers more protection from deficiency balances. California, for example, prohibits deficiency balances on loans to purchase your home or if the foreclosure is by a nonjudicial sale.

But if "junior" lien holders—creditors whose liens were filed after the foreclosing lender's lien was filed—don't receive full payment when that foreclosing lender forecloses, you may still owe them the deficiency and they can collect it from you.

In many states, a lender with a deficiency can use the collection techniques covered in Chapter 7 and will often accept less than the full amount if you can offer a lump sum settlement. If you owe a lot of money, or there's an easy target for collection (such as a large bank account or monthly wages), the lender is likely to pass your debt to a collection agency or a lawyer (to sue you).

If you plan to file for bankruptcy, you may not need to worry about a deficiency balance, because you will probably be able to discharge it in the bankruptcy.

Alternatives to Foreclosure

There are many options for homeowners in foreclosure, in danger of being in foreclosure, or just having trouble making monthly mortgage payments. What options might work for you depend on your individual situation. Some homeowners may be able to take advantage of government or lender-specific programs to modify loans or refinance. Some may be better off selling, doing short sales, or getting deeds in lieu of foreclosure. Others might be able to work out short- or long-term deals with their lenders.

Whatever your situation, if you have difficulty paying your mortgage, review all of your options before taking action. In almost all situations, you'll need to communicate with your lender or servicer.

Tips for Communicating With Lenders and Servicers

There are a number of strategies for dealing with mortgage payments or possible foreclosure. When you encounter trouble paying your mortgage, follow these tips.

Keep a log. It is critical that you keep a log of all contacts with the mortgage lender or servicer during your attempts to deal with your mortgage. Keeping copies of all documents submitted with a workout option could become key if you need to challenge a lender that improperly refused to allow you to modify your loan, or even to challenge a foreclosure.

Act quickly. Mortgage lenders and consumer credit counselors agree: When you know you're going to fall behind on your mortgage payments, you should call the servicer. The sooner you get in contact with the servicer, the more options you will have to cure the delinquency and save your house. Also, open and respond to all mail and phone calls from your servicer. These communications will contain information about foreclosure avoidance options. Understand that the lender would rather receive your monthly payments and the interest associated with them than the house. And, the servicer makes money by servicing

the loan on a monthly basis. You have a much better chance of working out a way to avoid foreclosure if you keep the lines of communication open.

Communicate with your lender. Don't stop communicating with the lender or servicer.

Consider all options. Carefully consider all of your options. Depending on your financial situation, this can mean agreeing to a payment plan to make up missed payments, getting a short-term break on interest or payments, or refinancing or modifying your loan so you can afford the payments over the long term. It may also make sense for you to get the lender to let you walk away if you either turn over the keys or sell the house for less than you owe. And some people might be better off letting the house go into foreclosure, and use the time during the foreclosure process to save money that would otherwise be spent on mortgage payments to accumulate a security deposit for a rental.

Federal Programs for Homeowners Facing Possible Foreclosure

Agencies such as the Department of Veterans Affairs (VA), Federal Housing Administration (FHA), Fannie Mae, and Freddie Mac have programs to help homeowners who have these types of loans avoid foreclosure. Or, you might be able to get help from the Hardest Hit Fund (such as a modification, mortgage payment assistance, or a transition assistance program) if you live in a state that received federal money designed to provide aid to struggling homeowners.

Getting Help From HUD

One of the best ways to get competent, free assistance to learn about ways to avoid foreclosure is to contact a housing counselor certified by the Department of Housing and Urban Development (HUD). To get a referral to a counselor in your area, contact HUD at 800-569-4287 or 800-877-8339 (TDD), or go to www.hud.gov or download the HUD mobile app.

Fannie Mae and Freddie Mac Flex Modification and Other Programs

The Flex Modification program is intended to help people who have a Fannie Mae or Freddie Mac loan, and who are about to default on a mortgage or are already behind on their payments. (If you're late by 60 days or more, you're likely eligible. Those less than 60 days delinquent, or current, might qualify in certain situations.) The program usually provides around a 20% payment reduction to eligible borrowers through a mortgage modification. To find out if Fannie Mae or Freddie Mac owns your loan:

- Contact Fannie Mae at 800-232-6643 or go to knowyouroptions.com/loan lookup.
- Contact Freddie Mac at 800-373-3343 or go to ww3.freddiemac.com/loan lookup.

Both Fannie Mae and Freddie Mac also offer rate reductions, term extensions, and other loan changes for people in financial distress, especially people experiencing involuntary money problems, such as an illness, death of a spouse, or a job loss. For information about Fannie Mae's various foreclosure avoidance programs, go to Fannie Mae's Know Your Options website at www.knowyouroptions.com. To get information about Freddie Mac's programs, go to myhome.freddiemac.com and click on "Foreclosures & Alternatives."

Options for Borrowers with Department of Veterans Affairs (VA) Loans

Borrowers with loans insured by the Department of Veterans Affairs (VA) who are in default might qualify for a loan workout option, such as a loan modification. Your servicer should be able to help you resolve the default using the programs available (when possible). Additionally, loan technicians located in various VA Regional Loan Centers can intervene with the servicer to ensure that all foreclosure avoidance options are explored. You can call 877-827-3702 or go to https://benefits.va.gov/benefits and click on "Home Loans" and then "Mortgage Servicing Assistance" to learn more. The website also has a link that will help you locate a Regional Loan Center.

Options for Borrowers with FHA-Insured Loans

Borrowers with an FHA-backed mortgage (a mortgage insured by the Federal Housing

Administration) are entitled to a particular loss mitigation (mortgage workout) process. Borrowers might qualify for a forbearance plan that allows the homeowner to temporarily suspend or reduce payments, or a repayment plan to bring the loan current. A borrower who isn't eligible for these options will be evaluated for a loan modification, partial claim (an interest-free loan from HUD to get caught up on the overdue payments), preforeclosure sale (a sale of the property for less than you owe, also called a "short sale"), or deed in lieu of foreclosure (where the lender takes ownership of the home and releases you from the mortgage obligation). If you have an FHA-insured loan, call your servicer for information about starting the process.

Federal Hardest Hit Fund

In 2010, the federal government created the Hardest Hit Fund in response to the ongoing foreclosure crisis. This federally funded program provides monetary help to homeowners in states most affected by the mortgage crisis.

As part of this program, $7.6 billion was allocated to help residents in 18 states (Alabama, Arizona, California, Florida, Georgia, Illinois, Indiana, Kentucky, Michigan, Mississippi, Nevada, New Jersey, North Carolina, Ohio, Oregon, Rhode Island, South Carolina, and Tennessee) plus the District of Columbia. Each state developed initiatives to help homeowners. Programs typically include:

- mortgage payment assistance for unem-ployed or underemployed homeowners

- principal reductions to help lower a homeowner's monthly payment
- payment assistance to bring a delinquent mortgage current
- funding to help eliminate a junior loan, such as a second mortgage, and
- help to transition into more affordable housing.

The Hardest Hit Fund program has been extended to December 31, 2020, though some states have ended their programs early because their allocated funds have run out. For more information, go to www.treasury.gov and search for "Hardest Hit Fund." You'll find links to each state's program. To reach an expert from a HUD-approved housing counseling agency, call 888-995-HOPE (4673).

Proprietary Loan Modifications

Almost all lenders offer proprietary (in-house) modifications to borrowers who are having difficulty making mortgage payments. Banks typically offer programs lowering interest rates (and thereby reducing the monthly mortgage payment), or you might be able to extend the length of your loan and add missed payments to the end. Each lender sets the eligibility criteria and guidelines for its in-house program. Call your mortgage servicer to learn about options available to you.

CAUTION

Don't get help from a "loan modifica-tion" company. If you need help trying to modify your loan, do not call one of the loan modifica-tion companies advertised on TV, mail, radio, by flyers, or on the Internet. These companies often try to sound like they are affiliated with government programs, but they are not. They will likely help themselves to some of your money, and leave you in a worse position than before. For help with loan modifications, contact HUD (see "Getting Help From HUD") for a list of legitimate housing counselors approved by HUD.

Other Mortgage Workouts

Even if you don't qualify for any of the government programs or your lender doesn't offer you a proprietary modification, you may be able to arrange another type of loss mitigation option or "mortgage workout." A workout is any agreement you make with the lender that changes how you pay the delinquency on your mortgage or otherwise keeps you out of foreclosure. Many lenders require a formal process even for short-term fixes. Be sure to submit all requested documents to the servicer in a timely manner.

Some workout options your lender might agree to include:

- spreading repayment of missed payments over a few months. For example, if your monthly payment is $1,000 and you missed two payments ($2,000), the lender might let you pay $1,500 for four months (called a "repayment plan")
- reducing or suspending your regular payments for a specified time, and then adding a portion of your overdue amount to your regular payments later on (called a "forbearance")

- deferring or waiving late charges, or temporarily reducing your interest rate, or
- allowing you to complete a short sale or a deed in lieu of foreclosure. (See "Short Sales and Deeds in Lieu of Foreclosure" below.)

It's best to start the workout discussions as early as possible. But before you contact the servicer about a workout, you should prepare information about your situation, including:

- a reasonable budget for the future and an assessment of your current financial situation (review Worksheets 1 and 2 and see Chapter 3 for help in making a budget)
- a plan to deal with other essential debts, such as utility payments and a car loan if you need it for work (see Chapter 5 for ways to meet those essential debts and reduce or eliminate other bills)
- a brief explanation about why you fell behind on your mortgage (typical hardships include job loss, a reduction in income, an increase in housing expenses, a divorce or legal separation, the death of a borrower or wage earner in the home, or a disability or serious illness of the borrower or dependent family member), and
- information about your loan, your income, and the amount of the default.

You should also find out if your mortgage is insured by the Federal Housing Administration (FHA) through the U.S. Department of Housing and Urban Development (HUD) or Department of Veterans Affairs (VA). As noted earlier, borrowers with these types of mortgages have some special rights that those with "conventional" mortgages don't have.

It's a good idea to look for a nonprofit debt counselor or lawyer who has experience with mortgage workouts to help you. (See "Getting Help From HUD," above, to find a HUD-approved counseling agency in your area.)

Be advised that workouts are not for everyone, nor will every lender agree to a workout. Be realistic about your situation before you approach the servicer. If it is likely that you will lose your house anyway because of your dire financial situation or because you have other pressing financial problems, it doesn't make sense to keep paying your mortgage through a workout. Also, be wary of agreeing to any workout arrangement that you do not understand, because it might make the situation increasingly difficult later.

Refinancing

If you can't afford your current mortgage payments, and you can't qualify for any of the government's special programs, a modification, or any other workout the lender may offer, but you still have equity in your home, your lender may let you refinance the loan to reduce the amount of the monthly payments. You'll have to convince the lender that you have enough income to make the reduced payments. Typically, a lender looks at both the ratio of your total monthly housing debt burden (principal, interest, real estate taxes, and insurance) to your monthly gross income and your total monthly expenses to your monthly gross income. For example, if your housing

debt ratio is 31% or less and your total debt ratio is 43% or less, you can qualify for an FHA-insured loan. If you have good credit, you may qualify for loans with even higher debt ratios. Be realistic when refinancing. If you can't afford your new payments, the process is likely to hurt more than it helps.

RESOURCE

Online mortgage calculator. If you need help figuring out how much mortgage payment you can afford—and what terms you'd need to qualify—visit Nolo's website at www. nolo.com/legal-calculators and check out the "How much home can I afford?" calculator.

If you are considering refinancing your home loan, try to avoid or minimize the following:

- **Rapidly increasing interest.** For example, the interest begins at an artificially low "teaser" rate (such as 1 or 2%), so that you think you can afford the loan. After six months to two years, the interest automatically rises by two points or so. Every six months or year after that, the interest rate adjusts, depending on the market. There are now some safeguards designed to protect you from getting in over your head because of a teaser rate. As of January 10, 2014, federal law requires lenders to consider a borrower's "ability to repay" when issuing a mortgage loan. (This applies to most mortgage loans.) The lender must determine whether you can afford a mortgage before making the loan and it can't base its evaluation of your ability to repay on teaser rates. This means that the lender must look at your ability to repay both the principal and the interest over the long haul—not just during the introductory period when the rate is lower.

- **Points.** Real estate loans usually come with points, an amount of money equal to a percentage of your loan, which you pay to your lender simply for the privilege of borrowing money. If you refinance with the same lender from whom you originally borrowed, the lender may waive the points. Loans with very high points and other charges are subject to the requirements of a federal law called HOEPA. (See Chapter 10 for more information.)

- **Insurance and other extras.** Consumer loans, including refinanced loans, are often loaded with extra products that most consumers don't need. You should especially look out for credit insurance charges. (See Chapter 10.)

- **Prepayment penalties.** A prepayment penalty usually applies if you pay the entire mortgage within a certain number of years. Most mortgages don't have prepayment penalty fees, but you should check your loan paperwork to be sure.

- **Predatory terms.** Predatory lenders target people whom they think are desperate, as well as consumers who could qualify for better loans. An offer often starts out okay but then turns sour at the last minute, when you're told that because

of your credit rating you will have to pay more. The lenders offer high interest rates (often with low teaser rates), large balloon payments (jumbo payments due at the end of the loan term), and sometimes negative amortization (loans where your monthly payment does not cover the interest due that period, so you owe more at the end than when you started). Negative amortization loans have mostly disappeared from the mortgage market, but you should still watch out for them.

Don't just accept what one lender tells you is available. Shop around before you apply for a loan. Websites like www.bankrate.com can give you an idea of the available rates for the type of loan you want. Contact several lenders that seem to have good rates. If a lender tells you that you don't qualify for the terms initially offered, ask the lender to give you a revised written statement of the terms it's offering. Review those terms before you make any decisions.

If you've already applied for a loan and discover that the terms are different from what the lender offered, or you decide you don't like the terms, in most cases you have a right to cancel the transaction within three business days after the terms are properly disclosed to you or three business days after you sign the loan documents, whichever is later. If you planned to pay your current lender with the new loan, and discover only at the last minute, or even after you sign, that the terms were misrepresented to you, act quickly. Tell your current lender, file a complaint against the company or person who misled you, and immediately look for another lender. If you missed only a few payments before the deal went sour, you can prevent foreclosure by making up the missed payments and then obtaining a new loan. If the original lender has accelerated the loan—declared the entire balance due because you've missed several payments—you'll have to refinance the entire loan to prevent foreclosure.

EXAMPLE: Jessica owes $213,000 on her mortgage, which has monthly payments of $1,400. She has missed four payments and received a letter from the lender stating that it has "accelerated" the mortgage as permitted under the loan agreement. All $213,000—not merely the $5,600 in missed payments—is due immediately. For Jessica to save her house, she will need to get a loan from a second lender to cover the full $213,000, unless the original lender agrees to reinstate her loan.

In such a situation, it may be difficult for you to get a new loan. The new lender will do a credit check and likely see a mortgage delinquency (if reported by your first lender). You'll have to convince the new lender that you won't default on the new loan.

 TIP

Be aware of the three-day right to cancel. Under federal law, for most loans secured by your home (such as a home equity loan or a refinance mortgage by another lender), you can cancel the contract within three business days of signing the contract, or sometimes longer if the lender fails to provide you with the proper disclosures. (15 U.S.C. § 1635.)

Selling Your House

If you don't want to keep your house, or you've come to the conclusion that you can't afford it, your best option may be to sell it. If you decide to do this, you can probably stop making mortgage payments.

Even at this late date, consumer credit counselors suggest that you contact the lender and ask for time to list the house with a real estate agent and sell it. If your payments aren't too far behind and you've kept in contact with the lender, it may agree.

If the lender chooses to foreclose, the process may take anywhere from a few months to a year or more. If you're willing to take any reasonable offer, you might be able to sell your house much sooner.

Short Sales and Deeds in Lieu of Foreclosure

There are two other options to consider if you decide you cannot keep your house—a short sale and a deed in lieu of foreclosure.

Short Sales

The lender may agree to a "short sale." This happens when the money you get from selling your house is less than the amount you owe to your lender. In a short sale, the lender agrees to accept the proceeds from the sale and forgo foreclosure. Some lenders require documentation of any financial or medical hardship you are experiencing before agreeing to a short sale. By accepting a short sale, the lender can avoid a lengthy and costly foreclosure, and you may be able to pay off the loan for less than you owe. (If your lender agrees to release you from having to pay back the remainder of the loan, make sure to get this release in writing.) These sales are common when the real estate market is depressed.

Most homeowners who complete short sales will face deficiency judgments. (See "Watch Out for Deficiency Balances," above.) To avoid a deficiency after short sale, make sure the short sale agreement expressly states that the transaction is in full satisfaction of the debt and that the lender waives its right to the deficiency. Though, if the lender forgives the deficiency and sends you a Cancellation of Debt form (Form 1099-C), you could face tax consequences. (See "Caution" below.)

Deed in Lieu of Foreclosure

If you don't get any offers for your house or the lender won't approve a short sale, your other option is to transfer your ownership interest in your home to the lender—this is called a deed in lieu of foreclosure, or "deed in lieu," for short. Keep in mind that ordinarily you won't get any cash back, even if you have lots of equity in your home. And this transaction may have negative tax consequences, unless you qualify for an exception. (See "Beware of the IRS If You Settle a Debt" in Chapter 6.) The deed in lieu will appear on your credit report as a negative mark for several years.

Most states don't prohibit the lender from going after you for a deficiency judgment after a deed in lieu. To avoid a deficiency judgment, make sure your deed in lieu agreement expressly states that the transaction is in full

satisfaction of the debt. If the deed in lieu of foreclosure agreement does not contain this provision, the lender may file a lawsuit to obtain a deficiency judgment. Again, if the lender forgives the deficiency and sends you a Cancellation of Debt form (Form 1099-C), you might be liable to pay taxes on the canceled amount.

If you opt for a deed in lieu, try to get concessions from the lender—after all, you are saving it the expense and hassle of foreclosing on your home. For example, ask the lender to eliminate negative references on your credit report or give you more time to stay in the house.

 CAUTION

A short sale, principal reduction, foreclosure, or deed in lieu could increase your tax bill. Any time a lender writes off $600 or more of the principal you owe, the lender must report it to the IRS on a Form 1099-C or 1099-A, a report of miscellaneous income. The theory is that you're receiving a gift of this amount, because you don't have to repay it. But in some cases, you may not have to pay income tax on the amount if you meet one of the exceptions. See Chapter 6, "Beware of the IRS If You Settle a Debt."

Finding Other Programs to Help Homeowners

The number and kind of programs to help homeowners in trouble on their home loans changes constantly as programs are tweaked or new programs added.

The bottom line: There may be other programs available. Talk with a HUD-certified housing counselor and your loan servicer to find out about other existing programs that might help. Ask your state or local representatives for information about state programs.

RESOURCE

Detailed information on foreclosure. *The Foreclosure Survival Guide*, by Amy Loftsgordon (Nolo), explains foreclosure from start to finish, includes 50-state laws, and suggests many strategies for keeping your house, or—at the least—lessening the financial blow of losing it. It discusses short sales, deeds in lieu of foreclosure, workouts, and how to get help from nonprofit housing counselors approved by the federal department of Housing and Urban Development.

Dealing With Debt Collectors

Not many years ago, debt collectors regularly threatened, scared, lied to, harassed, intimidated, and otherwise abused debtors. Debtors were falsely told they'd go to jail for not paying their bills; friends and relatives were often interrogated and threatened with financial and bodily harm if they didn't tell where absent debtors were living; and debt collectors published lists of people who didn't pay their debts. The Fair Debt Collection Practices Act (FDCPA) now makes abusive collection practices, including harassment, illegal—although an unfortunate number of collectors still resort to them.

When dealing with a debt collector, it's crucial to adopt a plan and stick with it. One choice—if you have no money, plan to file for bankruptcy, or choose not to pay right now—is to refuse to talk with the collector. As explained below, you can request that a debt collector from a collection agency stop contacting you. However, many credit counselors believe that whether you negotiate directly with the collector or obtain a lawyer's assistance, the best strategy almost always is to engage the collector, unless you're judgment proof or truly plan to file for bankruptcy. Don't just ignore the debt or try to hide from the collector. Usually, the longer you put off resolving the issue, the worse the situation and consequences will become.

If you really need more time to pay, another option is to contact the debt collector to negotiate a payment schedule. If you do contact a debt collector, realize that as nice as a debt collector may appear, he or she is not your friend and does not have your best interest at heart. The collector wants your money. To get it, he or she may ask you about your personal problems or may claim to be interested in saving you from ruining your credit. Don't believe it: The collector doesn't really care about your problems or your credit rating. The collector's only goal is to get your money. Stick to your plan. If you want extra time to pay or to lower your payments, insist on it.

> **SKIP AHEAD**
>
> **If you have already been sued.** If the creditor or a collection agency has sued you and won, the collection options are different. See Chapter 13 for more information.

Creditor or Debt Collector?

To understand your rights when dealing with a debt collector, you must keep in mind the difference between the creditor and a debt collector. This distinction is important, primarily because the federal law regulating debt collectors generally doesn't apply to original creditors, unless they take steps to act like third-party collectors.

Creditor. A creditor is a business or person who first extended you credit or loaned you money (the original creditor) or another company your debt was transferred to. The term does not include a company that has obtained debts after they are in default, solely to collect the defaulted debts for the creditor. Sometimes original creditors are called credit grantors.

RELATED TOPIC

If the creditor, not a debt collection agency, is collecting your debt, read Chapter 6. Chapter 6 discusses how to negotiate your debts when you are dealing directly with the creditor.

Debt collector. A debt collector, also referred to as a collection agency or third-party collector, is someone who regularly collects debts for others, or whose main business is collecting debts for others. Under the FDCPA (15 U.S.C. §§ 1692 and following), a debt collector also includes:

- a creditor that collects its debts under a different name or by sending letters signed by lawyers
- a lawyer who regularly collects debts owed to others (see *Heintz v. Jenkins*, 115 S.Ct. 1489 (1995)), and
- debt buyers, in some cases, like if the principal purpose of the business is the collection of debts (see *Henson et al. v. Santander Consumer USA Inc.*, 137 S.Ct. 1718 (2017), *Tepper v. Amos Financial, LLC*, 898 F.3d 364 (3d Cir. 2018)).

As mentioned above, creditors generally are not governed by the FDCPA. Several states, however, have debt collection laws that apply to both creditors and debt collectors. Also, many states have laws regulating debt collectors more strictly than the FDCPA. (See "State or Local Laws Prohibiting Unfair Debt Collections," later in this chapter.)

Efforts to collect past-due unsecured bills usually follow a standard pattern. Original creditors first try to collect their own debts.

When you initially owe money, you'll receive a series of letters or phone calls from the original creditor's collections or customer service department. Although most creditors make first contact a few weeks after you miss a payment, some more aggressive companies begin hard-core collection efforts within 24 to 36 hours after your payment is due, even before a late payment charge would apply. If you don't respond to the letters or calls or your efforts to negotiate with the creditor do not succeed, most creditors will hire a debt collector or sell your debt to a debt collector, and write it off as a bad debt.

CAUTION

Written-off debts could increase your tax bill. If a creditor stops collection efforts on a debt of $600 or more that you owe and abandons the debt, it is required to report to the IRS the amount of the cancelled debt on Form 1099C. You may have to report that amount as income and pay tax on it. If a creditor sends you a Form 1099C, but either it or a debt collector continues to try to collect the debt from you, talk to a tax adviser. You may not have to report the amount listed on the 1099-C as income. See Chapter 6 for more information.

TIP

General negotiating tips in Chapter 6. The information in Chapter 6 on how to negotiate with creditors is also useful when dealing with debt collection agencies.

Negotiating Secured Debts

This chapter deals mainly with collection efforts on unsecured debts. Why? Secured creditors rarely hound you to pay back debts. They don't have to. As long as they comply with state or federal laws that require them to notify you that you are behind on your payments and then follow the proper repossession procedures, they can simply come and take the property (collateral) that secures the debt. See Chapter 6 for information on how to negotiate secured debts and Chapter 7 for information on repossession of personal property.

Before Your Debt Is Sent to a Debt Collector

Do not let collection letters or phone calls from a creditor or a debt collector undo your plan for handling (or not paying) a debt. Here is what you can expect as your creditor first attempts to collect, before transferring the debt to a debt collector.

Creditors usually begin their collection efforts with a collection ("dunning") letter. At first, it will probably send a polite "past due" form letter. If you don't respond, subsequent letters will get firmer.

Some creditors will also suspend your credit at some point; the only way to get it back is to send a payment.

The last letter will likely contain a threat: "If we do not receive payment within ten days, your credit privileges will be canceled (if they haven't already been), your account sent to a collection agency, and your delinquency reported to the national credit reporting agencies. You could face a lawsuit, wage attachment, or lien on your property."

Creditors hate it when collection efforts reach this stage. They want you to pay your bill, but they also want to be nice so that you'll remain a customer. If the creditor's letter-writing campaign fails or the person assigned to your account prefers direct contact, you'll probably receive a phone call.

When the first overdue notice arrives, your first response may be to throw it away. And if the letter is from a creditor whose debt you marked as "low priority" (see Chapter 4 and Worksheet 2), not responding may be your best alternative. But don't throw it away. It may turn out to be evidence if you need to sue for violations of the debt collection laws.

 CAUTION
Don't write a letter or make a payment if the statute of limitations has run out. If your debt is so old that the creditor or collection agency is barred by law from collecting it—three to ten years from your last payment, in many states—then you shouldn't say anything in a letter or on the phone that acknowledges the debt, or even make a small payment on it. If you admit that you owe the money now or ever owed it in the past, or even if you make a payment on it, this could turn your debt into a brand new debt, which gives the creditor or agency another three to ten years to collect. Debt collectors often try to keep you on the phone until you say something that "revives" the statute of limitations. Don't fall for it—the best practice is simply not to talk to collection agencies about very old debts. See "How to Handle Time-Barred

or "Zombie" Debts," below, for more information. If you are not sure if the statute of limitations has run, consult an attorney before you act on debts you haven't paid on for a long time.

When Your Debt Is Sent to a Debt Collector

If you ignore the creditor's letters and phone calls, you are unable to work out an agreement to repay or settle the debt, or you set up a repayment schedule but fail to make the payments, your bill will most likely be turned over to a collection agency or sold to a debt buyer, and your delinquency reported to a credit reporting agency. This will probably take place within three to six months after you default. The types of debts most likely to be sent to a collection agency are credit card and telephone service debts, followed by other utilities, car, government, and medical debts.

TIP

If a debt collector contacts you by telephone, call back. If a debt collector first contacts you by phone, ask for the collector's name, telephone number, address, and the particulars of the debt. Write down the information and arrange a time when you can call back. That way, you will have a record of each person with whom you have contact. This information might be important if you later discover that the company has violated the FDCPA or if you sue the debt collector or it sues you. This will also allow you to talk to the debt collector when you are prepared, rather than when the debt collector catches you by surprise.

What to Expect

By taking some time to understand how debt collectors operate, you'll know how to respond when they contact you so that you can negotiate a payment plan or get the debt collector off your back. So keep these basic points in mind.

Debts may be assigned or sold. The creditor may continue to own the debt, but turn it over to a debt collection agency with a contract to collect. Or, the creditor may sell the debt outright to a collection agency.

Collection agencies with assigned debts take their cues from the creditor. If the debt is assigned to a debt collector, but still owned by the creditor, generally, the debt collector can't sue you without the original creditor's authorization. If the original creditor insists that the debt collector collect 100% of the debt, the debt collector cannot accept less from you without getting the original creditor's okay.

Debt collectors move quickly. You can expect to hear from a collection agency as soon as the original creditor passes on your debt. Professional debt collectors know that the earlier they strike, the higher their chance of collecting.

Debt collecting is a serious—and lucrative—business. Collection agents get paid for results. Some earn high salaries. Other companies pay their collectors meager wages plus commissions, which means you may be called by a stressed-out, rude collector who doesn't much care what the law allows.

Agencies with assigned debts usually keep between 25% and 60% of what they collect. The older the account, the higher the fee. Sometimes, the collector charges per letter it writes or phone call it places—usually about 50¢ per letter or $1 per call. That gives it an incentive to contact you repeatedly.

Debt collectors are choosy. Before an agency tries to collect, it evaluates its likelihood of success. It may carry thousands—or even tens of thousands—of delinquent accounts and must prioritize which ones to go after. If success looks likely, the agency will move full speed ahead. If the chances of finding you are low, the odds of collecting money from you are somewhere between slim and nil. If your credit file shows that you've defaulted on 20 other accounts, the agency may give your debt low priority.

Collection agencies that purchase debt may not have good information. Buying debts has become a huge business. Especially if your debt is old, you are likely to find yourself dealing with someone who has bought a bundle of debts for pennies on the dollar. Because the collector may not have any of the original credit documents and only a computer printout of the debt, the information it has may very well be incorrect. It may even have bought the debt from a previous debt collector, not the original creditor, which increases the likelihood that the collector doesn't have accurate (or any) information about the debt.

Just because a letter is on law firm letterhead doesn't mean an attorney is involved. Sometimes debt collectors send form collection letters on attorney letterhead with a mechanically produced lawyer's signature on the bottom. Although under the FDCPA an attorney must review your file before allowing the collector to send such a letter, some debt collectors do this anyway. (It might be allowable if the letter states that an attorney is not involved.) If you suspect foul play, contact the lawyer on the letterhead. If the lawyer does not appear to know about your case, you can: Use this possible FDCPA violation as a negotiating tactic, contact a lawyer for help in suing the debt collector and attorney, or complain to the FTC.

CAUTION

If you're behind in payments, open all mail. One of the biggest complaints from people who are behind in paying their bills is that the collector never notified them that a debt was in collection before suing. However, a debt collector will almost certainly mail you at least one letter, probably more, before starting a lawsuit. The problem is that debt collectors often send collection notices in plain, inconspicuous envelopes. This is because the FDCPA clearly states a debt collector may not use any language or symbol on a mailed envelope that indicates that the collector is in the collection business or that the communication relates to the collection of a debt. People often mistake these plain envelopes for junk mail and throw them away unopened. To avoid any surprise lawsuits, take the time to open your mail—even if you don't recognize the return address on a letter—to find out if it contains a debt collection notice.

How Debt Collectors Find You

Just because a collection agency calls or writes to you, don't assume that it knows where you live, especially if you've moved since you transacted business with the original creditor. All the debt collector knows is that it mailed a letter or left a phone message that wasn't returned.

You do not have to provide information to a debt collector. There are many reasons why you might not want to have contact with the debt collector (for example, the debt is old, you are judgment proof, it's a low-priority debt, or you want to protect the privacy of your information). But remember that if you don't deal with a debt collector, you are likely to wind up with a judgment against you. (See Chapter 13.) And chances are, the debt collector will find you anyway.

Often, debt collectors find you by relying on information you have voluntarily given to someone. For example, they can get your credit application from the original creditor, access your credit report, or for a small fee, get your location information from a credit reporting agency. Debt collectors also buy information from data aggregators. Data aggregators collect information from public records, surveys, purchases, and demographic data, then sell it. The Privacy Rights Clearinghouse has a lengthy list of online data sellers that allow opting out. You can get a copy of the list at www. privacyrights.org/data-brokers.

Beware of Debt Collectors Using Social Media to Get Information

Debt collectors are not always candid about their identities on social media, despite the law's requirement that a collector disclose its identity when contacting you (see "Illegal Debt Collection Practices," below). If you're in debt, beware of accepting friend requests or invitations to connect with anyone who you don't know. Collectors have been known to set up false identities and try to connect with consumers though Facebook or LinkedIn, and then fish around for information about whereabouts or assets. Unscrupulous debt collectors also use social media sites to coerce you to pay by posting messages that you owe a debt or otherwise harassing you. While debt collectors who violate the FDCPA face statutory damages of up to $1,000, you may not be able to trace the fake identity back to the debt collector.

In many cases, debt collectors simply look at your posts (without having to connect with you) and use that information to get your contact information or learn more about you. According to one former debt collector, "It's amazing what people leave open to the public on Facebook for everyone to see." For example, debt collectors can often find out where you work by viewing your Facebook page or your LinkedIn profile. Once debt collectors know that you have a job, they may be more motivated to seek a garnishment. To avoid this, you should change your privacy settings on your social media platforms to filter who can see what you post and limit what information appears in public.

!

CAUTION

Be sure to read the terms of service for any data brokers. The vendor will require you to provide documentation to verify your identity before removing your information from its database. Think twice before giving the broker additional information that it can disclose for its benefit. Also, opting out might not effectively remove your name or address if the information differs slightly in another record (for instance "Samuel" instead of "Sam," or "3131 First AVE NE" instead of "3131-1st Avenue Northeast").

Debt collectors also search the Internet for information you've provided to social networking sites, as well as clubs, churches, and other groups that post newsletters and other information online.

Debt collectors can also get location information from some government sources. For example, they can get forwarding address information from the Post Office. If you do not want a debt collector (or anyone else) to get your new address, privacy rights advocates recommend you file a temporary change of address. Or, only provide your new address to each person or business you want to find you (this could cause problems, however, if you forget to notify certain businesses and then don't receive bills). State motor vehicle address records are generally available to a creditor or debt collector. Voter registration records are generally publicly available.

Some debt collectors use skip tracers to find you. Skip tracers locate people using traditional and high-tech techniques, such as telephone directories, email address finders, Social Security number searches, telephone company call

records, public records, domain name lookups, military and Selective Service lookups, prison inmate lookups, professional license lookups, apartment locators, hotel/motel locators, business and corporate records, hunting and fishing licenses, and even eBay seller searches.

If You're the Cosigner of a Loan

When you cosign for a loan, you assume full responsibility for paying back the loan if the primary borrower defaults. In almost every state, the creditor can go after a cosigner without first trying to collect from the primary borrower. But most creditors try to collect first from the primary borrower. So, if you've been contacted by a debt collector, you can assume that the primary debtor defaulted.

If the debt and amount are correct, your best bet is to pay the debt if you can (and save your credit rating) and then try to collect from the primary debtor. For more information on cosigned debts, see Chapter 10.

Unscrupulous debt collectors may use pretexters. Pretexters get people's personal information illegally, using false pretenses. A pretexter might call you and say he's from a survey firm for example. He might ask you some questions to elicit basic personal information. When the pretexter has enough information, he calls your financial institution and pretends to be you or someone who is authorized to access your account. He gets more personal information from the bank.

Some Government Records Are Off Limits

Social Security, unemployment, disability, census, and other government records are not public documents, so bill collectors are not supposed to be able to get them. But as some well-publicized instances have shown, thieves search for Social Security numbers on the Internet and sell them. And companies are sometimes careless with their customers' Social Security numbers, making them vulnerable to being discovered.

TIP

Never disclose where you work or bank. If you are asked, simply say "no comment"—this isn't the time to worry about being polite. If the collection agency or original creditor later sues you and gets a judgment, knowing where you bank or work will make it easy to collect the judgment. If you do make a payment, don't send a check from your bank— get a money order or cashier's check from a different bank or the post office.

Collection Efforts Must Stop While You Verify Debt

One of the most powerful tools you have under the FDCPA is to require that a debt collector verify the amount and validity of the debt. In order to do this, however, you must act quickly once you are contacted by the debt collector. Normally, the collection

agency's first contact gives you the following information (if it doesn't, by law it has five days from the initial contact to tell you):

- the amount of the debt
- the name of the creditor or debt collector to whom the debt is currently owed
- that you have 30 days to dispute the validity of the debt
- that if you don't dispute the debt's validity, the collector will assume it is valid
- that if you do dispute the debt's validity in writing within the 30 days, the agency must send you verification of it, and
- that if you send a written request within that 30 days for the name and address of the original creditor, the agency must provide it, if different from the current creditor.

The debt collector may immediately take steps to try to collect the debt, but if you send a written request for verification of the name and address of the original creditor or dispute the debt, the collection agency must stop its collection efforts and cannot resume them before double-checking the debt information with the original creditor and mailing you the verification, including the original creditor's name and address. If you receive notice of a lawsuit, make sure your response is timely—the deadline may be different than the 30-day deadline to request verification of the debt. (See Chapter 13.)

Checking into who the original creditor is may help you decide whether you have grounds to dispute the debt. Collection agencies and original creditors are busy. While verification may seem as if it should take only a simple phone call, it may take several weeks or longer.

Requesting verification is particularly helpful if the debt has been sold. Often debt buyers have little information about the debts they own. They may try to collect the wrong amount or from people with similar names who don't owe the debt. If the debt collector cannot verify the debt, you may be able to reduce or even eliminate the debt.

If the debt is old, in your verification letter ask the debt collector for the date it claims your last payment was made. This can help you determine if the debt might be time barred, or if the collector has incorrect information about your debt. (See "How to Handle Time-Barred or "Zombie" Debts," below.)

If you don't dispute the validity of the debt (or part of it) or don't timely request verification, the agency can assume the debt is valid and continue collection efforts during the 30 days and after. The debt collector has a right to use all legal collection efforts against you. (See Chapter 13 for more on lawsuits seeking payment for questionable debts.)

To request verification, send a letter like the one below to get more information about the debt.

If the debt collector does not verify the debt, it cannot continue its collection efforts. If the debt collector does provide you with information about the debt, but you dispute the information or it is incomplete, and you believe you do not owe the debt or the full amount demanded, write again disputing the debt and explaining why you do not owe the debt.

Sample Letter to Collection Agency Requesting Verification of Debt

JB Collections, Inc.
245 Broadway
Salinas, CA 97245
Re: Verification Request on Account No. 27543

Dear JB Collections:

I received a letter from you about a debt for $250 owed to JB Collections, Inc. I dispute the validity of this debt. Please provide documentation verifying the debt, including the last date you claim I made a payment on this debt. Please also send me the name and address of the original creditor, and immediately return this account to the creditor and delete your tradeline from my credit file.

Sincerely,

Joe Brown

Joe Brown

Asking the Creditor to Take Back the Debt

If you are ready to negotiate on a debt, you will probably be better off talking to the creditor, not a collection agency. This is because the creditor has more discretion and flexibility in negotiating with you, and may see you as a former and possibly future customer. Ask the debt collector for the phone number of the collections department of the original creditor. Then call the creditor and ask if you can negotiate the debt.

Ideally, the creditor will immediately negotiate with you, and you'll work something out. Unfortunately, that's rare. It's more likely that the creditor will agree to take the debt back if you negotiate with the collection agency, establish a repayment plan, and make two or three payments under the plan. The creditor may eventually give you a new line of credit, helping you rebuild your credit.

Put any agreement you reach with the creditor in writing—preferably, in a letter from the creditor to you, although a letter from you to the creditor confirming the agreement and asking the creditor to correct any errors in your letter is better than nothing. Send a copy of the letter to the collector.

The danger in working with the creditor rather than the collector is that the collector may have bought the debt, and may refuse to give you credit for payments made directly to the creditor. Be sure to include in any written agreement with the creditor that it acknowledges that it (not the collection agency) owns the debt. Also, you may want to ask to have the negative credit information on the debt removed from your credit file, or shown as payment in full, if you make the payments under the new agreement.

How to Get a Debt Collector to Leave You Alone

Another powerful weapon against a collection agency is your right to demand to be left alone, whether you owe the debt or not. In writing, simply tell the collection agency to

cease all communications with you. It must do this, except to tell you either of the following:

- Collection efforts against you have ended.
- The collection agency or the original creditor may invoke a specific remedy against you, such as suing you.

Furthermore, if the collection agency does contact you to tell you that it intends to pursue a specific remedy, the agency must truly intend to do so. It cannot simply write to you four times saying, "We're going to sue you."

Below is a sample letter you can use to get a collection agency off your back. Although it is not required, you might also want to tell the collector why you are in financial trouble. Be brief. If you are judgment proof, which means you don't have anything that the agency can legally take from you (see Chapter 15 for more on this), you should let the collector know that. If the collection agency knows it can't get anything from you, it is less likely to sue.

 CAUTION

Asking a debt collector to stop contacting you is not always the best approach. If you don't negotiate with the collector, you run the risk that the collector will file a lawsuit that ultimately may require you to pay more than the amount of the original claim, and much more than a negotiated settlement. Plus, the judgment will stay on your credit record for seven years and will lower your credit score. Whether you negotiate directly with the collector or obtain a lawyer's assistance, many counselors feel the best strategy almost always is to communicate with the collector.

Sample Letter to Collection Agency to Tell It to Cease Contacting You

November 11, 20xx
Sasnak Collection Service
49 Pirate Place
Topeka, Kansas 69000

Attn: Marc Mist
Re: Lee Anne Ito
Account No. 88-90-92

Dear Mr. Mist:

For the past three months, I have received several phone calls and letters from you concerning an overdue Rich's Department Store account.

This is my formal notice to you under 15 U.S.C. § 1692c(c) to cease all further communications with me except for the reasons specifically set forth in the federal law.

This letter is not in any way an acknowledgment that I owe this money.

Very truly yours,

Lee Anne Ito

Lee Anne Ito

How to Handle Time-Barred or "Zombie" Debts

A creditor or collector has a limited number of years to sue you if you fail to pay a debt. This period is set by a law called the statute of limitations, and varies by state. (See Chapter 13 for more information.) In most states, the statute of limitations on debts is between three and ten years, but can be longer or shorter, depending on the state and the type of debt.

If a debt collector tries to collect a time-barred debt from you, the most important thing is not to say or do anything that in any way acknowledges that you owe the debt. Acknowledging the debt or making even a token payment can restart the statute of limitations in some states.

Debt Collectors in California Must Tell You If the Statute of Limitations Has Expired

As of January 1, 2019, California law requires a debt collector to inform the debtor if the statute of limitations for a particular debt has expired. The collector has to include the notice in the first written communication sent to the debtor after the statute of limitations passes.

The law also bans collectors from actually filing a lawsuit or initiating arbitration or any other legal proceeding to collect a time-barred debt.

If you're absolutely certain that the statute of limitations has expired on the debt, you can tell the collector to stop contacting you, and the collector must abide by your wishes. The only downside is that the debt will appear on your credit report until the seven-year reporting period ends, which may hinder your efforts to get a mortgage or car loan.

Why is someone coming after you for such an old debt, anyway? Aggressive debt collectors buy these debts from creditors for pennies on the dollar, so they make a tidy profit when they collect anything. Each year, debt buyers buy billions of dollars worth of charged-off consumer debt. It's legal to try to collect (after all, you still owe the debt), and the collector is only prevented from using the courts to try to collect it. The collector can seek voluntary payment of the debt, but most courts have held that suing you or threatening to sue you is a violation of the FDCPA, *unless* the statute of limitations has started anew. A collector cannot legally try to collect a debt that you discharged in bankruptcy. But that doesn't mean that debt collectors won't sue you anyway. (For more information on how to handle time-barred debts, go to the FTC website at www.ftc.gov and search for "time-barred debts." For more information on what to do if the collector sues, see Chapter 13.)

According to media reports, debt buyers have been known to harass debtors, re-age accounts on debtors' credit reports, and try to trick debtors into reaffirming debts so that the statute of limitations begins anew.

Particularly watch out when you are offered new credit. One way debt collectors try to trick you into reaffirming an old debt is to offer you a credit card. You may not realize that by signing up for the credit card you are reaffirming a debt by turning it into a new debt on your new credit card, which otherwise is so old the debt collector would be unlikely to ever be able to collect it. Often the credit card turns out to have a very low credit limit, so it is not useful as a credit card, anyway.

The collector should not be able to re-age your account so that the debt appears on your credit report for more than seven and one half years from the date of the first missed payment when you stopped paying the debt. The federal Fair Credit Reporting Act (FCRA) sets strict rules for the reporting of delinquencies and the start of the seven-year reporting period. At least in theory, the creditor should have reported that date, and the collector should not be able to change it. (See Chapter 16 to learn about disputing inaccurate information in your credit report.)

Negotiating Unsecured Debts

Most debts that go to collection agencies are unsecured debts, such as credit card, telephone, utility, and medical debt. If the creditor is flexible, it may be happy to accept a settlement below the full amount to avoid spending months futilely trying to collect the whole thing. As you negotiate, remember two key points:

- **The collection agency didn't lend you the money or extend you credit initially.** It doesn't care if you owe $250 or $2,500. It just wants to maximize its return, which may be a percentage of what it collects. or whatever it can collect over the pennies on the dollar it paid for the debt.

- **Time is money.** Every time the collection agency writes or calls you, it spends money. The agency has a strong interest in getting you to pay as much as you can as fast as possible. It has less interest in collecting 100% over five years.

Before you negotiate with a collection agency, review your debt priorities. (See Chapter 4 and Worksheet 2.) If you don't have the cash to make a realistic lump sum offer or to propose a payment plan, don't even talk to the collector—you may make promises you can't keep or give the agency more information than it already has. Or, worse, you may say something that turns an old time-barred debt into a brand-new debt.

Offer a Lump Sum Settlement

If you decide to offer a lump sum, understand that no general rule applies to all debt collectors. Some want 75% to 80% of what you owe. Others will take 50%. Those that have given up on you may settle for one-third or less. Before you make an offer, however, decide your top amount and stick to it. Once the collector sees you will pay something, it will try to talk you into paying more. Don't agree to pay more than you can afford.

A collection agency will have more incentive to settle with you if you can pay all at once. If you owe $500 and offer $300 on the spot to settle the matter, the agency can take its fee, pay the balance to the original creditor (who treats the amount you don't pay as a business loss), and close its books. If the collector owns the debt, it keeps the money, which usually ends up being a profit.

RELATED TOPIC

Thinking of mentioning bankruptcy? If you are considering mentioning bankruptcy when you negotiate, first review Chapter 6 for information on using this strategy.

Negotiate Improvement to Your Credit Report

After your debt has been transferred or sold to a debt collector, it will probably appear twice in your credit history. According to the credit reporting agency Experian, this is how it works: The debt starts as a current, never-late account. As you get behind on the payments, it is typically reported as being 30, 60, 90, and then 120 days late. At that point the creditor is likely to charge off the debt. Its status will be changed to "charged off" or "sold to collections." "Charged off" and "sold to collections" are both considered final statuses. Although the account is no longer active, it stays on your credit report.

When the debt is sold or transferred to a debt collector, a new collection account is added to your credit history. It appears as an active account, showing that the debt collector bought the debt from the original creditor. If the debt is sold again to another collection agency, the status of the first collection account is changed to show that it was sold or transferred. Once again, the final status shows that the first collection account is no longer active, but that status continues to appear as part of the account's history. All of the accounts—the original account and any subsequent collection accounts should be deleted at the same time, which is seven and one-half years from the original delinquency. (See Chapter 16.)

Before you start negotiating, decide what you want the debt collector and creditor to do to improve your credit file. If you want all references to the debt removed, you need to get both the debt collector and the creditor to agree to remove the tradeline reported by the creditor and the tradeline reported by the debt collector. This will remove any good history you had on the account before you stopped paying, as well as the negative history. For example, if you made on-time payments for ten years before you lost your job, you may not want the entire tradeline removed.

Alternatively, if the debt collector agrees to accept a reduced amount to settle the account, and you want to keep the history showing your years of on-time payments, you might ask the debt collector to report its tradeline as "satisfied in full" (the creditor's tradeline will still show that the account was charged off or transferred to collection).

Whichever way you settle the account, be sure to get written confirmation from the company you settle with (the creditor or debt collector) before you pay the money. See below for a sample letter you can adapt to the particular circumstances of your situation.

 TIP

Offer less if you're contacted by a second agency. If you're contacted by more than one collection agency for the same debt, it means the creditor has hired a secondary collection agency or that the first debt collector sold the debt to another debt collector. The creditor and at least one collection agency have given up on you. A collection agency that agrees to take your debt at this time will either insist on a generous fee (usually 50% to 60% of what's recovered) and substantial freedom in negotiating with you or have paid very little for the debt. At this point, you can probably settle the bill for 30¢ to 50¢ on the dollar or less. If the agency hasn't been able to reach you by phone but knows that you are receiving its letters, it may settle for even less.

Offer to Make Payments

If you offer to pay the debt in monthly installments, the debt collector has little incentive to compromise for less than the full amount. It still must chase you for payment, and it knows from experience that many people stop paying after a month or two.

Before a collection agency considers accepting monthly installments, it may have you fill out asset, income, and expense statements. Two points to keep in mind:

- You could be giving the collection agency more information about you than it previously had, and that might not be to your advantage.

Sample Letter to Creditor or Debt Collector to Make Lump Sum Payment If Negative Information Is Removed From Credit Report

[In your letter, use only the paragraphs that apply.]

[*Date* _____]

_____

_____

_____

Attn: Customer Service

Name(s) on account _____

Account Number: _____

To Whom It May Concern:

I am now in a position to resolve this matter. I can pay a lump sum amount of $_____ .
If I make a lump sum payment of $_____ by _____ , 20xx, you will agree
to do the following:

☐ *[If the amount of the debt is not disputed.]* You will release all claims against me and
anyone else arising from this account.

☐ *[If the amount of the debt is disputed.]* I dispute the amount of the debt. You will
acknowledge that the balance owed on the account is $ [*the amount of the lump sum
payment*], release all claims against me and anyone else arising from this account, and
accept that payment as payment in full.

☐ *[If you want the negative credit information about the original debt removed from your
credit report.]* You have authority to act for [*name of original creditor*], and [*name of
debt collector*] and you will submit a Universal Data or similar form to Experian, Equifax,
TransUnion, and any other credit reporting agency to which this account was reported
deleting all accounts/tradelines for this debt.

☐ *[If you want the debt collector to report the debt transferred or sold to it as paid in full.]*
You have authority to act for [*name of debt collector*], and you will report the debt
to Experian, Equifax, TransUnion, and any other credit reporting agency to which this
account was reported as satisfied in full when I have paid the amount of [*the lump sum
amount you agreed to pay*].

If my offer is acceptable to you, please sign the acceptance below, and return this letter
to me in the enclosed envelope.

Sincerely,

I agree to the terms and conditions in this letter.

_____   _____

Signature   Date

- Don't lie. You may be signing these forms under penalty of perjury. It's unlikely that you would ever be prosecuted for lying on the forms, but if the creditor later sues over the debt, lies on the forms can only hurt your case.

TIP

Beware of "urgency payment" suggestions. If your bill is seriously past due (90 days or more) and you've just agreed to a send a bill collector some money, don't be surprised if the creditor urges you to:

- Send the check by express or overnight mail.
- Wire the money, using Western Union or American Express.
- Put the payment on a credit or charge card. (If you're having debt problems, the last thing you need to do is incur more debt.)
- Have a bank wire the money.
- Visit the creditor directly and bring the payment.
- Let the collector come to your home to pick up the check.

Resist all urgency suggestions. Many will cost you money (using express or overnight mail or wiring the money) or time (visiting the collector in person) or are unnecessary incursions into your private life (the collector visiting you in person). Instead, get a cashier's check or money order from a bank other than yours (so the debt collector doesn't get your bank account information), and send by a method that will provide proof that the debt collector received the money. Do not send it before you get a signature from the debt collector on the agreement you have made.

Can a Lawyer Help You Negotiate?

If you're thinking of hiring a lawyer, remember that while a lawyer can carry clout, is probably experienced at negotiating, and can convincingly mention bankruptcy, a lawyer costs money. Don't hire one unless you owe a lot and the lawyer has a realistic chance of negotiating a favorable settlement, such as getting a debt reduced to $5,000 from $10,000. After all, if the amount you pay the collection agency and the lawyer totals what you originally owed, you should have just paid the full amount to the collection agency. Also, make sure the lawyer quotes you the fee and doesn't charge more, or you could have one more creditor at your door. If you dispute a debt and either the seller or the debt collector may have violated the law, you may be able to find an attorney who will take your case on contingency. See Chapter 18 for tips on hiring an attorney.

When Collection Turns Into a Lawsuit

Often, a creditor or debt collector will consider the following before filing a lawsuit:

- **The chances of winning.** Most debt collection lawsuits are filed only if winning is a sure thing. It's not worth it to the creditor to pay a lawyer if the chances of winning are small.
- **The chances of collecting.** If you are judgment proof and likely to stay that way (see Chapter 7), the creditor may not bother suing you.

- **The lawyers' fees.** The older or more difficult your debt will be to collect, the larger the lawyers' fee is likely to be. The creditor doesn't want to have to pay a lot to collect.
- **Any recent Chapter 7 bankruptcy discharge.** You can't file more than once every eight years. If you filed recently, you won't be able to discharge the debt in another Chapter 7 bankruptcy and are a good lawsuit target.
- **The relationship of the lawyer and the creditor.** Sometimes, a lawyer will take small debts along with several large ones to stay in good standing with the creditor.

These traditional bases for determining whether to sue no longer govern the conduct of numerous unscrupulous creditors and debt collectors, however. They use "robosigners," employees who prepare affidavits to file in court swearing to their familiarity with your credit account, even though they have never seen the file. Companies have also been known to submit affidavits to courts with attached documents that are purportedly the consumers' specific account contracts or records—even when they aren't. While actions like this are illegal, these types of practices have been widespread in the debt collections industry. Debt collectors using these improper methods, and lawyers who assist them, can file hundreds, or even thousands of lawsuits at very little expense. But it only works well if debtors don't answer the lawsuits. The vast majority of consumers who are sued for nonpayment of a debt don't respond to the lawsuit or show up in court.

So, many debt collectors routinely file lawsuits, perhaps in distant courts, knowing that chances are good they can get a default judgment. Don't be surprised if collection efforts quickly turn into a lawsuit.

> **CAUTION**
>
> **Don't ignore a lawsuit.** If you ignore a lawsuit, the creditor or debt collector will quickly get a judgment against you and possibly garnish up to 25% of your disposable wages each pay period. If you're not working, you risk having your bank accounts emptied and a lien recorded against your real estate. Keep in mind that many lawsuits by collectors are not backed by solid evidence of the debt, its amount, or even whether you really owe it. This means that your chances of winning the lawsuit may be better than you think. This isn't the time to bury your head in the sand. Find out how to fight back in Chapter 13.

Illegal Debt Collection Practices

Both federal and state laws restrict debt collectors' tactics. You can use your knowledge of these laws to protect yourself from harassment, negotiate a better settlement, file a complaint with the federal agencies that oversee debt collection agencies, or file your own lawsuit. The Consumer Financial Protection Bureau (CFPB) is the primary agency for enforcing the federal Fair Debt Collection Practices Act (FDCPA). The CFPB has authority over debt collectors with more than $10 million in annual receipts—about 60% of the debt collection business. The FTC enforces the law against smaller debt collectors.

(See Appendix A for information on how to file a complaint with the FTC or CFPB.)

Federal Law

The FDCPA requires that a collection agency make certain disclosures and prohibits the collector from engaging in many kinds of abusive or deceptive behavior. Here are some collection actions prohibited by the FDCPA.

Communications with third parties. For the most part, a collection agency cannot contact others about your debt. For example, for the most part, a debt collector cannot email you at work if someone else might have access to those emails, nor can it leave voicemail messages at your home that others living with you might hear.

There are a few exceptions to this general rule. Collectors are allowed to contact:

- your attorney. If the collector knows you are represented by an attorney, it must talk only to the attorney, not you, unless you give it permission to contact you, or your attorney doesn't respond to the agency's communications.
- a credit reporting agency, and
- the original creditor.

Collectors are also allowed to contact your spouse, your parents (only if you are a minor), and your codebtors. But they cannot make these contacts if you have sent a letter asking them to stop contacting you.

There is one other exception. Debt collectors are allowed to contact others for the limited purpose of finding information about your whereabouts. In these contacts, collectors:

- must state their own names and that they are confirming location information about you
- cannot identify the debt collection company's name unless asked
- cannot state that you owe a debt
- cannot contact one person more than once unless the person requests it, or unless the debt collector believes the person's earlier response was wrong or incomplete and that the person has correct or complete information, and
- cannot call other people for location information once they know an attorney represents you.

Communications with you. A debt collector's first written communication with you must tell you that he or she is attempting to collect a debt and that any information obtained from you will be used for that purpose. If the collector's first communication is oral, it must convey this same information as well. For example, a debt collector cannot leave a message from an unidentified company asking you to call back about "an important matter." In subsequent communications, the collector must disclose that it is a debt collector.

A collector cannot contact you:

- at a time or place that the debt collector knows, or should know, is inconvenient; calls before 8 a.m. and after 9 p.m. are presumed to be inconvenient (but, if you work nights and sleep during the day, a call at 1 p.m. may also be inconvenient). If a debt collector contacts you at an inconvenient time or place, say so. If the collector continues to contact you at that time or place, you have a stronger basis for a complaint or lawsuit.

- directly, if it knows or should have known that you have an attorney, or
- at work if it knows that your employer prohibits you from receiving collections calls at work. (If you are contacted at work and you are not allowed to have personal calls at work, tell the collector that your boss prohibits such calls, and send a confirming letter.)

Harassment or abuse. In general, a collection agency cannot engage in conduct that would naturally harass, oppress, or abuse. Specifically, it cannot:

- use, or threaten to use, violence, harm or threaten to harm you, another person, or your or another person's reputation or property
- use obscene, profane, or abusive language
- publish your name as a person who doesn't pay bills (this does not apply to state or federal child support agencies' deadbeat parents lists—see Chapter 12)
- list your debt for sale to the public
- call you repeatedly, or
- place telephone calls to you without identifying the caller as a bill collector.

You never have to put up with harassment. Just hang up the phone, or put the receiver down (without hanging up) and walk away.

False or misleading representations. A collection agency can't use any false, misleading, or deceptive statement in connection with collecting a debt. For example, it can't:

- claim to be a law enforcement agency or suggest that it is connected with the federal, state, or local government, for example, by using a badge or uniform to give that impression, or sending a document that looks as if it is from a government agency (a collector making this kind of claim is probably lying, unless it's trying to collect unpaid child support, or it's a private check diversion program under contract with a district attorney)
- falsely represent the amount you owe or the amount of compensation the collection agency will receive
- claim to be an attorney or that a communication is from an attorney
- claim that you'll be imprisoned or your property will be seized, unless the collection agency or original creditor intends to take action that could result in your going to jail or your property being taken (you can go to jail only for extremely limited reasons—see Chapter 7)
- threaten to take action that isn't intended or can't be taken—for example, if a letter from a collection agency states that it is a "final notice," it cannot write you again demanding payment
- falsely claim you've committed a crime to disgrace you
- threaten to sell a debt to a third party, and claim that, as a result, you will lose defenses to payment you had against the creditor (such as a breach of warranty)
- communicate false credit information, such as failing to state that you dispute a debt

- send you a document that looks like it's from a court or an attorney or part of a legal process if it is not
- use a false business name, or
- claim to be employed by a credit bureau, unless the collection agency and the credit bureau are the same company.

Unfair practices. A collection agency cannot engage in any unfair or outrageous method to collect a debt. For example, it can't:

- add interest, fees, or charges not authorized in the original agreement or by state law
- accept a check postdated by more than five days unless it notifies you between three and ten days in advance of when it will deposit the check
- deposit or threaten to deposit a postdated check prior to the date on the check
- solicit a postdated check for the purpose of then threatening you with criminal prosecution
- by concealing the true purpose of the communication, cause you to incur communications charges, such as by calling you on your cellphone, but not identifying itself as a debt collector
- threaten to seize or repossess your property if it has no right to do so or no intention of doing so
- communicate with you by postcard, or
- put any words or symbols on the outside of an envelope sent to you that indicate it's trying to collect a debt.

State or Local Laws Prohibiting Unfair Debt Collections

You may have additional protections from unfair debt collection practices, under state law. The most valuable state laws prohibit unethical and abusive collection practices by creditors as well as debt collectors. (Remember, the federal law applies only to debt collectors.) To learn whether your state offers additional protections, begin by going to your state government home page (www.[*state abbreviation*].gov, as in www.ca.gov), and look for a link to a consumer protection page. Chances are you'll find articles, FAQs, and booklets having to do with consumer rights, debt collectors, and creditors.

In addition, you may find that the collector has charged you too much interest. If your contract doesn't set forth an interest rate, most states impose a limit on the rate that debt collectors can charge. Some states also limit the interest rate for written contracts. Check your state law to see what that limit is and compare it to the rate charged by the collector. (See Chapter 18 to learn how to research your state's law.) Once the collector gets a judgment against you, however, a different interest rate limit set by the state may apply.

How to Fight Back If a Debt Collector Violates the Law

If a collection agency violates the law, you may be able to:

- Sue the agency in small claims or regular court.

- If you win in regular court, have your attorneys' fees paid by the other side.
- Bring up the violation if the agency sues you over the debt.
- Complain to the original creditor, which may be concerned about its own liability and offer to cancel or reduce the debt.
- Complain to the CFPB, FTC, and the state agency that regulates collection agencies in your state. (These agencies don't ordinarily represent you, but if the debt collector is routinely violating the law, they may prosecute the debt collector and seek an order that stops the violations or requires the collector to pay money to affected consumers; some agencies may also seek penalties or fines.)

See Chapter 3 for additional ways to assert your rights if the law was violated. See below for a sample letter to write to the creditor if you think the collection agency has violated the law.

Using Right to Verification Violations as a Bargaining Chip

If the debt collector's initial notice to you doesn't comply with its obligations under the law, you can use the violation as a bargaining chip in negotiations, or you can sue the collector and ask for damages and attorneys' fees.

One such violation often occurs with the verification notice. (See "Collection Efforts Must Stop While You Verify Debt," above, for information about the verification notice requirement.) Debt collectors know they may

continue to try to collect the debt during the 30 days you have to contest the debt, unless you ask for verification. Although collection agencies usually provide the required notice about verification, they often violate the FDCPA by overshadowing this notice with other statements, so as to discourage consumers from asking for verification.

For example, often, the first letter describes itself as an effort to collect a debt, and tells you that you have 30 days to dispute the debt's validity. Then the letter demands payment, usually immediately, or threatens that if payment is not received immediately, the debt will be reported as delinquent to credit bureaus, and you may be sued. Many courts have held that this kind of statement effectively overshadows or contradicts a debtor's right to dispute the debt for 30 days and therefore violates the FDCPA. (See, for example, *Swanson v. Southern Oregon Credit Services, Inc.*, 869 F.2d 1222 (9th Cir. 1988); *Owens v. Hellmuth & Johnson, PLLC*, 550 F.Supp.2d 1060 (D. Minn. 2008).) In such a situation, you are entitled to damages from the agency if you sue and win. Many cases settle, with the debt erased or greatly reduced in exchange for the debtor's dropping the FDCPA violation claim.

Bringing a Lawsuit

Under the FDCPA, you're entitled to compensation for any actual losses, including pain and suffering, that you suffer as a result of a collection agency's illegal tactics. And, depending on the circumstances you can recover up to $1,000 additional damages.

Sample Letter to Creditor About Debt Collector's Improper Collection Tactics

April 19, 20xx
Stonecutter Furniture Factory
4500 Wilson Boulevard
Bloomington, IN 47400

Dear Stonecutter:

On May 10, 20xx, I purchased a bedroom set from you for $2,000 ($500 down and the rest at $100 per month). I paid $900 and then lost my job, became ill, and was unable to pay you.

In early 20xx, I was contacted by R. Greene at the Drone Collection Agency. R. Greene called me twice a day for nearly three weeks and used profanity at me, my husband, and my 11-year-old son. In addition, he called my father and threatened him with a lawsuit, even though he is a 76-year-old diabetic with a heart condition and has had no connection with this transaction.

I am fully prepared to take the steps necessary to protect my family and me from further harassment. I am also filing a complaint with the Consumer Financial Protection Bureau and the Indiana State Attorney General, and I am considering seeing an attorney. I am writing you in the hope that you have not condoned Drone's practices and will instruct Drone to stop harassing and abusing my family and me. I also would appreciate any other assistance or consideration you may be able to provide.

Very truly yours,

Karen Wood

Karen Wood
57 Curtis Street
Bloomington, IN 47400

cc: Indiana State Attorney General, Consumer Protection
     Drone Collection Agency
     Federal Trade Commission

If you win, you can also ask the judge to order that the other side pay your attorneys' fees and court costs.

To win, you'll need to show repeated abusive behavior. If a collector calls five times in one day and then never again, you'll probably lose in court. You may also be able to collect punitive damages under other laws, including your state's laws if the collector's conduct was particularly horrible.

In truly outrageous cases, consider hiring a lawyer to represent you in court. Some private lawyers specialize in debt collection abuse cases. You may be able to find one through the National Association of Consumer Advocates' website, www.consumeradvocates.org.

Think about this strategy if the mental abuse inflicted on you is substantial and you have reports from therapists and doctors documenting your suffering.

In addition to bringing a lawsuit against a collector, you can also raise FDCPA violations in a collection lawsuit that a creditor or collection agency brings against you. These are called "counterclaims." See Chapter 13 for more on counterclaims.

Gathering Proof

Whatever route you decide to go, you'll need proof of the violation. Written threats are the best evidence, but collectors usually know better than to threaten you in writing. One effective way to collect evidence is to keep a log of all calls you get from the agency. Write down the agent's name, date and time of call, and any information you remember about what the collection agent told you.

In some states, you can tape the conversation without the collector's knowledge. In others, it's a crime to tape without consent. Only tape without consent if you are sure it's legal. To find out whether it's legal in your state, you'll have to do some legal research on your own. (See Chapter 18.) If it's not legal to tape without consent in your state (or you aren't sure), first tell the collector that you plan to tape-record the call or try to have a witness present during your conversations. If the collector knows you are recording the call, that may stop the abusive conduct. If you're loud enough about the abuse you suffered—and you've got proof backing you up—you have a chance to get the whole debt canceled in exchange for agreeing not to file a lawsuit.

Suppose the collector is foolish enough to leave a message with illegal content (profanity, for example) on your voicemail. The recording probably can be used as evidence, provided you can identify that the call came from the collector (perhaps because you recognize the voice, you call the number for the agency in response to the call and confirm the call was from the agency, or there is something in the message that identifies the caller).

Collectors also have trickier ways to collect that may not violate the law, such as by calling to say you have won a prize as a way to find out personal information about you, offering a credit card that obligates you to pay on a stale debt, or including your agreement to pay a stale debt in a refund anticipation loan.

Understanding Loan and
Other Credit Documents

Understanding the key terms in a credit agreement, whether it be for a credit card, car loan, home mortgage, or something else, is important. By knowing what certain terms mean and what to look for in the fine print, you can:

- avoid entering into a bad agreement or accepting terms that won't work for you
- know what to expect when you do enter into a credit agreement so that you can manage the account well and avoid pitfalls
- understand the consequences if you default on payments, and
- better negotiate with lenders and creditors when you are struggling with payments.

This chapter will help you identify and understand the terms you're likely to find in credit agreements.

Credit Disclosures

The federal Truth in Lending Act (TILA) requires lenders to give consumers clear and conspicuous information about the terms of credit before signing an agreement. (15 U.S.C. §§ 1631 and following.) By reviewing this information carefully, you can determine how much the credit will cost you and other important conditions that might affect you.

TILA applies to consumer credit cards and most other types of consumer credit if the creditor either charges for giving credit (such as interest and other fees) or if there is a written agreement requiring four or more installment payments. There are a few exceptions. (Visit Nolo.com to learn more about TILA.)

 RELATED TOPIC

Closed- and open-end credit. With open-end credit, you may make new charges to the account, such as with a credit card account. Closed-end credit is for a fixed purchase, such as a home or car loan, that you will pay off over a set period of time. Closed-end credit can be in the form of a credit contract with the seller (a car dealer that finances its cars) or in the form of a loan from a financial institution or another lender. For more information on the difference between the two, see "Is the Account Open- or Closed-End Credit?" in Chapter 13. And to learn about disclosures for open-end credit (such as credit cards), see Chapter 17.

In a closed-end credit transaction, the lender must give you lots of information. It's important to review this information carefully. Here are some of the things lenders must disclose about your transaction:

- the finance charge (the amount the credit will cost you, including interest and certain fees)
- the annual percentage rate or APR (the cost of the credit on a yearly basis)
- the amount financed (the amount of credit provided) including both the money you actually get and most of the charges for getting the loan, as well as any money used to pay off outstanding debts
- an itemization of the amount financed or a disclosure of your right to get an itemization, if you ask for it (which you should do so you can see what you are being charged for)

- the total of payments (the sum of the amount financed and the finance charge)
- the total number of payments needed to pay off the loan, the amount of each payment, and the payment schedule
- whether the lender is taking a security interest in the property being purchased
- the amount or percentage of any late fee
- any prepayment penalty or refund of unearned finance charge if the loan is refinanced or paid off early
- the total sales price of the item or service (plus all other charges), if the creditor is also the seller, and
- special disclosures for adjustable-rate residential mortgages (loans where the interest rate fluctuates), including the maximum possible interest rate.

RESOURCE

Additional disclosures if your home is involved. If your credit transaction involves your home, the lender must provide additional disclosures, depending on the type of mortgage and how high the rates and fees are. (To learn about these requirements, visit Nolo.com.)

Common Terms in Credit Agreements

Below are some other common terms that may appear in a credit agreement.

Acceleration

This clause lets the lender declare the entire balance due ("accelerate" the loan) if you

default—that is, miss a payment or otherwise violate a term of your loan agreement (by failing to pay taxes or maintain required insurance, for example). If you miss one or two payments, the lender will probably agree to hold off accelerating the loan if you pay what you owe and pay the remaining balance on time. If you miss additional payments, however, you can be sure you'll fall from the lender's good graces.

Once a mortgage loan is accelerated, it's sometimes difficult to get the lender to "unaccelerate" and reinstate your old loan. Under state law, you may be able to reinstate your loan by paying the past-due amounts and fees, even after the loan has been accelerated, up to a set deadline before a foreclosure sale. Also, if state law doesn't set the reinstatement period, Fannie Mae and Freddie Mac standard loan forms allow reinstatement up to five days before a nonjudicial foreclosure sale, or before a court enters a judicial foreclosure judgment.

Attorneys' Fees

Many creditors include a provision in a loan contract awarding them attorneys' fees if you default and they have to sue you to get paid. If your contract contains this provision but says nothing about your right to attorneys' fees if you win, most states give you the right to attorneys' fees if you are sued—or you sue—and you win. Several states prohibit the creditor's attorneys from collecting from you a fee in excess of 15% of the amount you owed.

Balloon Payment

To make loans seem affordable, or to qualify borrowers who can't afford the monthly payments when they apply for loans that require repayment in equal monthly installments for a set period, some loans are set up with regular payments too small to pay them off. However, they have a final large payment called a balloon payment. Balloon payments can be dangerous. Often, a borrower with a balloon payment cannot afford the large final payment when it comes due. If you don't pay, the lender may have the right to repossess or foreclose on the property that serves as security for the loan—often a house. Unscrupulous lenders or their agents may assure you not to worry because you can refinance with them before the large payment is due. Usually, however, nothing in the documents guarantees you that right. If you have been misled in this way, get help. (See Chapter 18.)

Many states prohibit balloon payments in loans for goods or services that are primarily for personal, family, or household use; others prohibit balloon payments on loans under a certain amount. Or they give borrowers the right to refinance these loans at the lender's prevailing rate when the balloon payment comes due. In practice, many lenders let borrowers refinance balloon payments as long as the borrowers have decent credit at the time of the refinancing. Balloon payments are not allowed in high-cost or higher-priced mortgage loans.

Confession of Judgment

A confession of judgment is a provision that lets a lender automatically take a judgment against you if you default, without having to sue you in court. Confessions of judgment are prohibited in consumer contracts. Few lenders try to include one in their loans. The laws limiting confessions of judgment don't apply to real estate purchases, but state laws generally govern the procedures to collect on real estate mortgages.

Cosigner or Guarantor

If you didn't qualify for a loan on your own, a lender may have let you borrow money because you had a cosigner or guarantor. This person assumed full responsibility for paying back the loan if you didn't. This person may be called a cosigner, a guarantor, or some other name. The cosigner or guarantor need not benefit from the loan to be liable for it.

Many young adults with no credit history have their parents cosign or guarantee loans. Under the CARD Act, credit card companies cannot provide credit cards to consumers under 21 years of age unless they can prove they have their own source of income or they have a cosigner. The cosigner rule was added to help prevent young people from getting into trouble with easy-to-get credit cards. You may feel pressure to cosign for a minor who is a relative, but think carefully before signing. It may not be the best financial decision for the minor or for you.

Another borrower, who may have had a serious financial setback (repossession, foreclosure, or bankruptcy) or simply doesn't earn enough to get a loan, may ask a friend or relative to cosign or guarantee. Cosigners and guarantors should fully understand their obligations before they sign on.

Credit Insurance

Credit insurance guarantees payment of a debt if the borrower is unable to pay. It is sold by credit card companies, car dealers, finance companies, department stores, and other lenders who make loans for personal property.

Credit insurance, for the most part, is a rip-off. Consumers spend billions each year on credit insurance, often without knowing what they have bought. Or they may believe it is required, when it's not. Sometimes all it takes to purchase it is to check a box on the credit agreement. And the seller or creditor may have already checked the box, without your knowing it, before you sign the credit agreement. The insurance may have limitations and exclusions so that in many instances when you might want insurance, you may not be covered anyway.

There are four main types of credit insurance:

- credit property insurance (insures against damage or loss to the collateral securing the loan)
- credit life insurance (ensures that the remaining debt on a loan or credit card account will be paid off if the consumer dies during the term of the coverage)
- credit disability/accident insurance (pays a limited number of monthly payments on a loan or credit card account if the borrower becomes disabled during the term of the coverage), and
- involuntary loss of income insurance (insures against layoff or other causes of involuntary loss of income).

Many lenders will tell you that insurance is required to get a loan. This is almost always wrong. For the most part, you cannot be required to buy insurance. The main exception is for property insurance: Creditors can require you to buy this type of insurance in certain circumstances. But even if property insurance is required, in most states, creditors cannot force you to buy the insurance from them. A creditor must allow you to shop around and buy from another company.

Mandatory Arbitration

More and more, businesses include a mandatory arbitration clause in many types of consumer contracts, including contracts for employment, credit, insurance, and even for doctors' services and hospital admission. These clauses require you to waive (give up) your right to a jury trial and even your right to go to court to resolve disputes.

Mandatory arbitration clauses require you to resolve any dispute by way of a private, and often costly, arbitration system usually selected by the business. Consumer advocates warn that arbitration clauses often disadvantage consumers. For example, one arbitration company reportedly decided in favor of the credit card company in 18,045 cases out of

18,075. Additionally, the Consumer Financial Protection Bureau (CFPB) found that in cases that were resolved by an arbitrator (and when the CFPB was able to ascertain the outcome), consumers obtained relief regarding their claims in just 32 out of 341 cases (tracked over a two-year period).

In arbitration, you also have less ability to find out information about the company that you may need to prove your case, and you may not be able to appeal the decision, even if the arbitrator made a serious mistake about the law. On the other hand, you may be able to get a decision sooner, at less expense.

Watch out for these clauses when you sign contracts. Sometimes the arbitration agreement is separate and sometimes it is hidden among the many paragraphs in a contract.

Sometimes the arbitration paragraph gives you a choice to avoid the arbitration clause, but you may have to write a separate letter saying you don't agree to the arbitration clause.

If the clause doesn't allow you to opt out, you can tell the person you are dealing with that you won't agree to arbitration. Sometimes he or she will let you strike that out of the contract. If you can't get out of the arbitration clause, and you want to purchase the product or service, you may want to write just above where you have to sign: "I don't want arbitration, but I was told I could not receive the *[product or service]* unless I signed agreeing to arbitration." Making it clear you did not want arbitration, but had no choice, may be helpful if there is a dispute later, and you or your attorney tries to prevent enforcement of the arbitration part of the contract.

Voluntary mediation and arbitration, on the other hand, can be helpful. (See Chapter 13.) These programs allow you to sue in court if you cannot resolve a dispute outside of court or if you don't like the arbitration or mediation result.

 SEE AN EXPERT

More on mandatory arbitration agreements. These websites may help: Public Citizen, www.citizen.org, Trial Lawyers for Public Justice, www.publicjustice.net, or the National Consumer Law Center, www.nclc.org.

Prepayment Penalties

Lenders make money on the interest they charge for lending money. If you pay off your loan early, they don't make as much as they had anticipated. To make up some of the loss, some lenders impose prepayment penalties; if you repay the loan before it is due, you have to pay a penalty, usually a percentage of the balance you paid early. This makes it very expensive for you to refinance if you are having trouble making the payments or if you find a lower interest rate.

When you are shopping for a loan, state that you want no prepayment penalty. Before you sign credit documents, ask the creditor to show you where it makes clear there is no prepayment penalty, then carefully check the documents you are asked to sign.

Some states have laws that limit the amount or duration of prepayment penalties. In states where prepayment penalties are allowed only on larger loans, a creditor might try to get you to borrow more money than you need so it can include a prepayment penalty. Be suspicious if a creditor offers you more money than you really need and, if you can, choose a loan without a prepayment penalty.

As of January 10, 2014, federal law prohibits prepayment penalties for most residential mortgage loans. (12 C.F.R. § 1026.43(g).) Prepayment penalties are only allowed for fixed-rate or step-rate qualified mortgages that are not higher priced and only when the law otherwise permits it. Even if a prepayment penalty is permitted, the penalty is only allowed during the first three years after the loan is consummated (that is, when the borrower becomes contractually obligated on the loan). After three years, a prepayment penalty is not allowed. In addition, if a lender offers you a mortgage loan that includes a prepayment penalty, the lender must also offer you an alternative loan that does not include a prepayment penalty. The alternative loan must be similar to the loan that has a prepayment penalty, and you can then choose between the two.

Pyramiding Late Fees

If you're late on a loan payment (such as a car loan or personal loan), the lender normally imposes a late fee. These fees are generally permitted unless the lender engages in an accounting practice known as pyramiding. Pyramiding takes place when the lender assesses a late fee that you don't pay and then applies your regular payment first to the late fee and then to partially cover the payment due. You will never fully catch up on the payments due and the lender will impose a late fee every month, even when you pay on time. For the most part, pyramiding is prohibited.

EXAMPLE: Sheila has a personal loan that requires her to pay $100 each month by the 5th. On May 6, when her payment has not yet been received, the bank assesses a $5 late fee. When the lender receives Sheila's $100 payment on May 17, it applies the first $5 to cover the late fee and the remaining $95 toward her $100 payment. In June, Sheila is automatically assessed another late fee on the $5 balance due for May, even though her June payment was on time. With this scheme, Sheila will always have a slight balance—and will continually be assessed a late fee.

If you find yourself being charged a late payment in the months after you make one payment late, immediately contact the creditor, and if you can't resolve it with the creditor, complain.

Right to Cancel

Some types of contracts must provide you with the right to cancel the contract within a certain number of days of signing. Examples include home equity loans, many home improvement contracts, and credit repair service contracts. Many states have other laws that allow you to cancel certain contracts within three (or more) days. Make sure you review the contract to see if you have a right to cancel, and if you change your mind about the contract, be sure to cancel within the allotted period.

Security Interest

When you take out a secured loan, you give the creditor the right to take your property that secures the loan, or a portion of the property if you don't pay. This is called a security interest. The two most common types of security interests are a mortgage, where you give the lender the right to foreclose on your home if you miss payments, and a car loan, where the lender can take the car if you default.

Some consumer loans, especially for large appliances and furniture, include a security interest in the item being purchased. Also, some personal loans that are not used to purchase a specific item—but are often used to pay off other loans—include a security interest in your home, car, or important items around your house. These personal loans can be hazardous to borrowers. The interest is usually very high, and if you default, the lender can take the item identified in the contract.

To protect borrowers, lenders are generally prohibited from taking security interests in the following, unless you use a loan or credit to buy the items: your clothing, furniture, appliances, linens, china, crockery, kitchenware, wedding ring, one radio, one television, and personal effects. Some states provide borrowers with additional protections and remedies.

Remember: You have three business days to cancel most loans secured by your principal residence.

Wage Assignment

If your loan or credit contract allowed creditors to collect past-due debts out of your wages, without having to get a court judgment, your creditors can collect much more easily. That kind of contract provision is called a wage assignment. Federal law and the law of some states prohibit creditors from including most wage assignments in consumer credit contracts. However, a creditor can include a wage assignment in your contract if the contract allows you to revoke the wage assignment whenever you want. Or, a wage assignment may be allowed if, when you first got the loan, you set up a payment plan, with payments to be paid out of your salary. The laws limiting wage assignments don't apply to real estate purchases.

Some lenders, especially credit unions, ensure your repayment of a loan by such a wage assignment payment plan. This means that each time you are paid, your employer deducts a sum of money from your paycheck and sends it to the lender. This kind of wage assignment is legal. You may find this method of payment is overly intrusive and prefer to pay on your own. On the other hand, you may be able to get credit from your credit union this way, when you cannot get credit elsewhere.

Wage assignments are further limited in a number of states. (See "State Laws Limiting Wage Assignments in Consumer Loans," above.) In many states, if you're married, your spouse must consent before a lender can take a voluntary wage assignment.

State Laws Limiting Wage Assignments in Consumer Loans

Many states protect consumers from wage assignments for certain loans, such as credit or installment contracts. If your state is not listed, check with your department of consumer credit or consumer affairs to see if there are similar laws or regulations in your state.

State and Statute	Spouse's Consent Is Required	Limit on the Amount of Wages That Can Be Deducted	Wage Assignment Must Be Notarized
Alabama Ala. Code 1975 § 8-5-21		Wage assignments for future wages are not enforceable.	
Arkansas Ark. Code Ann. § 11-4-101			
California Cal. Lab. Code § 300	Yes	50%	Yes
Colorado Colo. Rev. Stat. § 8-9-104	Yes		Yes
Connecticut Conn. Gen. Stat. Ann. § 52-361a		Assignment by employees of earnings shall be void other than for support obligations and union dues (§52-361a(i).	No
District of Columbia D.C. Code Ann. §§ 28-2305, 28-3804		Certain wage assignments, including wage assignments for future wages, are not enforceable.	
Florida Fla. Stat. Ann. §§ 516.17, 560.404		Wage assignments for consumer loans and certain consumer transactions are not enforceable.	
Hawaii Haw. Rev. Stat. Ann. § 476-15		Wage assignments for credit sale contracts are not enforceable.	
Idaho Idaho Code Ann. § 28-43-304		Wage assignments for certain consumer credit transactions are not enforceable.	
Illinois 740 Ill. Comp. Stat. 170/4		The lesser of 15% gross weekly salary, or the amount by which net weekly wages exceed 45 times the federal or Illinois minimum hourly wage (computed using whichever minimum wage is greater).	
Indiana Ind. Code Ann. § 22-2-7-4	Yes		

State and Statute	Spouse's Consent Is Required	Limit on the Amount of Wages That Can Be Deducted	Wage Assignment Must Be Notarized
Iowa Iowa Code § 539.4	Yes		
Kansas Kan. Stat. Ann. 16a-3-305		Wage assignments for consumer loans and certain consumer transactions are not enforceable by the assignee.	
Kentucky Ky. Rev. Stat. Ann. § 286.4–570		10%	
Louisiana La. Rev. Stat. Ann. § 23:731		Assignments of future wages enforceable against employer only if employer consents in writing. Employer cannot terminate or decline to hire because of a voluntary assignment or a single garnishment of earnings.	
Maine Me. Rev. Stat. tit. 9-A, § 3-305		Wage assignments for certain consumer credit transactions are not enforceable in Maine. Some authorized deductions are valid if the employee can revoke the authorization.	
Maryland[1] Md. Code Ann., Com. Law §§ 12-311, 12-607, 12-923, 15-302	Yes	Certain consumer wage assignments are not enforceable.	Yes
Massachusetts[2] Mass. Gen. Laws Ann. ch. 154, §§ 2, 3; Mass. Gen. Laws Ann. ch. 255B, § 20, Mass. Gen. Laws Ann. ch. 255D, § 10	Yes	Depending on the amount of the loan, $10 or 75% of the weekly wage may be exempted. Certain retail installment wage assignments are not enforceable.	Yes
Michigan Mich. Comp. Laws Ann. §§ 493.17, 445.864		Wage assignments for certain consumer loans and retail installment contracts are not enforceable.	
Minnesota Minn. Stat. Ann. §§ 56.17, 181.07, 325G.16 (West)	Yes	10% for regulated loans. Wage assignments for certain consumer credit sales are not enforceable.	
Mississippi Miss. Code Ann. § 71-1-45			

[1] In Maryland, a wage assignment may not remain in effect for more than six months.

[2] In Massachusetts, a wage assignment may not remain in effect for more than two years (or one year if the loan is for less than $3,000).

State Laws Limiting Wage Assignments in Consumer Loans (continued)

State and Statute	Spouse's Consent Is Required	Limit on the Amount of Wages That Can Be Deducted	Wage Assignment Must Be Notarized
Missouri Mo. Ann. Stat. §§ 432.030, 408.365, 408.551, 408.560		Wage assignments for future wages, for certain credit contracts, and for certain retail contracts are not enforceable.	
Montana Mont. Code Ann. §§ 31-1-306, 32-5-310	Yes	10%	Yes
Nebraska Neb. Rev. Stat. §§ 36-213, 25-1558, 45-1030	Yes	25% net weekly wages (15% for the head of a family), or the amount by which net weekly earnings exceed 30 times the federal minimum hourly wage, whichever is less	Yes
Nevada Nev. Rev. Stat. Ann. §§ 604A.435, 604A.440, 675.340		Wage assignments for certain consumer loans are not enforceable.	
New Hampshire N.H. Rev. Stat. Ann. § 361-A:7		Wage assignments for motor vehicle retail installment contracts are not enforceable.	
New Jersey N.J. Stat. Ann. §§ 17:11C-41, 17:16C-39, 17:16C-64		Wage assignments for certain consumer loans and retail installment contracts are not enforceable.	
New Mexico[3] N.M. Stat. Ann. §§ 14-13-11, 58-15-22	Yes, if loan is made by a small loan business	25%; 10% if loan made by a small loan business	Yes
New York N.Y. Pers. Prop. Law §§ 48-a, 302, 413		10% for certain wage assignments. Wage assignments for retail installment contracts and retail installment credit agreements are not enforceable.	
North Carolina N.C. Gen. Stat. Ann. § 53-180		Wage assignments for certain consumer loans are not enforceable.	
North Dakota N.D. Cent. Code Ann. § 51-13-02.1		Wage assignments for retail installment contracts are not enforceable.	
Ohio Ohio Rev. Code Ann. § 1321.31	Yes	25% if married; 50% if unmarried	
Oklahoma Okla. Stat. Ann. tit. 14A, § 3-403		Wage assignments for certain consumer loans are not enforceable. Certain authorized deductions are valid if the employee can revoke the authorization.	

[3] Under New Mexico law, a small loan business is one that makes loans under $2,500 to consumers.

State and Statute	Spouse's Consent Is Required	Limit on the Amount of Wages That Can Be Deducted	Wage Assignment Must Be Notarized
State Laws Limiting Wage Assignments in Consumer Loans (continued)			
Oregon Or. Rev. Stat. §§ 83.150, 83.670, 725.355		Wage assignments for certain consumer loans, retail installment contracts, and retail charge agreements are not enforceable.	
Pennsylvania 43 Pa. Stat. Ann. §§ 271, 274	Yes	Wages payable semimonthly can't be assigned.	
Rhode Island R.I. Gen. Laws § 19-14.1-7	Yes (unless spouses have been separated for at least five months)		
South Carolina S.C. Code Ann. §§ 37-2-410, 37-3-403		Wage assignments for certain consumer loans, credit sales, and leases are not enforceable. Some authorized deductions are valid if the employee can revoke the authorization.	
Tennessee Tenn. Code Ann. § 50-2-105			
Texas Tex. Fin. Code Ann. §§ 342.503, 345.354, 347.053, 348.410, 353.407		Wage assignments for certain consumer loans, retail installment contracts, and retail charge agreements are not enforceable.	
Utah Utah Code Ann. § 70C-2-202		Wage assignments for certain consumer loans are not enforceable.	
Vermont Vt. Stat. Ann. tit. 8 § 2235, Vt. Stat. Ann. tit. 9, § 2456	Yes	Wage assignments for certain consumer loans and contracts are not enforceable.	
Virginia Va. Code Ann. § 6.2-1526	Yes	10%	
Washington Wash. Rev. Code Ann. § 49.48.100	Yes		
West Virginia W.Va. Code §§ 46A-4-109(2), 46A-2-116		25% of net weekly earnings. Wage assignments for consumer loans made by regulated lenders are not enforceable.	
Wisconsin Wis. Stat. Ann. §§ 422.404, 241.09	Yes, plus signature of two disinterested witnesses		
Wyoming Wyo. Stat. § 27-4-111	Yes		

Waivers of Exemptions

If a creditor sues you and gets a court judgment, or you file for bankruptcy, some of your property is protected from your creditors—that is, it can't be taken to pay what you owe. This property is called exempt property. It usually includes your clothing and personal effects, household goods, and some of the equity in your home and car. (See Chapters 14 and 15.)

Some creditors try to get around the laws that let you keep exempt property by including a provision in a loan agreement whereby you waive your right to keep your exempt property. These provisions are prohibited in most non-real-estate consumer contracts.

Student Loans

With the cost of education skyrocketing, it's not surprising that student loan borrowing is on the rise. Most graduates these days face not only an uncertain economic future, but also mountains of student loan debt.

Because the government guarantees or provides most student loans, it is the government that will ultimately try to collect if you don't pay. This is significant, because the government can use far more aggressive collection tactics than private collectors.

The good news is that there are lots of options available for paying back student loans. And, in some circumstances, you may be able to get your student loan debt canceled.

Borrowing Is on the Rise

In 2004, approximately 23 million individuals held student debt. By 2015, this number grew to over 40 million. In 2016 alone, lenders originated one million student loans totaling $10.5 billion. Since then, the total amount of outstanding student loan debt has grown to over $1.5 trillion, with around 45 million students holding debt.

It's no wonder that these numbers continue to climb. As education costs go up, more students must finance their schooling.

This chapter reviews the basic types of student loans and ways to repay, defer, or cancel them.

What Kind of Loan Do You Have?

The first step to managing your student loan debt is understanding what types of loans you have. Many repayment options and other programs are available for only certain types of loans, so you need to know which type you have. This section covers the most common ones.

Federal Student Loans

In the past, most student loans were provided by private lenders and guaranteed by a guaranty agency and then by the federal government—these are called Federal Family Education Loans (FFELs). The "guarantee" means that the government will reimburse your lender if you default and can then go after you to collect on the loan. In 1993, the federal government began providing loans directly to students—called Direct Loans. As of July 2010, FFELs are no longer available to students. However, if you (like many Americans), took out a student loan prior to July 2010, you very well may have an FFEL. Through these and other programs, the federal government provides the majority of all student grants and loans, although private loan numbers are increasing.

Here are the details of FFELs, Direct Loans, and other common federal loans.

Federal Family Education Loans (FFELs)

FFELs may be one of the following:

- Stafford Loans, (previously called Guaranteed Student Loans or GSLs or Federal Insured Student Loans (FISLs) (the most common)

Student Loans: Where to Find Additional Resources

Here's where to find the student loan resources mentioned throughout this chapter.

The U.S. Department of Education. The Department of Education has lots of information about the different types of student loans, details about the various repayment plans, deferments and forbearances, cancellation and forgiveness options, as well information about consolidation loans. Go to the Department of Education's website at https://studentaid.ed.gov/sa and run a search for the specific topic you're interested in. Then follow the link. Or you can reach the department at 800-433-3243 (voice) or 800-730-8913 (TTY).

The Federal Student Aid Ombudsman Group. The Department of Education's student loan ombudsman helps borrowers with student loan problems. The ombudsman is a "last resource"; usually it will help you only after you have tried to resolve the problem yourself. You can contact the student loan ombudsman office at 877-557-2575 or go to www. studentaid. ed.gov. (Look for "How to Repay Your Loans" at the bottom of the page and then click on "Contact the Ombudsman.")

Consumer Financial Protection Bureau (CFPB). You can learn more about options for repaying your student loans at www. consumerfinance.gov/students. The CFPB also has an online form that you can submit to complain about a federal loan or private lender. Look for a link on the website.

Legal aid. If you are having problems making your student loan payments because you have a low income or because you have been a victim of fraud or abuse by a for-profit school, you may be able to get help from your local legal aid or legal services office. You can find a national listing of legal aid offices at www.lsc.gov.

National Consumer Law Center (NCLC) Student Loan Borrower Assistance Project. This valuable resource is for borrowers, their families, and advocates representing student loan borrowers; you can find it at www.studentloanborrowerassistance.org. This site is for people who already have student loans and want to know more about their options and rights. You can also find links to various federal student loan forms by hovering over "Resources" and then clicking on "Forms."

- PLUS loans (loans to parents or to graduate students)
- SLS loans (made before 1994), or
- consolidation loans.

If you got your loans after June 30, 2010, they are not FFELs.

Direct Loans

These loans are made directly by the federal government, rather than by a bank or another lender. A Direct Loan may be a:

- Direct Subsidized Loan (similar to a subsidized Stafford Loan)

- Direct Unsubsidized Loan (similar to an unsubsidized Stafford Loan)
- Direct PLUS Loan (available to credit-worthy parents and graduate students), or
- Direct Consolidation Loan.

Direct Loans have had a more favorable repayment option than FFELs for students who do not have sufficient income to pay the standard payments. But as of July 2009, both types of loans have similar flexible repayment plans available. If you are having trouble paying an older FFEL, it may be worthwhile seeing if you can switch to one of the more affordable payment plans now available.

Most existing federal loans are either FFELs or Direct Loans. (As mentioned above, loans made after June 30, 2010, cannot be FFELs.)

Perkins Loans

A Perkins Loan is a low-interest loan for undergraduate or graduate students with very low incomes. These loans were previously known as National Direct Student Loans, and before that, National Defense Student Loans. The federal government guarantees repayment of Perkins Loans but, unlike other loans, Perkins Loans are made by the school with a combination of federal and school funds. This means that the school, not a bank or the government, is the lender.

For more information about the different types of federal student loans and other aid, go to the U.S. Department of Education's website.

Private Loans

Many students have private loans from banks and other financial institutions without the guarantee of the federal government. Many of these loans are made by the Student Loan Marketing Association (Sallie Mae). For more information, go to www.salliemae.com.

For a list of other lenders making private student loans, go to FinAid's website, at www.finaid.org, click on "loans," then follow the link to private student loans to find a table comparing the different lenders.

Student Loan Terminology

A **guaranty agency** is a state or private nonprofit company that insured your FFEL student loan made before July 2010 and pays the holder if you default.

The **holder** owns your loan. The servicer is the company hired by the owner to collect and process payments. Your loan holder may be your lender or a company that purchased your loan from the lender. If you're in default, the holder (a guaranty agency, the Department of Education, or the school that made the loan) might place the loan with a collection agency.

The **lender** is the institution from which you obtained your loan. This may be a bank, a savings and loan, a credit union, your school, or the federal government.

CAUTION

Private loans are usually more expensive and have harsher repayment terms than the others described here. You should not get a private loan unless you have received all the government grants and federal Direct or guaranteed loans available. Some schools may not tell you about all the federal grants and loans for which you are eligible before trying to steer you to a more expensive private loan. Private loans may also have names, such as "signature loan," that do not clearly distinguish them from government loan programs.

State Loans

Many states have their own student loan programs. To find out about these programs, contact your state department of higher education. The Department of Education's website has contact information for each state guaranty agency at https://studentaid.ed.gov/sa/resources. Click on "Types of Aid" and then look for "Aid From Your State Government."

Figuring Out Who Holds or Services Your Student Loan

If you want to set up a repayment plan, postpone payments, consolidate your loans, cancel a loan, or apply for some other government program, you need to know both what type of loan you have and who holds or, in some cases, who services your loan. To find out, try these sources:

- The National Student Loan Data System (https://nslds.ed.gov/nslds/nslds_SA).

This is the Department of Education's central database for student aid. You can get information about what kind of loan you have, as well as loan or grant amounts, outstanding balances, loan status, and disbursements.

Identification information is required to access the database, including a user name and password that you can get online. You can also access the database by calling 800-999-8219.

- My Federal Student Aid (https://studentaid.ed.gov/sa/?login=true) provides information about your federal student loans and the servicer or lender for those loans. You'll need to create an FSA ID, which is a username and password that you can use to access federal websites like StudentLoans.gov and the myStudentAid mobile app. You may also call the Department of Education's Federal Student Aid Information Center at 800-433-3243 or 800-730-8913 (TDD).
- For loans in default, call the Department of Education's Default Resolution Group at 800-621-3115 or 877-825-9923 (TDD).

If you've tried all of these places and are still having trouble, consider contacting the Federal Student Aid Ombudsman office.

Canceling Your Loan

If you qualify for cancellation (also known as discharge), it is always your best option. It may completely wipe out the loan balance and allow you to get back any payments you have made or that have been taken from you through tax intercepts or wage garnishments, or it may eliminate some or all further payments.

Certain types of discharges treat your loan as if you never owed it (for example, closed school and false certification discharges) and wipe out all negative references in your credit report. If only a portion of your debt is wiped out due to the school's failure to pay a required refund on your loan, your credit report must state that a portion of the loan was discharged.

Below are several ways to cancel your loan. The first three—cancellation due to school closure, false certification, and unpaid refunds—are most likely to apply to students who attended private, for-profit schools.

If a school misled you, you may have a basis to sue or defend against collection actions, but only the types of conduct explained below qualify you to have your loan canceled without a lawsuit.

School Closure

Many former students were lulled into taking out student loans to attend schools with glowing descriptions of future careers and high salaries, only to have the schools deteriorate or close before the students could finish the programs. You can cancel an FFEL, a Direct, or a Perkins Loan (including an NDSL loan) if you received any of the loan proceeds after January 1, 1986, as well as the portion of a consolidation loan used to pay off any of these loans, if you were unable to complete the program because the school closed:

- while you were enrolled (and you did not complete your program because of the closure)
- while you were on an approved leave of absence, or
- within 120 days after you withdrew from the school. (The government may extend this period if there are exceptional circumstances.)

The Department of Education has a list of closed schools. Go to https://studentaid.ed.gov/sa/about/announcements/closed-school#list.

In most circumstances, your school must be on the list in order to qualify for a closed school cancellation. The list may not be entirely accurate. If you have information that can show a school closed earlier than the date indicated in the list, you should provide it.

Even if the school closes, you won't be eligible for this type of cancellation if you:

- withdraw more than 120 days before the closure
- are completing a comparable program through a teach-out agreement (an agreement between schools that allows students to finish their programs of study), or
- have completed all program coursework at the closed school (even if you didn't receive a diploma or a certificate).

To apply for the cancellation, you generally must submit an application but, in some cases, discharge is automatic.

False Certification

If the school did not make sure that you were qualified to attend the program, you may be able to cancel your loans based on "false certification." This program applies to FFELs or Direct Loans if you received any of the loan proceeds after January 1, 1986, as well as the portion of a consolidation loan used to pay off one of these loans. (If you had a Perkins Loan, you may have other grounds to have the loan canceled, but will need to contact an attorney familiar with the intricacies of student loan law for help.) Typically, the grounds for false certification are any of the following:

- You did not have a high school diploma or GED at the time of admission, and the school did not properly test your ability to benefit from the program (for example, the school did not properly time its entrance exam, did not properly score it, did not use an exam relevant to the course, did not use an approved exam, or improperly assisted you to pass the exam).
- At the time of enrollment, you could not meet the licensing requirements for employment in the field for which you were to receive training because of physical or mental condition, age, criminal record, or other reason the Department of Education accepts (for example, you had a felony record and enrolled in a security guard course, but your state doesn't permit prior felons to work as security guards).
- The school forged your signature on the loan papers or checks and you did not receive the loan proceeds.
- You are a victim of the crime of identity theft (shown by a verdict or judgment).

TIP

If someone steals your identity. Go to IdentityTheft.gov to report the theft, get an Identity Theft Report, and receive a personalized recovery plan. You should also contact the three nationwide credit reporting agencies and ask them to put a credit freeze on your file. To learn more about what to do if your identity is stolen, get *Nolo's Credit Repair,* by Amy Loftsgordon and Cara O'Neill.

Unpaid Refunds

You can cancel all or a portion of a loan if the school failed to pay you a refund that it owed you because you never attended the school or withdrew from the school and were owed a refund for the time left in the program. Loans must be GSL, Stafford, SLS, PLUS Loans, or Direct Loans, or the portion of a consolidation loan used to pay off one of these loans and must have been made after January 1, 1986. (If you had a Perkins Loan, you may have other grounds to have the loan canceled, but will need to contact an attorney familiar with the intricacies of student loan law for help.) In addition, some states have funds to reimburse students who didn't get refunds due them.

Permanent Disability

You can cancel any federal student loan if you are unable to work because of a total and permanent disability. In most cases, to qualify for this cancellation, you cannot have had the injury or illness at the time you signed up for the loan. If you did have the disability at the time you got the loan, you might be able to cancel your loans if you can show substantial deterioration of your condition.

You are eligible if the Secretary of Veterans Affairs has determined that you are unemployable due to a service-connected disability.

In 2018, the U.S. Department of Education began using the National Student Loan Data System and U.S. Department of Veterans Affairs (VA) databases to identify disabled veterans who have federal student loans and invite them to apply for a student loan discharge.

To qualify, you have to submit documentation showing that you:

- have a service-connected disability (or disabilities) that is 100% disabling, or
- that you're totally disabled based on an individual unemployability rating.

As part of the initiative, the Department of Education is sending veterans customized letters, which explain the disability cancellation program along with an application to get a discharge. If you don't receive a letter, but think you might qualify, go to Disability Discharge.com to get specific details about how to apply for a total and permanent disability discharge.

You can also show that you are totally and permanently disabled if you are receiving Social Security Disability Insurance (SSDI) or Supplemental Security Income (SSI) benefits and you submit a notice of award that states that your condition will be reviewed every five to seven years (meaning your condition is not expected to improve). Otherwise, you will need to get a statement from your treating physician on a form provided by the holder of your loan or by the Department of Education.

Your physician must certify that you are unable to engage in any substantial gainful activity due to a medically determinable physical or mental impairment that is expected to result in death, has continued for at least 60 months, or is projected to continue for 60 months or more.

For specific information about how to apply for a disability cancellation, go to www.disabilitydischarge.com/application-process. If you have questions, you can call Nelnet (the servicer that assists the Department of Education in administering the disability discharge process) at 888-303-7818 or send an email to DisabilityInformation@Nelnet.net.

If your documentation proves to the department that you are permanently and totally disabled, you will be discharged from making further payments. If you're approved for a discharge based on SSDI/SSI documentation or a physician's certification, you're subject to a three-year post-discharge monitoring period. During any of the next three years, if you earn over 100% of the poverty guideline for a family of two, or if you get certain educational grants or a new Direct or Perkins Loan, your discharge will be revoked and your loan debt reinstated. (For 2018, the poverty line for a family of two was $16,460 in the contiguous United States. To see the values for Alaska and Hawaii, and for updates to poverty line numbers, visit https://disabilitydischarge.com/PovertyGuidelines.)

Parents who took out PLUS loans together cannot both get disability cancellations unless both are disabled. If only one parent is disabled and both parents took out the loan, the nondisabled parent is still obligated to pay.

Death

A student's death wipes out any outstanding amount owed on student loans (including PLUS loans). If the loan has been consolidated with a spouse's student loans, this discharge wipes out only the portion owed by the spouse who died. (Although allowed in the past, a married couple can no longer combine their individual student loans into in a single, shared Direct Consolidation Loan.) If both parents signed for a PLUS loan, the death of one does not wipe out the remaining debt.

Participation in a Volunteer Program, a Teaching Program, Military Service, or Another Public Service

Different federal loans have different cancellation programs that apply if you are engaged in a particular type of work, such as volunteering for the Peace Corps, teaching needy populations, serving in the military, or providing another public service. Some programs allow you to postpone payments on your loans only while you are engaged in the service; others allow you to cancel all or a portion of a loan. Also check with your college counseling department—some colleges have their own loan cancellation programs for students employed in public service.

 CAUTION
To discharge or cancel a student loan —or to determine whether you qualify to do so— call the servicer of your loan. Be aware that your servicer might not inform you of all the options

available to you. For this reason, it pays to learn about your options before you call. Go to the U.S. Department of Education's Federal Student Aid website at https://studentaid.ed.gov/sa for the most recent information about available cancellation programs, including eligibility criteria.

Postponing Payments

If you don't qualify to have your loan discharged, and you can't afford to make any payments right now, you may be able to postpone student loan payments through either a deferment or a forbearance.

Deferments

Each type of federal loan program has different rules that allow you to postpone paying your loan in certain circumstances. Postponements that are available only if you are not in default when you apply are called "deferments." If you get a deferment, you will still have to pay the loan back at some point, but you can wait a while. Most important, interest will not accrue on a Federal Perkins Loan, a Direct Subsidized Loan, the subsidized portion of a Direct or FFEL Consolidation Loan, or Subsidized Federal Stafford Loan (the government pays it) during the deferment period. On unsubsidized loans, the unsubsidized portion of Direct or FFEL Consolidation Loans, and PLUS Loans, you will not have to pay the interest during the deferment, but it will be added to your loan, so you will have to pay more later. Deferments are available only if you aren't in default, which for most loans typically occurs once you're 270 days

(about nine months) behind and you meet the specific criteria for your type of loan. (With a Perkins loan, you're in default as soon as you miss a payment.)

A deferment is usually available if you are:

- enrolled in school at least half-time
- unemployed and seeking employment
- suffering an economic hardship
- serving in the military on active duty during a war, another military operation, or a national emergency, or performing qualifying National Guard duty during a war, another military operation, or a national emergency, and up to 180 days afterward
- called to service while enrolled in school or were enrolled within six months before being called up (the deferment continues for 13 months after the military duty ends)
- serving in the Peace Corps, or
- battling cancer.

You can find a chart and description of available deferment programs on the U.S. Department of Education's website.

Forbearances

If you don't qualify for a deferment but are facing hard times, you still might be able to postpone payment on your loans or temporarily reduce your payments with a forbearance. In theory, you should be able to get a forbearance even if your loans are in default. Unfortunately, the Department of Education doesn't agree with this interpretation of the forbearance rules and says they're not available after default.

Forbearances are less attractive than deferments because interest continues to accrue when you are not making payments. But if you can't make your loan payments, a forbearance will at least keep you out of default. In the long run, the cost of default is much higher than the interest that accrues during a forbearance. Even if you can't get a forbearance on all of your loans, a forbearance on some of them may give you enough breathing room to catch up financially.

CAUTION

Consider other options before agreeing to a forbearance. Some lenders and for-profit schools put a borrower into a forbearance agreement, even though another option, such as a flexible payment plan or deferment, would be better for the borrower.

RESOURCE

More information on deferment and forbearance. You can find more information on the Department of Education's website and the National Consumer Law Center (NCLC) website for student borrowers.

Changing Your Repayment Plan

If you don't qualify to have your loan canceled or for a deferment (in which interest doesn't continue to accumulate), before you decide on the forbearance alternative, check out the variety of repayment alternatives available. And even if you do qualify for a

deferment or forbearance, remember that these are short-term solutions only. If you can find a repayment plan you can manage (and which may eliminate part of your debt if you pay regularly), you'll end up with a long-term solution to your student debt problem.

Repayment Plans

There are many flexible options for repaying federal loans. The options are more limited for private loans. This section focuses on federally guaranteed or Direct Loans only. If you have a private loan, you should contact your loan holder for more information about repayment plans.

Standard plan. This is the basic payment plan for federal loans. These plans carry the highest monthly payments but cost less in the long run because you pay less interest. Most borrowers either choose this plan or end up with it because they fail to choose something else. In most cases, a standard plan requires that you pay at least $50 per month and repay your student loans in ten years.

Graduated plan. In a graduated plan, if you start after July 1, 2006, you have to pay the loan off in ten years (for all loan types except Direct Consolidation Loans and FFEL Consolidation Loans), but payments start out low and increase every two years. (Borrowers pay monthly payments for between 10 and 30 years for Direct Consolidation Loans and FFEL Consolidation Loans.) This may be your best option if you are just starting a career or business and your income is low but likely to increase over time.

Extended repayment plan. This plan allows a student with over $30,000 in principal and interest debt who is starting repayment after July 1, 2006, to stretch payments over a longer period of time, up to 25 years. In order to qualify, you must have more than $30,000 in outstanding Direct Loans or more than $30,000 in outstanding FFEL Program loans. Your monthly payments will be lower, but you'll pay more interest over the long term.

Plans if the regular payment plan causes hardship. There are other plans available for low- and moderate-income borrowers and those who have high student loan debts. You may be eligible for these plans even if your financial difficulties are only temporary. These plans require you to submit financial information annually to the loan holder. The lender will adjust payments according to your financial circumstances. Details of the income-driven plans follow:

- **Pay As You Earn repayment plan (PAYE).** This plan is available for Direct Loans only. To qualify, you must have high debt relative to your income and be a new borrower as of October 1, 2007. (You are a new borrower if you had no outstanding balance on a Direct Loan or FFEL Program loan when you received a Direct Loan or FFEL Program loan on or after October 1, 2007.) You must also have received a disbursement of a Direct Loan on or after October 1, 2011. This plan requires payments equal to 10% of your discretionary income, but never more than the 10-year standard repayment plan amount. And, if you can't pay the full amount after making

20 years of payments under the plan (instead of the 25 years required by some other repayment plans), the rest of the amount you owe will be forgiven. Depending on your income, your payments may be as low as $0. This payment plan cannot be used for PLUS loans made to a student's parent.

Direct Consolidation Loans that repaid PLUS loans made to parents, FFEL PLUS Loans made to parents, and FFEL Consolidation Loans that repaid PLUS loans made to parents, are not eligible for this plan.

- **Revised Pay As You Earn repayment plan (REPAYE).** The REPAYE Plan enables borrowers to cap their monthly student loan payment amount at 10% of their monthly discretionary income, without regard to when the borrower first obtained the loans. Under this plan, the repayment period is 20 years (if all loans you're repaying under the plan were for undergraduate study) or 25 years (graduate or professional study loans). Direct PLUS loans made to parents, Direct Consolidation Loans that repaid PLUS loans made to parents, FFEL PLUS Loans made to parents, and FFEL Consolidation Loans that repaid PLUS loans made to parents are not eligible for this plan.

- **Income-based repayment program (IBR).** The IBR (which is for both FFELs and Direct Loans) eliminates any remaining debt after 25 years of repayment, and the payment amount may be even less than the accruing interest. Payments make up to 15% of your discretionary income, which can be as low as $0. IBR is not available for parent PLUS loans or Perkins Loans.

- **Revised income-based repayment plan.** For new borrowers on or after July 1, 2014, the payment limit is 10% of your discretionary income and the period for repayment is 20 years. This revision makes the plan as favorable as PAYE if you are a new borrower.

- **Income contingent repayment plan (ICRP).** If you have Direct Loans, this plan may help you. Your monthly payments will be the lesser of 20% of your discretionary income or what you'd pay on a repayment plan with a fixed payment over the course of 12 years, adjusted according to your income. If you make payments on an ICRP plan for 25 years, the government will cancel the remaining balance. ICRis not available on PLUS loans made to a student's parent.

CAUTION

You may owe taxes if the government cancels your loan. If a government agency cancels the balance of your loan, you may owe income tax on the amount canceled. For more on this, see Chapter 6.

- **Income Sensitive Repayment Plan (ISRP).** This plan applies to Subsidized and unsubsidized Stafford Loans, FFEL PLUS loans, and FFEL Consolidation Loans. You pay a monthly amount that is affordable for you, based on your

annual income and the loan must be paid in full within ten years.

- **Perkins Loans.** Perkins Loans have different repayment options than Direct Loans and FFELs. Check with your school to get information about Perkins Loan repayment plans.

TIP

CFPB Fix-It Form. In 2016, the Consumer Financial Protection Bureau (CFPB) published an "Income-Driven Repayment Application Fix-It Form" designed to help borrowers request an income-driven repayment plan. Within ten days after the borrower submits the form, the loan servicer must indicate whether the borrower's application is accepted, denied, or incomplete. If approved, the response will include the borrower's new monthly payment amount and the due date. If denied, the servicer must provide one of three explanations:

- The loan is ineligible for the requested plan.
- The payment under the program would be higher than the payment under a standard plan.
- The borrower failed to provide necessary information within 60 days.

You can find the Fix-It Form on the CFPB website.

RESOURCE

More information. For a summary of the terms of the different repayment plans, links to details about each plan, and a repayment estimator, go to the Department of Education's website.

Direct Loan Consolidation

Consolidation is a good option if you are having trouble paying your loans. You can "consolidate" just one loan, or several loans. You can consolidate loans even if you're already in default. In fact, consolidation is one good way to get out of default. (See "Getting Out of Default," below, for more information.)

A consolidation loan allows you to combine your federal student loans into a single loan with one monthly payment. This may be a good option if any of the following are true:

- You can't afford the monthly payments on your federal student loans under any of the options described in "Repayment Plans," above and don't qualify for a postponement or for loan cancellation.
- You qualify for some of the payment plans described in "Repayment Plans," above, but you are so deep in debt that you still can't afford your monthly payments.
- You have older loans with higher interest rates that you want to refinance at a lower interest rate.
- You are in default on one or more of your student loans.

The vast majority of federal loans are eligible for consolidation, including Subsidized and Unsubsidized Stafford Loans (GSLs), Direct Loans, Supplemental Loans for Students (SLSs), Perkins Loans, FISLs, and Direct PLUS Loans. All borrowers with these loans are eligible to consolidate after they graduate, leave school, or drop below half-time enrollment.

However, there are some restrictions. Private student loans cannot be included in a federal consolidation loan. In addition, spouses cannot consolidate their loans into a single consolidation loan. And, borrowers who are in default must meet certain requirements.

Consider both the advantages and disadvantages of consolidation before obtaining a consolidation loan. Consolidation could also lead to the loss of certain benefits, such as repayment incentives or cancellation options. For example, if you make qualifying Public Service Loan Forgiveness (PSLF) payments on a Direct Loan and then consolidate that loan, you'll lose credit for the PSLF payments you made. Only qualifying payments that you make on the new Direct Consolidation Loan would count toward the 120 payments required for PSLF. Likewise, if you have a Perkins Loan and you're working in an occupation that qualifies you for Perkins Loan cancellation benefits, you shouldn't include your Perkins Loan in a consolidation. That way you'll keep the benefits associated with that loan. Another potential disadvantage is the possibility that your interest rate will go up. Consolidation will extend the repayment period, which means that you will pay more interest over the life of your loan. Consolidation will not completely clean up your credit report, either. If you were in default, your report will reflect that your previous loans were in default but are now paid in full through the new loan. However, if you can keep up your consolidation payments, your credit score will begin to improve.

Loan consolidation offers other potential advantages, too. If you are in default on any of your government loans, consolidation may offer the opportunity to get out of default and make affordable monthly payments.

And consolidation gives you the advantage of locking in a low rate on your student loans.

CAUTION

Beware if you have a PLUS loan. A PLUS loan made to a parent can't be transferred to a student to include in a consolidation loan. And if you have both a parent PLUS loan and other student loans in your name, you should not consolidate the parent PLUS loan with other student loans. PLUS loans made to parents are not eligible for most of the flexible payment plans (for example, IBR and PAYE), so if you consolidate a PLUS parent loan with other loans, the entire consolidation loan will be ineligible for these alternative payment plans. (For further details, go to https://studentaid.ed.gov/sa/repay-loans/understand/plans/income-driven.)

The federal government provides Direct Consolidation Loans. They come with flexible repayment options, including a standard plan, a graduated plan, and an extended plan, or an income-driven repayment plan. In order to get out of default through a Direct Consolidation Loan, you must either make three consecutive monthly payments on the loan before you consolidate or simply agree to an income-driven repayment plan on the consolidated loan. Borrowers are also eligible for deferment or forbearance in certain circumstances. If there is a delay in approval of your consolidation loan, or if the payment amount specified is not the lowered payment amount you should get under the income-driven repayment option you chose, you may need to apply to your loan servicer for a deferment or forbearance while the loan is being set up.

Each subsidized loan consolidated under the program keeps its interest subsidy benefit. This can be important if you return to school.

To qualify for a Direct Consolidation Loan, you must have at least one Direct Loan or FFEL. So, if you have only a Perkins Loan, for example, you don't qualify. For step-by-step information on Direct Consolidation Loans and how to apply, go to the Department of Education's website.

One other point to consider before you apply for a consolidation loan: Your right to assert a school-related claim against the lender of the consolidation loan is not clear. That right might be important, for example, if you got a loan to attend a for-profit school because it lied about the likelihood of your getting a job after graduation. If you think you have a claim against the school, it is better to consult an attorney experienced in bringing these kinds of cases before you consolidate your loan.

Reconsolidation

The circumstances under which you can consolidate a loan or loans that have already been consolidated are limited. Check the U.S. Department of Education's website for details.

CAUTION

Avoid private consolidation loans. Some private lenders offer consolidation loans that may sound like Direct government loans, but they do not have all of the benefits of a Direct Consolidation Loan, such as deferment, forbearance, cancellation, and affordable repayment plans. Your best bet is to apply for a Direct Consolidation Loan. To apply, go to the Department of Education's website.

Getting Out of Default

Generally, if you are more than 270 days behind in your student loan payments, you are considered in default. Getting out of default is key to dealing with student loans. Many repayment plans and most postponement options require that you not be in default. In addition, as long as you're in default, you are not eligible to get new loans or grants. As just discussed, you can get out of default if you qualify to have your loan canceled (discharged), or by getting a consolidation loan with a repayment plan matched to your income or by making three consecutive, voluntary, on-time, full monthly payments on the defaulted loan before you consolidate it.

You can also get out of default by "rehabilitating" the defaulted loan. To rehabilitate a defaulted Direct Loan or FFEL, you must agree in writing to make at least nine timely payments (within 20 days of when due) in a period of ten consecutive months. Once you've made the required nine payments, your loan will no longer be in default.

With a loan rehabilitation agreement, the loan holder determines a reasonable monthly payment amount that is equal to 15% of your annual discretionary income, divided by 12. Perkins rehabilitation does not specify that the payments must be reasonable and affordable, only that the nine required payment amounts are to be set by the holder. If you have a Perkins Loan, you should negotiate for reasonable and affordable payments.

Generally, if you rehabilitate a defaulted loan and then default on that loan again, you can't rehabilitate it a second time. (Though, if you rehabilitated a loan before August 14, 2008 and go back into default on that loan, you can rehabilitate it again.)

Loan rehabilitation also wipes out the default notation on your credit report. But your credit history will still show the late payments your loan holder reported before the loan went into default.

The option to rehabilitate (bring current) a loan is not automatically available if the creditor has already gone to court and obtained a judgment against you for the debt. Lenders have the choice to rehabilitate these loans but are not required to do so.

RESOURCE

More information. For more on getting out of default, go to the NCLC or U.S. Department of Education website.

TIP

Consider consolidation first. Loan consolidation is usually a faster way to get out of default than rehabilitation. Once you get a Direct Consolidation Loan, you will immediately be taken out of default status. You will stay out of default as long as you keep making payments. One downside to consolidation, though, is that the default status of the previous loan, as well as late payments, will remain on your credit report for the full amount of time allowed under the Fair Credit Reporting Act. (For more information on the Fair Credit Reporting Act, see Chapter 16.)

Filing for Bankruptcy When You Can't Pay

Eliminating your student loan debt in bankruptcy is another possibility, although it can be difficult to get rid of student loan debt this way.

You can discharge (cancel) student loans in bankruptcy if repayment would cause you "undue hardship." This standard applies to private loans, as well as to the federal Direct and federally guaranteed loans. This is a difficult, although not impossible, standard to meet. If you are considering bankruptcy primarily as a way to discharge student loan debt, you should talk to an attorney experienced in handling student loan debts.

In determining undue hardship, many bankruptcy courts look at the following three factors:

- **Poverty.** Based on your current income and expenses, you cannot maintain a minimal living standard and repay the loans.
- **Persistence.** It is not enough that you can't currently pay your loan. You must also demonstrate to the court that your current financial condition is likely to continue for a significant portion of the repayment period.
- **Good faith.** You've made a good-faith effort to repay your debt.

Some bankruptcy courts look at the totality of the circumstances (all relevant factors) and still others use a different test. For example, a court might consider whether you were misled and did not receive an education that would allow you to get a job with sufficient earnings to repay the loan. Examples include a vocational school that lacked necessary equipment; or a degree school that lacked adequate teaching staff and you could not transfer credits elsewhere to finish because the credits were not transferable.

Generally, courts look for reasons to deny student loan discharges. However, if you are older (at least 50 years old), are likely to remain poor, and have a history of doing your best to pay off your loan, you may be able to obtain a discharge.

The undue hardship standard for discharging student loans in bankruptcy applies only to loans used solely for "qualified education" for an "eligible student." Loans to attend unaccredited schools, loans used partially for something other than education expenses, and loans if you were not a qualified student (see "False Certification," above) can be discharged like any other unsecured loan in bankruptcy.

> **TIP**
>
> **Bankruptcy might still help.** Even if bankruptcy is unlikely to erase your student loans, it may help you get rid of other debts, freeing up money to pay your student loans. Another option is to file for Chapter 13 bankruptcy (see Chapter 14) and pay the amount you are behind on your student loan in a court-approved payment plan over three to five years.

Consequences of Ignoring Student Loan Debt

Student loans are not secured debt, and so you will not lose your home or car if you don't pay them. But they are also different from most other unsecured debts. If you don't pay your student loans, you won't be able to get additional student loans or grants or other government loans in the future. In addition, you will be subjected to a number of special debt collection tactics that only the government can use. These government collection tools can have very severe consequences.

First, the government can charge you hefty collection fees, often far in excess of the amount you originally borrowed. Second, unlike almost every other kind of debt, there is no statute of limitations for collection of student loans. This means that even 20 or 30 years after you went to school, the government can continue to try to collect your loans.

The government can also:

- Seize your income tax refund.
- Garnish up to 15% of your disposable income.
- Take some federal benefits that are usually exempt from collection, such as Social Security income, although the government must let you keep a certain amount of this income.

If you get notice of a wage garnishment or tax intercept, you have the right to challenge it by requesting a hearing. Sometimes just the act of requesting a hearing prompts the collector to agree to a payment plan. If you can pay a small amount, you should consider the various means of postponing payments or establishing a payment plan you can afford.

In some states, defaulting on your student loans could lead to the loss of your professional or other type of license. Around 20 states allow the government to suspend a state-issued professional license (like a nursing, teaching, or law license, for example) or other license (such as a driver's or even a fishing license), if a borrower misses too many student loan payments.

Refinancing Student Loans into Mortgage Debt

Nonbank lender SoFi offers a program that allows consumers to use home equity to pay off student loan debt at terms more favorable than a traditional refinance. Under SoFi's program, the lender consolidates your student loans with your existing mortgage. It then refinances the total amount and pays the student loans off by directly disbursing funds to the servicer. The upside is that your student loans are paid off and you might have a lower overall payment. However, you lose certain protections associated with federal student loans, such as deferments, cancellation possibilities, and income-based repayment options. Also, if you can't keep up with the mortgage payments, you could lose your home to foreclosure.

Private Student Loans

Private student loans are not made directly by the federal government or guaranteed by the federal government.

A private loan may be considered in default if you miss even one payment. And private student loan lenders are usually aggressive in their collection efforts. Private lenders are also not necessarily forthcoming with information about what alternative payment arrangements they will consider. Some will let you skip payments (usually called a forbearance) while you are in school, but may charge a fee to do so, or the lender might allow you to stop making payment for a short time (three to 12 months, for instance) if you lose your job. Some will modify your contract so you have smaller payments, although that may cost you more in the long run. Some will even cancel your loan in certain circumstances, such as if you become disabled or die, or if your school closes before you complete your program. Check your loan agreement to see if any alternatives are offered there. Read through the alternatives available for government Direct or guaranteed loans above before you attempt to negotiate with a private lender. Knowing what is available under those programs may give you ideas for what to ask the private lender to do.

The CFPB has created two new tools to help borrowers arrange a repayment plan with a private student loan lender: a financial worksheet and a sample letter. You can use the financial worksheet to figure out the monthly payment that you can afford. Once you figure out how much you can afford, customize the CFPB sample letter to ask your lender about repayment options. Then mail the letter and worksheet to the lender or send them through your private student loan servicer's website after you log in. It is also recommended that you include recent pay stubs, bank statements, or other documentation along with the letter to verify your income and expenses. (To find links to the financial worksheet and sample letter, go to the CFPB website and search for "Repay student debt." Follow the link and the click on "Non-Federal" and answer the questions. You'll then get access to the worksheet and sample letter.)

CAUTION

A 2016 report from the U.S. Government Accountability Office found that tens of thousands of older citizens have had their Social Security (mostly disability) benefits garnished to satisfy old, defaulted federal student loans. Most people lost around $140 per month to garnishment.

Remember, individuals who are totally and permanently disabled can eliminate federal student loans. Many people aren't aware of this option and continue to have their checks garnished.

Beware of Student Loan Debt Relief Services

With student loan debt weighing in at over $1.5 trillion, it's not surprising that businesses promising "student loan debt relief" are popping up all around the country. The National Consumer Law Center (NCLC) warns that you should be wary of companies that claim they will help you get your student loan debt under control. While these businesses say they'll help you get student loan relief under various government programs, they often engage in deceptive advertising and claims, charge high fees, and give bad information.

Instead of paying a company to help you with your student loan problems, you can get excellent free information about the various repayment and cancellation programs available to you on the U.S. Department of Education's website and from the NCLC Student Borrower Loan Assistance Project. After learning about your options, you may decide you'd like assistance in completing and submitting and application. If so, consider talking to an attorney or a consumer credit counselor. (See Chapter 18 for information on how to find a good credit counseling agency.)

CAUTION

Although you might be able to use a private lender to refinance private student loans along with your federal student loans, doing so will result in a loss of the federal protections. For example, you'll lose access to income-based repayment plans and public service loan forgiveness, as well as discharge programs, forbearance, and deferment options.

Most private student loans are taken out by students attending for-profit colleges. Some of these colleges have received a lot of negative publicity about misleading and unfair practices used to entice students to sign up for classes, failure to provide the training necessary for students to be able to get jobs in the occupations for which they trained, and other violations of law. If you are not able to negotiate payment arrangements you can afford with your lender, or if you believe the college engaged in improper conduct, you can submit a complaint through the CFPB, which has a Private Education Loan Ombudsman to assist private student loan borrowers. Go to the CFPB website to send your complaint.

If your school referred you to the lender or arranged the private loan, and you believe the school misled you or otherwise violated the law, the lender may not have a legal right to collect its loan. But proving this is complicated and requires an experienced attorney. See Chapter 18 for help in finding an attorney.

Child Support and Alimony

Benjamin Franklin once said that only two things in life are certain: death and taxes. To that short list we might add the obligation to support one's family.

This chapter will tell you:

- how child support and alimony are set and collected
- how you can seek to have your child support or alimony obligation modified, and
- what happens to child support and alimony obligations if you file for bankruptcy.

But first, a loud and clear warning: Regardless of the circumstances, you must pay your court-ordered child support. If you don't pay, you will be incurring the proverbial debt from hell. It never goes away. No bankruptcy judge can cancel past-due support. No state or federal judge can reduce it. It just sits there generating interest until it—and the interest—is paid in full. In the meantime, you are subject to intrusive collection techniques.

It's true that many parents who don't pay child support believe they have a good reason for not doing so, including:

- They have new families to support.
- The custodial parents won't let them see their kids.
- The custodial parents moved their kids far away.
- The custodial parents misuse the support.
- The custodial parents play all day while they have to work.
- The court ordered them to pay too much.

Understand, however, that it makes no difference to the judge. If you owe child support and have the apparent ability to pay (even if you aren't working at the time), you will be subject to harsh collection techniques and may also do a stretch of jail time if a judge gets angry enough.

 RESOURCE

Information on child support enforcement laws in your state. Visit the Office of Child Support Enforcement website at www.acf.hhs.gov/css.

How Child Support Is Determined

The federal Family Support Act of 1988 requires all states to use a formula or guidelines to calculate child support. Each state, and the District of Columbia, sets its own formula or guidelines. If you think your existing child support order isn't in line with your state's formula or guideline, you or your child's other parent can ask the court to review it. (See "Modifying the Amount of Child Support," below.)

 RESOURCE

Child support calculators. Judges and lawyers use fancy software to make precise support calculations, but you might be able to find simple support calculators for your state online. You can find a simplified version of your state's calculator at www.alllaw.com. You can also try searching online using the name of your state and "child support calculator." Another website, www.childsupportguidelines.com, has the actual guidelines for each state.

If You Are Owed Child Support or Alimony

This chapter addresses the concerns of people who pay child support or alimony, not those entitled to receive it. Many people, of course, have debt problems because they aren't receiving support to which they are entitled. This chapter doesn't explain how to get that support, but it should help you understand your rights and the strategies available to you.

The U.S. Department of Health and Human Services, Administration for Children and Families, Office of Child Support Enforcement, has a website full of information at www.acf.hhs.gov/css. You can find your state's child support enforcement agency there, as well as publications, information, and even help locating a missing parent.

Be cautious about private agencies offering to collect past-due support—they often charge exorbitant fees and can be less than reliable. Before signing up, find out how much it will cost and the agency's rate of success. Then call the local Better Business Bureau and your local district attorney's office to see whether the agency is legitimate.

While formulas differ from state to state, they almost always start with the parents' respective incomes and the amount of time the children spend with each parent. Other factors the formula may consider include:

- the number of children subject to the support order
- whether either parent is paying support from a previous marriage

- which parent is paying for health insurance, and the cost
- whether either parent receives irregular income, such as bonuses or incentive pay
- whether either parent is required to pay union dues or has other mandatory paycheck deductions, and
- which parent is paying day care costs and the cost of other necessities or programs.

Unpaid Child Support and Arrears

Unpaid child support is court-ordered child support that you failed to pay as it became due. This past-due support sometimes is referred to as arrears or arrearages. No matter what it's called, child support you failed to pay is a debt that cannot be reduced or discharged in bankruptcy. Although you can ask a judge to change the amount of support you will have to pay in the future (see "Modifying the Amount of Child Support," below), no judge can change the amount of unpaid support you owe. That debt will remain until you pay it off in full, period.

A court may require you to pay the following expenses as a part of, or in addition to, child support:

- health and dental insurance for your children or health and dental costs if neither parent has insurance covering the children (in fact, many states mandate that a parent pay for medical insurance if the costs are reasonable)

- life insurance naming your child's custodial parent as the beneficiary
- child care so that the custodial parent can work or go to school, and
- education costs for your children—sometimes including college.

Modifying the Amount of Child Support

Even before you fall behind on payments, you may realize that you can't afford to pay your court-ordered child support.

If so, you must take the initiative to change your child support order. This requires that you either make an agreement with your former spouse to change the order or go to court, request a modification, and show the judge that you cannot afford the ordered support or that some other significant change in circumstance warrants a reduction. If you don't get the order modified and your child support arrears build up, a court won't retroactively decrease it, even if you were too sick to get out of bed during the affected period. Once child support is owed and unpaid, it (and the interest on it) remains a debt until it is paid.

Legal Reasons That Justify a Support Change

To get a judge to reduce a child support order, you must show a significant change of circumstance since the last order. What constitutes such a change depends on your situation and the particular laws of the state that has jurisdiction over the case. Generally, the condition must not have been considered when the original order was made and must

affect the current standard of living of you, your child, or the custodial parent. Changes that qualify as significant include:

- **Your income has substantially decreased.** The decrease must be involuntary or due to reasons that will ultimately improve your child's situation, like training for a better job. If you quit your job to retire early or become a basket weaver, the court probably won't modify your support obligation. (In those cases, income may be "imputed" or assigned to you, based on your ability to work, your skills, and your earning capacity, even if you aren't actually working.) However, if you quit your job to attend business school, the court may temporarily decrease the amount, expecting you to earn more money and pay more child support after you graduate.
- **The custodial parent's income has substantially increased.** Not all increases in the custodial parent's income will qualify. For example, if your child's needs have increased as the custodial parent's income has risen, you probably won't get a reduction. Or, if the custodial parent's income increase is from a new spouse's earnings, most courts won't factor that in, because the new spouse has no obligation to support your child. However, if the new spouse is contributing significantly to the other parent's household expenses, you may be able to argue for a reduction of your payments on the basis that the other parent now has more income available for support.

Child Support and Visitation

If your child's custodial parent is interfering with your visitation rights, you don't have the right to withhold support. But you can schedule a court hearing where you can present evidence to a judge that shows there has been substantial interference with your visitation right and ask the judge to rectify the situation. This would be an "enforcement hearing" to enforce visitation only. The modification hearings discussed below only deal with modifying a support amount.

You'll need to document a persistent pattern of being denied access to your children. A good way to do this is to take notes on a calendar. Missing a weekend visit or two won't be enough. If you've only been allowed to see the kids once in eight months, however, a court may well hold the custodial parent in contempt of court for violating the court order allowing more frequent visitation. In addition, some judges will order your child's custodial parent to reimburse you for expenses you incur trying to exercise your visitation rights. And a judge may suspend your obligation to pay child support if your child's custodial parent and the child have disappeared altogether, leaving no one to whom you can send the support.

- **Your expenses have increased.** You may be entitled to a reduction, for example, if you have a new child or have developed an expensive, ongoing medical condition.

- **Your child's needs have decreased.** You may be entitled to a reduction if, for instance, your child is no longer attending private school. But as children grow older, their financial needs usually go up rather than down.
- **The children spend more time in your custody than when the court initially ordered the support.** In this situation, you may be entitled to a reduction because the other parent needs less money for the children.

As you can see, the judge won't be inclined to modify your support order unless conditions have changed substantially since the order was issued. If you just feel the court was wrong the first time, you're probably out of luck.

Step 1: Negotiate With Your Child's Other Parent

A child support modification hearing can be time-consuming, costly, and unpleasant if the other parent opposes it. In other words, you want to avoid a contested hearing if at all possible. If you believe a change in support is justified, call your child's other parent and talk about your changed circumstance before you file court papers. If you were laid off or in an accident, the other parent knows the court will probably order some change in the amount and may agree to your proposed amount ahead of time.

If you reach an agreement to reduce the amount of child support you owe, make sure to get your new agreement in writing. Then take it to the court for approval. You may need the help of a lawyer to do this. (See Chapter 18 for advice on finding legal help.) The judge's signature approving your agreement and making it into a court order is essential, because your informal modification (one that you haven't taken before a judge to approve) isn't binding. If your ex has a change of heart, you won't be excused from paying the difference between the court-ordered amount and the reduced amount (though you can always go to court and get a change that applies to future payments).

EXAMPLE: When Mia and Zander divorced, Mia got full custody of the children, and Zander paid child support. After Zander got a larger apartment, the children began to spend every other week with him, so Mia agreed to accept half as much child support but signed no written agreement. Later on, when Zander wanted the children for the whole summer, Mia went back to court to claim unpaid child support. Zander will be on the hook for the entire amount because the court didn't approve their agreement and issue a new child support order.

Step 2: If Negotiations Fail, File Modification Papers

If your child's other parent won't agree to a reduction in child support, you will have to convince a judge to grant your request. In most states, to modify child support, you must fill out and file court papers, schedule a hearing, and present evidence to a judge. You may need the help of a lawyer. (See Chapter 18 for advice about finding one.) The kind of evidence you need to show the court includes:

- information regarding your income, expenses, assets, and debts
- a sworn statement from your most recent employer, if you were recently let go
- previous and current paychecks to show a pay or hours cut
- records of your job search, if you've been looking unsuccessfully, and
- sworn statements from medical professionals if you are sick, injured, depressed, or otherwise unable to work.

Don't delay filing your request for child support modification. Under state and federal law, the effective date of a child support modification order cannot be earlier than the date that your formal request was served on the other parties.

In some states, paying parents can initiate a request to reduce child support at their local child support enforcement agency. Check your state's department of child support services for more information on this.

A special rule applies to members of the military. Parties eligible for a support modification due to military activation or out-of-state deployment may use a special "notice of activation and request" procedure. An order modifying or terminating support based on the servicemember's change in income takes effect on either the date of service of the notice on the opposing party, or the date of the member's activation, whichever is later. If you're in the military and need a support modification, it would be a good idea to talk to an attorney with experience in military divorce.

CAUTION

Remember: Past-due support debts will not go away. A modification of child support cannot change your obligation to pay past-due child support.

Simplified Modification Procedures

Some states try to make it easy for parents requesting an increase or decrease in child support.

The procedure is meant to be user friendly for parents without attorneys. But lawyers are welcome to take advantage of the procedure as well. Court clerks or case managers assist you in filling out the papers. The hearings often take place before a court magistrate or hearing examiner, not a judge. Decisions may be rendered on the spot or within about 30 days.

To find out whether your state has a simplified modification procedure, call the county court clerk, the state child support enforcement agency, or the district attorney's office.

If the judge denies your request and you can't come up with the necessary payments by reducing your living expenses, you'll need to consider your options, including finding ways to increase your income or decrease your expenses. You may need to consider filing for bankruptcy. It won't get you out of your support obligation, but it will let you get rid of some of your other debts—such as those owed to credit card companies and health care providers—and free up money to meet your child support obligation.

When You Can Stop Paying Child Support

You must pay child support for as long as your child support court order says you must. If the order does not contain an ending date, you must support your children as long as your state requires it. Some common state rules for supporting children are:

- until they reach 18
- until they are 19 or finished with high school, whichever occurs first (as long as they are full-time students and living with a parent)
- until they reach 21
- as long as they are dependent, if they are disabled, or
- until they complete college.

To find out exactly what your state law requires, you'll need to do a little legal research or talk to a lawyer. (See Chapter 18.)

RESOURCE

State laws on child support duration. You should be able to find information about when child support terminates in your state at www.divorcenet.com.

In addition, your child support obligation will probably end early if: Your child joins the military, gets married, or moves out of the house to live independently, a court declares your child legally emancipated, or your parental rights are terminated.

Even when you are no longer liable for support or your support obligation is reduced, you still must pay past-due child support. If the custodial parent goes to court and gets a judgment for unpaid support, that judgment can be collected for as long as your state lets a creditor enforce a judgment. This typically covers a period of at least five to 20 years, and the period is usually extended if the judgment is renewed. (Chapter 13 explains how long judgments can last.) In most states, judgments for unpaid child support can easily last your entire life.

If Paternity Is Disputed

If you have a child for whom you're not paying child support and you never married the child's mother or acknowledged paternity (for example, by signing a Declaration of Paternity, having your name put on the birth certificate, or supporting the child), you may find yourself in court on a paternity and child support action—up to 18 years after the child was born. The suit may be filed by the other parent, a child support services agency, or a prosecutor.

Most states make it easy and quick to get a paternity ruling. In many cases, the right to a hearing before a judge has been eliminated, and administrative agencies can hear cases. If you're served with notice of a paternity hearing and you fail to appear, a default paternity order can be entered.

The court may order blood or DNA tests to determine whether there is a biological relationship between you and the child. If the court finds that you are the father, you are likely to be ordered to pay support until the child turns 18. In some states, you may also be required to pay unpaid support, covering up to three years. In other states, you aren't responsible for support until the date that the custodial parent filed the support petition in court.

Enforcement of Child Support Obligations

If you owe a lot of unpaid child support, your child's other parent has a number of choices for how to enforce support. First, the other parent may go to court and ask a judge to issue a judgment for the amount of the arrears. This is called a judgment for child support.

EXAMPLE: Al was ordered to pay his ex-wife Cindy $550 per month in child support. He lost his job and hasn't made the last three payments. He is in arrears a total of $1,650 under the original child support order. Cindy can try to collect the arrears owed under the child support order, or she can go ask a judge to grant her a judgment for the amount Al owes.

Even without a judgment for past-due child support, a person owed child support can use the most effective and most commonly used collection methods.

It's possible that you are having money withheld from your paycheck or are required to send money to a state agency that in turn sends a check to the custodial parent. If that's not the case yet, your ex might try to get that set up now to ensure support is paid in the future.

Both the federal and state governments are now aggressively involved in enforcing child support orders. Parents that are owed payments under a child support order may turn to state child support agencies for help. State and local agencies are required to help parents collect child support, even if the parent who owes money has moved out of state. Extensive database and registry systems track parents who owe child support. Information is shared among states and between the states and the federal government. For example:

- Employers must report all new hires to their state's child support enforcement agency. The agency forwards this information to the National Directory of New Hires, a centralized registry that matches employee names with the names of parents who owe child support. The National Directory sets up income-withholding orders for delinquent parents.
- States must ask for the Social Security numbers of both parents when a child is born and must pass those numbers on to the state agency that enforces child support.
- Judges sometimes order noncustodial parents to pay child support to the state child support enforcement agency, which in turn pays the custodial parent. This method is often used when the noncustodial parent is without regular income (perhaps self-employed) or when parents agree to waive the automatic wage withholding (this is explained below).

CAUTION

You can run but you can't hide. Each state and the federal government maintains locators that search federal, state, and local records to find missing parents. The federal service has access to Social Security, IRS, and all other federal information records except census records. The state locator services will check welfare, unemployment, motor vehicle, and other state records.

Federal Child Support Enforcement

The Department of Health and Human Services (HHS) enforces federal laws having to do with child support through its Office of Child Support Enforcement in the Administration for Children and Families (ACF). For more information about these federal programs and links to state enforcement programs, visit www.acf.hhs.gov/css.

Your Income May Be Automatically Withheld

The federal Family Support Act requires all states to have an automatic income withholding program that seizes part of a parent's wages to pay child support orders that were made or modified on or after January 1, 1994. For pre-1994 child support orders, the court may order income withholding if the custodial parent goes back to court to complain that you are in arrears.

The income withholding is usually automatic unless the parties agree otherwise (for example, the custodial parent agrees not to serve the order on your employer, as long as you pay him or her directly) or unless there is good cause not to require immediate withholding. For example, in some states, if the parent has a reliable history of paying child support, income withholding is not automatic.

The automatic income withholding provisions also apply to orders that combine child support and alimony, but not to orders for alimony only. If income withholding is ordered in one state (for example, where your child lives), but you live in another, the state you live in will enforce the income withholding.

An automatic income withholding order works quite simply. After a court orders you to pay child support, the custodial parent sends a copy of the court order to your employer. Each pay period, your employer withholds a portion of your pay and sends it to the custodial parent or to the state agency that distributes child support.

If you don't receive regular wages but do have a regular source of income, such as income from a pension, a retirement fund, an annuity, unemployment compensation, or other public benefits, the court can order the child support withheld from that income. Instead of forwarding a copy of the order and the custodial parent's name and address to an employer, the court sends the information to the retirement plan administrator or public agency from which you receive your benefits.

If your income is from Social Security or a private pension governed by either ERISA (Employee Retirement Income Security Act) or REA (Retirement Equity Act), the administrator might not honor the court order. This is because Social Security and many private pensions have "antialienation" clauses that prohibit the administrator from turning over the funds to anyone other than the beneficiary (you).

Your Income Tax Refund Could Be Intercepted

If you owe more than $500 in child support and the custodial parent has contacted the state's child support enforcement agency for help, or if you owe $150 and the custodial parent receives welfare, the child support enforcement agency in the state where the custodial parent lives will notify the U.S. Department of the Treasury. The IRS will then take money out of your tax refund to pay the amount due, or at least part of it.

If you are now married to someone other than the custodial parent to whom you owe support, the IRS will take the refund from your joint income tax return. In some states, however, your new spouse won't be liable for your child support debts. If you live in one of those states, your new spouse can request a reimbursement from the IRS by completing Form 8379, *Injured Spouse Claim and Allocation,* and filing it with Form 1040 or 1040A. You can obtain a copy of this form and directions for filling it out at the IRS website at www.irs.gov.

States that impose income taxes also intercept tax refunds to satisfy child support debts.

Liens May Be Placed on Your Real and Personal Property

A custodial parent who is owed child support can place a lien on your property. A lien is a notice that tells the world that there are claims against you for money. Usually the custodial parent files a lien with the same office where the property is registered or recorded. For example, a lien on your house would be filed with the county recorder in the county where your house is located. The lien remains until your child is no longer entitled to support and you've paid all the arrears, or until the custodial parent agrees to remove the lien. With a lien, the custodial parent can force the sale of your property or wait until the property is sold or refinanced and then get the money that's owed. Although some states require that the custodial parent obtain a judgment for the arrears before putting a lien on property, most states allow liens to be imposed on property when you miss court-ordered support payments. To check the lien requirements in your state, go to the Office of Child Support Enforcement website at www.acf.hhs.gov/css.

Your best defense is to schedule a hearing before a judge and claim that the lien impairs your ability to pay your current support. For example, if the lien is on your house and is going to keep you from borrowing money to pay the child support arrears, make that clear to the judge. You'll probably need to bring copies of loan rejection letters stating that your poor credit rating—due to the lien— was the reason for the rejection.

To help locate the assets of parents who owe child support, all states are required to maintain what is known as a "data match

system." Under this system, financial institutions that do business in a state, such as banks, insurance companies, and brokers, must provide that state's child support enforcement agencies with account information on clients who have past-due support obligations. The agency can then use this information to place a lien on and seize assets of people who owe child support.

You May Be Required to Post a Bond or Assets to Guarantee Payment

Some states allow judges to require a parent with child support arrears to post a bond or assets, such as stock certificates, to guarantee payment. In some states, for example, if a self-employed parent misses a child support payment and the custodial parent requests a court hearing, the court can order the noncustodial parent to post assets (such as by putting money into an escrow account).

Most states' child support enforcement agencies have the power to require parents to post bonds or assets. But not all agencies use this measure, and others use it for extreme cases only. In practice, few bond companies will write bonds for child support debts. Most parents will find that they must put property into an escrow account or, in some states, into a trust account that is managed and invested for the child's benefit.

You must be given notice of the action seeking to require you to post assets or a bond and have an opportunity to oppose it. You may have a good defense if posting the assets or bond would impair your ability to pay your current support or to borrow money to pay the arrears.

The Arrears May Be Reported to Credit Bureaus

The law requires credit bureaus to include information about overdue child support in your credit report. Creditors and lenders may deny credit based on this information. In addition, sometimes creditors and lenders report the whereabouts of missing parents to child enforcement agencies.

Child support arrears remain on your credit report for up to seven years, unless you make a deal with the child support enforcement agency. An agency may agree not to report negative information to the credit bureau if you pay some or all of the overdue support. But few child support enforcement agencies will agree to eliminate all negative information. Most will at least report that you were delinquent in the past. (See Chapter 16 for information on how to correct your report if information reported is wrong or obsolete.)

Many states require child support enforcement agencies to notify you before reporting overdue child support information to the credit bureaus. Usually, the enforcement agency must give you a reasonable opportunity to dispute the information. Many states require agencies to report only overdue amounts exceeding $1,000. (For information on how to find your state law, see Chapter 18.)

You May Be Publicly Humiliated

Congress has encouraged states to come up with creative ways to embarrass parents into paying the child support they owe. One method used nationwide by an association of state child support enforcement agencies is the publishing of "most wanted" lists of parents who owe child support.

In some areas, for example, the family court lists the names of parents not paying child support on cable television 300 times a week and in a full-page newspaper advertisement once a month. One county using this technique claims to have located over 50% of the parents owing support. Similarly, the Iowa attorney general reports that 90% of missing fathers who owe child support have been located through the state's "most wanted" poster program.

If your name is included on a most wanted list, the only way to get your name removed is to turn yourself in and begin paying your child support. You'll be ordered to make monthly payments henceforth, your wages will be attached, and the court will take steps to see that you pay your back child support. But that may be better than having this kind of notoriety in your community.

You Might Be Denied a State License or U.S. Passport

In most states, parents with child support arrears will be denied original or renewed driver's or professional licenses (for doctors, lawyers, contractors, and the like) and, if they owe $2,500 or more, may be denied U.S. passports. You are also at risk of having your current driver's license suspended.

You Might Be Held in Contempt of Court and Jailed

Failure to obey a court order is called contempt of court. If you owe unpaid child support, the other parent can ask for a hearing before a judge and ask that you be held in contempt of court. You must be served with a document ordering you to attend the hearing, and then must attend and explain why you haven't paid the support you owe. If you don't attend, the court can issue a warrant for your arrest. Many courts do issue warrants, making county jails a resting stop for parents who don't pay child support and fail to show up in court.

If you attend the hearing, the judge can still throw you in jail for violating the order to pay the support. And the judge might do so, depending on how convincing your story is as to why you haven't paid.

To stay out of jail, go to the hearing prepared to show that you have not deliberately disobeyed the court's order to pay child support. You may have to convince the judge that you're not as irresponsible as it appears. Preparing evidence is a must. Your first step is to show why you didn't pay. If you've been out of work, get a sworn statement from your most recent employer stating why you were let go. If you went job searching but had no luck, provide records of when you interviewed or filled out an application and with whom you spoke. Remember: Disputes with the custodial parent about custody or visitation are never an acceptable excuse for not paying child support.

Next, you must explain why you didn't request a modification hearing when it became evident that you couldn't meet your support obligation. For example, if you've been in bed or otherwise immobilized—depressed, sick, or injured—get sworn statements from

all medical professionals who treated you. Also, get statements from friends or relatives who cared for you. Emphasize your most compelling arguments (for example, you couldn't get out of bed), but never lie.

If you spoke to lawyers about helping you file a modification request but couldn't afford their fees, bring a list of the names of lawyers you spoke to, the date you spoke to each one, and the fee the lawyer quoted you. If you tried to hire a legal aid lawyer to help you but you make too much money to qualify for such assistance (or the office had too many cases, or doesn't handle child support modifications), make sure you bring the name of the lawyer and the date of the conversation.

The judge may put you in jail or may instead order you to make future payments and set up a payment schedule for you to pay any unpaid support. The judge won't reduce the amount of your unpaid support—arrears cannot be modified retroactively—but may decrease your future payments. The judge may also order that your wages be withheld, that a lien be placed on your property, or that you post a bond or other assets.

Judges rarely put a parent in jail for contempt of court. Usually, it happens only if an income-withholding order and a wage garnishment won't work. Courts recognize that a jailed parent cannot earn money to make child support payments.

Your Wages May Be Garnished and Other Assets Seized

Child support arrears that are made into a court judgment can be collected by the various methods described in Chapter 14. Even if the judgment was obtained in one state and you have since moved to another state, the custodial parent can register the judgment in the second state and enforce it there.

The most common method of collecting a judgment for overdue support is wage garnishment. A wage garnishment is similar to income withholding. A portion of your wages is removed from your paycheck and delivered to the custodial parent before you ever see it. In many states, the arrears need not be made into a judgment to be collected through wage garnishment.

To garnish your wages, the custodial parent obtains authorization from the court in a document usually called a writ of execution. Under this authorization, the custodial parent directs the sheriff to seize a portion of your wages. The sheriff in turn notifies you and your employer.

The amount garnished is a percentage of your paycheck. What you were once ordered to pay is irrelevant. The court simply wants to take money out of each of your paychecks—and leave you with a minimum to live on—until the unpaid support is made up.

Under federal law, if a court orders that your wages be garnished to satisfy any debt except child support or alimony, a maximum of roughly 25% of your net wages can be taken. For unpaid child support, however, up to 50% of your net wages can be garnished, and up to 60% if you are not currently supporting another dependent. If your check is already subject to wage withholding for your future payments or garnishment by a different creditor, the total amount taken from your paycheck cannot exceed 50% (or 65% if you are not currently supporting another dependent and are more than 12 weeks in arrears).

Some state laws protect more of your wages than does federal law. Check your state's department of labor website for information on child support wage garnishment amounts in your state. Or look up the law yourself (see Chapter 18, "Help Beyond This Book," to learn how to find state statutes).

To put a wage garnishment order into effect, the court, custodial parent, state agency, or county attorney must notify your employer. Once your employer is told to garnish your wages, your employer tells you of the garnishment. You can request a court hearing, which will take place shortly after the garnishment has begun. At the hearing, you can make only a few objections:

- The amount the court claims you owe is wrong.
- The amount will leave you with too little to live on.
- The custodial parent actively concealed your child, as opposed to merely frustrating or denying your visitation (not all states allow this objection).
- You had custody of the child at the time the support arrears accrued.

If the wage garnishment doesn't cover the amount you owe, or you don't have wages or other income to be garnished, the custodial parent may try to get the unpaid support by going after other items of your property. Examples of the type of property that may be vulnerable include cars, motorcycles, boats, airplanes, houses, corporate stock, horses, rents payable to you, and accounts receivable. In some cases, even spendthrift trusts and your interest in a partnership may be used for payment.

The Arrears Might Be Sent to the State Enforcement Agency

If the custodial parent receives welfare, the state's child support enforcement agency is required to help collect unpaid child support. For a $25 fee, the agency will also help any parent trying to collect child support. If you move out of state while you owe unpaid child support, state laws require that when the custodial parent contacts the local state child support enforcement agency, that agency must contact the agency in the state where you now live. The agency in your state then contacts you and orders you to pay the child support. If you pay that money to the state agency in your state, the agency will send it to the agency in the state where the custodial parent lives.

When the state agency is involved, you'll receive a notice requesting that you attend a conference. The purpose of the conference is to establish your income and expenses, including support for other children, and how much you should pay. The agency is likely to propose that you pay a lot. You should emphasize, truthfully, your other necessary expenses— food, shelter, clothing, other kids, and the like. Bring receipts, bills, and all other evidence of your monthly costs. If you don't show up, the agency may initiate criminal charges against you for failure to appear.

You Might Be Criminally Prosecuted

In many states, it's a misdemeanor to fail to provide support for your child. While criminal prosecution isn't all that likely, the involvement of a county attorney increases the possibility. Also, if you have violated a judge's order enough times, the judge may report you to prosecutors.

In addition, under the federal Child Support Recovery Act of 1992, failure to pay support for a child living in another state is a federal crime. To be prosecuted under this law, the parent must have failed to pay a support obligation for more than one year, or owe more than $5,000, and the failure to pay must be deliberate.

Alimony

Alimony, also called spousal support or maintenance, is money paid by one ex-spouse to the other for support. No federal law requires states to have guidelines for setting the amount of alimony. In some courts, however, there are formal guidelines, and in others, judges have adopted informal written schedules to help them determine the appropriate level of support.

It's very likely that when you got divorced, you signed a settlement agreement that said when alimony would end; usually, it will be when your ex-spouse gets married to someone else or when a specific date arrives. If that's the case, you're stuck with your payments until then. But if there's no provision like that in your divorce papers, you can ask for a modification of the amount of alimony you are required to pay.

To do this, file a motion for modification. You must show a material change in circumstances since the last court order. Depending on your state's law, such changes might include:

- your ex-spouse's living with someone
- your ex-spouse's remarriage
- a decrease in your income (unless it was voluntary—for example, you quit work, took a lower-paying job, or have become a perpetual student)
- a significant increase in your expenses because of your health or the requirement that you care for someone else, like an aging parent, or
- a substantial increase in your ex-spouse's income.

If you have voluntarily decreased your income, the judge may consider your ability to earn, not just your actual earnings.

If child support and alimony are lumped together in one payment, the collection techniques allowed for child support may be used against you. If they are kept separate, however, only the following techniques can be used to collect alimony:

- interception of income tax refunds
- court hearings
- wage garnishments, and
- other judgment collection methods, such as property liens.

As with child support, alimony arrearages can be incorporated into a court judgment and collected while the judgment is in effect.

Bankruptcy and Child Support or Alimony Debt

As discussed, bankruptcy won't cancel arrears or a support judgment. These debts and obligations survive bankruptcy.

How Bankruptcy Affects Marital Debts

Child support and alimony are never discharged (wiped out) in bankruptcy. However, other types of debt created in the course of a divorce or separation may be discharged—in Chapter 13 bankruptcy only, not Chapter 7—as long as they are not "in the nature of support." An example of a debt that can't be discharged would be one spouse's agreement to pay the children's school tuition as part of a divorce settlement agreement. A debt that typically would not be considered in the nature of support would be an agreement by one spouse to pay off the other spouse's credit card debts as part of an overall division of the marital assets and liabilities. (For more on bankruptcy, see Chapter 14.)

The primary advantage of filing for Chapter 7 bankruptcy is that you can get rid of many of your other debts, thus freeing up money to meet your current support obligation and to pay off the arrearage.

If you file a Chapter 13 "repayment plan" bankruptcy, you also can get rid of many of your debts, but you will have to pay off the entire support arrearage over the life of your plan—between three and five years. You will also have to remain current on your support obligation during that period, and if you don't, your Chapter 13 case will be dismissed. (Both kinds of bankruptcies are discussed in Chapter 14.)

Taxes, Child Support, and Alimony

Child support and alimony are treated differently for tax purposes. Child support is a tax-neutral event, meaning it is neither taxable nor deductible—you do not need to report it on either end. However, alimony owed pursuant to a divorce settlement agreement or judgment entered on or before December 31, 2018, is tax deductible to the payor and is considered taxable income to the recipient. For any alimony agreement executed after December 31, 2018, paying spouses will not be able to deduct these payments on their taxes, and supported spouses will not have to report alimony as income. This tax treatment could affect decisions you make about the amount, duration, or payment schedule for alimony, so check with a tax professional if you think the tax consequences might be important to you.

CHAPTER

Lawsuits and Collection of Judgments

f you don't pay your debts, eventually you'll probably be sued unless any of the following are true:

- You aren't available for service. A creditor or collection agency that can't find you might not be able to serve you with a complaint. (See Chapter 9.)
- You're judgment proof. As explained in Chapter 7 (under "Lawsuits"), you don't have any property or income that the creditor can legally take to collect on a judgment, either now or in the foreseeable future.
- You file for bankruptcy. One way to prevent a collection lawsuit is to file for bankruptcy. (See Chapter 14.) Filing for bankruptcy temporarily stops most collection efforts, including lawsuits, dead in their tracks, and you might be able to erase (discharge) many debts in your bankruptcy case.

Being sued can be scary and can cause sleepless nights, but in large part that's because few people actually know what goes on in a lawsuit. Our perceptions, which typically have been shaped by television shows, movies, and famous trials, are usually off the mark.

If you owe someone money and haven't paid, it's usually considered a breach of a contract. This chapter explains how to negotiate the debt and the types of defenses you can raise if you're sued for breaching a contract.

There are other reasons you could be sued, too—for example, you cause a car accident, slander someone, or infringe a copyright. These kinds of suits claim that you have injured someone's person, property, reputation, or intellectual property. This kind of injury is called a "tort." These suits are not based on a contractual obligation to pay someone money or failure to pay a preexisting debt.

If you are sued, don't ignore it. Not responding (called "defaulting") is often a mistake. If you want to do nothing, consider talking to an attorney to make sure it is the best option for you.

How a Lawsuit Begins

A lawsuit starts when the creditor, or a lawyer for a creditor or collection agency, prepares a document called a complaint or petition, claiming that you owe money. The lawyer or creditor files the document with a court clerk and pays a filing fee. The lawyer or creditor then has a copy of the complaint, along with a summons, served on you. The summons is a document issued by the court, notifying you that you are being sued. It usually provides additional information, such as how soon you need to file a written response in court.

The complaint identifies:

- the plaintiff—that's the creditor or collection agency, or possibly another third party the creditor sold the debt to
- the defendant—that's you and anyone else liable for the debt, such as your spouse, a cosigner, or a guarantor
- the date the complaint was filed (this is important if you have a statute of limitations defense, as explained below)
- the court in which you are being sued
- why the creditor is suing you, and
- what the creditor wants from the lawsuit.

Should You Hire a Lawyer or Represent Yourself?

In civil court, a lawsuit can be time-consuming and expensive, although routine debt collection cases rarely are. You are required to follow formal procedural and evidentiary rules. While it can be extremely difficult to represent yourself in civil court, more and more people are doing it.

If you decide to represent yourself in court, you will have to educate yourself and do some legal research. You'll also need patience to learn and follow the rules. For example, if you raise an argument or a defense at the wrong time, or try to make a comment not allowed under the rules, the court may refuse to consider it.

Unless you are being sued for a very small amount, you are almost always better off getting an experienced attorney, especially if he or she will represent you for free or for a low cost. First, check to see if you qualify for legal aid. (See Chapter 18 for information on legal aid.) If you don't qualify, there are several other options for low-cost legal service. You might be able to hire a lawyer and keep your expenses down by doing some of the work yourself. Some lawyers today "unbundle" their services and will assist you with specific tasks (such as preparing an answer) or in portions of the lawsuit for less than if you hired them to defend the entire lawsuit.

If you have a strong claim against the creditor that could generate substantial money for you if you win, or if the creditor might have violated a law that pays a consumer's attorneys' fees if the consumer wins, the lawyer may take your case on a contingent fee basis—which means you don't pay attorneys' fees unless you win. Finally, a lawyer might file a class action lawsuit representing you and many others who have been the victims of the same unlawful conduct relating to your debt (for example, a class action based on a debt collector's violation of the FDCPA).

 RESOURCE

Resources for representing yourself in court. People who decide to handle their own cases—in any state—will find *Represent Yourself in Court: How to Prepare & Try a Winning Case*, by Paul Bergman and Sara Berman (Nolo), indispensable. Many state courts also provide useful self-help information on their websites.

Service of Court Papers

After filing papers with the court, the creditor must serve them on you. In most civil courts, you must be handed the papers personally. If you can't be found, usually the papers can be left with someone over the age of 18 at your home or business, as long as another copy is mailed to you. The creditor cannot serve the papers on you personally, because a party to a lawsuit can't do the actual serving. Most creditors hire professionals called process servers or have a local sheriff or marshal do the job.

Sometimes, a creditor will mail you a copy of the summons and complaint with a form for you to sign and date, acknowledging that you have received the papers. If you sign and date the form you are deemed to have been served according to the rules in your state.

It's often a good idea to sign the form and send it back promptly, because you can save money. If you refuse to sign and the creditor can later prove that you declined the opportunity to do so, you might have to pay whatever costs—frequently between $35 and $150—the creditor incurred in hiring a process server or sheriff to serve the papers on you personally. Plus, you can avoid uncomfortable situations, such as being served at work.

Trying to avoid service is not helpful. Usually, if you avoid service, the creditor can serve you by publishing a notice in some small newspaper, which you may never see. It is better to receive the court papers so you will know how soon you have to respond.

Understanding the Complaint

Skim through the complaint and see if you agree or disagree with the facts. To find out what the creditor or collector wants from you, turn to the final pages. Find the word "WHEREFORE," or a section called "Relief Requested," and start reading. You'll not only learn how much the creditor says you owe, but, most of the time, you'll also find out that the creditor is claiming you must pay interest, court costs incurred, possibly attorneys' fees, and "whatever other relief the court deems appropriate." This last phrase is a catchall added in the event the court comes up with another solution.

> ### Warning—Fraud Allegations
>
> When you receive a complaint, one of the first things you'll want to do is to determine whether the creditor is suing you for fraud. It's important. If the creditor receives a judgment, including a default judgment, you won't be able to wipe out the debt in bankruptcy. In most cases, you'll want to put up a robust defense or file for bankruptcy immediately. Either way, it's imperative that you seek legal counsel as soon as possible.

When Is Your Response Due?

You probably will have between 20 and 30 days to respond in writing (in a document usually called an answer) to the creditor's complaint, but it could be less depending on your state law. The summons will likely tell you how much time you have. You probably will have to pay a filing fee in order to file your answer. If you can't afford the filing fee, you might qualify for a fee waiver. After you file the formal response with the court, you'll have to serve it on the creditor. To learn how to prepare, file, and serve the answer, you'll have to hire an attorney or, if you're comfortable representing yourself, get a good self-help book. (See "Resources for representing yourself in court," above.)

If you don't respond in time, the creditor can ask the court to enter a default judgment against you. Usually the default judgment is granted for the amount the creditor requested plus fees, interest, and perhaps attorneys' fees if legal fees are allowed under your contract or state law.

Being Sued in Small Claims Court

Virtually every state has a small claims court to hear disputes involving modest amounts of money. The range is typically from $5,000 to $10,000. Small claims courts handle matters without long delays or formal rules of evidence and are designed for people to represent themselves without a lawyer.

In most states, you don't need to file a written response to a lawsuit in small claims court. You simply show up on the date of the hearing. If, however, you plan to file your own claim against the creditor you have to do that before the hearing.

Be sure you show up at the hearing. If you don't, you can expect to lose the case automatically because the court will enter a default judgment against you.

If you lose, the judge might let you set up a schedule to pay off the judgment in monthly payments—but don't count on it. Depending on your state's law, you might also have the right to appeal to a higher court.

The rest of this chapter assumes that you are not sued in small claims court, but in your state's civil court of general jurisdiction (often called district court, county court, court of common pleas, or something similar).

If you're sued in small claims court, use *Everybody's Guide to Small Claims Court*, by Cara O'Neill (Nolo), as a guide to representing yourself.

Should You Default?

Many defendants think they have no real defense and no money to hire a lawyer—and in some cases, it's true. If you owe the money, it's likely that there won't be much to fight about. In fact, in most routine debt cases (80% to 95%), the creditor wins by default. Even so, in some of these cases, if the defendant had responded, he or she might not have lost or might have ended up with a judgment in a lesser amount. In fact, the FTC and consumer attorneys warn that debt buyers (companies that buy debts for pennies on the dollar) often get default judgments even when the debt is so old that the creditor doesn't have the right to a judgment (time barred) or they cannot prove that they own the debt.

Before you decide to default, be sure to review the complaint carefully to see if it accurately reflects a debt you owe, if the amount is correct, and how old the debt is. It may be worthwhile to consult with an attorney to determine if you have any defenses. On a final note, always seek legal advice right away if the creditor alleges that you committed fraud. The consequences can be severe, but you'll have a good chance of avoiding them if you file for bankruptcy before the creditor receives a judgment against you. If you don't file for bankruptcy, you'll likely want to either settle the matter or aggressively defend the case.

Negotiate a Deal

Even if you've avoided your creditor or a collection agency up to this point, it's never too late to try to negotiate. If you call and offer to settle the matter, the collector might agree to give you additional time to file your response while you attempt to settle the matter for an amount you can both live with. Keep in mind that unless you get an extension in writing you should file your responsive pleading when it's due, even while you are negotiating. For tips on negotiating, see Chapters 6 and 9.

As you decide whether to settle or fight the lawsuit, keep this in mind: If you lose, you might have to pay the plaintiff's attorneys' fees and court costs, and this can be expensive. If the plaintiff's lawyers conduct discovery or file a summary judgment motion (explained below), or have to make repeated court appearances, you could wind up having to pay more in fees and costs than the amount you owed in the first place. This does not mean you should give up if you have a good defense. You should just be realistic about the strength of your case and the amount of expenses you may face if you lose.

Lump Sum Settlement

You will be in the best position to settle with a creditor or collector (the plaintiff) if you can offer a lump sum of cash to settle the case. How much the plaintiff will accept depends on many factors, including how likely you are to be able to pay more in the near future. The plaintiff, not wanting to

start all over if you miss the payments, is less likely to stop a lawsuit in exchange for a promise to pay in installments. And for good reason. Once the creditor has a money judgment against you, the creditor can force you to pay monthly installments through a wage garnishment, and take money out of your bank account, too.

If the plaintiff agrees to take your lump sum offer, make sure it's accepted as a complete settlement of what you owe. Further, make sure the plaintiff agrees to dismiss—and in fact *does* dismiss—the lawsuit filed against you. Ask that the plaintiff dismiss the lawsuit "with prejudice," which means that the plaintiff cannot sue you again on the same claim. (See "Sample Settlement Agreement or Release," below.) Of course, get all agreements in writing. The plaintiff should give you a copy of the dismissal. If you don't receive one, you can check the case status by visiting the courthouse filing office and looking up your matter using the case number located on the first page of the complaint.

It would be unusual for the plaintiff to fail to file a request for dismissal. If it happens, you will have to take some action yourself. If you can't get the plaintiff (or plaintiff's lawyer) to file the dismissal, prepare one yourself for the plaintiff to sign. Go to your court's self-help center and ask for the forms you should use to request a dismissal. Once your request is completed, make a copy and send the original to whoever sued you.

Sample Settlement Agreement or Release

This Agreement is entered into on the date below between Christopher's Contracting Company, Creditor, and Donna Markell, Debtor.

Creditor has alleged that Debtor owes him $7,745 for construction work he did on Debtor's home;

Creditor has filed Civil Action No. C49903 in the Superior Court for the County of Fairfield, State of California, seeking a money judgment; and

Creditor and Debtor want to settle their differences and end the above-identified litigation.

Creditor and Debtor agree as follows:

1. Within 20 days of the date this Agreement is entered into, Creditor will file in the Superior Court for the County of Fairfield, State of California, a Dismissal With Prejudice in the above-identified litigation.

2. Creditor further agrees not to make any future claim or bring any future action against Debtor or another person for the acts alleged, or which could have been alleged, in Civil Action No. C49903, occurring up to the time of the entry of that Dismissal With Prejudice.

3. Debtor agrees not to make any future claim or bring any future action against Creditor for acts alleged, or which could have been alleged in a cross complaint, in Civil Action No. C49903.

4. Debtor will, at the time of executing this Agreement, pay to Creditor the sum of $5,000 as full settlement of any claim of Creditor against Debtor.

5. Creditor agrees to submit a Universal Data form, or similar document, to each credit reporting agency to which Creditor has submitted information related to this contract advising the credit reporting agency to remove all negative information related to this debt from their files.

6. Creditor and Debtor will bear their own costs, expenses, and attorneys' fees.

7. This Agreement embodies the entire understanding between Creditor and Debtor relating to the subject matter of this Agreement.

Dated: May 30, 20xx

Creditor's signature, address, and phone number:

Stephen Christopher

1782 Main Street, Fairfield, CA

707-555-9993

Debtor's signature, address, and phone number:

Donna Markell

98 South Acorn Ave., Fairfield, CA

707-555-0081

Ask that the form be signed and sent back to you. Once it comes back, file it with the court clerk yourself. You might have to pay a fee to file the document. Be sure to take a few copies with you and have the clerk stamp them to show you filed it. Keep the file-stamped copy in your records.

Settlement Involving Installment Payments

Assuming the plaintiff does agree to settle the case based on your promise to make installment payments, chances are he or she will insist that you agree ("stipulate") to having a court judgment entered against you if you fail to make payments. The stipulated judgment will be for an amount that you and the plaintiff agree on to settle the case. Sign the stipulated judgment if it is acceptable to you, but make sure the collector promises *in writing* not to file it with the court unless you fail to make the installment payments. This way, your credit report won't show that there's a judgment against you. Of course, if you stop making the payments, the plaintiff can file the judgment and collect the amount you haven't paid. Also watch out for other terms the plaintiff wants in the settlement, especially if you have not consulted an attorney. For example, you should not have to admit that you owe the money or that you have no defense. You are just agreeing that to settle the plaintiff's claim, you will pay the agreed amount.

If the Negotiations Hit a Sour Note

If your negotiations are going nowhere, or you're uncomfortable handling them yourself, consider hiring an attorney to negotiate for you. An attorney carries clout that might lead the collector to settle for a good deal less than you owe. But don't hire an attorney unless it's cost-effective. If a lawyer charges $250 to negotiate a $700 debt down to $500, you've actually lost $50. Plus, depending on the amount forgiven, there could be tax consequences, as well. (See Chapter 6 for information about debt settlement taxation.)

Alternative Dispute Resolution

Alternative dispute resolution (ADR) refers to methods used to settle a disagreement short of going to court. If you clearly owe a debt and are looking for some way to avoid court, most creditors won't agree to using ADR. If you really don't think you owe the money or have some other credible defense to the creditor's lawsuit, however, the creditor might agree to resolve the lawsuit through ADR.

ADR can be informal, fast, and inexpensive. Because of the informality of ADR, you generally don't have to follow formal procedural and evidentiary rules. You just tell your story and provide any documents you might have that support your case.

However, some types of ADR are rarely helpful for consumers. And sometimes ADR can be expensive, although it's usually significantly cheaper than traditional litigation.

You'll have to decide whether you want to use binding or nonbinding ADR. If you choose nonbinding arbitration, both sides can still go to court if they don't like the result. Binding arbitration is a good choice if you believe you'll get a fair shake and want the case resolved in an expedient manner.

The following are the main ADR options.

Arbitration. This is the most formal type of ADR. You and the creditor or collector agree to submit your dispute to at least one neutral third person—often a lawyer or retired judge. If a lot of money is at stake, arbitrators usually let the parties use attorneys at arbitration hearings and impose formal rules of evidence. In other disputes, arbitration is less formal and can take place without lawyers. You often have to pay the arbitrator's fees in advance, and they can be high. If you win, however, you might be reimbursed.

If arbitration is voluntary and nonbinding (meaning you can appeal the decision in court if you don't like it), it can be a good thing. However, many creditors and businesses include clauses in contracts that require you to submit to binding arbitration instead of going to court. In these types of arbitration, you can rarely challenge a bad arbitration decision in court, even if the arbitrator decides not to follow the law or makes a mistake of fact. Usually, the creditor will know much more about potential arbitrators than you and suggest ones likely to rule in favor of the creditor. If you have any defense, especially a defense based on the creditor's improper conduct, most consumer advocates believe consumers do better in court than in arbitration. If your contract requires that you go to arbitration, you might be able to get out of arbitration and go to court instead—but to do so is often complicated. You'll have to get help from a lawyer. If you are stuck with arbitration, find out as much as you can about the panel of arbitrators (the group from which your arbitrator will be selected). Look for any that might be sympathetic to consumers rather than creditors and businesses. For example, many arbitrators are also practicing lawyers— find out if they represent mostly creditors or mostly consumers.

Mediation or conciliation. This is the second-most common type of ADR. You and the creditor or collector work with a neutral third party to come up with a solution to your dispute. Mediation is informal, and the mediator does not have the power to impose a decision on you. An excellent resource on mediation is *Mediate, Don't Litigate*, by Peter Lovenheim (available as a downloadable book only at www.nolo.com).

Minitrial. A third option is for you and the creditor or collector to present your positions to a neutral third person who acts as a judge and issues an advisory opinion. You can agree to be bound by that opinion. Your state might have "rent-a-judge" programs to encourage the use of minitrials to settle disputes.

Many states encourage mediation or arbitration and encourage the court to make ADR available. These programs are usually not binding and can provide a quick way to resolve problems without battling it out in court. Keep in mind, however, that you'll likely have to reject the arbitration award within a certain period. If your court has such a requirement, and you fail to reject the award in a timely manner, it will become binding and you'll be stuck with it.

If your state doesn't assign cases to mediation or another form of ADR, you can find someone to resolve your dispute yourself. The Better Business Bureau operates a nationwide system for settling consumer disputes through arbitration and mediation. For information on the program, go to www.bbb.org/bbb-dispute-handling-and-resolution. To find your local BBB, go to www.bbb.org and then fill in your zip code. One advantage to BBB arbitration over more formal arbitration is that it is free to consumers and is geared toward operating without lawyers.

If you would like to use ADR instead of going to court, write to the creditor and emphasize the advantages of ADR. (See "Sample Letter to Creditor Requesting Mediation," below.) *Even if you send a letter requesting ADR, file a response to the complaint.* As explained above, if the deadline passes and you haven't filed a response, the creditor can ask the court to have a default judgment entered against you. Protect yourself by filing your answer even while you're negotiating.

Finally, before agreeing to a mediator or an arbitrator, do a bit of online research and ask for references. Call the references and find out if they were satisfied with the service.

Defenses and Claims

When you respond to the lawsuit, you do two things:

- Deny any facts or conclusions that you disagree with.
- State any other reason why the creditor should not recover all or part of what the complaint asks for. These are called affirmative defenses.

You might also want to raise a separate claim against the creditor, called a counterclaim. Below are some common affirmative defenses and counterclaims that might apply in a debt collection lawsuit.

Statute of Limitations

The creditor has a limited number of years to sue you after you fail to pay your debt. This period is set by state laws called statutes of limitations. The time allowed varies greatly from state to state and for different kinds of debts—written contracts, oral contracts, promissory notes, or open-ended accounts like credit cards.

Written contract. A written contract is a legally binding agreement involving two or more people or businesses (called parties) that sets forth what the parties will or will not do. A contract is formed when competent parties—usually adults of sound mind or business entities—mutually agree to provide each other some benefit (called consideration), such as a promise to pay money in exchange for a promise to deliver specified goods or services.

Sample Letter to Creditor Requesting Mediation

March 15, 20xx
Merrily Andrews, Esq.
Legal Department
Presley Hospital
900 Hollis Boulevard
Carson City, NV 88888

Re: Shawn Smith Account # 7777-SMI
Civil Case # 07-0056

Dear Ms. Andrews:

I have just been served with the Summons and Complaint for the lawsuit filed by Presley Hospital against me for $7,400. I would very much like to resolve this matter and suggest that we mediate the dispute with the help of a mediator from the Nevada Consumer Council. I know that the Consumer Council has helped many people resolve their differences quickly, informally, and inexpensively.

I hope you'll agree to mediate this dispute. If so, please contact me by April 10, 20xx.

Some examples of written contracts are car leases, vehicle purchase agreements, and contracts to buy and sell real estate. (Some states consider a credit card agreement to be a written contract when determining the statute of limitations, but others don't. For example, your state might apply the statute of limitations for oral contracts or for open-ended accounts to credit cards. If you have unpaid credit card debt and are concerned about the statute of limitations, you should speak to an attorney about the specific laws in your state.)

Oral contract. An oral contract is an agreement based on spoken words that is valid and enforceable, provided that it is provable, meets the condition of contract formation, and is not in violation of statutes that prohibit oral agreements (for example, state statutes that require sales of real property and agreements whose performance takes more than one year must be in writing). Say you tell your neighbor that you would like to buy her old television for $200. She agrees and delivers the television to you, but you don't pay. This is an enforceable oral contract. If she sues you for the unpaid amount, a court will order you to pay up (so long as your neighbor proves her case).

Promissory note. A written promise by one party (called maker, obligor, payor, or promisor) to pay a specific amount of money (called principal) to another party (called payee, obligee, or promisee), which often includes a specified amount of interest on the unpaid principal amount and penalties for failure to pay according to its terms. If you borrow $10,000 from your in-laws and sign a document promising to pay them back within a specified amount of time at a certain rate of interest, for instance, three years at 5%, the document is a promissory note. The statute of limitations generally starts on the day the debt was due, or the first payment you missed when you stopped paying on an open-ended account.

If the creditor has waited too long to sue you, you must raise this as a defense in the papers you file in response to the creditor's complaint. Raising a statute of limitations problem is an easy way to get rid of a case. Instead of an answer, you'll likely want to file a special motion asking the court to dismiss the case because the cause of action is stale. You'll learn more in the next section

When the Statute Has Run

Be diligent if you think the creditor has sued you after the statute of limitations has run. It's common for credit card issuers to sell their uncollected debts to debt collectors. Those companies aggressively try to collect, ignoring the fact that the statute of limitations may have expired. If the debt collector sues you (or threatens to sue you) once the statute of limitations has run, the debt collector has probably violated the federal Fair Debt Collection Practices Act (FDCPA), by misrepresenting that you still must pay the debt when it is time barred, or by threatening to take an action (file a lawsuit) it cannot legally take.

The FTC has sued debt collectors for filing cases on time-barred debts and has helpful information on time-barred debts (enter "time-barred debts" in the search box). If you are sued on a debt you think is time barred, ask the plaintiff if the statute of limitations has run on the debt. The plaintiff does not have to answer, but if it does, and doesn't answer truthfully, it violates the FDCPA.

Ordinarily, a statute of limitations does not eliminate the debt—it merely limits the judicial remedies available to the creditor or collection agency after a certain period of time. A debt collector can still seek voluntary payment of an old debt, but the law cannot force you to pay it.

This means you very well might receive collection letters or phone calls about a debt even if the statute of limitations has expired. (See Chapter 9 for more information about debt collection rights.)

In response to your claim that the statute of limitations prevents the creditor or collector from going forward with the lawsuit, the plaintiff might claim that you waived, extended, or revived the statute of limitations in your earlier dealings.

Waiving the Statute of Limitations

If you waive the statute of limitations on a debt, it means you give up your right to assert it as a defense later on. The law makes it very difficult for a consumer to waive the statute of limitations by accident. A court will uphold a waiver only if you understood what you were doing when you agreed to waive the statute of limitations for your debt. In certain circumstances, even then, a waiver may be unenforceable. If you think you may have waived the statute of limitations, you should still raise it as a defense (and force the creditor to demonstrate that you waived it).

Extending or Reviving the Statute of Limitations

Extending and reviving the statute of limitations are two different things. Extending the statute is often called "tolling." Tolling or extending the statute temporarily stops the clock for a particular reason, such as the collector's agreeing to extend your time to pay.

EXAMPLE: Emily owes the Farmer's Market $345. The statute of limitations for this type of debt in her state is six years. Normally the statute would begin to run when Emily stopped paying the debt, but Farmer's gave her an additional six months to pay (and therefore tolled or extended the statute of limitations for six months). After six months, Emily still cannot pay the debt. The six-year statute of limitations begins to run at this point.

Reviving a statute of limitations means that the entire period begins again. Depending on your state, this can happen if you make a partial payment on a debt or otherwise acknowledge that you owe a debt that you haven't been paying. In some states, partial payment will only toll the statute rather than revive it.

EXAMPLE: Ethan owes Memorial Hospital $1,000. The statute of limitations for medical debts in his state is four years. He stopped making payments on the debt, and the four-year statute began to run. Three years later, Ethan made a $300 payment and then stopped making payments again. In Ethan's state, his partial payment of $300 revived the statute of limitations. The hospital now has four years from the date of the $300 payment to sue Ethan for the remainder of the debt.

A new promise to pay a debt may also revive the statute of limitations in some circumstances. In most states, an oral promise can revive a statute of limitations, although in a few states the promise must be in writing.

Other Defenses

Listed below are some other examples of affirmative defenses you might be able to state in your answer:

- You never received the goods or services the creditor claims to have provided.
- The goods or services were defective.
- The creditor damaged your property when delivering the goods or services.
- The creditor threatened you or lied to you to get you to enter into the agreement.
- You legally canceled the contract and therefore owe nothing.
- You cosigned for the loan and were not told of your rights as a cosigner. (See Chapter 10.)
- The creditor was not permitted to accelerate the loan. (See Chapter 10.)
- The contract was too ambiguous to be enforced.
- The contract is illegal.
- The contract or the creditor has violated a consumer protection statute that makes the contract unenforceable.
- After repossessing your property, the creditor did not sell it in a "commercially reasonable manner." (See Chapter 7.)
- The case was filed in the wrong court (wrong jurisdiction or venue).

Counterclaims

A counterclaim is the basis of a lawsuit you have against a creditor or collector. It might be based on different issues from those in the complaint. You might even be asking for more money than the plaintiff wants from you. In many states, however, the counterclaim must arise out of the same transaction for which you are being sued.

To raise a counterclaim, you will usually have to serve and file your own complaint and pay a filing fee within the time you have to respond to the complaint. If you succeed on a counterclaim, you might be entitled to money damages from the creditor or collector, or at least to rescind (cancel) the contract with the creditor. Here are examples of some counterclaims you might want to make against a creditor or collector:

- The creditor breached a warranty.
- The creditor violated the Fair Credit Reporting Act (see Chapter 16), Truth in Lending Act (see Chapter 10), or Equal Credit Opportunity Act (see Chapter 18).
- A collection agency violated the federal or a state debt collection law. (See Chapter 9.)

Is the Account Open- or Closed-End Credit?

The statutes of limitations for open-end and closed-end credit are often different. Unfortunately, determining whether an account is open-end or closed-end is not always easy. Generally, if you can use the account repeatedly, it is open-end credit (also called "revolving credit"). Your payments vary, depending on how much credit you have used in a certain period of time. The most common example of open-end credit is a credit card. Closed-end credit usually involves a single transaction, such as the purchase of a house or car, and the payments are fixed in amount and number.

Many creditors try to characterize a closed-end account as open-end, either to take advantage of a longer statute of limitations or to avoid providing the more extensive disclosures required for closed-end credit.

To complicate matters even more, the statute of limitations for an open-end account is not always clear. Some states specify limits for credit card accounts only. In others, if you have a written contract with the credit card company, the statute of limitations for written contracts applies to credit card accounts. In still other states, the statute of limitations for oral contracts governs open-end accounts. In order to find the statute of limitations for an open-end account in your state, you'll have to do some legal research or check with a local attorney. (See Chapter 18 for help finding an attorney or for tips on doing legal research.)

EXAMPLE: Bart lives in Delaware, where the statute of limitations on open-end accounts is three years. Bart had a large balance on his Visa card, made a small payment in July 2016, and then paid no more. His August Big Bank Visa statement included a payment due date of August 15, 2016. Bart was sued in September 2019, three years and a few days after he first missed the payment. Bart has a statute of limitations defense. Bart must raise this defense in the papers he files opposing Big Bank's lawsuit. If Bart doesn't, he loses the defense.

Statutes of Limitations*

State	Written Contracts	Oral Contracts	Promissory Notes
Alabama	6 years	6 years	6 years
Alaska	3 years [1]	3 years	3 years [1]
Arizona	6 years [2]	3 years	6 years
Arkansas	5 years	3 years	5 years
California	4 years	2 years	4 years
Colorado	6 years [3]	6 years [3]	6 years
Connecticut	6 years	3 years	6 years
Delaware	3 years [4]	3 years	6 years
District of Columbia	3 years	3 years	3 years
Florida	5 years [5]	4 years	5 years
Georgia	6 years	4 years	6 years
Hawaii	6 years	6 years	6 years
Idaho	5 years	4 years	5 years
Illinois	10 years	5 years	10 years
Indiana	10 years [6]	6 years	6 years
Iowa	10 years	5 years	10 years
Kansas	5 years	3 years	5 years
Kentucky	10 years [7]	5 years	15 years [8]
Louisiana	10 years	10 years	5 years
Maine	6 years [9]	6 years	6 years [9]
Maryland	3 years [10]	3 years	12 years [11]
Massachusetts [12]	6 years	6 years	6 years [13]

[1] Ten years for sealed instruments
[2] Includes credit card debt
[3] Three years if the contract is not related to a debt
[4] Contract may provide for up to 20 years for a transaction involving $100,000 or more
[5] One year in certain situations, see Fla. Stat. Ann. § 95.11
[6] For all cases other than payment of money, which is six years
[7] 15 years for contracts entered into on or before July 15, 2014
[8] Except when the note is attached to a bill of sale, in which case five years
[9] The statute of limitations on a debt owed to a bank, or on a promissory note signed before a witness is 20 years.
[10] 12 years if the contract is under seal
[11] Three years if the note is not under seal
[12] The statute of limitations on a debt owed to a bank, or on a promissory note signed before a witness is 20 years.
[13] 20 years if witnessed and claim brought by original payee
* This chart does not include the statute of limitations for foreclosures or deficiency judgments after foreclosure. The statute of limitations that applies to home foreclosures may be the one for written contracts, but some states have a specific statute of limitations for foreclosure. A state may also have a specific statute of limitations for a deficiency judgment after foreclosure or state law may prohibit a deficiency judgment. (A "deficiency" is the difference between the foreclosure sale price and what you owe the foreclosing lender.) To find the statute of limitations for foreclosure or a deficiency judgment where you live, check your state statutes (which are often available online at your state legislature's website) or talk to a local attorney.

Statutes of Limitations (continued)

State	Written Contracts	Oral Contracts	Promissory Notes
Michigan	6 years	6 years	6 years
Minnesota	6 years	6 years	6 years
Mississippi	6 years	3 years	6 years [14]
Missouri	10 years[15]	5 years	10 years
Montana	8 years	5 years	8 years
Nebraska	5 years	4 years	5 years
Nevada	6 years	4 years	6 years
New Hampshire	3 years	3 years	3 years
New Jersey	6 years	6 years	6 years
New Mexico	6 years	4 years	6 years
New York	6 years	6 years	6 years
North Carolina	3 years[16]	3 years	3 years
North Dakota	6 years	6 years	6 years
Ohio	8 years[17]	6 years	8 years[18]
Oklahoma	5 years	3 years	5 years
Oregon	6 years	6 years	6 years
Pennsylvania	4 years	4 years	4 years
Rhode Island	10 years	10 years	10 years
South Carolina	3 years	3 years	3 years
South Dakota	6 years	6 years	6 years
Tennessee	6 years	6 years	6 years
Texas	4 years	4 years	4 years
Utah	6 years	4 years	6 years
Vermont	6 years	6 years	6 years[19]
Virginia	5 years	3 years	6 years
Washington	6 years	3 years	6 years
West Virginia	10 years	5 years	10 years
Wisconsin	6 years	6 years	6 years
Wyoming	10 years	8 years	10 years

[14] Six years from date of demand for payment; if no demand, ten years from last payment made

[15] If contract is for something other than payment of money or property, then the statute of limitations is five years.

[16] One year in certain circumstances, see N.C. Gen. Stat. Ann. §§ 1-52, 1-54

[17] Eight years generally; statute is four years for contracts of sale (for claims accruing on or after 9/28/2012. If you have a claim that accrued between 9/28/2005 and 9/28/2012, you have until the statute of limitations period in effect at the time expires, or until 9/28/2020, whichever is sooner, to bring an action.)

[18] For claims accruing on or after 9/28/2012. If you have a claim that accrued between 9/28/2005 and 9/28/2012, you have until 9/28/2020 to bring an action.

[19] Statute of limitations on a promissory note signed before a witness is 14 years.

What to Expect While the Case Is in Court

After you file your answer, you must serve it on the creditor. From that point on, you should get written notification of further proceedings in your case. Depending on the type of case and how litigious the creditor's attorney is, a whole lot can go on between the time you file your answer and the date of the trial. Below is a brief description of the most common proceedings in a civil lawsuit. If you intend to represent yourself, you should get detailed information about litigation procedures. See "Resources for representing yourself in court," above.

Discovery

Discovery refers to the formal procedures used by parties to obtain information and documents from each other and from witnesses. The information is meant to help the party prepare for trial or settle the case. In routine debt collection cases where you don't have any defense, don't expect the plaintiff to engage in discovery.

If you raise a strong affirmative defense or file your own counterclaim, however, the plaintiff might want to do some discovery. And you might want to do some discovery yourself, especially if you are sued by a debt collector. For example, you could request that the debt collector produce documents demonstrating that you owe the debt, such as a copy of the contract, or that the collector owns the debt, such as the agreement by which the debt collector claims it bought your debt.

The most common types of discovery include:

- **Depositions.** You, the plaintiff, or another witness answers questions under oath.
- **Interrogatories.** You and the plaintiff answer written questions.
- **Demands for inspection or production of documents.** You or the plaintiff require the other one to provide documents.
- **Demands for a property inspection.** In some cases, you or the plaintiff can arrange a time to view land or other property that wouldn't otherwise be accessible, often accompanied by an expert.
- **Requests for admission.** You or the plaintiff ask the other to provide written responses admitting or denying certain facts or conclusions.

Summary Judgment

If either side believes the case has no merit, that party might file a summary judgment motion. It's a complicated motion because in essence, the filing party must lay out the facts, evidence, and law. It's akin to a trial on paper. Here's how it works.

Suppose the creditor wants to avoid a trial by filing a summary judgment motion. The creditor must first convince the judge that none of the facts of the case are in dispute. For example, the creditor would need to provide evidence establishing that you signed a legal loan agreement, made no payments, and have no defense as to why you're not paying. But that's just the first half. The creditor also must convince the judge that the law says that the plaintiff is entitled to judgment when that set of undisputed facts exists. If the judge agrees with the creditor, the judge can enter a judgment against you without any trial taking place.

If you don't file a formal opposition to the summary judgement motion, you'll probably lose. To defeat the summary judgment motion, you'll need to prove to the judge that there is a disagreement on an important fact, for instance, that you had a valid reason for not paying the debt. You can also demonstrate that the creditor applied the wrong law, and that you're not culpable under the proper legal standard. In either case, you'll have to follow rigorous procedural requirements and will likely need the assistance of an attorney. Considering that a lawyer could easily bill 40 hours of time to prepare or defend a summary judgment motion, it might make more sense to pay the debt.

Settlement Conference

Several states and the federal court system require that the parties come together at least once before the trial to try to settle the case. To assist you in settling, you'll be scheduled to meet with a judge or an attorney who has some familiarity with the area of law your case involves. You don't have to settle, but the judge or attorney will usually give you an honest indication of your chance of winning in a trial.

Trial

The vast majority of cases do not go to trial. They settle or end in summary judgment or a similar proceeding. However, if the case doesn't resolve, you will eventually find yourself at a trial. In a trial, a judge makes all the legal decisions, such as whether or not a particular item of evidence can be used, and the law that governs the case. Either a judge or a jury will examine the evidence, decide whether it's credible, and apply the law to the facts.

At the trial, you will be required to present your case according to very specific rules of procedure and evidence. As mentioned before, the book that can help you in any trial is *Represent Yourself in Court*, by Paul Bergman and Sara Berman (Nolo). It's best to consult with a lawyer before the trial to get some help.

When the Creditor Gets a Judgment Against You

The creditor might get a judgment against you in any of the following situations:

- You don't respond to the complaint.
- You don't comply with a judge's order to respond to a discovery request.
- You lose a summary judgment motion.
- You lose a trial.

The judgment is a piece of paper issued by the court stating that the plaintiff wins the lawsuit and is entitled to a certain amount of money. The judgment must be "entered"— that is, filed with the court clerk—shortly after the judge issues it. After it is filed, the court or the creditor's attorney sends you a copy.

Components of a Money Judgment

When you get a copy of the judgment, your first step is to determine how much you owe to whom and for what reason. Keep in mind that the judge might have knocked off some money in response to a defense or counterclaim you raised.

A judgment usually consists of the following components.

The debt itself. This is the amount of money you borrowed from the creditor, charged on a credit card, or owe on a repossession deficiency balance.

Interest. Part of the judgment will be the interest the creditor is entitled to collect under the loan agreement or contract. If you defaulted on a $1,000 loan at 9% annual interest and the creditor obtains a judgment a year later, the court will award the creditor $90 in "prejudgment" interest ($1,000 x .09 = $90).

Interest can be added after judgment from the time the judgment is entered into the court clerk's record until you pay the judgment in full. Usually the postjudgment interest rate is set by your state's law, generally in the 8% to 12% range.

Court costs. Almost every state awards the winner of a lawsuit the costs incurred in bringing the case, such as filing fees and service costs.

Attorneys' fees. If your original contract with the creditor includes the creditor's right to collect attorneys' fees in the event the creditor sues you and wins, these fees will be added to the judgment. They can add up to thousands of dollars. Even without an attorneys' fees provision in a contract, the creditor may be entitled to attorneys' fees if a state law allows it.

How Long Judgments Last

Depending on the state, a creditor may have from five to as many as 20 years to collect a court judgment. Also, in most states, the judgment can be renewed for a longer time, and in some states, indefinitely, if it is not collected during the original period, so the creditor may have an unlimited amount of time to collect a judgment.

How Creditors Collect Judgments

Once a judgment is entered against you, the creditor is now called a judgment creditor, and you are called a judgment debtor. Judgment creditors have many more collection techniques available to them than do creditors trying to collect debts before getting a court judgment. For example, in some states, a judgment creditor can order you to come to court and answer questions about your property and finances. Also, a judgment creditor can direct a sheriff to seize some of your property to pay the judgment.

What property the creditor can take varies from state to state. Usually, the creditor can go after a portion of your net wages (up to 25%, more if the judgment is for child support), bank and other deposit accounts, and valuable personal property, such as cars and antiques.

Not all of your property can be taken, however. Every state has certain property it declares "exempt." This means it is off limits to your creditors, even judgment creditors. Just because you owe money, you shouldn't have to lose everything. You still need to eat, keep a roof over your head, clothe yourself, and provide for your family. If you have very few possessions, you may find that most of what you own is exempt. Exempt property is covered in Chapter 15.

Debtor's Examination

Most states let a judgment creditor question you about your property and finance, in a procedure called a "debtor's examination." You'll be required to come to the courthouse and give the judgment creditor the opportunity to review financial documents and ask questions about your assets under oath. The examination usually takes place in the hallway outside of a courtroom. If there's a dispute about the propriety of a question, the judge will make a ruling on the spot. The judgment creditor is looking for money or property that can be legally taken to pay the debt. High on the list of property the creditor looks for are deposit accounts (such as savings, checking, certificate of deposit, and money market accounts), tax refunds, and other easy cash. The creditor will also want to know about business holdings, investments, and valuable property.

Written Questions

In some states, a judgment creditor will send a form for you to fill out and return. You'll include you employer's name and address, your assets, and other financial information. You must do this under penalty of perjury. If you don't comply or the judgment creditor believes you're not disclosing information, the judgment creditor can ask the court to issue an order requiring you to come to court and answer the questions.

Penalties for Noncompliance

If you receive an order to appear in court and you don't show up, the court can declare you in contempt and issue a warrant for your arrest.

In a few states, if the judge issues an order for you to come to court, serving that order on you creates a lien on your personal property. The lien may make it difficult for you to sell the property without first paying the judgment. Also, in some states, if the judgment creditor believes you are about to leave the state or conceal your property to avoid paying the judgment, the creditor can ask the judge to issue a prejudgment order freezing your assets. This is quite drastic, but it's been known to happen when a lot of money is owed.

If you receive an order to appear but can't take the time off from work or otherwise can't make it, call the judgment creditor or the lawyer and explain your situation. Explain that you're willing to answer questions at another time. If the creditor thinks you're telling the truth, the creditor might send you a form about your finances and property, or agree to move the appearance date.

If the judgment creditor agrees to any change, ask for a letter to you and the court verifying that you don't need to appear at the hearing. If the creditor won't write the letter, then you'll want to appear as scheduled or file a motion with the court asking for a rescheduling of the appearance.

If you can attend the hearing, or you reschedule it to a convenient time, do not take any money or expensive personal items with you. The judgment creditor can ask you to empty your pockets or purse and ask the court to order you to turn over any nonexempt money or valuable personal property in your possession, such as a college ring or leather jacket.

Can You Be Fired for a Wage Attachment?

Your employer might consider a wage attachment a hassle and threaten to fire you if you don't settle the debt right away. Under the law, however, an employer cannot fire you because your wages are attached to satisfy a single debt. (15 U.S.C. § 1674(a).) But, if two judgment creditors attach your wages or one judgment creditor attaches your wages to pay two different judgments, this law does not protect you from being fired. Some states protect you until you have three or more attachments; find out how to research your state's law in Chapter 18.

Most employers will work with employees who are honestly trying to clear up their debt problems. If your wages are attached, talk with your employer and explain that you are working hard to settle the matter as soon as possible. If, however, you are fired because your employer was not aware of the law or because your employer was "suddenly" unhappy with your work, consider filing a complaint. (See Chapter 18 for tips on finding a lawyer.)

Wage Garnishment

The first asset most judgment creditors will go after is your paycheck, through a wage attachment (or wage garnishment). Your employer takes a portion of your wages each pay period and sends it to your creditor before you ever see it.

Federal law allows the judgment creditor to take up to 25% of your net earnings or the amount by which your weekly disposable earnings exceed 30 times the federal minimum wage (currently $7.25 an hour times 30, equals $217.50), whichever is less. Disposable earnings are your gross earnings less all legally mandated deductions, such as withheld income taxes, Social Security, and unemployment insurance.

Some states offer greater protections for judgment debtors about to lose their wages. To find out the limits in your state, see "State Limits on Wage Garnishments by Judgment Creditors," below.

CAUTION

For certain debts, you have to pay more. The wage attachment laws and limitations described in this section do not apply to:

- **Child support.** Up to 50% of your wages may be taken to pay support (more can be taken if you don't currently support another dependent or are behind in your payments). Your child's other parent usually does not have to first sue you.
- **Income taxes.** If you ignore all attempts by the IRS to collect taxes you owe, the government can grab a large amount of your wages. The weekly garnishment amount (called a levy) is based on the standard income tax deduction and your personal exemption, divided by 52 weeks. If you don't verify the calculations, you could stand to lose more than necessary.

State Limits on Wage Garnishments by Judgment Creditors

State	State Limits Equivalent to Federal Limits?	Wages Judgment Creditors Can Garnish Under State Law
Alabama	Yes	
Alaska		Residents: Federal limits apply, but not more than $473 per week ($743 if you are the sole wage earner in your household and submit an affidavit to that effect). Alaska Stat. Ann. §§ 9.38.030, 9.38.050; Alaska Admin. Code tit. 8, § 95.030(d)(e). Nonresidents: Federal limits apply.
Arizona	Yes	
Arkansas		Laborers and mechanics: 60 days of wages are exempt; then, no more than $25 per week (or federal limits, whichever is less). Ark. Code Ann. §16-66-208. All others: Federal limits apply.
California		The lesser of: (1) 25% of your disposable earnings, or (2) the amount by which your weekly disposable earnings exceed 40 times the federal or state hourly minimum wage. Cal. Civ. Proc. § 706.050
Colorado	Yes	
Connecticut		The lesser of (1) 25% of your disposable earnings, or (2) the amount by which your weekly disposable earnings exceed 40 times the federal or state hourly minimum wage, whichever is greater. Conn. Gen. Stat. Ann. § 52-361a
Delaware		The lesser of (1) 15% of your disposable earnings, or (2) your disposable earnings less 30 times the federal minimum wage. Del. Code. Ann. tit. 10 § 4913
District of Columbia	Yes	
Florida		Head of family with weekly disposable earnings less than $750: All wages are exempt. Head of family with weekly disposable earnings more than $750: only if agreed to in writing, and then federal limits apply. Not head of family: Federal limits apply. Fla. Stat. Ann. § 222.11
Georgia		The lesser of (1) 25% of your disposable earnings, or (2) the amount of your weekly disposable earnings that exceed $217.
Hawaii		Employer must use calculation (federal or state law) that is most favorable to employee. Under state law, creditors can garnish: (1) 5% of your first $100 of disposable earnings per month, (2) 10% of your second $100 of disposable earnings per month, and (3) 20% of your disposable earnings exceeding $200 per month (or an equivalent portion of this amount per week). Haw. Rev. Stat. § 652-1, Hawaii District Court Rules of Civil Procedure, Form DC27
Idaho	Yes	

State	State Limits Equivalent to Federal Limits?	Wages Judgment Creditors Can Garnish Under State Law
		State Limits on Wage Garnishments by Judgment Creditors (continued)
Illinois		The lesser of (1) 15% of your gross wages, or (2) the amount of disposable income that remains after deducting the state minimum wage (or federal minimum wage if it's greater) multiplied by 45. 735 Ill. Comp. Stat. 5/12-803
Indiana		Federal limits apply, but if individual shows good cause the garnishment amount may be reduced to less than 25% of disposable earnings, as long as the amount is at least 10%. Ind. Code Ann. § 24-4.5-5-105.
Iowa		Federal limits apply, but also has annual limits: If your income is: -below $12,000 per year: up to $250 may be garnished -between $12,000 and $15,999 per year: up to $400 may be garnished -between $16,000 and $23,999 per year: up to $800 may be garnished -between $24,000 and $34,999 per year: up to $1,500 may be garnished -between $35,000 and $49,999 per year: up to $2,000 may be garnished, or -$50,000 or more per year: no more than 10% of your wages may be garnished. Iowa Code § 642.21
Kansas	Yes	
Kentucky	Yes	
Louisiana	Yes	
Maine		The lesser of (1) 25% of your weekly disposable earnings, or (2) the amount by which your weekly disposable earnings exceed 40 times the federal hourly minimum wage. Me. Rev. Stat. Ann. tit. 14 § 3126-A
Maryland		In Kent, Caroline, Queen Anne's, and Worcester Counties: The lesser of 25% or 30 times federal minimum hourly wage. In other counties: The lesser of (1) 25% of disposable earnings, or (2) the amount by which your weekly disposable earnings exceed $145 per week, or (3) the amount by which your weekly disposable earnings exceed 30 times the federal hourly minimum wage. (Note: These amounts could change to reflect the decision in *Marshall v. Safeway*, 437 Md. 542 (2014).) In all counties: Any medical insurance payment deducted from a payment is exempt. Md. Code Ann., Com. Law § 15-601.1
Massachusetts		The lesser of (1) 15% of gross wages or (2) the amount that exceeds 50 times the greater of the federal or state hourly minimum wage per week. Mass. Gen. Laws Ann. 235 § 34
Michigan		Mostly equivalent to federal law, with minor exceptions (see Mich. Comp. Laws Ann. §§ 408.476, 600.4031)

State Limits on Wage Garnishments by Judgment Creditors (continued)

State	State Limits Equivalent to Federal Limits?	Wages Judgment Creditors Can Garnish Under State Law
Minnesota		The lesser of (1) 25% of your disposable earnings, or (2) the amount by which your weekly disposable earnings exceed 40 times the federal hourly minimum wage. Minn. Stat. Ann. §571.922
Mississippi		Federal limits apply, but creditors cannot garnish wages for the first 30 days after the garnishment order is served. Miss. Code Ann. § 85-3-4
Missouri		Federal limits apply, unless you are the head of a family, in which case the limit is the lesser of (1) 10% of your disposable earnings, or (2) the amount by which your weekly disposable earnings exceed 30 times the federal hourly minimum wage. Mo. Ann. Stat. 525.030
Montana	Yes	
Nebraska		Federal limits apply, unless you are the head of a family, in which case the limit is the lesser of (1) 15% of your disposable earnings, or (2) the amount by which your weekly disposable earnings exceed 30 times the federal hourly minimum wage. Neb. Rev. Stat. § 25-1558
Nevada		The lesser of (1) 25% of your disposable earnings, or (2) the amount by which your weekly disposable earnings exceed 50 times the federal hourly minimum wage. Nev. Rev. Stat. 21.090
New Hampshire		Federal limits apply. However, judgment creditors may only garnish earned but unpaid wages. So creditor must keep renewing wage garnishment in order to attach more than one paycheck. N.H. Rev. Stat. Ann. 512:21
New Jersey		Federal limits apply, unless you earn no more than 250% of the federal poverty level for a household of your size, in which case the limit is 10% of your income. The 10% limit doesn't apply if the creditor is the state. N.J. Stat. Ann. 2A:17-56
New Mexico		The lesser of (1) 25% of your disposable earnings, or (2) the amount by which your weekly disposable earnings exceed 40 times the federal hourly minimum wage. N.M. Stat. Ann. § 35-12-7
New York		The lesser of 10% of your gross wages or 25% of your disposable income to the extent that this amount exceeds 30% of minimum wage. If your disposable income is less than 30 times the federal minimum wage, it cannot be garnished at all. N.Y.C.L.P.R. § 5231
North Carolina		No wage garnishment except for taxes, student loan debt, child support, alimony, overpayment of unemployment benefits, and charges for ambulance services in some North Carolina counties. If garnishment is allowed, federal limits apply.

State	State Limits Equivalent to Federal Limits?	Wages Judgment Creditors Can Garnish Under State Law
\multicolumn{3}{c}{**State Limits on Wage Garnishments by Judgment Creditors (continued)**}		
North Dakota		The lesser of (1) 25% of your disposable earnings, or (2) the amount by which your weekly disposable earnings exceed 40 times the federal hourly minimum wage. Additionally, the maximum amount that can be garnished will be reduced by $20 for each dependent that lives with you. N.D. Cent. Code 32-09.1-03
Ohio	Yes	
Oklahoma	Yes	
Oregon		The lesser of (1) 25% of your disposable earnings, or (2) the amount by which your disposable earnings exceed $218 per week, $435 per two-week period, $468 per half-month period, and $936 per month. Or. Rev. Stat. § 18.385
Pennsylvania		No garnishments except for child or spousal support, obligations relating to a final divorce distribution, back rent on a residential lease, certain types of taxes, student loans, and court-ordered restitution in criminal matters. Garnishments to satisfy judgments for back rent on a residential lease are subject to federal limits, but cannot be more than 10% of net wages provided the garnishment does not cause your salary to fall below the poverty guidelines as set out by the federal government. Pa. Consol. Stat. tit. 42 § 8127
Rhode Island		Federal limits apply, but Rhode Island garnishment law also allows you to protect all of your wages or salary for a period of one year after you have been receiving assistance from any state, federal, or municipal corporation or agency, such as public assistance or welfare benefits. Rhode Island law also prohibits the wages of a sailor from being garnished. R.I. Gen. Laws § 9-26-4
South Carolina		No garnishments for consumer debts. S.C. Code Ann. § 37-5-104.
South Dakota		The lesser of (1) 20% of your disposable earnings, or (2) the amount by which your weekly disposable earnings exceed 40 times the federal hourly minimum wage, less $25 per week for each dependent family member who resides with you. S.D. Codified Laws § 21-18-51
Tennessee		Federal limits apply, but state law also allows you to protect an additional $2.50 per week for each dependent child you support that also lives in Tennessee. Tenn. Code Ann. § 26-2-106, Tenn. Code Ann. § 26-2-10.

State Limits on Wage Garnishments by Judgment Creditors (continued)

State	State Limits Equivalent to Federal Limits?	Wages Judgment Creditors Can Garnish Under State Law
Texas		Judgment creditors cannot garnish wages except for child or spousal support debts. Tex. Civ. Prac. & Rem. Code Ann. § 63.004; V.T.C.A., Civil Practice & Remedies Code § 63.006; Tex. Const. Art. 16 §28
Utah		Mostly equivalent to federal law, with minor exceptions (see Utah Code Ann. § 70C-7-103)
Vermont		(1) 25% of the your weekly disposable earnings, or your weekly disposable earnings less 30 times the federal minimum hourly wage, whichever is less, (2) 15% of your weekly disposable earnings, or your weekly disposable earnings less 40 times the federal minimum wage, whichever is less, if the debt arose from a consumer credit transaction (such as a credit card), (3) 0% of your wages if you received assistance from the Vermont Department for Children and Families or the Department of Vermont Health Access in the last two months. Vt. Stat. Ann. tit. 12 § 3170
Virginia		The lesser of (1) 25% of your disposable earnings, or (2) the amount by which your disposable earnings exceed 40 times the federal minimum hourly wage. Va. Code Ann. tit. § 34-29
Washington		The lesser of (1) 25% of your weekly disposable earnings, or (2) your weekly disposable earnings less 35 times the federal minimum hourly wage. Wash. Rev. Code Ann. 6.27.150
West Virginia		The lesser of (1) 20% of your disposable earnings for that week, or (2) the amount by which your disposable earnings for the week exceed 50 times the federal minimum hourly wage. W. Va. Code, § 38-5A-3, W. Va. Code, § 46A-2-130
Wisconsin		No garnishment if (1) you receive, or have received in the past six months, public assistance, or (2) your income is below the federal poverty line, or (3) 25% of your disposable wages are being garnished for support. Otherwise, garnishment is limited to the lesser of (1) 20% of your weekly disposable income , or (2) the amount by which your weekly disposable income exceeds 30 times the federal minimum wage. If the resulting amount causes your income to fall below the poverty line, the garnishment is limited to only that amount above the poverty line. Wis. Stat. Ann. 812.34
Wyoming	Yes	

To attach your wages, a judgment creditor obtains authorization from the court in a document usually called a writ. Under this authorization, the judgment creditor directs the sheriff to seize a portion of your wages. The sheriff in turn notifies your employer of the attachment, and your employer notifies you. Unless you object, your employer sends the amount withheld each pay period to the sheriff, who deducts his or her expenses and sends the balance to the judgment creditor.

You can object to the wage attachment by requesting a court hearing. In some states, the attachment can't begin until after the hearing, unless you give up your right to a hearing. In most states, however, as long as you have the opportunity to have your objection promptly considered, the attachment can take effect immediately.

Property Liens

One collection device commonly used by judgment creditors is a property lien. In about half the states, a judgment entered against you automatically creates a lien on the real property you own in the county where the judgment was obtained. In the rest of the states, the creditor must record the judgment in the county in which you own real estate. The recorded judgment creates a lien on the real property in that county only. In a few states, the lien is on your real and personal property. A lien remains until the property is refinanced or sold, or until the judgment debtor pays the judgment amount (more below).

If a judgment creditor does not get a lien on personal property after the judgment is entered or recorded, the judgment creditor might be able to get a lien on your personal property by recording the judgment with the secretary of state. This usually applies to property with title papers, such as a car or a business's assets. If, for example, you tried to sell your car, the lien would appear, and you'd have to pay off the judgment creditor before selling.

Once the judgment creditor has a lien on your property, especially your real property, the creditor can safely anticipate payment. When you sell or refinance your property, title must be cleared—that is, all liens must be removed by paying the lienholder—before the deal can close.

Instead of waiting for you to sell your property, the creditor can "execute" on the lien. That means having the sheriff seize your property—typically a house—and arrange for a public sale from which the creditor is paid out of the proceeds. However, if your property is exempt, the creditor cannot do this. Even if your property is not exempt, many creditors don't want to go through the expense and hassle of a public sale. This is especially true if the creditor won't get much money through the sale. Any mortgage holder, government taxing authority, or other creditor who placed a lien on your property before the judgment creditor will be paid first. Then you get any homestead exemption to which you are entitled. (See Chapter 15.) Only then does the judgment creditor get his or her share.

EXAMPLE: Lin lives in Wisconsin and owns a house worth $200,000. Child-Aid Medical Clinic obtained a judgment against Lin for emergency treatment of his daughter for $2,500 and, consequently, got a lien on Lin's house. Child-Aid considers seizing his house to sell it and be paid but realizes that it won't get any money because:

- Lin owes $125,000 on his first mortgage.
- Lin owes $23,000 on a home equity loan.
- Lin owes the IRS $17,000 on a tax lien.
- Lin's homestead exemption is $75,000.

These items total $240,000, more than the value of Lin's house.

A creditor who places a judgment lien on your property must do so according to the rules in your state for judgment liens. It's not unusual for creditors to make mistakes, which may make the lien unenforceable. You'll need to consult with an experienced consumer attorney if you suspect that the lien was placed inappropriately. See "How to Stop Judgment Collection Efforts," below, for additional reasons the lien may not be enforceable.

Property Levies

A judgment creditor can get a "writ of execution" from the court and go after your personal property by instructing the sheriff or marshal to "levy" on it. Levy basically means that the officer takes the property (your baseball card collection, for example) or instructs the holder of the property (your bank, for example) to turn it over to the officer. After taking your property, the sheriff or marshal sells it at public auction and applies the proceeds to your debt. In the case of a bank account, the amount taken from your account is applied to your debt. You must be notified any time the sheriff or marshal levies against your property. You can request a hearing to show that the property is exempt or that the seizure will cause you financial hardship.

Here is how the levying process generally works:

1. The judgment creditor gets a court order authorizing a levy on your property. This order is usually called a writ of execution.

2. The judgment creditor directs the sheriff to seize (levy on) a particular asset, such as your car.

3. The sheriff comes to your home. If you are present, the sheriff explains that he or she has an order to take a particular item of your property to sell to pay off your debt. You do not have to let the sheriff into your home, however, unless the sheriff has a special court order allowing entry.

4. If you aren't home or don't cooperate, the sheriff can use a duplicate car key or hotwire a car, as long as it is not in a locked garage. Stay calm; in most states you can be arrested for interfering with the sheriff. The sheriff can't enter your house without your authorization to take other property without a special court order allowing entry. But again, if the sheriff insists on entering anyway, don't interfere.

5. The sheriff puts the item into storage.

6. If you don't file an objection (often called a "claim exemption") within the time allowed by your state, the sheriff will put the item up for sale.

7. After the sale, the proceeds are used to pay whatever you still owe the original lender, then to pay the sheriff's costs (seizing, storage, and sale), and then to pay the judgment. If the sale doesn't cover all of what you owe, the judgment creditor can still come after you for the rest.

Assignment Orders

An assignment order lets creditors go after property you own that can't be subjected to a levy, such as an anticipated tax refund, the loan value of unmatured life insurance, or an annuity policy. Independent contractors and other self-employed people who have no regular wages to be garnished are particularly susceptible to an assignment order against their accounts receivable.

An assignment order is straightforward: The judgment creditor applies to the court for an order prohibiting you from disposing of money you have a right to receive—such as a tax refund, insurance loan, royalties, dividend payments, or commissions. You are given the date and time of the court hearing and an opportunity to oppose issuance of an assignment order. If the creditor gets the order, the creditor serves it on whomever holds your money. When payment to you comes due, the money is sent to the judgment creditor instead.

Contempt Proceedings

Sometimes, a judgment issued by the court will include a schedule for installment or periodic payments. In a few states, if a judgment doesn't include such a schedule, the judgment creditor can go back to the court and ask the judge to make an order requiring periodic payments on a debt.

If you violate a court order, the creditor can seek a contempt order. In a handful of states, if a judge issues an order requiring periodic payments on a debt and you miss any payments, the judge can hold you in contempt. You could be fined, sentenced to community service, or, in theory, at least, the judge could issue a warrant for your arrest and you could be jailed.

As you might hope, arresting a debtor on this kind of warrant is usually a very low priority for law enforcement agencies, and in most situations, the warrants become old and moldy without anyone being arrested. But the threat of arrest and jail can be a serious incentive for many judgment debtors to send a check ASAP.

How to Stop Judgment Collection Efforts

It's miserable enough to owe money; it's worse to have your creditors take what little property you may have left.

Fortunately, in many situations you can take steps to try to head off collection efforts, the most common of which is filing for bankruptcy (See Chapter 14.).

Debts for Necessities

In most states, you cannot request a claim of exemption to protect your wages if your debt was for basic necessities, such as rent or mortgage, food, utilities, or clothing. The law says that you should pay for your necessities, even if you suffer a hardship in doing so.

Still, you can request a claim of exemption hearing if the debt (now part of the judgment) was for a basic necessity. The creditor might not challenge your claim. Or, the judge might not care whether the debt was for a basic necessity and consider only whether you need the money to support your family.

Also, it's never too late to negotiate. A judgment creditor who receives a reasonable offer will settle and stop a lien, levy, wage attachment, garnishment suit, or assignment order. (For tips on negotiating, see Chapters 6 and 9.) Or, consider contacting a debt counseling agency for help in negotiating and setting up a repayment plan. (See Chapter 18.)

Most important, just because a judgment creditor levies on your property or attaches your wages doesn't mean that the creditor is entitled to take the property. Every state exempts certain property from creditors. This means that creditors simply cannot have that property, no matter how much you owe. In addition, you might be able to keep property that isn't exempt if you can prove to the court that you need it to support yourself or your family.

Exempt property is described in detail in Chapter 15. In most states, your clothing, furniture, personal effects, and public benefits can't be taken to pay a debt—nor can some of the equity in your car and house, most of your wages, and most retirement pensions. What follows is a discussion on how to claim that your property is exempt (or that you need nonexempt property) when the judgment creditor pursues a lien, a levy, a wage attachment, or an assignment order.

Any time the sheriff or marshal levies against your property, you must be notified. You can request a hearing, which is usually called something like a claim of exemption hearing, to argue that it will be a financial hardship on you if the property is taken, or that your property is exempt under state law. If you lose that hearing and your wages are attached, you can request a second hearing if your circumstances have changed, causing you hardship (for example, you have sudden medical expenses or must make increased support payments).

Here is an overview of how a claim of exemption hearing normally works:

1. When your employer notifies you of a wage attachment request, or you are notified of a property levy (such as a bank account attachment) or an assignment order, you will be told in writing how to file a claim of exemption—that is, how to tell the judgment creditor you consider the property unavailable. The period in which you must file your claim is usually short and strictly enforced—don't miss it.

2. Complete and send a copy of your claim of exemption to the judgment creditor. (See Chapter 15 to learn how to figure out what is exempt.) In some states, you'll also have to serve it on the levying officer, such as the sheriff. The judgment creditor will probably file a challenge to your claim. The judgment creditor may abandon the attachment, levy, or assignment order, however, if it's too expensive or time-consuming to challenge you. If the creditor does abandon it, your withheld wages or taken property will be returned to you.

3. If the judgment creditor doesn't abandon the attachment, levy, or assignment order, the creditor will schedule a hearing before a judge. If you don't attend, you'll probably lose. On the day of the hearing, come early and watch the way the judge handles other cases. If you're nervous, visit the court a day earlier to get accustomed to the surroundings.

4. At the hearing, you'll have to convince the judge that your property is exempt or that you need it to support yourself or your family. This is your opportunity to defend yourself from having your wages or other property taken. You must do all that you can to prepare for this hearing if you want to keep your property.

For example, if the creditor tries to take your "tools of trade," which are exempt to a certain value in most states, bring along someone who works in your occupation. A supervisor, union boss, or shop leader can say that you use the items in your job. You'll need to show that the items' value does not exceed the exemption amount. If you have high income one month, bring in pay stubs to show that you usually make less. Or, if your bills are higher than average, bring copies. Think carefully about your income and financial situation. There may be other ways to show the judge that your property is exempt or necessary to support yourself or your family.

5. The judge will listen to both you and the judgment creditor, if the judgment creditor shows up. Sometimes the judgment creditor relies on the papers already filed with the court. The judge will rule for or against your claim. The judge might also set up an arrangement for you to pay the judgment in installments.

Bankruptcy: The Ultimate Weapon

ankruptcy can be a good way to deal with your debt problems. Most bankruptcy filers can wipe out (discharge) all—or a good portion—of their outstanding debts. But deciding whether bankruptcy will be a good idea isn't always easy. You need to understand how the different types of bankruptcies work and what bankruptcy can and cannot do.

The two types of bankruptcy that most consumers use are Chapter 7, or liquidation bankruptcy, and Chapter 13. Although there are two other types of bankruptcies that consumers might use—Chapter 12 for family farmers and fishermen and Chapter 11 for individuals with unusually high debts—this chapter discusses Chapter 7 and Chapter 13 only.

Chapter 7 Bankruptcy

In Chapter 7 bankruptcy, you discharge (wipe out) most or all of your debts without the need to repay creditors through a payment plan. In exchange, the bankruptcy trustee sells your nonexempt property (property you can't legally protect) and uses the money to repay your unsecured creditors. You get to keep all of your exempt property. (See "Bankruptcy Exemptions," below.) Many Chapter 7 filers are able to keep all or most of their property by using exemptions.

The Chapter 7 Bankruptcy Process

The Chapter 7 bankruptcy process takes about three months, currently costs $335 in filing and administrative fees (which may be waived or paid in installments in certain circumstances), and usually requires only one trip to the courthouse. To begin a Chapter 7 bankruptcy case, you fill out a packet of forms that ask for detailed information about your property, income, debts, monthly living expenses, and recent financial transactions. You must also take a credit counseling course prior to filing and a financial management course before getting a discharge.

When you file for bankruptcy, a bankruptcy trustee is appointed to administer your case. The trustee will hold a short hearing, called the creditors' meeting or 341 hearing, about 20 to 40 days after you file.

You must attend the hearing and answer the trustee's questions under oath. Most hearings last about five minutes and creditors rarely attend. After the hearing, the trustee collects your nonexempt property, sells it, and distributes the money to your unsecured creditors. If you want to keep an item of nonexempt property, you can pay the trustee the property's value in cash (often minus the costs of sale) or see if the trustee is willing to accept exempt property of roughly equal value instead.

At the end of your bankruptcy case, the court will wipe out all of your "dischargeable" debts, which means you no longer owe anything to those creditors. For most people, this ends up being most or all of their debts. Not all debts are dischargeable in bankruptcy however. To learn which aren't, see "Which Debts Will Remain," below.

Who Can File for Chapter 7 Bankruptcy

Not everyone is eligible for Chapter 7 bankruptcy. Here are some of the criteria to qualify for Chapter 7.

The means test. If your average monthly gross income within the last six months is lower than the median income in your state for a family of the same size, then you'll qualify for a discharge under Chapter 7 bankruptcy (assuming you meet the other eligibility criteria). However, if your income is higher than the median income in your state, you must pass something called the "means test." You can find median income tables, by state and family size, on the U. S. Trustee's website at www.justice.gov/ust; choose "Means Testing Information."

The purpose of the means test is to determine if you have enough income to fund a Chapter 13 plan. You'll find out by subtracting certain allowed expenses and required debt payments from your income. If the remaining amount, called your disposable income, is enough to pay back a meaningful amount of your unsecured debts over a five-year repayment period, you fail the means test. You won't qualify for a debt discharge under Chapter 7, but you can file for Chapter 13, instead.

Previous bankruptcy filings. You cannot get another Chapter 7 discharge if you:

- received a Chapter 7 discharge within the last eight years, or
- received a Chapter 13 discharge within the last six years.

There are a few exceptions to these rules.

Previous bankruptcy dismissals. You cannot file for Chapter 7 or Chapter 13 bankruptcy if the court dismissed a previous Chapter 7 or Chapter 13 case within the past 180 days because you violated a court order, you failed to appear in court as required, the court found that your filing was fraudulent or was an abuse of the bankruptcy system, or you requested a dismissal after a creditor asked the court to lift the automatic stay.

Chapter 13 Bankruptcy

In a Chapter 13 bankruptcy, you keep your property whether it's exempt or not. In exchange, you pay off your creditors (some you pay in full, some you pay in part) through a court-approved repayment plan that lasts three to five years.

If you qualify for Chapter 7 but want to take advantage of one of the benefits unique to Chapter 13, you can opt for a three-year plan. Otherwise, you'll pay the greater of either your disposable income or the value of your nonexempt property over five years.

The Chapter 13 Bankruptcy Process

To begin a Chapter 13 bankruptcy, you fill out a packet of forms—much like the forms in a Chapter 7 bankruptcy—listing your income, property, expenses, debts, and financial transactions. You file them with the bankruptcy court along with the current filing fee of $310. As with Chapter 7, you must take a credit counseling course before bankruptcy, and a financial management course before receiving your discharge.

In Chapter 13, you must also submit a repayment plan. This plan indicates how much you will pay to the bankruptcy trustee each month and how that money will be divided among your creditors. Generally, you must devote all of your disposable income to your plan for three to five years. Your plan length depends on several factors, including whether your income is higher or lower than the median income in your state.

As in Chapter 7 bankruptcy, you are required to attend a creditors' meeting. You or your attorney must also attend a confirmation hearing where the judge reviews your plan and either confirms or denies it. Often, repayment plans go through several revisions before being confirmed. Once your plan is confirmed, you make payments to the bankruptcy trustee, who in turn distributes the money to your creditors. At the end of the plan period, the court will wipe out the remaining unpaid balance on your dischargeable debts.

Who Is Eligible for Chapter 13 Bankruptcy?

Only individuals can file for Chapter 13 bankruptcy, not businesses (unless you are a sole proprietor). In addition, you cannot file for Chapter 13 if your unsecured debts are more than $419,275 and your secured debts are more than $1,257,850. (These amounts are valid as of April 1, 2019 and won't change again until April 1, 2022.)

The Chapter 13 Plan

You typically pay the following through your plan.

Administrative claims—100%. These include your filing fee, the trustee's commission, and attorneys' fees.

Priority debts—100%. These include back alimony and child support, most tax debts, wages, salaries, or commissions you owe to employees, and contributions you owe to an employee benefit fund.

Secured debts—regular monthly payments. You must continue to make your regular payments on secured debts, such as your mortgage or car loan, if you want to keep the property.

Mortgage and car loan arrears—100%. If you are behind on secured debt payments and want to keep the property (such as your house or car), you have to make up the back payments through your plan.

Unsecured debts—between 0% and 100% of what you owe. The exact amount depends on the total value of your nonexempt property, the amount of disposable income you have each month to put toward your debts, and how long your plan lasts. Again, if you don't qualify for Chapter 7 and must file for Chapter 13, you'll pay either the value of your nonexempt property or your disposable income, whichever is greater, over the course of five years. For instance, if you have $1,000 of disposable income each month and $15,000 of nonexempt property, you'll pay the greater of the two, or $60,000 of disposable income over five years.

If you qualify for Chapter 7 and are choosing to file for Chapter 13 instead, you'll pay certain nondischargeable debts in full, such as your support obligation, a recent tax debt, or mortgage or car loan arrearages.

The Automatic Stay

When you file for Chapter 7 or Chapter 13 bankruptcy, the automatic stay immediately goes into effect. The automatic stay is one of the most powerful features of bankruptcy. It prohibits most creditors, debt collectors, and government entities from engaging in collection actions during your bankruptcy case. This means creditors and collectors cannot proceed with a lawsuit, make collection calls, send collection letters, repossess your property, or turn off your utilities, among other things.

However, there are some exceptions to this general rule.

Criminal proceedings. Criminal proceedings will proceed, but the collection of criminal fines and penalties might be stayed.

Foreclosures. Foreclosure proceedings are initially stayed when you file for bankruptcy. However, the lender can ask the judge to lift the stay and allow it to proceed with the foreclosure—and in Chapter 7, the judge will probably do so. Also, in some circumstances, the stay will only last 30 days, or not kick in at all, if in the recent past you filed for bankruptcy and the case was dismissed or the court previously lifted the stay on the foreclosure proceedings.

Evictions. In most states, the automatic stay doesn't stop an eviction if the landlord already had a judgment allowing it to evict you before the bankruptcy was filed. (In a few states, you might be allowed to stay the eviction if you bring your rent current.) And if the landlord alleges in its eviction action that you endangered the property or illegally used drugs on the property, the automatic stay won't last long if you filed for bankruptcy before the landlord got a judgment for possession. What's more, most bankruptcy judges will lift the automatic stay and allow an eviction upon the landlord's request.

Utilities. Companies that provide you with utilities, such as gas, heating oil, electricity, telephone service, and water, may not discontinue service because you file for bankruptcy. However, they can shut off your service 20 days after you file if you don't give them a deposit or another means to assure future payment.

Tax debts. The IRS can continue certain actions, such as conducting a tax audit, issuing a tax deficiency notice, demanding a tax return, issuing a tax assessment, or demanding payment of an assessment, and can take your tax refund to pay a prior year's tax debt. The automatic stay stops the IRS from issuing a lien or seizing any of your other property or income, however.

Domestic relations proceedings. Almost all proceedings related to a divorce or paternity action continue as before; they are not affected by the automatic stay.

TIP

You don't need bankruptcy to stop debt collectors from harassing you. Many people consider bankruptcy when debt collectors start phoning them at home and at work. As explained in Chapter 9, under federal law if you tell a debt collector, in writing, to stop contacting you, it must do so (with a few exceptions).

Bankruptcy Exemptions

When you file for Chapter 7 bankruptcy, you don't have to give up all of your property. Federal and state laws allow you to keep certain types of property; these are called exemption laws. It's important to understand exemptions and learn which ones apply to you, because they can determine what you get to keep and what you must give up in Chapter 7. Exemptions play a role in Chapter 13 bankruptcy as well. They help determine how much you'll pay through your plan. The more property you can claim as exempt, the better off you'll be.

Each state has its own bankruptcy exemptions. Federal law also has a set of exemptions. Some states require you to use their exemptions; others give you the option of choosing either the state exemptions or the federal system (you cannot mix and match from both sets).

Sometimes, exemption laws allow you to exempt the entire value of an item of property, no matter how much it's worth. For example, many states allow you to exempt the full value of your wedding ring. If that's the case in your state, you'd get to keep your ring if you filed for Chapter 7.

Other times, an exemption covers your property up to a certain dollar amount. For example, your state might exempt up to $5,000 in car equity. If your car equity (equity is the value of the car minus any car loan balance) is worth $4,000, you'd get to keep it in Chapter 7. If your car equity is worth $6,000, only $5,000 would be exempt.

This means the trustee could sell your car, pay you the amount of the exemption, deduct the costs of sale, and distribute the rest to your creditors.

Still other exemptions, called "wildcard" exemptions, can be applied to any type of property. For example, if your state has a $1,000 wildcard exemption, you could use it to protect artwork worth $1,000 or less. In many cases, you can also add the wildcard exemption to another exemption (such as a motor vehicle exemption) to protect more equity in an item of property.

States allow you to use exemption laws to protect property from collection by judgment creditors as well. Sometimes the exemptions you can use against judgment creditors (those creditors that have sued you and obtained a judgment against you) are the same as those you can use in bankruptcy, and sometimes they differ. If all of your property and income is protected from judgment creditors, you might not need, or want, to file for bankruptcy. (Chapter 15 discusses exemptions in the judgment creditor context.)

TIP

Finding state and federal exemptions. Some of Nolo's bankruptcy books have tables that list the federal bankruptcy exemptions and each state's bankruptcy exemptions. (See "Nolo's bankruptcy resources," below.) You can also find exemption amounts online, at www.nolo.com/legal-encyclopedia/bankruptcy-exemptions.

Will Bankruptcy Solve Your Debt Problems?

Bankruptcy is good at wiping out unsecured debt, but you might have trouble eliminating some other kinds of debts, including child support, alimony, most tax debts, and student loans. Also, if you want to save your home or car, both of which are considered secured property that you must relinquish if you don't stay current on the payment, Chapter 13 is often a better choice than Chapter 7. Unlike Chapter 7, Chapter 13 provides a mechanism that allows you to catch up on your missed payments.

Which Debts Will Be Wiped Out

In Chapter 7, the bankruptcy discharge will wipe out most of your unsecured debts, including credit card debt, medical bills, utility payments, memberships, and personal loans. (For more on which debts are secured and unsecured, see Chapter 4.) Some unsecured debts, however, can't be discharged. Those debts are listed below in "Which Debts Will Remain."

In Chapter 13, you repay some unsecured debts in full (called priority debts) and some in part (called dischargeable debts). For others, like student loans, you don't have to repay them in full during the plan, but you remain liable for the remaining balance when your plan is over. Once you complete your repayment plan, the court will wipe out the remaining balance on your dischargeable unsecured debts.

Which Debts Will Remain

In both Chapter 7 and Chapter 13 bankruptcy, the following debts will not be discharged:

- child support and alimony
- student loans, except in limited circumstances (see Chapter 11)
- most recent income tax debts
- debts you forgot to list in your bankruptcy papers, unless the creditors knew about your bankruptcy case (there is an exception in certain Chapter 7 cases)
- debts for personal injury or death caused by your intoxicated driving, and
- fines and penalties imposed for violating the law, such as traffic tickets and criminal restitution.

There are a few types of debts that you can discharge in Chapter 13 but not in Chapter 7, such as marital debts created by a divorce or settlement agreement and HOA fees incurred after you file, to name a few.

In addition, some types of debts won't be discharged if the creditors convince the judge that they should survive your bankruptcy. These include debts incurred through fraud, such as lying on a credit application, recent credit card charges for luxury items or cash advances, and debts resulting from your willful and malicious injury to another or another's property.

What Happens to Secured Debts?

A bankruptcy discharge eliminates debts, but it doesn't eliminate liens, except in a few instances. A lien is a property interest that gives a creditor the right to take the loan collateral if you don't pay the debt. So, if you have a secured debt, such as a mortgage or car payment, bankruptcy can eliminate the debt, but it won't prevent the creditor from repossessing the property if you fail to make payments. Here's how it works.

If you're caught up on your secured payment, you'll likely be able to keep the property if you file for Chapter 7 or 13, as long as you remain current going forward. If, however, you want to wipe out your mortgage or car payment in Chapter 7 or 13, you'll have to give up the house or car. If you're behind on your payment but want to keep the collateral, you can catch up in Chapter 13 and keep the property, assuming that you have sufficient income to do so.

What Only Chapter 13 Bankruptcy Can Do

In some situations, Chapter 13 bankruptcy offers more help than Chapter 7.

Stop a home foreclosure permanently. Though Chapter 7 bankruptcy can delay a foreclosure, it won't stop it for long. In Chapter 13, however, you can stop the foreclosure, pay off the missed payments through your plan, and continue to make your regular mortgage payments.

Allow you to keep nonexempt property. In Chapter 7, you'll give up nonexempt property so that the trustee can sell it and use the proceeds to pay off your creditors. If you have nonexempt property that you really want to keep, and a steady source of income,

Chapter 13 might make more sense because you can keep all of your assets.

Repay nondischargeable debt. If you have debts that are difficult or impossible to discharge in bankruptcy—such as child support or student loans—you can use Chapter 13 to come up with a workable plan to repay these debts over time. You don't have to pay student loan debt in full through your plan, but you'll have to fully repay most other nondischargeable debts in your plan.

"Cram down" secured debts that exceed the value of the property that secures them. You can use Chapter 13 to reduce a debt (including, in some cases, a loan secured by your home) to the current retail value of the property securing it, and then pay off the debt through your plan. For example, if you owe $10,000 on a car loan and the car is worth only $6,000, if you've had it for at least 910 days, you can propose a plan that pays the creditor $6,000 through the plan. The remainder of the debt ($4,000 in this case) gets lumped with your unsecured property, and you'll most likely pay just a small part of it. You can't cram down a loan on a car you bought within 910 days (about 2 ½ years) of your bankruptcy. For household goods, the time limit is one year.

Getting Help With Bankruptcy

Some people choose to file for bankruptcy without an attorney. If yours is a simple Chapter 7 case and you aren't worried about losing valuable property, you might consider this option. Before you take the plunge, however, arm yourself with a detailed self-help bankruptcy book. (See "Nolo's bankruptcy resources," below.) You'll need to know details about how Chapter 7 works, which debts will be discharged, how to complete your paperwork, trouble you might run into, and much more.

Many people prefer to use a lawyer, however. If you are filing for Chapter 13 bankruptcy, it's an excellent idea to get legal help. In many districts, people who file for Chapter 13 on their own have a very low success rate—and most courts strongly encourage filers to retain counsel. Even when filing for Chapter 7, a lawyer can provide valuable expertise that could help you pass the means test, keep more property, get more debts discharged, and avoid fraud claims, among other things. Some lawyers and nonprofit law offices provide bankruptcy help for free, or at a reduced rate if you meet income guidelines that qualify you for services. You can find a list of offices providing free bankruptcy services on the American Bankruptcy Institute's Bankruptcy Pro Bono Resource Locater at http:// bankruptcyresources.org. For more tips on finding a bankruptcy lawyer, see Chapter 18.

Once you start looking for help, you'll probably encounter many ads for bankruptcy "petition preparers." Under the law, non-attorney petition preparers can only act as typing services; they cannot provide legal advice, tell you what to put on your bankruptcy papers, answer legal questions, or do anything other than type your forms. (See "Watch Out for Nonattorneys Offering Legal-Like Services" in Chapter 18.)

RESOURCE

Nolo's bankruptcy resources.

- *The New Bankruptcy: Will It Work for You?* by Cara O'Neill, contains all the information you need to figure out if bankruptcy is right for you, and, if so, which type of bankruptcy case you should file.

- *How to File for Chapter 7 Bankruptcy,* by Cara O'Neill and Albin Renauer, contains all the forms and instructions necessary to file for Chapter 7 bankruptcy.

- *Chapter 13 Bankruptcy: Keep Your Property & Repay Debts Over Time,* by Cara O'Neill, provides detailed information about how Chapter 13 works and how it will affect your debts and property.

Property Creditors Can't Take

This chapter will help you figure out what property you can protect if a creditor has obtained a judgment against you and seeks to enforce it by taking your cash, or by seizing and selling other property.

The good news is that you can almost certainly keep at least some of your property, no matter what. Certain types of property are "exempt," or free from seizure, by judgment creditors. For example, clothing, basic household furnishings, your house, and your car are commonly exempt, as long as they're not worth too much. However, any property you have that is *not* exempt *can* be taken to pay your debts.

In this chapter we're going to walk you through a worksheet where you can list your property and compare the exemptions available in bankruptcy and figure out what is safe from judgement creditors.

Certain Property Can Always Be Taken Away From You

If you are still making payments on a major purchase—typically, a home or car—your creditor most likely has a lien on the property to secure repayment. This is called a "secured" debt. If you fall behind on your payments, you face the real possibility of foreclosure or repossession of the property that is the security for the loan.

Property Subject to Collection

This section discusses what property a creditor can seize when enforcing a judgment —that is, when the creditor gets a court order allowing it to seize your property to satisfy the debt. Some of your property should be protected, or exempt, from collection. State and federal law determine which property you're entitled to exempt, and in almost every state, you'll use the same exemptions to protect property from debt collectors and bankruptcy creditors.

TIP

You may be "judgment proof." You are considered judgment proof if your property and wages are "exempt" and cannot be taken by a creditor. You can determine whether your property is exempt by checking your state's exemption laws (see below).

Property You Own and Possess

When a creditor seeks to collect a judgment against you, all of your nonexempt property that isn't protected under state law could be taken to satisfy the judgment. As a practical matter, few judgment creditors go after tangible personal property, such as furniture and clothing. The exception would be if an item is quite valuable, like a boat or a plane, for example. What a judgment creditor is really looking for is cash, usually in the form of deposit accounts, paychecks, stocks, and bonds. Real estate with substantial equity can also be at risk, but only if the creditor can't satisfy the judgment with assets that are easier to obtain. It takes significantly more time and money to seize and liquidate real estate.

Property that belongs to someone else is not available to judgment creditors—even if you control the property—because you don't have the right to sell it or give it away.

How Creditors Seize Property

A creditor who has a judgment against you can get a writ of execution from the court and ask the sheriff to seize some of your property and put it up for auction. This is called "an attachment and execution" or a "levy of execution." (See Chapter 13.) The property doesn't have to be property that the creditor took as collateral for a loan.

Unless you act, the sheriff will seize and sell property even if it's protected by an exemption. (See "Is Your Property Exempt?" below, for a discussion of exemptions.) The sheriff won't know what property is exempt without your help. You can prevent the sale of exempt property by filing a notice of exemption or by taking similar steps specified by your state law. In some states, you need to file papers with the sheriff or an official by a deadline. In other states, the sheriff will let you set aside exempt property at the time of seizure.

EXAMPLE: A parent establishes a trust for her child and names you as trustee to manage the money in the trust until the child's 18th birthday. You control the money, but it's solely for the child's benefit under the terms of the trust; you cannot use it for your own purposes. It can't legally be seized by your judgment creditor.

Property You Own But Don't Have on Hand

Any nonexempt property you own is legally available to a judgment creditor, even if you don't have physical possession of it. For instance, you might own a share of a vacation cabin in the mountains but never go there yourself. Or you might own furniture or a car that someone else is using. Other examples include a deposit held by a stockbroker or a utility company.

Property You Have Recently Given Away

People facing judgments are often tempted to give property to friends and relatives or to pay favorite creditors before the other creditors show up.

If you give away your property or sell it for less than it's worth, a judgment creditor could sue you and the recipient of the property for deliberately attempting to defraud the creditor. This might result in the property's being recaptured for the creditor's benefit, and you could be severely fined or prosecuted for your fraudulent activity.

How Do Creditors Find Out About Your Property, Anyway?

A creditor with a judgment against you can find out what property you have, used to have, or anticipate having at a court-ordered hearing. In some states, this is called a debtor's examination. Because it is a court-ordered appearance, you can be arrested, cited for contempt, and put in jail if you fail to show up.

You will have to answer the creditor's questions under oath—and lying under oath is a crime known as perjury. If the creditor learns about assets that belong to you that are not exempt, it can get a court order to make you turn over the assets. If you refuse to obey the order, you could be held in contempt of court and sent to jail. (For more discussion of debtors' examinations, see Chapter 13.)

You can generally choose what property to sell and which creditor to pay first. The exceptions to this rule are:

- If you make a payment shortly before bankruptcy that favors one creditor over another, it will likely be undone.
- If you sell property serving as a security interest, such as a car or home, you must repay the secured debt in full before repaying other obligations.
- You can't defraud a creditor by hiding funds or engaging in other actions intended to deprive the creditor of the amount owed.

Property You Are Entitled to But Don't Yet Possess

A creditor with a judgment against you can go after any assets coming your way, once your right to the property is firm. The most common examples are salary and commissions, earned before or after the creditor got the judgment. Other examples are refunds, vacation and severance pay, insurance payouts, royalties, inheritances, and guaranteed payments (such as from trusts or annuities). The procedure a creditor uses to seize property held by a third person is called "garnishment" or "attachment."

 CAUTION

Sometimes, the money in a trust isn't protected from the beneficiary's creditors. If you are a beneficiary who gets payments from a trust, check with a lawyer regarding the terms of distribution. Trusts often make payments until the beneficiary reaches a certain age and then give the beneficiary the remaining principal. Your creditors will probably be able to seize that money when it becomes due to you.

Federal law limits how much of your earnings can be taken directly from an employer—usually depending on the kind of debt. Taking part of your earnings is called "garnishment" or "wage attachment." Some states protect even more of your wages. To find the wage garnishment limits in your state, see "State Limits on Wage Garnishments by Judgment Creditors," in Chapter 13.

Future Claims

Creditors are not only interested in the property you own now—they sometimes set their sights on property or money that you might own in the future.

For example, you might have a claim against a third party that you haven't acted on and you have yet to apply for the refund, make an insurance claim, or bring a lawsuit.

Occasionally, a creditor will accept the rights to such a claim to satisfy a judgment. This is called an assignment of rights, and it lets the creditor pursue the claim in your place. Typically, because the value of the claim won't be definitely settled or known when you make the assignment, you and the creditor will negotiate what you think it might be finally worth, plus interest, but minus what it will cost to pursue the claim. The claim's value might be further modified, depending on how easy or difficult it looks to successfully collect on the claim.

Stock options are another kind of future right that might have some value to a creditor. However, you won't be able to assign an option unless, at the time you make the assignment, you have a right to exercise the option. In legalese, the right must be "vested." Even if the right has vested, it is not always assignable.

Partially Exempt Property

State and federal laws protect certain kinds of property from seizure by creditors. This protection is called an "exemption." Sometimes, property is protected only up to a certain value. Property is partially exempt if its value is greater than the amount protected by the exemption. A creditor can seize and sell an asset that is only partially exempt, if the creditor pays you the value of your exemption.

When Is Bankruptcy Better?

Many people find that they can keep all or most of their property after filing for bankruptcy. In contrast, when a judgment is granted, the first thing your creditors will look for is cash, and will likely seize wages and the money in your bank accounts.

In a Chapter 7 bankruptcy, creditors generally can get their hands only on the property you own on the day you file for bankruptcy (with a few exceptions). By contrast, a creditor with a judgment hangs around for years, waiting for any event that leaves you with money in your hands, whether it's a new job, sale of a major asset, or an inheritance. As long as the judgment hasn't expired, a creditor won't go away until the judgment is satisfied, with interest.

Many people decide to file for bankruptcy rather than struggling to pay judgments. Not only will bankruptcy protect future income from seizure, but it allows for a fresh start. To learn more about bankruptcy, see Chapter 14.

A creditor can also wait for your fully exempt property to increase to a value greater than the amount protected under your state's exemption law; this would also make your property partially exempt.

EXAMPLE 1: You bought your house for $190,000 in cash, just before a creditor got a judgment against you. In your state, a primary residence with a value of up to $200,000 is exempt from seizure. After a number of years, a similar house in your neighborhood sells for $250,000. The creditor still has a valid judgment and forces the sale of your house, which sells for $250,000 as well. You get the first $200,000 from the proceeds. The costs of sale and the creditor's judgment are paid next. You get any money left over.

EXAMPLE 2: You bought your house for $90,000 with $10,000 in cash and a mortgage for $80,000, just before a creditor got a judgment against you. Your state's exemption protects a primary residence up to $100,000. After a number of years, the mortgage has been paid down to $75,000 and the house is worth $150,000, giving you $75,000 of equity. The creditor won't bother to force the sale at this time, because after the sale the mortgage holder would be paid the first $75,000 of the sale proceeds, then you would be paid $75,000 for the exempt equity. Nothing would be left for the creditor.

Forcing the sale of a noncash asset can be expensive and not very productive for a creditor. Creditors frequently choose to wait for you to die or sell the property yourself, knowing that they'll be paid from the proceeds.

This is one reason why a judgment lien could sit on a house for years after the owner's equity has exceeded the exemption cap. The lien protects the creditor's interest until the property gets sold.

Your Share of Marital Property

If you are or have been married, a creditor can collect its judgment out of your share of marital property. What constitutes your share of marital property depends partly on:

- whether you live in a "community property" state or an "equitable distribution" state
- whether the property being seized was a gift or an inheritance
- when the debt was incurred (before, during, or after the marriage), and
- why the debt was incurred.

Chapter 2 identifies which states use community property law and which ones go by equitable distribution. In Chapter 2, under the headings for "Community Property States" and "Equitable Distribution States," review the sections on "Who Owes What Debts?" and "What Property Is Liable for Payment of Debts." These explain which property is subject to collection, that is, which property a creditor may reach to collect a debt or judgment it has against one spouse, even if it doesn't have a judgment against the other spouse.

Types of Exemptions

Exempt property is the property you can keep in spite of a collection judgment or bankruptcy. Nonexempt property is the property that the creditors are entitled to take away from you. Therefore, the more property you can claim as exempt, the better off you are. Each state has a set of exemptions for use by people who face collection of a judgment and who file for bankruptcy.

TIP

You might be able to negotiate to keep certain nonexempt property. You might not have to surrender a specific item of nonexempt property to creditors if you can pay the property's value in cash, or if you can strike a deal to substitute exempt property of roughly equal value instead. It's possible to negotiate with a creditor about which property gets taken. However, you should anticipate revealing the source of any money involved in the transaction, such as a loan from a relative or earnings. If the source isn't exempt, you might end up turning the funds over along with the property.

There are several types of exemptions:

- exemptions of a type of property, up to a specified value
- exemptions of a type of property, regardless of value, and
- "wildcard" exemptions that can be applied to any property.

Specific Property, Up to Specified Value

The first kind of exemption protects the value of your ownership in a particular item or type of property, but only up to a set dollar limit.

EXAMPLE: If your state exemptions allow you to keep $4,000 of equity in a motor vehicle and you are subject to collection by a judgement creditor, you can keep your car if the equity is worth $4,000 or less.

Even if the property is worth more than the dollar limit of the exemption amount, you can keep the property if selling it would not raise enough money both to pay what you still owe on it and to give you the full value of your exemption.

EXAMPLE: You own a car worth $20,000 but still owe $16,000. Selling it would raise $16,000 for the lender and $4,000 for you, thanks to the $4,000 state exemption. Since there would be nothing left over to pay your judgement creditor, the creditor wouldn't take the car.

However, if your equity in the property exceeds the dollar amount of the exemption, the judgment creditor can sell the property to raise money. A judgment creditor would return your exemption amount to you, plus any money left over after the sales costs are deducted and the judgment is paid.

EXAMPLE: You own a car worth $20,000. You owe $10,000 to the lender and you can exempt up to $4,000 of your equity. Selling the car for $20,000 would pay the lender $10,000 in full and pay your $4,000 exemption, leaving the remaining $6,000 for the judgment creditors, minus sales costs. In this scenario, you are entitled to the full value of your $4000 exemption but not to the car itself.

Specified Property, Regardless of Value

Another type of exemption allows you to keep specified property, regardless of its value. For instance, a given state's exemptions might allow you to keep a refrigerator, freezer, microwave, stove, sewing machine, and carpets with no limit on value.

Wildcard Exemption

Some states provide a wildcard exemption that gives you a dollar amount that you can use to protect any property of your choosing. A wildcard exemption is often used to protect luxury property that wouldn't otherwise be exempt.

EXAMPLE: Suppose you own a $3,000 boat. Your state doesn't have a boat exemption, but does have $5,000 wildcard exemption. You can apply $3,000 of the wildcard exemption to the boat and protect it fully. And, if you have other nonexempt property, you can apply the remaining $2,000 to that property.

Or, you can use a wildcard exemption to increase an existing exemption.

EXAMPLE: If you have $5,000 worth of equity in your car but your state only allows you to exempt $1,500 of its value, you will likely lose the car. However, if your state has a $5,000 wildcard exemption, you could use the $1,500 motor vehicle exemption and $3,500 of the wildcard exemption to exempt your car entirely. And you'd still have $1,500 of the wildcard exemption to use on other nonexempt property.

Is Your Property Exempt?

Figuring out exactly what property you're legally entitled to keep takes some work, but it's very important. It's your responsibility—and to your benefit—to claim all exemptions to which you're entitled. If you don't claim property as exempt, you could lose it to your creditors.

Here's how to figure out what you can protect.

List Your Property

Go through the property checklist (Worksheet 3 online) and check off everything that you have. Then enter the things you have into Column 1 of Worksheet 4: Property Exemptions.

When you complete Column 1 of Worksheet 4, you will have a complete inventory of your property. For the most part, judgment creditors won't go after anything that won't be worth their time to sell. For example, judgment creditors won't try to get small household items, clothing, books, used furniture, gardening tools, old DVDs, cleaning equipment, board games, and the like. So you can skip these things on the worksheet. However, if you have designer clothes, expensive furs, expensive furniture, a vintage book collection or board game, or anything else of value, be sure to list those items.

Value Your Property

In Column 2 on Worksheet 4, enter a value for each item of property listed in Column 1. Keep in mind that many items you originally paid hundreds of dollars for are now worth much less. For your cash, deposits, publicly traded stock holdings, bonds, mutual funds, and annuities, enter the cash amount. For shares of stock in small business corporations, any ownership share in a partnership, business equipment, copyrights, patents, or other assets that may seem hard to sell, do your best to assign a reasonable dollar amount.

If you own an item jointly, put its entire value here. In Column 3, you'll enter your share.

Here are some suggestions for valuing specific items.

Real estate. If your interest is ownership of a house, get an estimate of its market value from a local real estate agent or appraiser. If you own another type of real estate—such as land used to grow crops—put the amount it would sell for.

If you don't know how to arrive at a value, or if you have an unusual asset, such as a life estate (a current right to live in a house until you die) or a lease, leave this column blank.

Older goods. A local thrift store or online resources are good places to look for prices.

Jewelry, antiques, and other collectibles. Any valuable jewelry or collection should be appraised if you aren't certain of its value.

Life insurance. Put the current net cash surrender value; call your insurance agent to find out that amount. Term life insurance has a cash surrender value of zero. Don't put the amount of benefits a policy will pay, unless you're the beneficiary of an insurance policy and the insured person has died.

Stocks, bonds, and so on. You can check the stock's current value by looking it up online or in a newspaper business section. If you can't find the listing, or the stock isn't traded publicly, call your broker and ask. If you have a brokerage account, use the value from your latest statement.

Cars. Start with the *Kelley Blue Book*. You can find this book at the public library or online at www.kbb.com. You can also find price information at www.nada.com. If the car needs substantial repairs, reduce the value by the amount it would cost you to fix the car.

Total Column 2 and enter the figure in the space provided.

Calculate Your Ownership Share

In Column 3, enter two amounts: the percentage of your separate ownership interest in the property and the dollar value of your ownership interest in the property.

If you own an item alone, your percentage is 100%. If you are married and own an item together, your ownership share depends on several factors, including the form of title (for example, joint tenancy or tenancy by the entirety) and the laws in the state where you live or where the property is located. Whether a collector or creditor can get property held by your spouse depends on the type of debt. For example, usually a creditor cannot take the separately owned property of one spouse to pay the separate debts of the other spouse. (See Chapter 2 for more on property rights and debt liability of married, divorced, or separated people.)

EXAMPLE: Audrey and her brother jointly bought a music synthesizer currently worth $10,000. They still owe the music store $3,000, but that is not subtracted in this column. Audrey's ownership share is one-half, or $5,000.

List Liens

In Column 4, put the value of any legal claim (lien) against the property. For example, if you owe money on your house or car, the creditor probably has a security interest in that property. The property is collateral for the debt. Even if you own only part of the property, for example, and your spouse or partner owns a share, enter the full value of the lien. If you didn't sign a security agreement or the creditor has not put a lien on your property, there is no lien, even if you still owe money.

EXAMPLE: Marian owns a house and owes her mortgage lender $135,000. Last winter Marian had a new roof put on her house. She was not satisfied with the roofer's work and didn't pay all of his bill. He recorded a mechanic's lien on her house for $5,000. Marian also has an IRS lien of $25,000 on her house. In Column 4, Marian enters the total of all liens: $135,000 + $5,000 + $25,000 = $165,000.

Liens must be paid off before property can be transferred to a new owner. If the value of the lien exceeds the property's value, you're probably in luck—at least for now. The judgment creditor won't want the property because once the lienholders are paid, there won't be anything for the judgment creditor. This situation will change if the equity increases and opens up funds for the judgment creditor.

Include all liens in Column 4, for example:

- mortgages and home equity loans
- personal loans for which you pledged items of property that you already own as security for your repayment
- security agreements with a department store that specifically take a security interest in items purchased
- motor vehicle loans
- liens held by contractors who worked on your house without getting paid what they claim you owe (mechanic's liens)
- liens placed by the IRS after you fail to pay a bill for past taxes, and
- judgment liens recorded against you by someone who won a lawsuit.

Calculate Your Equity

Your equity is the amount you would get to keep if you sold the property. If you own the property alone, calculate your equity by subtracting the amount in Column 4 from the property's total value (in Column 2). Put the amount in Column 5. If you get a negative number, enter "0."

If you own the property with your spouse and you both owe a judgment creditor, calculate your equity by subtracting the amount in Column 4 from the property's total value in Column 2. If you co-own the property with someone other than a spouse, use the following formula:

1. If the liens in Column 4 are from debts jointly incurred by you and the other owner of the property, figure the total equity (Column 2 less Column 4). Then multiply that number by your ownership share (the percentage you figured in Column 3). Enter this figure in Column 5.

EXAMPLE: Bill and Lee, brother and sister, inherited their parents' $150,000 house in equal proportions. Bill and Lee owe $100,000 on the house's mortgage. Bill owes money to several judgment creditors and wants to figure out his equity in the house. It's $25,000—the total value of the house ($150,000) less what he and Lee owe on the mortgage ($100,000), multiplied by Bill's percentage share (50%). ($150,000 − $100,000 = $50,000; $50,000 x 50% = $25,000.)

2. If the liens in Column 4 are from debts incurred solely by you, then deduct the total amount of the lien from your share of the value of the property (Column 2 multiplied by Column 3). Only your assets—not a co-owner's—will go to pay your secured creditors.

EXAMPLE: Now assume that Bill and Lee inherited the $150,000 house free and clear of any mortgage. Bill owes the IRS $30,000, however, and the IRS placed a lien for that amount on the property. Now Bill's equity is $45,000—the total value of the house ($150,000), multiplied by Bill's percentage share (50%), less the lien ($30,000). ($150,000 x 50% = $75,000; $75,000 − $30,000 = $45,000.)

Determine What Property Is Exempt

Each state has exemption laws that determine which items of property can't be taken away from people with debt problems and what amounts are protected.

TIP

Focus on the property you really want to keep. If you have a lot of property and get bogged down in exemption jargon and dollar signs, start with the property you would feel really bad about losing. Focus on finding exemptions for that. Later, if you like, you can search for exemptions that would let you keep property that is less important to you.

Step 1: Find Your State's Exemptions

Finding the specific state exemptions that apply against judgment creditors will require some legwork. Here are some tips for finding the exemption laws that apply in your situation:

- **Check your state bankruptcy exemptions.** Exemptions play a big role in bankruptcy, particularly in Chapter 7, where they determine what property you can keep and what property you must turn over to the trustee. In many states, the exemptions that you may use against judgment creditors are the same as the ones you can use in bankruptcy. Unfortunately, however, some states (about nine) have different exemptions for bankruptcy and for use against judgment creditors. Other states use the same exemptions for most property, but have different exemptions for certain types of property. For example, some states have different homestead exemption amounts for bankruptcy and for use against judgment creditors, but the same exemption amounts for other types of property.

What does this mean? You can get a good start on finding state exemptions by checking your state's bankruptcy exemptions. (See Chapter 14, "Finding state and federal bankruptcy exemptions.") But then you'll need to do some more research to make sure the exemption applies in the judgment creditor context. For example, if you live in one of the states that have exemptions specific to bankruptcy only, you'll have to find the separate list of judgment creditor exemptions in the state law. Even if you don't live in one of those states, you should still make sure that a particular exemption applies to judgment creditors in your state. Doing so can be tricky. Sometimes the statute is clear that a particular exemption applies only in the bankruptcy context. But other times, that determination has been made by case law. (To learn more about finding state statutes and case law, see Chapter 18.)

- **Check with your local law library.** The librarian can point you to publications that list the most common exemptions that apply against judgment creditors. You might find resources at some public libraries, too.
- **Talk to a local attorney.** A local consumer or debtor's rights attorney should know the applicable exemption amounts for your situation.
- **Do some research on your own.** Generally, most state exemptions are grouped together in the state legal codes. But some types of state exemptions are listed elsewhere, most often where the law covers other issues dealing with that type of property. For example, the exemption for pensions, workers compensation payments, or insurance may be listed in the sections of the law that govern those kinds of property. So be sure to check the code sections that deal with judgment creditor exemptions along with other sections that cover particular types of property. And finally, you will want to learn about any case law that affects what your exemptions may be. For more information on how to research the law, see Chapter 18.

Step 2: Figure Out Which Property Is Exempt

Go though each item on Worksheet 4 and see whether it fits in an exemption category. If an exemption has no dollar limit, apply it to all items that fit the description.

EXAMPLE: The exemption system you're using exempts "furnishings and household goods." You could argue that all of your household furniture, fixtures, appliances, kitchenware, and electronic equipment are exempt.

In evaluating whether or not your cash on hand and deposits of money are exempt, look to the source of the money, such as welfare benefits, disability benefits, insurance proceeds, or wages. Most government benefits already received will also be exempt.

CAUTION

It's important that you keep exempt funds, such as your Social Security benefits, separate from any nonexempt money that you might receive. Once mixed in the same account (comingled), it becomes impossible to tell which funds get withdrawn and, therefore, the exempt funds lose all protection. For instance, if you use the account's debit card at the grocery store, the court won't be able to tell whether exempt or nonexempt funds covered the purchase. You can avoid this problem—and preserve the exempt status—by keeping exempt funds in a dedicated account used for those funds exclusively.

If you use your state exemptions, you can also select from a list of federal nonbankruptcy exemptions. (See Chapter 14, "Finding state and federal exemptions.") These exemptions are mostly survivors' benefits and pensions for federal employees. Despite their name, you can use them both in bankruptcy and against judgment creditors. You can use both your state and the federal nonbankruptcy exemptions, unless they're duplicative. If both your state and the federal nonbankruptcy exemptions allow you to exempt a certain amount in one category, such as 75% of unpaid wages, you cannot add them together; 75% is all you can claim.

TIP

Err on the side of exemption. If you can think of a reason why a particular property item might be exempt, list it even if you aren't sure that the exemption applies. However, don't try to game the system. If it's clear that an item isn't exempt, don't claim it.

Where's Your Domicile?

To figure out which exemptions you can use in bankruptcy, you need to know where your domicile is. As Congress defines it, your domicile is where you make your permanent home: the state where you vote, send your children to school, pay taxes, apply for your driver's license, register your car, receive your mail, and so on. This means something more than your residence, which generally means wherever you are living at any given time. Even if you reside in one state, your domicile may be elsewhere if you consider another state to be your true home. This might be the case if you must move temporarily for military service or to take a temporary position in another state: The state where you are staying temporarily is your residence, while the state to which you will return home is your domicile.

Step 3: Double Your Exemptions If You're Married and State Law Allows It

Some states allow you to double exemption amounts if you are married. This means that you and your spouse can each claim the full amount of each exemption (assuming you both own the property). For example, if your state allows you to double a $4,000 exemption for a car, you and your spouse could exempt $8,000 from a judgment creditor's collection efforts. In some states, you can double all of the state exemptions; other states allow you to double only certain types of exemptions, and still others don't allow you to double any exemptions.

To find out if you can double exemptions, check your state exemption laws.

Step 4: Apply Any Available Wildcard Exemption

If the exemption system you are using has a wildcard exemption, apply it to property you couldn't otherwise exempt, such as property worth more than the exemption limit or an item that isn't exempt at all.

Step 5: Determine the Value of Nonexempt Property

If an item (or group of items) is exempt to an unlimited amount, put "0" in Column 6.

If an item (or group of items) is exempt to a certain amount (for example, household goods to $4,000), total up the value of all items that fall into the category using the values in Column 5. Subtract from the total the amount of the exemption. What is left is the nonexempt value. Enter that in Column 6.

EXAMPLE: Jeremiah lives in a state where the exemption amount for household goods is $2,500. Jeremiah adds up the value of all his household goods listed in Column 5 of the worksheet. The total is $4,000. To find the nonexempt amount, Jeremiah subtracts the exemption amount from the total value: $4,000 – $2,500 = $1,500. The nonexempt amount in this example is $1,500. Jeremiah enters this amount in Column 6 of the worksheet on the line for household goods.

If an item (or group of items) is not exempt at all, copy the amount from Column 5 to Column 6.

When you're done, total up Column 6. This is the value of your nonexempt property.

Unless you file for bankruptcy, you remain indebted to your judgment creditors. This doesn't mean, however, that you must willingly turn over your property to your creditors, (unless a court orders you to). You can sell your property and use it for necessary living expenses, such as food, a mortgage or rent payment, utilities, or car repairs. Of course, it's a good idea to document the sale and keep track of your purchases.

You should be aware that converting property from nonexempt to exempt might seem to make sense, but it can be tricky. If you sell or convert property, a creditor might accuse you of attempting to defraud it of payment. Depending on the circumstances, a court might agree. And, if you give away nonexempt property or sell it for less than it is worth, a creditor may claim that you were fraudulently trying to hide assets. Selling property to close friends and relatives is especially suspicious. The creditor can sue the recipient of the property and ask the court to order the recipient to turn the property over to the creditor. In addition, you could be criminally prosecuted, fined, or jailed.

Before pursuing either of these options, it's best to consult with an attorney who is familiar with the practices of your local bankruptcy court.

CAUTION

See an attorney before converting or transferring property. If you plan to sell—or have already sold—some nonexempt property, consult with a local attorney in order to avoid problems.

Claiming Exemptions

In a few states, to take advantage of the state exemptions, you must file an exemption declaration with the court clerk, county recorder, county clerk, or similar official. The declaration is a simple form in which you describe (or list) your property and give its location. In the states where you must file a declaration, you can sometimes file it even after you've been sued or you've filed for bankruptcy.

The court clerk, county recorder, or county clerk may be able to tell you whether the office has an exemption declaration form. If it does, fill it out and file it. If the clerk's office doesn't have a form, the clerk may be able to tell you whether people file exemption declarations there anyway. Keep in mind, however, that clerks aren't allowed to give legal advice. If you don't get the answer you need, find out whether your court offers a walk-in legal clinic.

In most states, any real estate or personal property in which you reside, such as a mobile home or boat, will qualify for the homestead exemption. To take advantage of the homestead protection, you usually must be living in the homestead when you claim it as exempt in your declaration.

This puts your creditors on notice that they shouldn't bother to go after that particular property. If they do, you need only point out your filed a declaration for protection.

If you don't have to file an exemption declaration, you still must act to take advantage of your state's exemptions. If a judgment creditor goes after your exempt property, you must file a claim of exemption. (To learn how, see Chapter 13.)

Rebuilding Your Credit

f you've gone through a financial crisis—bankruptcy, repossession, foreclosure, history of late payments, or something similar—you may think that you'll never get credit again. Not true. If you get your finances in control and work to rebuild your credit, within a few years you'll likely have access to credit cards, car loans, and other forms of credit, as well as save money by getting better interest rates and paying lower fees.

The first step to rebuilding your credit is to get your finances under control—which is what most of this book is devoted to. Next, learn what goes into your credit reports and credit scores, get rid of incorrect or outdated information, and add positive information to your reports. Then, when you are on the road to recovery, you can take other steps to start establishing good payment history.

RESOURCE

Want more information on rebuilding your credit? This chapter provides a bare-bones introduction to credit reports, credit scores, and rebuilding credit. For detailed information on how to improve credit, get *Credit Repair*, by Amy Loftsgordon and Cara O'Neill (Nolo).

Credit Scores and Credit Reports: What's the Difference?

When a creditor or lender is considering offering a credit card, car loan, mortgage, or another extension of credit to you, it will look at your credit score. Some will review your credit report as well. What's the difference between the two?

Your credit report is a compilation of information about you, your credit accounts, your home or other real property, and employment (sometimes), among other things. Your credit score is a number that a credit scoring company assigns to you. It's a numerical calculation that indicates the risk that you will default on credit payments. The higher the score, the less likely you'll default and therefore the better the credit risk.

The two are intertwined. Your credit score is based on information in your credit report—so if one is good, the other is too. When it comes to rebuilding credit, steps you take to improve the information in your credit report will serve to boost your credit score.

If you've been having financial difficulties (late payments, defaults, bankruptcy, foreclosure), your credit score and credit report will reflect this. Taking steps to improve your payment history, establish new payment history, and show stability in your life and employment will improve your credit. But your credit reports might also have errors that make your credit look worse than it is—so cleaning them up can also help you rebuild credit.

Credit Reports

The first step in rebuilding credit is to review what's in your credit reports and understand what factors will help or hurt your credit.

Credit Reporting Agencies

Your credit reports (you have more than one) are created by credit reporting agencies (CRAs), also called consumer reporting agencies and credit bureaus. These for-profit companies gather information about you and your credit and sell it to banks, mortgage lenders, credit unions, credit card companies, department stores, insurance companies, landlords, and employers. These buyers use the information, along with your credit application, to determine whether to extend credit to you and at what rate.

What's In Your Credit Report?

CRAs get information for your credit report from creditors and public records. There are five categories of information in your credit report.

Personal information. This includes things like your name, former names, past and present addresses, Social Security number, and employment history. You supply this information to creditors on credit applications and they, in turn, report it to the CRAs.

Accounts reported monthly. CRAs get most of their account data from creditors such as department stores, mortgage lenders, banks, and credit card issuers. Some creditors will report the status of your account to the CRAs on a monthly basis.

Accounts reported when you are in default. Other creditors will only report to CRAs if you get behind in payments.

Public records. CRAs will search court and county records for things like evictions, child support orders, lawsuits, bankruptcies, judgments, and tax, judgment, or mechanic's liens.

Credit inquiries. Your report will have the names of creditors and others (such as a potential employer) who requested a copy of your report during the previous year or two.

Some special credit reports, called investigative reports, contain even more information.

Credit reports do not contain information about race, religious preference, medical history, personal lifestyle, political preference, friends, and other information not related to credit. They may or may not include information about your income or your employment history.

The bulk of your credit report consists of credit accounts. Each entry (called a tradeline) contains the name of the creditor, the type of account (such as credit card, student loan, or mortgage), your account number (or partial account number), when the account was opened, your credit limit or the original amount of the loan, whether anyone else is obligated on the account, your current balance, your payment pattern for the previous 24 to 48 months (whether you pay on time or have been 30, 60, 90, or 120 days late), whether you dispute a charge, and whether a particular debt has been wiped out in bankruptcy. The report will have separate tradelines for any accounts that have been turned over to collection agencies.

Many credit reports also contain a credit score—but usually the score is available to creditors only, and not you.

Who Can See Your Credit Report?

The federal Fair Credit Reporting Act (FCRA) (15 U.S.C. §§ 1681 and following) and state fair credit reporting laws regulate who can look at your credit report and how that information can be used.

In general, only a person or a business with a "permissible purpose" can access your credit report. The most common people and businesses with a reason for access are:

- **Creditors and potential creditors.**
- **Employers.** But only under certain circumstances and only if you provide written authorization.
- **Government agencies.** To determine whether you are eligible for a license or public assistance or can make child support payments, or to investigate international terrorism.
- **Insurance companies.**
- **Collection agencies.** If trying to collect an overdue debt from you.
- **Judgment creditors.** To decide whether to begin collection efforts or to locate you or your assets.
- **Landlords and mortgage lenders.**
- **Utility companies.** Although in most situations a utility cannot deny service due to bad credit.
- **Student loan and grant lenders.** For PLUS loans (most other federal loans do not consider your credit). Also, you cannot get a new federal loan or grant if you are in default on another student loan.

Apart from those listed above, most other people and businesses cannot legally request a copy of your credit report. For example, without a court order, your credit report may not be used in divorce, child custody, immigration, and other legal proceedings.

The Three Cs

Creditors use your credit application, your credit report, and/or or credit score to evaluate the three Cs.

Capacity. This refers to the amount of debt you can realistically pay given your income. Creditors look at how long you've had your job, your income, and the likelihood that it will increase over time. They also look to see that you're in a stable job or at least a stable industry.

Creditors also look at your existing accounts and loans, paying particular attention to your credit limits (you may be denied additional credit if you already have a lot of open credit lines), your current credit balances, how long you've had each account, and your payment history—whether you pay late or on time.

Collateral. Creditors like to see that you have assets they can take if you don't pay your debt.

Character. Creditors develop a feeling of your financial character through objective factors that show stability. These include the length of your residency, the length of your employment, whether you rent or own your home (you're more likely to stay put if you own), and whether you have checking and savings accounts. Some specialty credit reporting agencies include information on whether you have bounced checks.

Cleaning Up Your Credit Report

You can't clean up your credit unless you know exactly what's in your credit report. Get a copy, review it, and take steps to get rid of incorrect or outdated items.

Get Free Copies of Your Credit Reports Regularly

You are entitled to a free copy of your credit report once every 12 months from each of the three nationwide CRAs—Equifax, Experian, and TransUnion. Contact the AnnualCreditReport.com service:

- by phone at 877-322-8228
- by mail at Central Source LLC, P.O. Box 105283, Atlanta, GA 30348-5283, or
- online at www.annualcreditreport. com/index.action (be sure to use this exact URL—the Internet is saturated with imposters with similar sounding names that charge a fee for getting your credit report).

There are also a number of nationwide specialty credit reporting agencies that keep records on particular types of transactions, such as tenant histories, insurance claims, medical records or payment, and check writing. You are also entitled to a free credit report each year from these agencies, but there isn't a centralized service for requesting them. Instead, you have to contact each agency individually to ask for your report— you may need to call different phone numbers for different types of reports.

You can get a list of most credit reporting agencies in the country and their contact information from the CFPB's website at www.consumerfinance.gov (search for "How many consumer reporting companies are there," and follow the link to the list).

The free annual credit reports you receive will not include your credit score unless you pay extra.

Additional Times You Can Get Free Credit Reports

You can also request a free copy of your credit report in a number of other situations:

- You are unemployed and planning to apply for a job within 60 days following your credit report request.
- You receive public assistance.
- You reasonably believe your credit file contains errors due to someone's fraud, such as using your credit cards, Social Security number, name, or something similar.
- You are a victim of identity theft or fraud or think that you may be.
- Because of information in your credit report, you were denied credit, didn't get credit on the terms you requested, a creditor terminated an account or took some other unfavorable action regarding your credit or account. (There are lots of details and exceptions—check out the Federal Trade Commission's article "Free Credit Report" at www.consumer. ftc.gov/articles/0155-free-credit-reports or get Nolo's *Credit Repair*.)

To request your credit report based on any of these circumstances, contact one or more of the credit reporting agencies.

Contact Information for the Three Nationwide Credit Reporting Agencies

Equifax Information Services LLC
P.O. Box 740241
Atlanta, GA 30374
866-349-5191
www.equifax.com/personal

Experian
P.O. Box 4500
Allen, TX 75013
866-200-6020
www.experian.com

TransUnion LLC
P.O. Box 1000
Chester, PA 19016
800-916-8800
www.transunion.com

If you've already gotten your free report for the year, and don't qualify for another free one, you can pay a small fee to get your credit report (about $20).

Review the Contents of Your Credit Report

Review your report carefully. One of the biggest problems with credit reports is that they contain incorrect or out-of-date information. Investigations by public interest groups and government agencies show that most credit reports contain errors. In some studies, 25% to 30% of the reports reviewed included errors serious enough that they might result in the denial of credit.

As you read through your credit report, make a list of everything that is incomplete, inaccurate, or improperly included in your report. In particular, look for the following:

- incorrect or incomplete name, address, phone number, Social Security number, marital status, or birthdate
- incorrect, missing, or outdated employment information
- credit inquiries by automobile dealers when you simply test drove a car or from other businesses when you were only comparison shopping (these creditors cannot lawfully pull your credit report without your permission until you indicate a desire to enter into a sale or lease)
- credit accounts that are not yours
- incorrect account histories—look especially for late payments when you've paid on time
- a missing notation when you disputed a charge on a credit card bill (some CRAs require you to file a written statement of dispute)
- duplicate entries, for example, when a collection agency is listed separately from the original creditor without showing the debt was transferred, making it appear that you are delinquent on more than one debt
- closed accounts incorrectly listed as open—making it look as if you have too much open credit
- any account you closed that doesn't have a "closed by consumer" notation; a necessity to avoid having it look like the creditor closed the account

- an account reported by a debt collector that lists the date it first received the account as the date the account was charged off, rather than the date required (see below)
- lawsuits you were not involved in, and
- bankruptcies not identified by the specific chapter of the bankruptcy code.

Other common snafus include:

- commingled accounts—credit histories for someone with the same or similar name
- premarital debts of your current spouse attributed to you
- voluntary surrender of your vehicle listed as a repossession
- paid tax, judgment, mechanic's, or other liens listed as unpaid
- accounts that incorrectly list you as a cosigner, and
- paid accounts listed as unpaid.

If credit reporting agencies report information about medical providers, they must not identify the provider or disclose your medical condition.

You should also review your credit report for out-of-date information. Credit reporting agencies are prohibited from reporting certain kinds of negative information after certain periods of time. Here are the basic rules:

- **Bankruptcies** can be reported for up to ten years. A Chapter 13 bankruptcy is generally deleted after seven years from the filing date. By contrast, a Chapter 7 bankruptcy will remain on your report for 10 years.

- **Lawsuits** may be reported for seven years from the dates the lawsuits were filed or until the statute of limitations expires, whichever is longer. Judgments may be reported from the date of the entry of judgment for up to seven years.
- **Paid tax liens** may be reported from the date of the last payment activity for up to seven years.
- **Most criminal records**, such as information about indictments or arrests, may be reported for only seven years (or until the statute of limitations has expired, whichever is longer). But records of criminal convictions may be reported indefinitely.
- **Delinquent accounts** may be reported for seven years after the date of the last scheduled payment before the account became delinquent.
- **Accounts sent to collection** (within the creditor company or to a collection agency), accounts charged off, or any other similar action may be reported from the date of the last activity on the account for up to seven years plus 180 days after the delinquency (the last missed payment) that led to the collection activity or charge-off. The clock does not start ticking again if the account is sold to another collection agency, you make a payment on it, or you file a dispute with the credit reporting agency. Creditors must include the date of the delinquency when they report past-due accounts to credit bureaus.

- **Overdue child support** may be reported for seven years.
- **Adverse information about student loans** made or insured by the U.S. government may be reported for much longer than seven years.
- **Exceptions for certain loans and jobs.** Bankruptcies, lawsuits, paid tax liens, accounts sent out for collection, criminal records, overdue child support, and any other adverse information may be reported beyond the usual time limits if you apply for $150,000 or more of credit or life insurance, or if you apply for a job with an annual income of at least $75,000. However, as a practical matter, credit reporting agencies usually delete all items after seven to ten years.
- **Positive information** may be reported indefinitely.

Dispute Incomplete or Inaccurate Information in Your Report

Once you've compiled a list of all incomplete, inaccurate, or out-of-date information you want changed or removed, complete and submit a dispute to the CRA. The three nationwide CRAs allow you to submit your dispute online or, if you prefer not to use the online process, you can mail in a request for reinvestigation. To find a sample form to use, see Nolo's *Credit Repair* or look online.

The CRA must reinvestigate and either delete the information you dispute or report back to you within 45 days (if you dispute information after receiving your free annual report) or 30 days otherwise (which can be extended to 45 days if you send the agency

additional relevant information during the 30-day period). You can also send a written dispute to the creditor (called a furnishing creditor) that supplied the incorrect information to the CRA. The furnishing creditor must investigate within 30 days and correct or update the information it sends to the CRA if it determines that it was incomplete or inaccurate.

There are exceptions to the periods for the CRAs and furnishing creditors to respond, situations when they don't have to respond at all (for example, they don't have to respond to "frivolous" disputes), and various obligations for reporting corrected information and notifying other interested parties about the corrections. To learn about these details, as well as steps you should take along the way, get *Credit Repair*, by Amy Loftsgordon and Cara O'Neill (Nolo).

Consider Adding a Brief Statement to Your Credit File

If the credit reporting agency's investigation doesn't resolve the dispute to your satisfaction, you have the right to include in your report a brief statement describing the dispute. Most creditors don't pay much attention to these explanations (or just look at your credit score), so if you are applying for new credit, explain the inaccuracy to the lender yourself.

Add Other Information to Your Report

It never hurts to add information to your report that makes you look more creditworthy. However, the CRA does not have to include this information, and if it does it can charge you a fee. Consider adding the items listed below.

How Debts Discharged in Bankruptcy Should Be Reported

Once a debt is discharged in bankruptcy, the creditor is supposed to update the way it reports the debt to the CRAs by removing any notation of "past due" or "charged off" (which means the debt is still owed, but the creditor has given up on collecting it). The debt will still show up on your credit report, but the notation should be "included in bankruptcy" or something like this. The debt should not show up as currently owed or active.

Unfortunately, some creditors routinely refuse to update the reports—possibly as a debt collection tactic. The creditor essentially holds your credit hostage until you pay up on a debt you don't legally owe. If you don't pay, the creditor continues to report the debt which damages your credit. You could then lose out on getting a new mortgage, job, or housing, for example, years after the debt was eliminated through bankruptcy because your credit report makes it look like you're still not paying your debts. Many consumers simply give in and pay off the debt to stop the negative reporting.

After a bankruptcy, you should review your credit report carefully to ensure that the debts are being reported accurately. Dispute any discharged debts that are reported incorrectly using the dispute procedure discussed in this chapter. If the creditor refuses to change how it reports the debt, you should speak to your bankruptcy attorney about how to enforce your rights, possibly by filing a lawsuit. Some creditors have responded to recent lawsuits claiming they do not have an obligation to update outdated or incorrectly reported debt. However, the bankruptcy code and the FCRA indicate otherwise, particularly in cases where the creditor willfully reports a discharged debt as "charged off" or "past due" to coerce you to pay the debt. Courts tend to side with debtors in this type of situation. You can also file a complaint with the CFPB at www.consumerfinance.gov.

Positive Account Histories

Not all creditors report to credit reporting agencies, and some report infrequently. If your credit report is missing accounts you pay on time, send the CRA a copy of a recent account statement and copies of canceled checks showing your payment history and ask to have the information added to your file.

Information Showing Stability

Consider asking the CRA to add the following:

- your current and previous employment
- your current residence (if you own it, say so) and previous residence
- your telephone number—a creditor who cannot verify a telephone number is often reluctant to grant credit

(although once your phone number is in your credit report, any debt collector who wants to collect from you will be able to call you)

- your date of birth—a creditor will probably not grant you credit if it does not know your age; however, creditors cannot discriminate based on age, and
- your Social Security number—this helps distinguish between people with similar names.

 CAUTION

If a creditor has a judgment or might sue you. Don't volunteer employment or residence information if a creditor might sue you or already has a judgment against you. Such information will make it easier for the creditor to garnish wages or place a lien on your home.

Your Credit Score

Credit scores are numerical calculations that are supposed to indicate the risk that you will default on your payments. To come up with your score, a company gathers information about your credit history, such as how many accounts you have, whether you pay on time, collection actions against you, and so on, then compares you to others with a similar profile and awards you points based on your creditworthiness. A high credit score indicates that you are a low risk—in other words, that you are more likely to repay a loan—and a low score indicates potential problems.

The vast majority of mortgage lenders rely on credit scores, as do car dealers, credit card issuers, and insurance companies. Your credit score determines not only whether you'll get the loan, but also what your interest rate will be: The lower your score, the higher your interest rate.

How Credit Scores Are Calculated

Credit scoring companies use criteria similar to the Three Cs when calculating scores. The largest and most ubiquitous credit scoring company is FICO, the company that generates "FICO" scores. The factors FICO considers in coming up with credit scores include:

- **Payment history** (about 35% of the score). The company looks at such things as whether you've paid on time, have any delinquent accounts, or have declared bankruptcy, how old past-due accounts are, and whether you have judgments against you.
- **Amounts owed on credit accounts** (about 30% of the score). FICO looks at such things as the amounts you owe and how many of your accounts carry balances. The more you owe compared to your credit limits, the lower your score.
- **Length of credit history** (about 15% of the score). Generally, a longer credit history yields a higher score.
- **New credit** (about 10% of the score). FICO likes to see an established credit history rather than a lot of new accounts, and, if you have had payment problems in the past, that

you have positive credit history after that. Opening several accounts in a short period of time might indicate a higher risk. Inquiries on your account may also lower your score slightly, depending on the reason.

- **Types of credit** (about 10% of the score). FICO is looking for a "healthy mix" of different types of credit, both revolving accounts (such as credit cards) and installment accounts (like a mortgage or car loan).

FICO scores do not rely on information about your income, your employment history, or whether you are in credit counseling.

Your credit score may differ depending on the company that generates it, the information considered, and the reason why the score is created. Although FICO is the largest credit scoring company, it isn't the only one. Lenders and credit reporting agencies may use different scoring programs that yield different results. Even your FICO scores may differ depending on which scoring model or industry-specific score is used. For example, auto lenders typically use FICO auto scores, whereas a credit card issuer is more likely to use FICO bankcard scores. FICO also offers a variety of scoring formulas that emphasize different aspects of your credit, which means the score one creditor sees may be different than the score you or another creditor might see.

FICO scores range from 300 to 850. In 2018, FICO reported that the average score in the United States was 704.

Another scoring system, VantageScore, has scores ranging from a low of 501 to a high of 990 in its older versions (which some lenders still use) and 300 to 850 (the same as FICO) in the newest versions. And each of the three nationwide credit reporting agencies, as well as others (for example, CreditXpert) offer their own versions of credit scores.

How to Get Your Credit Score

Unlike with credit reports, you aren't entitled to get a free credit score every year. But you can get your score for free in connection with certain types of credit transactions. If you are supposed to get a credit score and you don't, ask for it. Here's when you can get a free score:

- You apply for a residential mortgage.
- A creditor charges you a higher APR than other similar customers or when, based on your credit score, a creditor denies credit, refuses to raise your credit limit, terminates your account, or makes another unfavorable decision related to your credit that it doesn't make for other similar customers.
- It is required by a state law. Some states require creditors and others using your credit report to disclose your credit score to you in certain circumstances. For example, in California, if a car dealer gets your credit score in connection with your application for a car loan or lease, the dealer must give you your score. (Cal. Veh. Code § 11713.20.)

Should You Pay for Your Credit Score?

You can pay to get your score from FICO and VantageScore retailers, like the three major credit bureaus (Equifax, Experian, and TransUnion), and many credit card companies, loan companies, and banks have started providing credit scores to their customers for free. Keep in mind, though, that the score you get may not be the one that a particular creditor uses. On the upside, if you have a good score from one scoring system, your other scores are likely good as well.

RESOURCE

Want more information on credit scores? Check out the booklet, "Understanding FICO Scores," available from FICO's website, www.myfico.com.

Rebuilding Credit Without Getting New Credit

Getting new credit while you are still recovering from financial difficulties may land you back into trouble, especially because creditors and lenders will only offer you credit and loans with very high interest rates and fees.

Instead of getting new credit, start improving your credit in other ways. Here's how.

Open Bank Deposit Accounts

Creditors look at bank accounts as a sign of stability and as a source for how you will pay your bills. When reviewing a credit application from someone with poor credit, most creditors look for a history of maintaining a checking and savings account since the financial setback.

While a checking account and other bank account information will not appear in the credit reports prepared by the three major CRAs, if you bounce a check to a creditor, that creditor will most likely report the late or missed payment to the CRAs. Your bank or credit union may also report the bounced check to a type of credit reporting agency that specializes in checking account information.

Use Credit Cards Carefully

If your financial problems are behind you and you managed to hold onto one of your credit or charge cards, use it and pay your bills on time. Your credit history will improve quickly. Most credit reports show payment histories for two to four years. If you charge something every month or so, no matter how small, and pay every month, your credit report will show steady and proper use of revolving credit.

Add Joint Accounts to Your Credit Report

If you are married, separated, or divorced, and most of your accounts are in your spouse's or ex-spouse's name only, request that all joint accounts appear on your credit report too (if they are in good standing).

Rebuilding Credit by Getting New Credit

If you have recovered financially and have a track record of making your regular payments on time, it may be time to get new credit.

Get a Secured Credit Card

With a secured credit card, you deposit money into a savings account in a credit union or bank. It freezes the account while you have the card, and you will get a credit limit for a percentage of the amount you deposit—as low as 50% and as high as 120% (usually as a promotional incentive—you should read the cardholder agreement carefully to make sure that you fully understand the credit limit you'll receive). Depending on the credit union or bank, you'll be required to deposit as little as a few hundred dollars or as much as a few thousand. If you fail to pay your credit card debts, the bank or credit union can use the money in your account to cover your charges.

Keep in mind that secured credit cards are expensive—they often come with hefty application and processing fees, annual fees, and high interest rates. And some don't have a grace period. And before you get a secured card, ask the card issuer if it reports to the three national credit reporting agencies. Some don't, and if that's the case, it won't help your credit. Although if you really need a card—for example, to reserve hotel rooms and rent cars—then getting a secured credit card may still be worthwhile.

Get a Regular Credit Card

It's often easiest to obtain a regular (unsecured) charge card from a department store or gasoline company. Don't carry a balance on your card. Instead, make small charges and pay them off in full.

After you have successfully used a store or gasoline card for a few months to a year, you may be able to get a regular bank credit card, such as a Visa card, MasterCard, American Express card, or Discover card. (See Chapter 17 for tips on how to avoid costly traps when applying for credit cards.)

Get a Cosigner or Become an Authorized User

If you can't get a secured or unsecured credit card on your own, you still have other options to start rebuilding your credit.

Become an authorized user on someone else's account. Ask a friend or relative to add you to one of their accounts as an "authorized user." Once you are on the account, the creditor should report it to your credit file as an authorized user account. If it's not reported, ask the creditor and credit reporting agency to include it.

Should you get a cosigner? A cosigner is someone who promises to repay a loan or credit card charges if the primary debtor defaults. If your credit is not good enough, the creditor is likely to want a cosigner. Usually a credit account will be reported under both your name and the cosigner's name. But to be sure, ask the creditor if it will report the account to credit reporting agencies under your name, as well as under the cosigner's name, and request a written statement to that effect.

Work With Local Merchants

Another way to rebuild your credit is to approach a local merchant (such as a jewelry or furniture store) and arrange to purchase an item on credit. Many local stores will work with you in setting up a payment schedule, but be prepared to put down a deposit of up to 30% or to pay a high rate of interest. Ask the merchant if it reports payments to a credit reporting agency. If it doesn't, this tactic won't help rebuild your credit.

Get a Loan From a Credit Union or Bank

One way to rebuild your credit is to take some money you've saved and open a savings account. Then, ask the credit union or bank to give you a loan against the money in your account. In exchange, you have no access to your money—you give your passbook to the bank and the bank won't give you an ATM card for the account—so there's no risk to the bank if you fail to make the payments. If the bank doesn't offer these loans, called passbook loans or credit builder loans, apply for a personal loan and offer either to get a cosigner or to secure it against some collateral you own *(not your house)*.

Don't Use a Credit Repair Organization

You've probably seen ads for companies that claim they can fix your credit, qualify you for a loan, or get you a credit card. Their pitches are tempting, especially if your credit is bad and you desperately want to buy a car or house.

Don't be fooled by the ads. Many of these companies' practices are fraudulent, deceptive, and illegal. Even if a credit repair company is legitimate, it can't do anything that you can't do by yourself or with the help of a nonprofit credit counselor (see Chapter 18). What they will do, however, is charge you between $100 and $5,000 for unnecessary services.

Choosing and Managing Credit Cards

By now you understand that paying your unsecured credit card bills is usually a low priority if you are struggling to save your home or car or if you have other higher-priority bills. Even so, there are some things you can do to avoid increased credit card bills while you dig yourself out of your financial troubles, to choose which card(s) to keep or get, to successfully get rid of cards that have onerous terms, and to dispute credit charges you should not have to pay. This chapter explains how. (See Chapter 6 for the basics on how to negotiate on a delinquent credit card bill.)

Avoiding Credit Card Traps

Credit cards are convenient, but they can also be traps that spiral you into increasing debt for years. A handful of companies provide almost all of the credit cards used in this country. Their cards often have a number of the traps listed below, but not all do, and some cards are worse than others. Credit unions and smaller banks may offer better terms.

The descriptions below will help you recognize traps when choosing a card or deciding which card to get rid of.

Consumer Credit Card Rights

The Credit Card Accountability, Responsibility, and Disclosure Act, often referred to as the CARD Act, provides protections to consumers using credit cards.

The law sets forth rules about the time you get to pay your bill, grace periods, disclosures that credit card companies must provide, when a credit card company can and cannot increase your interest rate, the notice the company must provide when it does increase your rate or change the terms of the agreement, and more.

Although this law eliminates many of the credit card abuses that plagued consumers for years, it does not get rid of all of them.

Use Credit Card Disclosure Forms to Identify Traps

Because of the CARD Act, it is now much easier to comparison shop for credit cards. Credit card companies must display their credit agreements online. When you go to a credit card company's website, look for a link that says "Terms and Conditions" or "Pricing and Terms" (you may have to hunt around). Use this information to compare terms between cards.

When you get a credit card application or preapproved solicitation, the company must also disclose certain terms of the agreement. They may be tucked away on the back of one of the documents, so you may have to comb through the packet of papers to find them.

Finally, charge cards (cards that don't charge interest but require you to pay the balance in full each month) must include all applicable terms and any fees or interest charged if the company grants you an extension to pay.

TIP

Interest rates, APRs, and finance charges. Interest rates are often referred to as "annual percentage rates" or "APRs." And the dollar amount you are charged each month for interest is called the "finance charge."

Avoid Over-Limit Fees

Credit card companies can't charge you over-limit fees unless you "opt in," that is, agree in advance that the company can allow transactions that would put your balance over the credit limit. Even if a credit card company processes a transaction over your limit, if you did not opt in, the company cannot charge you an over-limit fee.

If you do opt in, the company can charge over-limit fees. The CARD Act places some limits on those fees. The company can only charge you one over-limit fee per billing cycle, but it can charge for the same over-limit transaction in a total of three billing cycles if you do not bring the outstanding balance below the limit before the bills are due.

The best strategy to avoid over-limit fees is simple—*don't opt in!* And don't add an over-limit protection plan. This may require some diligence on your part, so that you don't accidentally opt in. For example, a credit application may have a box to check or a line to initial or sign that is really an agreement to allow over-limit transactions.

Not sure if you may have opted in by mistake? If you opt in, the company must provide a written statement confirming you agreed to let them process over-limit transactions. You can revoke this agreement at any time. (The over-limit fees would still apply to over-limit transactions already processed.) You can revoke the agreement with the same method you used to opt in. So, if you opted in by phone, you can revoke your agreement with a phone call. Not certain how you opted in? Contact your credit card company and find out. As always, send a confirmation letter in case there is a dispute later.

Limits on Penalty Fees

Many credit card companies charge penalty fees for:

- late payments
- over-limit charges (if you opt in), and
- payments returned for insufficient funds.

The CARD Act limits these fees to the actual amount the violation cost the company, or to a maximum of $28 for the first violation and $39 for a second violation if it occurred within six billing cycles of the first violation (2019 figures). Of course, you want to always pay on time, but if you sometimes pay late, carefully compare how much different companies charge for these fees.

Watch Out for Multiple Interest Rates

Many cards have different rates (APRs) for balance transfers, purchases, and cash advances. Sometimes there are different introductory APRs on the three types of use, as well. It can become very confusing to figure out what rate you are paying or to compare rates when you want to get rid of cards or get a new card.

Also, many cards today charge variable rates that are linked to an index that moves with market forces. So from one year to the next, the cost of not paying off your balance each month may change dramatically, for example, from 13% to 25%, depending on how volatile the index is. Even cards with "fixed" annual percentage rates may only be fixed for a period of time, and then change to a variable rate. A credit agreement should specify how long the fixed rate applies. If it doesn't, the fixed rate should apply for as long as you keep the card. At the end of a fixed rate period, the company generally has to give you at least 45 days' notice before it can change the rate.

As a general rule, look for the lowest and most stable APR that will apply to the way you plan to use the credit card (for example, if you plan to use the card to get cash advances, look at that APR). If you carry a balance from month to month, even a small difference in the APR can make a big difference in how much you'll pay over a year.

EXAMPLE: Suppose that you have a credit card with an APR of a whopping 28% and that your balance last month was $1,250. To calculate this month's finance charge, the credit card issuer multiplies the outstanding balance by one-twelfth of the annual rate (28% ÷ 12) x $1,250 = $29.16). If you make the minimum payment required, let's say, $32, then $29.16 pays off this month's finance charge, so only about $3 goes to reducing your outstanding balance. If your APR was 13%, only about $13.54 would go to pay off the finance charge for the month and $18.45 would go toward paying off the balance. Exactly how much goes to pay off your balance depends on the method of computation the card issuer uses. (See below, "Balance Computation Methods.")

High Cash Advance Interest Rates and Fees

Using a credit card to get cash advances, or using "convenience" checks a card issuer sends you, can be very expensive.

Additional transaction fees. Most banks charge a fee of up to 5% or so for taking a cash advance. Some waive the fee on convenience checks.

No grace period. Most banks charge interest from the date the cash advance is posted, even if you pay it back in full when your bill comes. A few banks give grace periods for convenience checks.

Very high interest rates. Usually the highest APR is charged for cash advances. APRs of 25% are not uncommon. Even so, you may think it is a way to go, compared, say, to pawnshops, payday loans, or refund anticipation loans. By comparison, this rate could be much better, and an alternative if you can't get a lower interest loan elsewhere. The catch is that you pay both a fee and interest, so the interest rate (APR) doesn't really tell you the full cost for comparison. So, for example, say you get a cash advance or use a convenience check for $500 and the company charges a 5% fee plus an APR of 25% from the date of the transaction. You will pay a $25 fee, plus about $10.42 in interest, for a total of $35.42, assuming you pay it off within one billing cycle. That amounts to an annual percentage rate of about 85%!

Introductory "Teaser" Interest Rate Offers

Credit card companies know that consumers compare interest rates (APRs), so they frequently offer very low APRs, often on balance transfers. The very low APR applies for only a few months and is followed by a very high APR afterwards. If you still have a balance outstanding when the low rate ends, the high rate applies to the balance as well as new transactions.

You may lose the low introductory rate even sooner, for example, if your payment is even one day late. Check the company's disclosures of terms and conditions to see if the APR is an "introductory" rate and, if it is, how long it lasts. If you get a card with a low introductory rate, be sure you can pay it all off before the higher rate kicks in.

Balance Computation Methods

Different cards may seem to offer the same APR, but cost you very different amounts. Credit card disclosures have to tell you which method the company uses to figure your monthly charge (the finance charge). The method that results in the lowest balance each month will be the cheapest card for you.

> **TIP**
>
> **The adjusted balance method is usually best for consumers.** You are also better off if the method used includes payments you make before the due date and excludes purchases during that time.

Adjusted balance. The company determines your balance by subtracting payments you made during the current billing period from the balance at the end of the previous billing period. Purchases made during the billing period aren't included.

Daily balance method. The company takes the beginning balance for each day and adds new purchases and subtracts payments made. The company calculates the finance charge for each day's balance, then adds those figures together to get the finance charge for the whole billing cycle.

Average daily balance (including or excluding new purchases). To calculate the balance due, the issuer totals the beginning balance for each day in the billing period and subtracts any payments made to your account that day. New purchases may or may not be added to the balance. Cash advances typically are added to the balance. The resulting daily balances are added for the billing cycle. Then, the total is divided by the number of days in the billing period to get the "average daily balance." An average daily balance that doesn't include new purchases is better for consumers than one that does include new purchases.

Previous balance. This is the amount you owed at the end of the previous billing period. Payments and purchases made during the current billing period are not included.

Here's an example of how these methods of calculating finance charges affect the cost of credit. In this example, the monthly interest rate is 1.5%, the APR is 18%, and your previous balance is $600. On the 15th day of your billing cycle, the card issuer receives and posts your payment of $400. On the 15th day, you also make a $100 purchase. Using the:

- adjusted balance method, your finance charge would be about $2.96
- average daily balance method (excluding new purchases), your finance charge would be about $5.92
- daily balance method, your finance charge would be about $6.60
- average daily balance method (including new purchases), your finance charge would be about $6.66, or
- previous balance method, your finance charge would be about $8.88.

An explanation of the balance computation method must appear on your billing statements, as well as on online disclosures.

Beware of Balance Transfer Offers

Low- or no-interest balance transfer offers can be a boon, but they can also trip you up. Here's how.

First, if all you pay on your card is the minimum required payment, the credit card company can apply it wherever it wants, which is usually to the balance with the lowest interest rate. The company does not have to split the payment among the various balances or follow your directions to apply it to a particular balance. Say you have an introductory 0% APR (interest rate) on your transferred balance and a 15% APR on purchases you make on the card. The company makes more money if it uses your payment to pay the balance transfer because it isn't earning any interest on that, but it is earning interest

on the purchases you make on the card. So, it applies your minimum to the transferred balance. However, the CARD Act does generally require that any amount you pay above the minimum payment be applied to the balance with the highest interest.

Second, credit card companies sometimes use low interest rate offers on balance transfers to get you to reinstate stale debts (debts you already owe the company or ones they purchased from another creditor), on which they could not legally collect by suing you. Check the fine print on any cards on which you transferred a balance. If you didn't realize you were renewing an old, stale debt, write the company and tell it to cancel the card and remove the old debt from it. Explain you did not understand that you were agreeing to pay a debt that was too old to be collected. (Also see Chapter 9 "How to Handle Time-Barred or "Zombie" Debts.")

Third, the offer may tell you in huge print that the APR is 0%, and you might reasonably think that means there is no charge on the transfer. Not true. Usually there is a "balance transfer fee" of up to 4% or so of the transferred amount. So on a transfer of $1,000, you would immediately owe $1,040.

If you do get a low interest rate on a balance transfer, don't put any new purchases on the card, and be sure to pay off the balance before it resets to a much higher interest rate.

High Penalty Interest Rates

According to the U.S. Government Account-ability Office (GAO), beginning in the late

1990s, companies started charging default or penalty rates. Your regular interest rate might be around 14% on a fixed-rate card. But you can easily trigger a "default" rate that is much higher. Around 30% is common.

What may trigger a default rate? Usually, going over limit or one or more late payments. The default rate applies to any new balance, not just to the late payment. As explained above, after a credit card company raises your annual percentage rate, it must reevaluate it every six months. But you could still wind up paying the default rates for months, years, or indefinitely. And if you are more than 60 days late with a payment, the default rate can apply to the outstanding balance as well (but you can get it reduced on the outstanding balance by making the next six payments on time).

Avoid Deferred Interest Deals

Stores sometimes offer credit card promotions that promise "no interest if paid in full in [xx] days." Be wary of these promotions. If you do not pay off the entire balance by the end of that period, the card issuer may charge interest (usually at a high rate) on the entire amount from the day you made the purchase. So, if you buy a stove for $500 and pay only $400 by the end of the zero-interest period, the store can charge you interest on $500 from the day you purchased the stove.

It gets trickier if you already have a balance on the card you use to make the "no-interest" purchase. In that case, any payments on the card will not necessarily go toward the no-interest purchase. The company can

apply the minimum required payment as it likes. Anything you pay above the minimum payment amount will be paid on the balance with the highest interest rate, with one exception. The company must apply the two payments that come due right before the end of the zero-interest period to the zero-interest purchase balance.

For example, say you have a $300 balance with a higher interest rate on the card before you buy the stove. The company can apply your minimum payments to either balance, but will apply any additional amounts you pay (except your last two payments) to the higher-interest balance, not to the balance for the stove purchase. That means that you may pay $500 on your card before the end of the zero interest period, but still have an outstanding balance for the stove purchase. You can always ask the creditor to apply all of your payments to the no-interest purchase first, but the credit card company does not have to comply with your request.

Annual and Other Fees

Only about 5% of credit cards charge annual fees, so look for one that doesn't. But, you also have to look out for other fees. New fees seem to pop up all the time. Now that the CARD Act has limited the amount of fees for late payments, returned payments, and over-limit charges, credit card companies may get even more creative in finding ways to add fees. For example, one card targeting people with poor credit charges a one-time $95 "processing fee." Some of these fees may not even be included in the written disclosures.

No Grace Period

A grace period lets you avoid all finance charges if you pay your balance in full before the date it is due. Before the CARD Act, you had to pay the balance in full to avoid finance charges on the entire balance. Now the CARD Act prohibits finance charges on any part of the balance you pay within the grace period. So for example, if you start with a zero balance, then charge $300 and pay $200 within the grace period, the company can charge interest on the remaining balance of $100, but not on the $200 you paid.

If you can pay, or want to try to move toward paying your balance down, having a grace period is very important. Without a grace period, the card issuer may impose a finance charge from the date you use your card or from the date each transaction is posted to your account, even if you pay your bill in full each month. The CARD Act does not require that companies offer a grace period, but many credit card companies do, at least on purchases. If they do have a grace period, they must send the bill at least 21 days before the end of the grace period. Most grace periods are from 21 to 30 days. Avoid cards that offer no grace period.

The Minimum Payment Trap

If you opt to pay only the minimum (or less) each month, you'll need years to get out of debt. For example, if you charge $1,000 on a 17% credit card and pay it off by making the minimum payments of 2% of the balance each month, you'll take more than 11 years to pay off the loan and will end up paying more

than $2,171. If the balance is $8,000, it will take over thirty years and cost over $25,000 to repay.

As of February 22, 2010, the federal CARD Act requires credit card statements to show you how long it will take to pay off your balance if you pay just the minimum payment (and don't add any more charges) and the total amount you would pay over that period of time. Your statement also must show the amount your monthly payments would have to be in order to pay off the balance in three years. You can also check out Nolo's credit card repayment calculator, at www.nolo.com, to find out how long it will take you to pay off your balance (and your total cost) for various payment amounts.

It might make sense to make minimum payments in certain circumstances. For example, if you have more than one credit card, consider making minimum payments on all of your cards except one, and then put any extra cash into paying off completely the outstanding balance on that one card. Once you've paid that balance off, start with another card, and so on, until you pay off the outstanding balances on all your cards.

Rewards, Points, Discounts, and Other Perks

Don't be fooled by cards that offer bonuses, let you design the card, or give you discounts. If you will pay high interest or could get hit with high fees of various sorts, or if the card uses one of the worst computation methods, you are better off without the perks.

RESOURCE

Where to complain about credit card abuses. You can file a complaint about a credit card company with the Consumer Financial Protection Bureau, the Consumer Response Center of the FTC, or your state's attorney general or consumer protection department. (See Appendix A for contact information.)

Trouble Paying Your Bill

Credit card issuers want you to pay your bill—or do they? In fact, they depend on customers who don't pay—or rather, who pay late or pay just a little each month.

Americans, in total, have around a trillion dollars in revolving credit debt, most of which is credit card debt. Around 40% of households have outstanding credit card debt. Some consumers have switched to debit cards to try to avoid the traps and costs of credit cards, but debit cards have their own problems (see below). Credit card companies are eager to get more customers. In fact, billions of credit card solicitations are sent out each year.

Should You Get Rid of Unnecessary Credit Cards?

Especially if you've found it hard to rein in your credit card balances, you should avoid using too many cards. But you should also consider the effects of closing accounts on your credit rating (see below). Go back through the list of traps, review the credit card disclosures you received for your cards, or if you can't find

them, check online, call and ask the creditors about the different APRs, fees, and charges, compare the various costs on the cards you have, and try to choose the card with the best terms for how you use a card.

Some credit card issuers offer you an additional card, even if you are in default on a card from the same credit card issuer. These cards are known as "fee-harvesters." The offer may tout credit limits "up to $5,000" or more, but the consumer who applies often winds up with a much lower credit limit, often as low as a few hundred dollars. In the past, fee-harvester cards had so many high fees that consumers would be near the credit limit just with the fees, even before making a purchase. Although the CARD Act limits fees during the first year you own the card—they cannot be more than 25% of your credit limit—the rule doesn't apply to application fees, late charges, returned payment charges, or over-limit charges. And it doesn't apply after the first year. The end result: You'll end up paying high fees on not just one, but two, credit cards.

Here are some rules to follow:

- Close accounts on which you are delinquent or maxed out, and ask the creditors to identify them to credit reporting agencies as "closed by customer request"—otherwise, the credit card issuer may close them for you with a negative notation in your credit record. A card issuer will close your account and cancel your privileges. It might also demand that you pay off the balance. Ask that it send you monthly statements allowing you to pay the balance off over time (and any interest and fees that accumulate on it) and suggest a reduced lump sum payment or a payment plan you can afford. Or contact the bank whose card you are keeping and ask it to transfer the balance on the account you are closing to the account you are keeping. If you're delinquent on all your accounts, keep open the most current account.

- If you pay your bill in full each month—that is, you don't carry a balance—close the accounts with the highest annual fees. Make sure that the accounts you keep open have a grace period in which you can pay off your bills and not incur any interest.

- If you carry a balance, close the accounts with the highest interest rates, shortest grace periods, and least favorable balance computation method. Check your credit agreement disclosures to see which method the company uses to calculate interest. (See "Balance Computation Methods," above.) Keep the cards that use the adjusted balance method, or if none do, your next best choice is to keep one that uses the average daily balance method, including your payments but not your purchases during the billing cycle.

- If you sometimes find yourself needing to pay at the last minute by phone, get rid of ones that charge extra if you talk to a customer service person to expedite payment. If you think you might make late payments here and there, get rid of ones with the highest late fees and penalty rates.

Closing an account, especially one you have had for a long time, may affect your credit score. On the one hand, if you close an account you haven't used and that has no, or only a small, outstanding balance, your credit rating may decrease. Why? The credit report may show your overall debt is now larger in relation to your total available credit. FICO (see Chapter 16) recommends against closing unused credit card accounts if your purpose is to raise your FICO score. See FICO's "Will closing a credit card account help my FICO score?" in the FAQ at www.myfico.com/credit-education/faq.

On the other hand, many creditors refuse credit to people they believe already have too much credit and some are even closing unused accounts themselves. Having an unused account could be grounds for denying you any future accounts you do want or limiting increases on existing accounts. And a notation in your credit report of "closed by consumer request" may be better than a notation that the creditor closed your account.

So, to maximize the benefit of closing accounts, close the accounts on which you are in default already, or ones with large outstanding balances owed, particularly ones that are maxed out. But be aware that a creditor may close out an unused account, so you may want to either (1) make a small purchase every few months and pay it off in the grace period, or (2) close the account before the credit card company closes it.

How to Close a Credit Card Account

If you want to close a credit card account, make sure you do it the right way:

- If you have any bills automatically deducted from your credit card, such as a credit card protection plan, gym dues, or online video streaming fees, cancel those billing arrangements directly with the billing company before closing your account.

- Write a letter to the credit card company and request a "hard close." (You'll find the appropriate address online.) If you don't do this, the company may give you a "soft close," which means new charges can go through, even though you asked that the account be closed. With a soft close, you are susceptible to credit card fraud or merchants—even ones affiliated with the credit card company—continuing to bill you monthly for services you don't need or want and may not even have realized you were paying for.

- Some creditors may refuse to do a hard close until a certain amount of time has passed. If yours is one of them, find out how long you'll have to wait and demand that the company send you a letter then, confirming that the account has been hard closed. As soon as you have paid off any outstanding balance, also ask for confirmation that the balance is zero.

- Request, in writing, that the credit card company report to the credit reporting agencies that your account was "closed by consumer request." Ask the company to send you written confirmation that the account was closed at your request.

- After 30 days, check your credit report to ensure that it reflects that the account in question was "closed by consumer request."

- Once you cancel the card, if you receive a credit card bill for items you canceled directly with the seller or for charges you dispute, use the dispute procedures described below to challenge those charges.

- You should continue to receive billing statements until your balance is zero. If you don't, ask the creditor to send you regular bills to show the balance and your payments. When you have paid the account off, ask the creditor to send confirmation that your account balance is zero.

Shopping for a New Card

Hopefully, you've shed any excess cards and any with terrible terms. Or perhaps, because of your money troubles, you have no cards remaining. Having dealt with your troubles, you are now ready to apply for a new card. Take a careful look at both the protections and traps outlined in this chapter. Use the disclosure tables on each company's website to compare offers. Some information won't be in the table, like minimum payment amounts. To find missing information, search online or call the credit card company. Also, because many credit card companies base your interest rate and credit limit on your creditworthiness, you may not know which card will give you the best rate just by reviewing the disclosures.

Now that you're starting fresh, look for a card that matches your needs. For example, if you think you might carry a balance, look for the card with a low APR even after any introductory rate expires. If possible, get a card with a fixed rate rather than a variable rate. If you sometimes pay late, compare fees for late payments. If you are considering a balance transfer, consider not just the introductory rate, but the interest rate that will apply after any introductory period is over. Avoid cards with high start-up, annual, or other periodic fees, and, of course, don't agree to allow over-limit transactions.

A number of websites compare card features. Keep in mind that the websites don't compare all cards available, and some might only include cards that have paid a fee to be on the website. If you find a card that looks good, check the card's website to read the terms and conditions. Credit cards offered by credit unions usually must be secured by a deposit account at the credit union.

Watch out for preapproval solicitations for nonbank cards. A gold or platinum card with a high credit limit may be nothing more than a card that lets you purchase items through catalogs provided by the company itself. No other merchant accepts these cards, and the company won't report your charges and payments to the credit bureaus. You usually have to pay a fee for the card and then another one for the catalog. And the items in the catalogs are usually high priced and of poor quality.

If you can't qualify for a regular credit card because of your poor credit history, you may want to consider a secured credit card. Credit unions often offer credit cards with lower interest rates and fees, but they are usually secured by your account. (See Chapter 16 for more on using secured credit cards to reestablish your credit.)

If you are inundated with credit card offers, it's probably wise to stop the flow. If you need a card, you'll do better to shop around yourself. And if you are trying to get out of debt, you probably don't want to be tempted by a flurry of credit card offers. You can opt out of receiving unrequested "prescreened" credit offers for five years or permanently. To get details about how to opt out, go to the Federal Trade Commission's website at www.consumer.ftc. gov/articles/0148-prescreened-credit-and-insurance-offers. You can also contact the national credit reporting agencies at 888-567-8688 or online at www.optoutprescreen. com. The website is managed by the three credit reporting agencies, which earn money by selling lists to credit card companies. Not surprisingly, the website attempts to persuade you not to opt out. But, if you call or log onto the website, you can opt out for five years. To opt out permanently, download the form from the website and mail it back.

Using Credit Cards Wisely

Here are some tips for wise credit card use:

- **Check billing statements to keep tabs on your balance.** Generally, if you have an outstanding credit card balance, your monthly statement must show:
  - how long and how much it will cost to pay off the balance if you make only the minimum required payments
  - how much you would have to pay to eliminate your balance in three years or less, and
  - how much you would save by paying off the balance in three years, instead of paying only the minimum payment.

- By reviewing this information, you can better stay on top of the debt before it gets out of control. To review this information, examine the part of your statement that looks like the "Sample Credit Card Billing Statement," below.

- **Send your creditors a change of address when you move.** Many creditors provide change of address boxes on their monthly bills or allow you to change your address online. For your other creditors, you can send letters, call the customer service phone numbers, or use post office change of address postcards. Don't let your monthly statements go to your old address. You may miss making

Sample Credit Card Billing Statement

Payment Information	
New Balance	$1,784.53
Minimum Payment Due	$58.00
Payment Due Date	4/20/17

Late Payment Warning: If we do not receive your minimum payment by the date listed above, you may have to pay a late fee of up to $35 and your APRs may be increased up to the Penalty APR of 28.99%

Minimum Payment Warning: If you make only the minimum payment each period, you will pay more in interest and it will take you longer to pay off your balance. For example:

If you make no additional charges using this card and each month you pay...	You will pay off the balance shown on this statement in about...	And you will end up paying an estimated total of...
Only the minimum payment	10 years	$3,284
$62	3 years	$2,232 (Savings=$1,052)

payments on time, or someone may steal your statement and use your identifying information to gain access to your account or obtain credit in your name.

- **Watch your credit limit.** Creditors may close accounts if you exceed your credit limit. Pay close attention; if you're charging to the limit on your credit card, you may be heading for financial trouble.

- **Sign your cards and protect your PINs.** Sign your cards as soon as they arrive. If you have a personal identification number (PIN) that allows you to take cash advances, keep the number in your head; never write it down near your credit card. Make a list of your credit card issuers, the account numbers, and the issuer's phone numbers so you can quickly call if you need to report a lost or stolen card. Keep this list in a safe place at home.

- **Don't give your credit card or checking account number to anyone over the phone, unless you placed the call and are certain of the company's reputation.** Never, never, never give your credit card or checking account number to someone who calls you and tries to sell you something or claims to need your account number to send you a "prize." Never give your credit card number, checking account number, or personal information to a caller who claims to represent a company you do business with and wants to "confirm" or "update" your account information. The same is true for Internet inquiries like this. *These are all scams.*

Cards You Didn't Request

It is illegal to send you a credit card you did not request. These days, most companies don't violate the law by sending out straightforward unsolicited credit cards. Instead, a bank may send out a "replacement" credit card for a store card that is no longer active, or a sales company may send out a prepaid card that can be linked to a credit account. These are also illegal unsolicited cards. (But a company is allowed to send a replacement card for an active credit card, even if the new card is usable at more stores or has different features.)

Don't just throw an unsolicited card in the trash. It could be the result of identity theft. Or, your credit file may show that you have an account with an open line of credit for whatever amount you were granted by the card issuer. Some creditors refuse credit to people they believe already have too much credit. Having an unused account could be grounds for denying you future accounts you do want or limiting increases on existing accounts.

Before you cut up and toss the card, make a copy and then call the company and inform it of the following:

- that you believe its sending you the unsolicited card violated the law
- that you don't want the card
- that it must cancel the account, and
- that it must provide you with written evidence that it did not, and will not, report the account to any credit reporting agency.

After you call, send a confirmation letter to the company—keep a copy for your files, along with information about the credit card, such as the account number and name on the account. Also send a complaint to the CFPB or FTC (see Appendix A). Wait a few weeks, then get your credit report (see Chapter 16) and check to be sure the account is not on your report.

Rejected and Blocked Cards

In the regular course of using your cards, you may find merchants telling you that the card is "blocked" or has been refused. Here's what's going on.

Blocked Credit or Debit Cards

Have you had a credit or debit card purchase rejected when you were sure you were well under the credit limit? Here's what may have happened. People often use a credit or debit card to buy gas at a "pay first" station, rent a car, or pay for a hotel stay after giving the card to the hotel at check-in as security that they will pay the bill. All of these transactions have one thing in common: The customer is offering the card as payment for a transaction, but because the business doesn't yet know the total that will be billed, the business puts a "hold" on your debit or credit card for the estimated amount you will spend. Usually the amount withheld is not that large and is held only for a short time. Unfortunately, some businesses have been known to hold much more than the estimated amount you'll spend and keep the hold in place for up to 45 days.

Whenever you pay with a credit or debit card at a gas station, hotel, rental car agency,

or anywhere else you provide your card before the amount of the bill is certain, you can protect yourself in one of two ways:

- Pay with the same card, not with cash or a different card than the one you gave initially. That way the hold should come off within a short time after you pay.
- When you pay, remind the business to remove the hold from the card you provided, now that you have paid your bill.

Rejected Credit Cards

When a merchant swipes your card, it's contacting a credit card verification company that has a record of your credit status. One purpose is to check to see if you are over your credit limit or delinquent in your payments. But credit card and verification companies also use guidelines to help them predict when fraud may be involved. If you charge a much larger amount than usual or charge from a different location than usual, your card may not be accepted.

To avoid a declined card when you are not over your credit limit and not delinquent, contact your credit card company before you make an unusually large credit card purchase and before you leave on a trip.

Liability If Your Credit Card Is Lost or Stolen

Most credit card issuers don't hold you liable for any charges made by a thief, as long as you're fairly prompt to report the card stolen. (The same is true for debit cards.) Under federal law, how much you could be liable for depends on whether the thief presented the card in person or not.

Must You Provide Personal Information When You Use a Credit Card?

When you use your credit card, can the merchant record your address and phone number on the credit card slip? No. In fact, Visa and MasterCard do not require a customer to furnish a phone number when paying with Visa or MasterCard (although you may have to provide your zip code). Also, several states bar merchants from recording personal information when you use a credit card. The purpose of these state laws is to make it more difficult for unauthorized persons to obtain personal and financial information about credit card users. Try to not give your address, phone number, driver's license number, or other identifying information when you use your credit card. The credit card issuer already has this information, and the merchant normally does not need it (unless, for example, you want your purchase delivered).

If the card was personally presented to make the purchase, the issuer could hold you liable for up to $50 in fraudulent charges. (15 U.S.C. § 1643; 12 C.F.R. § 1026.12(b).) That's why you don't need to pay extra for loss or theft protection. The most you could

be liable for is $50. But, you should report the theft or loss as soon as possible anyway. If you don't, the creditor may not believe that the card was lost or stolen.

If the thief didn't present your card in person, but, for example, used your card by phone or on the Internet, you have no liability. (12 C.F.R. § 1026.12(b) Official Staff Commentary.) Even so, if you don't report the loss as soon as possible, the creditor may not believe that the card was really lost or stolen. So, be sure to report it right away.

CAUTION

Your liability is greater if you lose a debit card. Debit card rules don't provide as many protections as do credit card rules—so if you lose the card you may lose a lot more money. See below to learn more about the disadvantages of using debit cards.

Where to Call If You Lose Your Card

Your monthly billing statement or credit card disclosure lists the phone number and address for reporting lost or stolen credit cards. Or call toll-free information, 800-555-1212, and ask for the number of your credit card issuer. Better yet, make a list of the customer service numbers for all of your credit cards and keep the list in a safe place at home and take it with you if you travel.

When you discover that a credit or charge card is lost or stolen, call the customer service department of the card issuer at once. Get the name of the person you speak to and get an address. Then, send a confirming letter like the one shown below, keeping a copy for your records. If the credit card issuer doesn't agree to remove the fraudulent charges within a few days, you need to send a letter to trigger the dispute protection measures explained below.

Because the credit card issuer is liable for unauthorized charges once it's notified, it will usually act fast. The issuer will cancel your existing account, open a new one for you, or issue you a new card and number (and may send it by overnight mail), and remove all fraudulent charges from your statement.

TIP

Skip the credit card "protection." Some credit card issuers urge cardholders to buy credit card protection to guard against unauthorized use of credit and charge cards. Given that your liability for unauthorized charges is $50 maximum, and then only for charges made in person before you notify the card issuer, this "protection" is a waste of money. Even worse, the FTC warns that scammers contacting consumers to sell bogus credit protection plans may use the information you provide to defraud you, including stealing your identity.

Sample Letter Confirming Telephone Notice of Lost or Stolen Card

March 2, 20xx
Large Oil Company
Customer Service Department
1 Main Street
Enid, OK 77777

Attn: Natalie Revere
Re: Account No. 1234 5678 9012

Dear Ms. Revere:

This is to confirm my telephone call of March 1, 20xx, notifying you that I lost my Large Oil Company credit card on February 26, 20xx, while I was on vacation at the Grand Canyon.

I understand that under the law, my telephone call serves as timely notice to your company. I further understand that I am not liable for any unauthorized use of this card from the time of my telephone call, and the maximum I am liable for on charges made before my notification is $50.

Please contact me immediately if you have any questions.

Sincerely,

Amalia Kiran

Amalia Kiran

Unauthorized Use of Your Card by an Acquaintance

The rules that apply to lost or stolen cards apply when someone has used your card without your authorization, but here the question is whether you authorized the use. If you implicitly, or apparently, gave authority to the other person, the company can hold you liable.

Suppose you sometimes allow your 25-year-old son to use your card, or gave him a card to use for emergencies, but he has been using it for beer and pizza, and you have allowed those purchases previously. From the credit card issuer's viewpoint, it appears you gave your son authority to use the card, including for the purchase of a very expensive TV or audio system that now appears on your statement. On the other hand, if your adult daughter, who you never allowed to use your card, took your card without your knowledge and charged a trip to Hawaii, you should be able to argue successfully that the company has no basis to believe you authorized her, and the law limits your liability in the same way as if your card was lost or stolen by a stranger.

Your biggest obstacle will be convincing your card issuer that you did not authorize your son, your daughter, or any other person you know to use your card. If such a person takes your card, or uses your card number, take the same steps to call and report it and get a new card as if a stranger had stolen your card. Then, your best bet is to send a letter explaining the situation to the card issuer. For example, emphasize that you never allowed your daughter to use it in the five years you have had the card, and that when you were not at home, your daughter went to your bedroom, took your card, and used it without your ever knowing it. (See below for how to dispute charges on your bill.)

If you follow the measures explained below to dispute a bill and the credit card issuer still claims you owe the bill, you can choose not to pay. The issuer will no doubt close your account and, if the amount is high enough, sue you. If you want to fight it, you'll probably need a lawyer to help you defend yourself. (See Chapter 18 for tips on finding a lawyer.) You may be best off paying the bill and buying a safe into which you can put your cards—and all papers with the account numbers—to keep them from getting into the hands of people who shouldn't be using them.

To Dispute a Credit Card Bill

Although credit cards can trap you with high, hidden, or unexpected interest and fees, you do get better protection (at no extra cost) when you dispute a credit card charge than if the payment were by check or cash. You have two different ways to challenge charges for goods or services on your credit card:

- disputing a "billing error" (which covers a lot more than you might think) (12 C.F.R. § 1026.13), and
- asserting a claim or defense when you are dissatisfied with your credit card purchase, and you have a legal reason why you shouldn't have to make the payment (12 C.F.R. § 1026.12(c)).

Each way has different requirements and limits. Sometimes one way applies, sometimes the other, sometimes both. So, consider both options when you have a problem with a credit card purchase or with a charge that shows up on your credit card bill.

Resolving Disputed Charges With the Credit Card Billing Error Process

Because the definition of "billing error" is fairly broad, you can use this process to dispute many types of problems.

Billing errors include:

- an extension of credit not clearly identified on your bill
- a math error
- a charge on your bill for which you need more information
- failure to mail you a periodic statement
- charges by someone who was not authorized to use your card
- charge for property or services that were never delivered to you
- the company's failure to credit your account properly, and
- charges for items that you returned because they were defective or different from what you ordered.

If you find a billing error in your credit card statement, immediately write to the company that issued the card. Send a separate letter; don't just scribble a note on the bill. The credit card company must receive your letter within 60 days after it transmitted or mailed the bill to you. (If you missed the 60-day time limit, you may be able to dispute

the bill under the claim and defense right explained in the next section.)

You can write a letter like the one shown here, "Sample Letter to Notify of Credit Card Billing Error." Give your name, your account number, an explanation of the error, and the amount involved. Also enclose copies of supporting documents, such as receipts showing the correct amount of the charge. Send the letter to the particular address designated by the creditor for this purpose. Check the back of your statement for this address, look online, or call the company to get it. You can withhold the portion on the credit card bill that you dispute, including finance charges, but you must pay the portion that you do not dispute.

The credit card company must acknowledge receipt of your letter within 30 days, unless it corrects the error within that time. The card issuer must, within two billing cycles (but in no event more than 90 days after it receives your letter), correct the error or explain why it believes the amount to be correct.

If your bank issued the card and you have authorized automatic payments from your deposit account, the bank cannot deduct the disputed amount or related finance charges from your account while the dispute is pending if it receives your billing error notice at least three business days before the automatic payment date.

During the two-billing-cycle/90-day period, the card company cannot report the disputed amount as delinquent to credit reporting agencies or other creditors. Likewise, the card issuer cannot threaten

Sample Letter to Notify of Credit Card Billing Error

May 20, 20xx
Eighteenth Bank of Cincinnati
1 EBC Plaza
Cincinnati, OH 44444

Attn: Customer Service
Re: Billing Error on Bradley Green
Account Number 123 456 789 0000

To Whom It May Concern:

I have found a billing error on my MasterCard statement dated May 15, 20xx.

There is a charge on my MasterCard, dated March 25, 20xx, for $1,000 for a spa located in Cincinnati. I did not make that purchase. I was on vacation from March 20 through March 30 in Nashville. You will notice charges on my statement during that period for businesses in Nashville. Please delete the charge for the spa. I will pay the rest of my bill, excluding that charge. I understand that the law requires you to acknowledge receipt of this letter within 30 days unless you correct this billing error before then. Furthermore, I understand that within two billing cycles (but in no event more than 90 days), you must correct the error or explain why you believe the amount to be correct.

I have also enclosed a copy of the receipt for my hotel in Nashville, for your information.

Sincerely,

Bradley Green

Bradley Green

or actually take any collection action against you for the disputed amount. But it can include the disputed amount on your monthly billing statements. And it can apply the amount in dispute to your credit limit, lowering the total credit available to you. The card company can also add interest to your bill on the amount you dispute, but if the card company later agrees you were correct, it must drop the interest accrued.

If the credit card company sends you an explanation but doesn't correct the error, and you are not satisfied with its reason, you have ten days to respond. Send a second letter explaining why you still refuse to pay. If the card company then reports your account as delinquent to a credit reporting agency or anyone else, it must also state that you dispute that you owe the money. At the same time, the card company must send you the name and address of each credit reporting agency and anyone else to whom it reports the delinquency. When the dispute is resolved, the issuer must send a notice to everyone to whom it has reported the delinquency.

If the credit card company doesn't comply with any of these error resolution procedures, it must credit you the amount you disputed, plus the interest on that charge, up to a total of $50, even if the bill was correct. States may provide greater protection. In California, for example, if the card company doesn't comply by the two-billing-cycle/90-day time limit, you don't have to pay any portion of the disputed balance and may be able to collect triple damages. (Cal. Civil Code § 1747.50.)

Another option is to sue the company for a violation of the Fair Credit Billing Act. (15 U.S.C. § 1640.) Suing a credit card company can be difficult. If the amount is small, you can use small claims court. If you decide not to sue, you should still report the problem to the appropriate government agency. (See Appendix A for contact information.) You may also want to cancel the card if you don't like the way the company treated you. (See "How to Close a Credit Card Account," above.)

Resolving Disputed Charges With the Credit Card "Claim or Defense" Process

If you have a dispute with the seller about an item or service you purchased with a credit card, you may be able to withhold payment on the credit card up to the amount outstanding for that purchase. There are a few exceptions to this rule as well as conditions you must meet before you withhold payment.

You can often withhold payment (subject to the limits and conditions below) if you believe you shouldn't have to pay a certain credit card charge because the seller refuses to replace or repair an item, or otherwise refuses to correct a problem. (15 U.S.C. § 1661i and 12 C.F.R. § 1026.12(c).) Some examples of when this might happen include:

- The item you bought was defective.
- The business sent the wrong item.
- You did not authorize the person who made the purchase to use your card.

Before withholding payment, you must:

- make a good-faith effort to resolve the dispute with the seller, and

- explain to the credit card company, in writing, why you are withholding payment.

There are limits to using this process for certain types of credit cards. If you used a Visa, MasterCard, or another card not issued by the seller, you can refuse to pay only if the following apply:

- The purchase cost more than $50.
- You made the purchase in the state where you live or, if you live in a different state, within 100 miles of your home. (Your state's law determines whether a purchase you made via home telephone or the Internet is considered a purchase made in your state or in the state where the merchant is located.)

These distance and amount conditions don't apply in these cases:

- The seller issued the credit card (such as a department store card issued by the store).
- The seller controls the card issuer or vice versa.
- The seller obtained your order by mailing you an advertisement in which the card issuer participated, urging you to use the card to make the purchase.

You get one year to use this dispute process to raise a claim or defense to payment. But, you can withhold only the balance on the disputed item or service that is still unpaid when you first notify the seller or card issuer of the problem. If you already paid part of the bill, the amount you paid is applied first to late charges, then finance charges, then your purchases, starting with the oldest. So, if you owe a lot of fees and charges, you may not have paid off much—if any—of the disputed amount.

If you conclude that you are entitled to withhold payment, here's what to do.

Write a letter. Write a letter to the credit card company explaining why you aren't going to pay. Describe the steps you took to resolve the problem with the merchant. You can write a letter like the one shown below, "Sample Letter Disputing Credit Card Charge."

Mail to the correct address. Before mailing the letter, look at the back of your bill for the correct address to use. It will probably be listed under a heading like "Your Rights If You Are Dissatisfied with Your Credit Card Purchases." Or call the credit card company to find out where to send it. Credit card companies have special addresses they use for this type of correspondence. If you don't send it to the correct address, the company can disregard your letter.

Keep a copy. And don't forget to keep a copy of the letter for your records.

The credit card company is not allowed to report the amount in dispute as delinquent until the dispute is settled or the matter is decided by a lawsuit.

If you can't resolve the dispute, it can form the basis of a claim in a lawsuit you file or a defense if you are sued for the debt (see Chapter 13), but only up to the amount you have not paid on the disputed debt.

Sample Letter Disputing Credit Card Charge

June 1, 20xx
VISA International
1000 Visa Place
Kreditt City, South Dakota 70502

Re: Claim for defective purchase from Cliff's Department Store
To Whom It May Concern:

I charged on my VISA card a winter coat that I bought from Cliff's Department Store in South Dakota for $89. It was supposed to be washable. I wore the coat for a couple of months; then I washed it, according to the instructions, but it shrank. I took the coat back to Cliff's and was told to leave it there so they could have their buyer look at it. After several telephone calls with different people over a couple of weeks, Cliff's finally said they would not refund my money or replace it with another coat. I still owe for that coat on my VISA card. I am making a claim under 15 U.S.C. § 1661i & 12 C.F.R § 1026.12(c). Because the item was not as represented, and Cliff's refused to replace it or refund my money, I do not believe I am required to pay for the coat. Please deduct that amount ($89) from my credit card bill. Thank you.

Sincerely,

Marge Bright

Marge Bright

cc: Cliff's Department Store

CAUTION

Check your credit report following a dispute or an error. Despite laws designed to protect consumers, a credit card issuer may negligently report an outstanding balance it removed from your card, fail to report that you dispute a charge, or fail to report that the dispute is resolved. Be sure to check your credit file. (See Chapter 16.)

Debit Cards

Consumers use debit cards nearly as much as credit cards according to the CFPB. Unlike a credit card, a debit card directly—and pretty much immediately—withdraws money from your bank account.

Some believe that debit cards are a good alternative to credit cards, because they may help you curb spending. Does that mean debit cards are a good deal for consumers? Not necessarily, at least, not yet. Although the federal Electronic Funds Transfer Act (15 U.S.C. § 1693; 12 C.F.R. § 1005 et seq.) provides some protections for people using debit and ATM cards, it still leaves a lot of traps that can end up costing consumers lots of money.

Here's why you should be extremely careful when using debit cards.

No grace period. With a debit card, the money is taken almost immediately from your account.

No protection for defective purchases. Unlike credit cards, if you have a dispute with a store or another seller about a product or service you bought with a debit card, there is no process to dispute the bill or assert a claim or defense because the product or service was not as promised, defective, or never provided. If you do have a debit card, don't use it for major purchases, especially one that requires a large up-front deposit.

Banks are required to have a process for reporting errors for things like mistaken transfers, transfers from the wrong account, or transfers in the wrong amount. An explanation of how to report such an error is provided either on your initial agreement or with each statement.

Less protection for lost or stolen cards. With a credit card, your maximum liability if a lost or stolen card is used to charge items is either $50 or nothing. Period. With a debit card, if you report the loss or theft within two business days after you discover it, your maximum loss for unauthorized debits is $50. If you do not report the loss or theft within two business days after discovering it, your loss could be up to $500 of unauthorized debits. If there is an unauthorized debit on your monthly statement that you don't report within 60 days after your statement is sent to you, your loss for unauthorized debits from your account is unlimited and continues from 60 days until you do report the unauthorized transaction listed on your statement. If you can convince the bank that there were extenuating circumstances preventing you from notifying it, it must extend the period for reporting for a "reasonable period." And while the bank is investigating your claim that a debit was unauthorized or in error, the money is gone from your account and isn't available to pay your bills. If you do use a debit card, it is imperative that you check the monthly statements carefully.

Fees and notice of changing terms. There is no limit on the kind or amount of fees that banks may charge for debit cards. Often you have to pay a fee when you use your debit card at an ATM or a store. You only get a 21-day notice if the bank increases fees or limits your privileges. And, if necessary for the safety or security of the account or the system, the bank may make changes with no notice.

Theft. Debit cards are reportedly more susceptible to theft than credit cards because thieves can set up readers to get your PIN when you enter it at a store or another location. To avoid this, choose the "credit" button if you do use a debit card—usually this will prompt the system to ask for a signature, instead of a PIN.

Overdraft fees. Overdraft fees are one of the most expensive features of debit cards. Banks often allow you to use more money than is in your account, and then charge a high overdraft fee. Some banks charge an overdraft fee for each purchase that is above the amount in your account, even if you make several purchases in one day. And reportedly, some banks purposely debit the largest purchase first in order to trigger an overdraft on that and each of the smaller amounts that would not otherwise have triggered an overdraft. Overdraft fees of up to $35 are not uncommon. Banks also often offer so-called overdraft or

"bounce" protection plans: Instead of paying a fee for each overdraft, you pay a high fee for the plan.

However, banks cannot charge you for overdraft fees or an overdraft plan on a debit or an ATM card unless you opt in. Don't opt in.

Many consumers opt into overdraft protection without meaning to. Check all solicitations you have received or signed. If you have already opted into overdraft protection or a plan, you can opt out, whenever you want.

Even if you are careful not to opt into overdraft protection, banks can still charge overdraft fees for checks and for regularly scheduled debits that you have authorized (for example, when you authorize a utility company to automatically debit your account each month). This means that you must keep track of how much money you have in your debit account.

Prepaid Cards

Another alternative to cash or a credit card is a prepaid card. These look like debit cards and usually have a bank or credit card name brand even though they are not connected to your bank account. Prepaid cards are reloadable cards that can be used to make payments. The cards are sold at various stores and major retailers, and offered by businesses, such as tax preparation companies to pay your tax refund. With some, you can even have your wages loaded on the card.

In 2016, the Consumer Financial Protection Bureau (CFPB) attempted to strengthen cardholder rights and make prepaid cards more consumer friendly by issuing what's called the "Prepaid Card Rule." Among other things, the CFPB rule requires financial institutions to:

- provide certain disclosures before you get the card
- limit your losses if the card is stolen or lost
- investigate and resolve errors, and
- give consumers access to account information.

The rule was scheduled to go into effect in 2017, but the CFPB postponed it until April 2018. Then, in early 2018, the CFPB announced it was delaying the rule's effective date yet again—until April 1, 2019. So, these protections will not have gone into place until April 2019 at the earliest, assuming there were no more delays.

Prepaid cards often come with monthly fees, activation fees, fees to get cash, fees for customer service, overdraft fees, and more. In combination, the fees might cost you more than a credit card with a very high interest rate. If offered a prepaid card, take cash instead. Or find a credit union or local bank where you can open an inexpensive checking account. (See Chapter 16, "Open Bank Deposit Accounts.")

Help Beyond This Book

This book gives you strategies for coping with your debts. But the suggestions outlined here may not be enough—bill collectors might continue to harass you even after you tell them to stop, you might want help in negotiating with your creditors, you might be sued, you may want to sue a creditor, or you may decide to file for bankruptcy.

Here are some ways to get more information or advice.

Looking Up the Law

Sometimes, you can handle a legal problem yourself if you're willing to do some research. The trick is to know where to turn for the type of information you need. Both the Internet and law libraries are full of valuable information, such as state and federal statutes. For example, you could read the Fair Debt Collection Practices Act, find out that harassment by collection agencies is illegal, and then read court cases that have decided what types of behavior constitute harassment by a bill collector.

If you decide to take the library route, you must first find a law library that's open to the public. You might find such a library in your county courthouse or at your state capitol. Publicly funded law schools generally permit the public to use their libraries, and some private law schools grant access to their libraries—sometimes for a modest fee.

Don't overlook the reference department of the public library if you're in a large city. Many large public libraries have a decent legal research collection. Also, be sure to ask the law librarian for help. Doing so is often the quickest way to find the answer you're looking for.

RESOURCE

Want detailed advice on legal research? We don't have space here to show you how to do your own legal research in a comprehensive fashion. To go further, get a copy of *Legal Research: How to Find & Understand the Law*, by Stephen Elias (Nolo). This nontechnical book gives easy-to-use, step-by-step instructions on how to find legal information.

State and Federal Statutes

Debt collection and credit reporting are governed by state and federal law.

State Statutes

We refer to many of the state laws affecting debtors throughout this book and include citations so that you can do additional research. State laws or codes are collected in volumes and are available in some public libraries and in most law libraries. Depending on the state, statutes may be organized by subject matter, title number (with each title covering a particular subject), or by numbers unrelated to subject matter.

"Annotated codes" contain the text of the laws plus brief summaries of some of the court decisions interpreting the laws and/or references to treatises and articles that discuss them. Annotated codes have comprehensive indexes by topic and are kept up to date with paperback supplements ("pocket parts") stuck in a pocket inside the back cover of each volume.

TIP

Try your state consumer protection agency. Your state consumer protection agency or attorney general's office may provide publications at little or no cost that explain state laws on debt, credit, and general consumer matters. You can find an excellent list of state consumer protection agencies at www.usa.gov/state-consumer.

Federal Statutes and Regulations

Congress has enacted laws—and federal agencies, such as the CFPB and FTC, have adopted regulations related to those laws—covering most of the topics in this book. We include citations for many of the federal laws referenced throughout this book. The *U.S. Code* is the starting place for research on most federal laws. It consists of separately numbered titles. Each title covers a specific subject matter. For example, Title 15 covers most of the federal laws protecting consumers in credit transactions, including the Truth in Lending Act (including the CARD Act amendments), the Fair Credit Reporting Act, the Fair Debt Collection Practices Act, the Equal Credit Opportunity Act, the Credit Repair Organizations Act, the Electronic Fund Transfers Act (dealing with debit cards), and the Consumer Leasing Act (automobile leases). Title 11 contains the Bankruptcy Act. Two versions of the *U.S. Code* are published in annotated form: the *United States Code Annotated* and the *United States Code Service*. Most law libraries carry both.

Most federal regulations are published in the *Code of Federal Regulations* (C.F.R.), organized by subject into 50 separate titles.

Court Decisions

The law is made up of more than just federal and state statutes. Published court decisions play a large role in the law as well. They are important in the two following contexts.

Interpreting Statutes. It's not always clear what a statute means or how it would apply to a specific set of facts. Part of a judge's job is interpreting statutes and telling parties what they mean in particular circumstances. If a judge publishes an "opinion" or "decision" that interprets a statute, that decision becomes part of the law.

The Common Law. Some parts of the law don't have statutes or regulations. Instead, they are made up of common legal principles derived from hundreds of years of American and English cases. This body of law is referred to as the common law, and it's made up entirely of court decisions.

Which Court Decisions Matter in Your Case?

There's a hierarchy that judges must follow when weighing other court's decisions. Some published opinions may be binding on your judge (meaning he or she has to follow the law as set forth in the opinion). Others are not binding, but might serve as a guide or otherwise influence your judge. To get a good grasp on how the courts relate to each other, and which opinions are binding on which courts, get a copy of *Legal Research: How to Find & Understand the Law*, by Stephen Elias (Nolo).

Finding Published Court Decisions

Finding court opinions related to your case is trickier than looking up a statute. Here are some ways to find relevant court decisions.

Practice guides. These are written for lawyers in various subject areas. For example, *California Foreclosure Law* or *Debtor-Creditor Law in New Jersey*. They compile the law and present it in an organized fashion. Ask the law librarian where they are kept (some are kept behind the reference desk). If the guide refers to a case that you'd like to read, use the case citation to find it (ask the librarian where the volumes of books containing cases are located).

RESOURCE

Check out the NCLC manuals. The National Consumer Law Center (NCLC) publishes comprehensive manuals on various consumer and debt topics. Because they are written for attorneys, they contain an abundance of statute and case citations as well as in-depth analysis of the law. Some law libraries carry these volumes. You can also order them from NCLC, but they are pricey. Go to www.nclc.org or call 617-542-8028.

Is the case still good law? You'll have to make sure any opinion you read has not been overruled or questioned by another case (or perhaps by a statute that became law after the case was published). Use a case-checking system, like Shepard's, or an online tool, to make sure the decision is still good law.

How to Read a Citation to a Case, Statute, or Rule

If you find a citation to a law (statute), regulation, or case that looks important, you should read the statute, regulation, or opinion. For cases, you'll need the title of the case and its citation, which is like an address for the set of books, volume, and page where the case can be found. Ask the law librarian for help.

Although it may look about as decipherable as hieroglyphics, once understood, a citation gives lots of useful information in a small space. A citation to a statute or regulation tells you the volume of the legal code, the abbreviation for the legal code, and the numbered section where the statute or regulation is found. So, for example, 16 C.F.R. § 310.4(a)(5) tells you the regulation is found in Title 16 of the *Code of Federal Regulations* at the paragraph numbered 310.4(a)(5). Likewise, a citation to 15 U.S.C. § 1601 sends you to Title 15 of the *United States Code*, Section 1601, which is the first section of the Truth in Lending Act. (You will notice that we sometimes refer to statute and regulation citations in the text of this book.)

A case citation tells you the names of the people or companies involved, the volume of the reporter (series of books) in which the case is published, the page number on which it begins, and the year in which the case was decided. So, for example, *Nielsen v. Dickerson*, 307 F.3d 623 (7th Cir. 2002) tells you one plaintiff was Nielsen, one defendant was Dickerson, the case is found in Volume 307 of the 3rd set of the *Federal Reporter* set of federal court cases, starting at page 623. It also tells you the year the case was decided and which court decided it—the 7th Circuit Court of Appeals.

Online Legal Research

You can accomplish a good deal of legal research using the Internet. But you can't do it all—not every court decision is available online. Furthermore, unless you know what you are looking for—the case name and citation or the code section—you may have difficulty finding it.

Finding Debt, Credit, and Consumer Information Online

Often, the best place to start your quest is with websites that contain information about debt, credit, finance, consumer protection, and bankruptcy. Unfortunately, websites on these topics are not always reliable sources of good information. Some are published by companies trying to sell things like debt settlement and loan consolidation services, or charge you for credit reports that you can get for free. Others are by attorneys who may not be specialists in the field. And often the information is not regularly updated. Here are a few, reliable websites to check:

- **www.nolo.com**
  Nolo's site includes a vast amount of legal information for consumers. Check out the "Bankruptcy," "Debt Management," "Foreclosure," "Personal Finance," and "Social Security and Retirement" areas for free information on credit repair, debt, bankruptcy, foreclosure, and more. You'll find articles, FAQs, online calculators, checklists, and blogs.

- **www.nclc.org**
  This is the website of the National Consumer Law Center.

- **www.consumerfinance.gov**
  The Consumer Financial Protection Bureau has lots of information for consumers, including a list of regulations it has published, FAQs on credit topics, information for students and the military, and more.

- **www.bbb.org**
  The Better Business Bureau allows you to file consumer complaints online, to check the reputation of businesses, and to get dispute resolution services for a variety of products and services. Don't put all of your trust in a BBB business rating though. In 2010, the Connecticut attorney general criticized the BBB for awarding ratings points to companies that paid dues (the AG later reported the BBB stopped this practice). The AG also alleged that the BBB doesn't have enough resources to adequately verify much of the information it relies on to evaluate businesses. In addition, businesses can change names and continue with unsavory practices before BBB complaints catch up to them.

- **www.fdic.gov, www.ftc.gov, www.federalreserve.gov**

  The Federal Deposit Insurance Corporation, Federal Trade Commission, and Federal Reserve Board offer extensive consumer protection rules, guides, and publications.

- **www.irs.gov**

  The Internal Revenue Service provides tax information, forms, publications and online interactive tax assistance. (The information is fairly generic but will help you get started researching a question.)

Finding Statutes and Regulations Online

You can find federal statutes, the entire *Code of Federal Regulations*, and state statutes by visiting the Library of Congress at www.loc.gov/law/help/guide.php. You can also find federal statutes on Cornell University Law School's website at www.law.cornell.edu. The Government Printing Office (www.gpo.gov) offers an excellent website that contains the entire *Code of Federal Regulations* (www.ecfr.gov), the *Federal Register* (in which notices of proposed or recently finalized regulations, and updated dollar amounts for fees that are based on an index, among other items, are contained), bills pending before Congress, Congressional reports on pending or passed bills, and the *U.S. Code*, among other legal resources.

There is often a delay between the time a statute is passed and the time it is included in the overall compilation of laws. Almost every state maintains its own website for pending and recently enacted legislation. These sites contain not only the most current version of a bill, but also its history. To find your state's website, see "Finding Court and Government Agency Websites," below. Finally, the United States Library of Congress maintains a website at www.congress.gov that contains all pending federal bills and a link to the *U.S. Code*.

RESOURCE

Information for Californians. You can get the text of appellate court decisions at www.courts.ca.gov and the text of all California statutes and pending legislation at https://leginfo.legislature.ca.gov/. For a catalog of University of California libraries, the California State Library, and law school libraries, as well as libraries worldwide, do an Internet search for "WorldCat Discovery." It can locate libraries near you that have the book you are searching for.

Finding Cases on the Internet

Here are some useful sites for finding cases by name or citation, and sometimes by key words or terms:

- Google Scholar (https://scholar.google.com). You can search by name, citation or key word. It includes state appellate and Supreme Court cases since 1950, U.S. District, Circuit Court of Appeal, Tax, and Bankruptcy Court opinions since 1923, and U.S. Supreme Court cases since 1791.

Finding Court and Government Agency Websites

Many courts and government agencies have websites that provide statutes and case law, plus other useful information, such as forms, answers to frequently asked questions, and downloadable pamphlets on various legal topics. To find your state's website, go to www.usa.gov.

Once you find your state's website, look for links to the state legislature or to state statutes, state courts, and state court decisions. Also, look for websites of university libraries and your state library.

Local, state, and federal court websites are also available at the National Center for State Courts' website, www.ncsc.org. The federal judiciary's website is www. uscourts.gov. And, of course, Nolo's website, www.nolo.com, provides all kinds of useful links.

- Supreme Court of the United States. You'll find recent Supreme Court opinions, arguments, and bound volumes of cases dating back to 1991.
- Cornell University Law School's Legal Information Institute (www.law. cornell.edu). This site has Supreme Court cases from 1992, a collection of important older Supreme Court cases, U.S. Appellate and District Court cases for the last ten to 25 years, and bankruptcy and tax court cases, or

links to other websites that have them. It also links to sites for state cases.
- VersusLaw (www.versuslaw.com). VersusLaw offers different monthly fee levels for research. You can try a search as a guest for free.
- LexisNexis (www.lexisnexis.com) and Westlaw (www.westlaw.com). These online legal databases contain almost all reported cases from state and federal courts. These websites are the easiest to use and include pretty much all cases you might rely on. But they are expensive. You might be able to find a law library near you that allows free or inexpensive access to Westlaw or LexisNexis to the public.

Lawyers

As a general rule, you should get an attorney involved in your situation if the dispute is of high enough value to justify the attorney's fees. For example, if you owe a creditor $1,200, but the goods were defective and you feel you shouldn't have to pay, and an attorney will cost $800, you're probably better off handling the matter yourself, even though this increases the risk that the creditor will win. If, however, you owe $10,000 and the attorney will cost $1,000, hiring the attorney may make sense. You also may want to consult an attorney if the stakes are high—for example, you are facing foreclosure.

If you believe a creditor has violated the law or if you think you were treated unfairly, but don't know if the conduct violated the law, you may want to have an initial consultation with a lawyer. Some consumer protection laws provide attorneys' fees if you win. Also, if you were victimized by a common unlawful practice, the attorney may be able to handle the case as a class action, even if each individual's stake in the case is relatively small. Depending on the law and circumstances, an attorney may take your case on contingency, so all you would have to pay before the case is over are costs. Even costs can mount up, so before you agree, find out how much you can expect to pay.

What Lawyers Can Do for You

There are four basic ways a lawyer can help you.

Consultation and advice. A lawyer can analyze your situation and advise you on your best plan of action. Ideally, the lawyer will describe all your alternatives so you can make your own choices. Get this kind of assistance early because you may lose options if you wait.

Negotiation. A lawyer can help you negotiate with your creditors, particularly if the lawyer has experience settling disputes through negotiation. If the creditor has an attorney, that attorney may be more apt to settle with your lawyer than with you. And an attorney's letterhead itself lets a creditor know you are serious about settling.

Representation. If you are sued or want to sue, especially if you have a good defense or a claim against the creditor, you may want

to hire a lawyer to represent you. You also may consider hiring a lawyer to assist you if you decide to file for bankruptcy. While many bankruptcies are routine and debtors can often represent themselves when armed with a good self-help book, in some cases, an experienced bankruptcy attorney may be able to point out rights and advantages that you might not figure out on your own.

Unbundled services. Some lawyers "unbundle" their services. This means that they will assist you with a certain task (such as preparing a response to a lawsuit filed against you) or a certain portion of a lawsuit (such as discovery) for a fee that is less than if you hired them to handle the entire lawsuit.

How to Find a Lawyer

Here are several ways to find a lawyer.

Legal Aid. Legal Aid offices offer legal assistance in many areas, especially for people with debt problems. To qualify for Legal Aid, you must have a low income. Usually that means your household income cannot exceed 125% of the federal poverty level, about $32,118 for a family of four, although some offices have different guidelines. To find a Legal Aid office, go to the federal Legal Services Corporation's website at www. lsc.gov. You can look elseware, too, but be careful. Some unscrupulous nonlawyers have been known to pose as legal aid organizations, even using "legal aid" in their names. These groups may take your money and not do anything or may take actions that you haven't authorized.

Legal clinics. Many law schools sponsor legal clinics and provide free legal advice to consumers. Some legal clinics have the same income requirements as Legal Aid offices—others offer free services to low- to moderate-income people.

Personal referrals. If you know someone who was pleased with the services of a lawyer, call that lawyer first. If that lawyer doesn't handle debtor's rights matters or can't take your case, ask for a recommendation to someone else. Be careful, however, when selecting a lawyer from a personal referral. Just because a lawyer performed satisfactorily in one situation doesn't guarantee the same performance in your case.

Group legal plans. Some unions, employers, and consumer action organizations offer group plans to their members or employees, who can obtain comprehensive legal assistance free or for low rates. If you're a member of such a plan, check with it first for a lawyer, but be wary of so-called group legal plans that solicit you, if they are not affiliated with a group such as your union or with your employment. Some are not legitimate. They charge high fees and may provide unlawful legal assistance by unskilled nonattorneys.

Prepaid legal insurance. Prepaid legal insurance plans offer some services for a low monthly fee and charge more for additional or different work. These too, can be used for running scams. Participating lawyers may use the plan as a way to get clients who are attracted by the low-cost, basic services, and then sell them more expensive services. If the lawyer recommends an expensive course of action, get a second opinion before you agree.

But if a plan offers extensive free advice, or you can use the lawyer to write several letters to your hounding creditors, the consultation or service you receive may be worth the cost of membership.

There's no guarantee that the lawyers available through these plans are of the best caliber. Check out the plan carefully before signing up. Ask about the plan's complaint system, whether you get to choose your lawyer, and whether or not the lawyer will represent you in court.

Consumer organizations. Many national or local consumer organizations can recommend attorneys who handle debtors' rights cases. One place to start is the National Association of Consumer Advocates (www.consumeradvocates.org). In some large urban areas, consumer advocates publish guides of consumer-oriented legal organizations and lawyers. Check the library to see if it has such a guide.

Lawyer referral panels. Most county bar associations will refer you to attorneys who practice in your area and who have at least some knowledge of the subject you need help with. But bar associations don't always provide meaningful screening for the attorneys listed, which means those who participate may not be the most experienced or competent.

State bar organizations. State bar organizations are often quasi-governmental bodies that are responsible for policing lawyers' conduct. Some of them establish standards for attorneys to become specialists in particular fields and may have lists on their websites of attorneys in your area who are specialists in particular areas, like bankruptcy or tax law.

Nolo's Lawyer Directory. This online directory provides detailed profiles of attorney advertisers, written by the lawyers themselves, including information about each lawyer's education, experience, practice areas, and fee schedule. Go to www.nolo.com/lawyers.

What to Look for in a Lawyer

Here are some suggestions on how to make sure you have the best possible working relationship.

Keep in mind that you're hiring the lawyer to perform a service for you; shop around if the price or personality isn't right.

Make sure you are comfortable with a lawyer before you hire him or her. When making an appointment, ask to talk directly to the lawyer. If you can't, this may give you a hint about the lawyer's accessibility.

If you do talk to the lawyer, ask some specific questions. Make a list ahead of time, and include questions about how many times the attorney has handled your type of case, what the results were, costs and fees, and what services will be covered. Do you get clear, concise answers? If not, try someone else. If the lawyer says little except "I can take care of it"—with a substantial fee—watch out. Don't be a passive client or hire a lawyer who wants you to be one. If the lawyer

admits to not knowing an answer, that isn't necessarily bad. In most cases, the lawyer must do some research.

When you've narrowed your search to several lawyers, check their disciplinary history on your state bar's website. This website also may say where the lawyers went to school, how long they've been in practice, and whether they're certified as specialists in any areas of practice.

Once you find a lawyer you like, make an appointment to discuss your situation fully. Your goal at the initial conference is to find out what the lawyer recommends and how much it will cost. Go home and think about the lawyer's suggestions. If they don't make sense or if you have other reservations, call someone else.

Keep in mind that the lawyer works for you. Once you hire a lawyer, you have the absolute right to switch to another—or to fire the lawyer and handle the matter yourself— at any time, for any reason.

How Much Lawyers Charge

If all you want is a consultation with an attorney to find out where you stand and what options you have, be sure to find out the hourly fee ahead of time. Some charge as little as $100 an hour, while others charge $500 or more per hour.

A letter doesn't take that long to write, however, and as long as you are clear about what you want the lawyer to do and not do, you can keep the bill low. If you want the lawyer to do some negotiating, the fee could add up.

If you're sued by a creditor and hire a lawyer to represent you, the lawyer's fee will probably add up fast. A few lawyers might represent you for a flat fee, but most charge by the hour. If you have a claim against a creditor and might win damages—for example, if a debt collector posted your name throughout the town as a "deadbeat"—the lawyer might take your case on a contingency fee basis. That means the lawyer gets paid only if you win your case. If you don't win, the lawyer doesn't get paid a cent, but will probably expect you to reimburse costs. Most lawyers tend to take only those cases they think they have a good chance of winning on contingency.

Watch Out for Nonattorneys Offering Legal-Like Services

Some companies pose as experts in some area of law, like bankruptcies or landlord-tenant, and charge high fees to provide services that seem like legal services, even though the services are usually provided by unskilled salespeople, not attorneys. They will likely claim that they are cheaper or better than attorneys. Or they may hire an attorney, supposedly to represent clients if needed, but the attorney's loyalty is to helping the company sell you expensive services, not to working for your best interests. Companies like this are illegal in most states. The "help" they provide may make your situation worse, besides being as expensive as a real attorney. If you may need an attorney, do the looking and selecting yourself. Don't be taken in by one of these companies.

One final word: No matter why you hire a lawyer, and for whatever fee, be sure the lawyer puts the fee arrangement in a written contract for both you and the lawyer to sign. If the lawyer doesn't mention a written fee agreement, insist on one. You don't want your lawyer's fee to become another debt you can't or won't pay.

Debt and Credit Counseling Agencies

Traditional credit and debt counseling agencies are organizations funded primarily by major creditors, such as department stores, credit card companies, and banks. They can work with you to help you repay your debts and improve your financial picture. Most are nonprofit companies.

To use a credit or debt counseling agency to help you pay your debts, you must have some disposable income. A counselor contacts your creditors to let them know that you've sought assistance and need more time to pay. Based on your income and debts, the counselor, with your creditors, decides on how much you will pay to your creditors each month. If you agree to the plan, you then make one payment each month to the counseling agency, which in turn pays your creditors. The agency asks the creditors to return a small percentage of the money to fund its work. This arrangement is generally referred to as a debt management program. It generally takes three to five years to repay debts through a debt management program.

Some creditors will make concessions to help you when you're on a debt management program. But few creditors will reduce your accumulated debt, such as waiving a portion of the accumulated interest to help you repay the principal. More likely, you'll get late fees dropped, interest rate reductions, and the opportunity to reinstate your credit if you successfully complete a debt management program.

Participating in a credit or debt counseling agency's debt management program is a little bit like filing for Chapter 13 bankruptcy. (See Chapter 14.) Working with a credit or debt counseling agency has one advantage: No bankruptcy will appear on your credit record.

But a debt management program also has two disadvantages when compared to Chapter 13 bankruptcy. First, if you miss a payment, Chapter 13 protects you from creditors who could otherwise start collection actions immediately. A debt management program has no such protection, and any creditor can pull the plug on your plan. Also, a debt management plan usually requires that your debts other than late fees be paid in full (with no interest or at a reduced rate). In Chapter 13 bankruptcy, the amount you have to pay depends on your disposable income and the value of your nonexempt property; you may end up paying back only a small percentage of your unsecured debt.

Consumer Credit Counseling Service

Consumer Credit Counseling Service (CCCS) is the oldest credit or debt counseling agency in the country. Actually, CCCS isn't one agency. CCCS is the primary operating name of many credit and debt counseling agencies affiliated with the National Foundation for Credit Counseling (NFCC). CCCS may charge you a start-up fee and a small monthly fee for setting up a repayment plan. CCCS also helps people make monthly budgets for a small fee or sometimes free. If you can't afford the fee, CCCS will waive it. In most CCCS offices, the primary service offered is a debt management program. Some offices have additional services, such as helping you save money toward buying a house, prebankruptcy counseling, or reviewing your credit report.

CCCS has more than 700 offices, located in every state. To connect with a consumer credit counselor, call 800-388-2227, or go to www.nfcc.org.

Shopping for a Credit or Debt Counseling Agency

The combination of high consumer debt and easy access to information (via the Internet) has led to an explosion in advertising by new credit and debt counseling companies. Some provide limited services, such as budgeting and debt repayment, while others offer a range of services, from debt counseling to financial planning and education. Shop carefully. Some of these agencies were established primarily to sell you products and services and don't provide good-quality counseling.

Many of these newer credit counseling companies claim to be nonprofits, but such claims may not be accurate. A company must meet IRS restrictions to be considered a nonprofit credit counseling agency. According to the rules, a nonprofit credit counseling company:

- cannot solicit contributions from you while counseling you or providing any other services to you

- cannot refuse to provide credit counseling services to you because you can't pay, you aren't eligible for the debt management plan the company offers, or you choose not to enroll in a debt management plan
- can only collect reasonable charges for its services (including a debt management plan)
- must allow a waiver of fees if you can't pay for the services, and
- unless state law allows it, cannot charge you a percentage of your debt, your plan payments, or the projected savings to you from a debt management plan.

The IRS has revoked the nonprofit status of many so-called nonprofit credit counseling companies. To find out whether a credit counseling company is really a nonprofit, go to www.irs.gov/charities, and click on "Search for Charities." In most cases, if the company is listed there, it's a nonprofit. The website was having technical problems when this book was last updated.

When choosing a credit or debt counseling agency, look for a company that is truly a nonprofit. Do not pay "voluntary contributions" or large up-front fees. At a minimum, always ask about all fees and get a quote in writing before agreeing to give your business to a particular counselor. And review "Checklist for Choosing a Credit or Debt Counseling Agency," below.

Finding Credit and Debt Counseling Agencies Through the U.S. Trustee

With a few exceptions, all bankruptcy filers are now required to get credit and debt management counseling. Filers must get this counseling from a nonprofit agency that meets a number of requirements and has been approved by the Office of the U.S. Trustee. If you decide to get help with debt management, you would do well to choose one of these agencies—the U.S. Trustee's office oversees their operation, which gives you some protection against fraudulent practices. You can find a list of approved agencies at the U.S. Trustee's website, at www.justice.gov/ust.

Before you sign up with any agency, ask if there are people who are currently in the debt management program (and who have finished the program) who are willing to speak to you regarding their experiences. Finally, you might be in this program for years, so make sure you feel comfortable with the people you'll be dealing with. Look for friendly, courteous staff who are willing to answer your questions.

CAUTION

Make sure your bills get paid. If you sign up for a debt management plan, keep paying your bills directly until you know that your creditors have approved the plan. Make sure the agency's schedule will allow it to pay your debts before they are due each month. Check your statements or call each of your creditors the first couple of months to make sure the agency paid them on time and that the statements reflect any reductions in interest, fees, or amounts owed that are to be included in the plan.

Checklist for Choosing a Credit or Debt Counseling Agency

Here are some tips for choosing a credit counseling or debt management company:

- Use companies affiliated with the National Foundation for Credit Counseling (www.nfcc.org) or listed on the U.S. Trustee's list (www.justice.gov/ust).
- Then, check with the Better Business Bureau where the company is located, the FTC, and the state agency that regulates this type of business (the attorney general's office, the corporations department or another state agency) to find out whether complaints have been made against an agency you're considering. Even if there are no complaints, don't assume the company is fine. Sometimes companies change names so the complaints don't show up under their names. And because many people don't complain, others can be victimized before a lot of complaints show up or companies are prosecuted.
- If the company claims to be nonprofit, check with the IRS to see if it really is (www.irs.gov/charities, then click on "Search for Charities").
- Consider an agency located in your community so you can visit the agency in person before signing up.
- Find an agency that offers a range of services and counseling options, not just enrollment in a debt management plan.

- Ask about *all* costs. Fees can vary a lot among agencies. Find out what you'll have to pay to set up your account, monthly fees, percentages taken based on your debt, the reduction in your debt, or anything else. Ask whether they have a sliding scale. Get a quote in writing.
- Get a copy of all documents you are asked to sign and take time at home to read them before you sign and return them.
- Make sure your information will remain private. Find out whether the agency sells or distributes information. Get that in writing.
- Ask how employees are compensated and get that in writing. If employees are paid more for signing up customers for a debt management plan, for example, take your business elsewhere.
- Ask how credit counseling will affect your credit report or score. Some creditors will report your participation in a debt management plan to the credit reporting agencies. Ask the agency how your credit report and score will be affected if you decide to get counseling or management services, then compare that with the information about credit reports and scores in Chapter 16 to see whether the agency line seems correct.

Checklist for Choosing a Credit or Debt Counseling Agency (continued)

- To protect yourself from embezzlement, find out who handles the money you pay, and how. The company should separate money you pay toward creditors from money it receives for its services. Ideally, the money should be kept in a trust account. That means the company cannot use the money for anything other than to make your payments to creditors. Also, if the money is placed in a bank account, ask for written confirmation that each customer's money is separately FDIC insured. (If it is not, there may not be enough to cover all the money the company receives from customers if the bank fails.) Ask how much insurance the company has to protect against embezzlement by its employees. Ask for a written proof of coverage (the agency can get that from the insurance company and provide you a copy).

- Ask how many companies are involved and what they do. To avoid limits on nonprofit companies, or to evade state laws regulating prorating, some companies have part of the fees paid to different companies or have different companies provide part of the service. If more than one company is involved, it may suggest the business is trying to avoid legal restrictions meant to protect consumers.

Glossary

This glossary defines certain terms that appear frequently in this book.

Acceleration clause. A provision in a contract requiring the debtor to pay the entire balance of the contract immediately because of a failure to meet some condition, such as a failure to make payments on time.

Arrears. A general term used to describe any loan payment or debt that is past due. It's most often used to describe back-owed child support or alimony. Some people use the term "arrearages," which means the same thing.

Balloon payment. A final lump sum payment on an installment contract, such as a mortgage or car loan, that is larger than the earlier payments.

Bankruptcy. A legal proceeding in which you are relieved from paying your debts. There are two kinds of bankruptcies for individuals: Chapter 7 and Chapter 13. In Chapter 7 bankruptcy, you may be required to give up some property in exchange for the erasure of your debts. In Chapter 13 bankruptcy, you don't have to give up any property, but you must pay off a portion of your debts over three to five years. At the end of the three-to-five-year period, the balance of what you owe is wiped out.

Closed-end credit. Credit that usually involves one transaction, such as a car loan or a mortgage, with a fixed amount borrowed and a fixed repayment plan. (Compare *Open-end credit.*)

Collateral. Property pledged as security for repayment of a secured debt.

Cosigner. A person who signs a loan agreement or credit application along with the primary debtor. If the primary debtor does not pay, the cosigner is fully responsible for the loan or debt. Many people use cosigners to qualify for loans or credit cards.

Credit repair. As we use this term, the legitimate steps that people take to rebuild their credit. It also refers to getting outdated, incorrect, or incomplete information removed from one's credit report.

Credit repair organization. A business that charges substantial money and claims to be able to remove negative information from someone's credit report.

Credit score. A numerical rating that predicts how creditworthy a consumer is—that is, how likely the consumer is to repay a loan and make payments when due. A credit score is created, using a statistical program, from information about a consumer and his or her credit experiences, such as bill-paying history, the number and type of accounts, late payments, collection actions, outstanding debt, and the age of accounts, collected from the consumer's credit applications and credit report.

Default judgment. If you are sued and you do not file papers in response to the lawsuit within the time allowed, the plaintiff (the person who sued you) can ask the court to enter a default judgment against you. When a default judgment is entered, you have lost the case. You can try to get the default judgment set aside, but it can be difficult to do so.

Deficiency balance. The difference between the amount you owe a creditor who has foreclosed on your house or repossessed an item of personal property and the amount that the sale of the property brings in.

Discharge. When a bankruptcy court erases your debts.

Exempt property or exemption. Items of property you are allowed to keep if a creditor gets a judgment against you or you file for bankruptcy.

Foreclosure. The forced sale of a house by the mortgage lender or another creditor with a lien on the house (such as the IRS or an unpaid contractor) to recover what the homeowner owes.

Guarantor. A person who pledges to repay a loan or debt in the event the primary debtor does not pay. Many people use guarantors to qualify for loans or credit cards.

Installment contract. A written agreement to pay for purchased goods or services by making regularly scheduled payments of principal and interest.

Judgment. The decision issued by a court at the end of a lawsuit.

Judgment creditor. A creditor who has sued you and obtained a court judgment.

Judgment debtor. Once a creditor sues you and gets a court judgment, you may be referred to as a judgment debtor.

Judgment proof. Having little or no property or income that a creditor can legally take to collect on a judgment, now or in the foreseeable future.

Lien. A notice a creditor attaches to property telling the world that the property owner owes the creditor money.

Necessities. Articles needed to sustain life, such as food, clothing, medical care, and shelter.

Nonexempt property. The property a debtor is at risk of losing if a creditor gets a judgment against the debtor or the debtor files for bankruptcy.

Open-end credit. A credit plan that involves repeated transactions, a fluctuating balance, and no fixed repayment period. The creditor sets a credit limit and allows the consumer to charge up to that limit as long as he or she makes required payments. Open-end credit plans are often called "revolving credit," and include retail installment accounts and bank credit cards.

Postjudgment interest. Interest on a court judgment that a creditor may add from the time the judgment is entered in the court clerk's record until it is paid.

Prejudgment attachment. A legal procedure that lets an unsecured creditor tie up property before obtaining a court judgment. The attachment freezes the property—it can't be sold, spent (in the case of money), or given away.

Prejudgment interest. The interest a creditor is entitled to collect under a loan agreement or by operation of law before obtaining a court judgment.

Prepayment penalty. A fee imposed by some lenders if loans are paid off early and the lenders don't earn all the interest they had anticipated.

Repossession. When a secured creditor takes property used as collateral because the debtor has defaulted on the loan secured by the collateral.

Secured credit card. A credit card obtained by depositing some money into a savings account while the consumer has no access to that account. The money deposited is security for paying the charges on the card.

Secured creditor. A creditor owed a secured debt—that is, a debt for which payment is guaranteed by a specific item of property (collateral). If the debt isn't paid, the secured creditor can take the collateral.

Secured debt. A debt for which a specific item of property (called "collateral") guarantees payment of the debt. If the debt isn't paid, the creditor can take the collateral.

Security agreement. A contract a consumer must sign when taking out a secured loan. The agreement specifies precisely what property (collateral) can be taken by the creditor in case of default.

Security interest. The right of a secured creditor to take property in the event of default.

Statute of limitations. The time limit to file a lawsuit, as determined by state law.

Unsecured creditor. A creditor who is owed an unsecured debt. If the debtor doesn't pay, an unsecured creditor's primary recourse is to sue, obtain a court judgment, and then attach wages or seize property.

Unsecured debt. A debt for which no specific item of property guarantees repayment.

Wage assignment. A method of voluntarily paying a debt through deductions from the debtor's paycheck.

Wage attachment. A method of involuntarily paying a debt through deductions from the debtor's paycheck, commonly used to collect court judgments and back-owed child support.

Wage withholding. A method of collecting child support through withholding a portion of the debtor's paycheck.

Where to Complain

Consumer Financial Protection Bureau

P.O. Box 2900
CInton, IA 52733-2900
855-411-2372; 855-729-2372 (TTY/TDD)
www.consumerfinance.gov

The Consumer Financial Protection Bureau is the go-to federal agency for most questions related to consumer credit, including credit discrimination. It oversees the largest banks and others lenders (over $10 billion in assets), payday lenders, and the largest credit reporting agencies and debt collectors (over $10 million in assets). You can file a complaint online. Its website has a wealth of information about credit card companies, home mortgage lenders, credit reporting agencies, debt collectors, private student loan lenders, and payday lenders, among others. It has a user-friendly "Ask CFPB" that answers many questions about consumers' rights in a wide range of credit transactions. It also has a variety of reports, and invites you to weigh in on rules it proposes to better protect consumers.

Department of Housing and Urban Development

Office of Fair Housing and Equal Opportunity
451 7th Street, SW
Washington, D.C. 20410
800-669-9777; 800-927-9275 (TDD)
www.hud.gov

Click on "File a Discrimination Complaint" to file a complaint about discrimination related to housing, including applying for a mortgage loan.

Department of Justice
Civil Rights Division

Washington, D.C.
202-514-4609; 202-514-0716 (TTY)
www.justice.gov/crt

You can complain to the Justice Department about any type of discrimination.

Federal Communications Commission

Washington, D.C.
888-225-5322; 888-835-5322 (TTY)
www.fcc.gov

If you were defrauded by a telephone company, cable company, or a telemarketer, or sucked in when a communication company aired a fraudulent advertisement on radio or television, tell the FCC. States also have utility commissions or agencies that take complaints about utilities, such as telephone, water, gas, electric, and moving companies.

Federal Lending Institution Regulators

Several different agencies regulate smaller financial institutions (the larger ones are regulated by the CFPB). If you aren't sure which one regulates the lender or credit card company about which you have a complaint, send your complaint to the CFPB.

Federal Trade Commission

Consumer Response Center
Washington, D.C. 20580
877-382-4357; 866-653-4261 (TDD)
www.ftc.gov

The FTC has authority to investigate many types of consumer complaints, including credit discrimination by car dealers, stores, the smaller financial institutions, debt collectors, credit reporting agencies, and others. Although the FTC doesn't intervene in individual disputes, the information you provide may show a pattern of violations on which it can act.

Media

Contact your local newspaper, radio station, or television station "action line." Especially in metropolitan areas, these folks often have an army of volunteers ready to try to right consumer complaints.

National Consumers League

1701 K Street, NW, Suite 1200
Washington, D.C. 20006
www.fraud.org/complaint

The nonprofit National Consumer League's Fraud Center can help if you've been defrauded by a telemarketer or online. It sends copies of your complaint to local, state, and federal law enforcement agencies. You can call, write, or fill out an online complaint form.

State Consumer Protection Agencies

To find your state's consumer protection agency (sometimes called "units" or "divisions"), go to www.usa.gov/directory/stateconsumer/index.shtml.

State and Federal Legislators

Legislators often are very sensitive to the welfare of their constituents: Yours may send a letter on your behalf if your efforts have been unsuccessful. After all, it's their job to see that the laws and the agencies work well to prevent and stop fraud. To find your representatives at the state and federal level, go to www.votesmart.org and enter your zip code.

State Licensing Boards

These boards cover licensed professionals like contractors, lawyers, doctors, mechanics, and funeral directors. To find addresses and phone numbers, check your state government's website, call directory assistance for your state capital, or ask the local prosecutor's office.

State and Local Prosecutors

You may find your local or state prosecuting offices more responsive than federal agencies (local prosecutors recognize you as a voter, not just a consumer). Contact the government prosecuting attorney (often called a district attorney) in the county where you live. Contact the attorney general's office in your state. You can find contact info for the state attorney general where you live at www.naag.org. Click on "Who's My AG?" Then check the website or call the office and ask how and where to file a consumer complaint.

U.S. Postal Service

Criminal Investigations Service Center
Attn: Mail Fraud
222 S. Riverside Plaza, Suite 1250
Chicago, IL 60606-6100
877-876-2455
https://postalinspectors.uspis.gov

If you were cheated by a mail-order company or any other seller who used the U.S. mail—including a magazine advertiser—contact the U.S. Postal Inspector. You can call, mail a complaint to your local postal inspector (check the government listings of your telephone white pages for the address) or to the address listed above, or fill out an online complaint form.

Contact Information for Useful Agencies, Organizations, and Other Entities

AARP
www.aarp.org

Annual Credit Report Service
www.annualcreditreport.com
877-322-8228
P.O. Box 105283
Atlanta, GA 30348-5283

Association for Children for Enforcement of Support
www.cocommunity.net/agency/aces-assoc-children-enforcement-child-support.html

Autopedia
www.autopedia.com

Bankrate
www.bankrate.com

BenefitsCheckup (sponsored by the National Council on Aging)
www.benefitscheckup.org

Better Business Bureau
www.bbb.org

California Courts
www.courts.ca.gov

California Legislative Counsel
www.leginfo.legislature.ca.gov
https://leginfo.legislature.ca.gov

Car Talk
www.cartalk.com

CardTrack.com
https://cardtrack.com

Center for Auto Safety
www.autosafety.org

Center on Budget and Policy Priorities
www.cbpp.org

Certegy Check Services
www.askcertegy.com

Chexsystems
www.consumerdebit.com
800-428-9623

Consumer Action
www.consumer-action.org

Consumer Credit Counseling Service
www.nfcc.org

Consumer Credit Reporting Industry/OptOutPrescreen
www.optoutprescreen.com
888-567-8688

Consumer Financial Protection Bureau
www.consumerfinance.gov

Consumer Product Safety Commission
www.cpsc.gov
800-638-2772
301-595-7054 (TTY)

Consumer Reports
www.ConsumerReports.org

Consumers Union
www.consumersunion.org

Cornell Law School Legal Information Institute
www4.law.cornell.edu

Debtors Anonymous
www.debtorsanonymous.org
800-421-2383

Department of Labor
www.dol.gov

Equifax
www.equifax.com/personal
866-349-5191

Experian
www.experian.com
866-200-6020

Fannie Mae
www.fanniemae.com
800-232-6643

Federal Communications Commission
www.fcc.gov
888-225-5322
888-835-5322 (TTY)

Federal Deposit Insurance Corporation
www.fdic.gov

Federal Judiciary
www.uscourts.gov

Federal Reserve
www.federalreserve.gov

Federal Student Aid Information Center
www.studentaid.ed.gov
800-433-3243
800-730-8913 (TTY)

Federal Trade Commission
www.ftc.gov

FICO
www.myfico.com

FinAid
www.finaid.org

Freddie Mac
www.freddiemac.com
800-424-5401

Google Scholar
http://scholar.google.com

Government Printing Office
www.gpo.gov

Internal Revenue Service
www.irs.gov

**International Association of
Lemon Law Administrators**
www.ialla.net

Kelley Blue Book
www.kbb.com

Legal Services Corporation
www.lsc.gov

Lexis
www.lexisnexis.com (for legal research)

LexisNexis
https://personalreports.lexisnexis.com
888-497-0011 (for credit reports)

LIHEAP Clearinghouse
http://liheapch.acf.hhs.gov

Making Home Affordable
www.makinghomeaffordable.gov

National Association of Consumer Advocates
www.consumeradvocates.org

National Association of Attorneys General
www.naag.org

National Automobile Dealers Association
www.nada.com

National Center for Home Equity Conversion
www.reverse.org

National Center for State Courts
www.ncsc.org

National Consumer Law Center
www.nclc.org
617-542-8010

National Consumer Law Center's Student Loan Borrower Assistance Project
www.studentloanborrowerassistance.org

National Consumers League
www.fraud.org
202-835-3323

National Foundation for Credit Counseling
www.nfcc.org

National Highway Traffic and Safety Administration
www.safercar.gov
888-327-4236
800-424-9153 (TTY)

Office of Child Support Enforcement
www.acf.hhs.gov

Official State Websites
www.[*state abbreviation*].gov

Privacy Rights Clearinghouse
www.privacyrights.org

Project Vote Smart
www.votesmart.org

Public Citizen
www.citizen.org

Sallie Mae
www.salliemae.com
800-472-5543

Social Security Administration
www.ssa.gov
800-772-1213
800-325-0778 (TTY)

SupportGuidelines.com
www.supportguidelines.com

TransUnion
www.transunion.com
877-322-8228

Trial Lawyers for Public Justice
www.publicjustice.net

University of California California Digital Library
www.cdlib.org

U.S. Bankruptcy Courts
www.uscourts.gov/services-forms/bankruptcy

U.S. Department of Education
www.studentaid.ed.gov/sa
800-433-3243
877-825-9923 (TTY)

U.S. Department of Energy
www.energy.gov

U.S. Department of Health and Human Services, Medicare/Medicaid
www.cms.hhs.gov

**U.S. Department of Health and Human
Services/Office of Child Support Enforcement
in the Administration for Children and Families**
www.acf.hhs.gov

**U.S. Department of Housing and
Urban Development**
www.hud.gov

**U.S. Department of Transportation/
Aviation Consumer Protection**
www.transportation.gov/airconsumer

U.S. Government Accountability Office
www.gao.gov

U.S. Library of Congress
www.congress.gov

U.S. Trustee
www.justice.gov/ust

VersusLaw
www.versuslaw.com

Westlaw
www.westlaw.com

Worksheets

You'll find the worksheets online on this book's companion page at:

www.nolo.com/back-of-book/MT.html

Worksheet 1: Monthly Income

You need to compute your monthly net income. Net income is your gross income less deductions, such as federal, state, and local taxes; FICA; union dues; and money your employer takes out of your paycheck for your retirement plan, health insurance, child support, or loan repayment.

To figure out your monthly net income, do the following calculations (unless you are paid once a month):

- If you're paid weekly, multiply your net income by 52 and divide by 12.
- If you're paid every two weeks, multiply your net income by 26 and divide by 12.
- If you're paid twice a month, multiply your net income by 2.
- If you're paid irregularly, divide your annual net income by 12.

Net Wages or Salary	You		Spouse		Total Monthly Income
Job 1	$	+	$	=	$
Job 2		+		=	
Other Monthly Income					
Bonuses		+		=	
Commissions		+		=	
Tips		+		=	
Dividends or interest		+		=	
Rent, lease, or license payments		+		=	
Royalties		+		=	
Note or trust payments		+		=	
Alimony or child support		+		=	
Pension or retirement pay		+		=	
Social Security		+		=	
Disability pay		+		=	
Unemployment insurance		+		=	
Public assistance		+		=	
Help from relatives or friends		+		=	
Other		+		=	
Total Income	$	+	$	=	$

Worksheet 2: Your Debts

Combine for you and your spouse

1	2	3	4	5	6
Debts and other monthly living expenses	Outstanding balance	Monthly payment	Total you are behind	Is the debt secured? (If yes, list security)	Priority (1 = highest; 4 = lowest)
Home loans—mortgages, home equity loans					
Homeowners' association dues					
Motor vehicle loans/leases					
Personal and other secured loans					
Department store charges with security agreements					
Judgment liens recorded against you					
Statutory liens recorded against you					
Total this page	$	$	$		

1	2	3	4	5	6
Debts and other monthly living expenses	Outstanding balance	Monthly payment	Total you are behind	Is the debt secured? (If yes, list security)	Priority (1 = highest; 4 = lowest)
Tax debts (liens recorded)					
Student loans					
Unsecured personal loans					
Medical bills					
Lawyers' and accountants' bills					
Credit card bills					
Total this page	$	$	$		

1	2	3	4	5	6
Debts and other monthly living expenses	**Outstanding balance**	**Monthly payment**	**Total you are behind**	**Is the debt secured? (If yes, list security)**	**Priority (1 = highest; 4 = lowest)**
Department store (unsecured) and gasoline company bills					
Alimony and child support					
Back rent					
Tax debts (no liens recorded)					
Unpaid utility bills					
Other					
Total this page	$	$	$		
Total Page 1					
Total Page 2					
Total all pages					

Worksheet 3: Property Checklist

1. **Real estate**

   ☐ Residence

   ☐ Condominium or co-op apartment

   ☐ Mobile home

   ☐ Mobile home park space

   ☐ Rental property

   ☐ Vacation home or cabin

   ☐ Business property

   ☐ Undeveloped land

   ☐ Farm land

   ☐ Boat/marina dock space

   ☐ Burial site

   ☐ Airplane hangar

   ☐ Time-share

2. **Cash on hand**

   ☐ In your home

   ☐ In your wallet

   ☐ Under your mattress

3. **Deposits of money**

   ☐ Bank deposit

   ☐ Brokerage account (with stockbroker)

   ☐ Certificates of deposit (CDs)

☐ Credit union deposit

☐ Escrow account

☐ Money market account

☐ Money in a safe deposit box

☐ Savings and loan deposit

4. **Security deposits**

   ☐ Electric

   ☐ Gas

   ☐ Heating oil

   ☐ Prepaid rent

   ☐ Security deposit on a rental unit

   ☐ Rented furniture or equipment

   ☐ Telephone

   ☐ Vehicle lease

   ☐ Water

5. **Household goods, supplies, and furnishings**

   ☐ Antiques

   ☐ Appliances

   ☐ Barbecue

   ☐ Carpentry tools

   ☐ Cell phones, PDAs

   ☐ China and crystal

☐ Clocks

☐ Electronic entertainment devices and equipment

☐ Furniture

☐ Gardening tools

☐ Home computer (for personal use)

☐ Home printer, fax, or copier

☐ Lamps

☐ Lawn mower or tractor

☐ Microwave oven

☐ Patio or outdoor furniture

☐ Rugs

☐ Sewing machine

☐ Silverware and utensils

☐ Small appliances

☐ Small electronics

☐ Snow blower

☐ Security system

☐ Telephones

☐ Televisions

☐ Tools

☐ Vacuum cleaner

Worksheet 3: Property Checklist (continued)

6. **Books, pictures, art objects; stamps, coin, and other collections**

   - ☐ Art prints
   - ☐ Bibles
   - ☐ Books
   - ☐ Coins
   - ☐ Collectibles (such as political buttons, baseball cards)
   - ☐ Compact discs, records, and tapes
   - ☐ Family portraits
   - ☐ Figurines
   - ☐ Original artworks
   - ☐ Photographs
   - ☐ Sculpture
   - ☐ Stamps
   - ☐ Videotapes, DVDs

7. **Apparel**

   - ☐ Clothing
   - ☐ Furs
   - ☐ Sports clothes

8. **Jewelry**

   - ☐ Bracelets, necklaces, and earrings
   - ☐ Engagement and wedding rings
   - ☐ Gems

   - ☐ Precious metals
   - ☐ Watches

9. **Firearms, sports equipment, and other hobby equipment**

   - ☐ Bicycles
   - ☐ Board games
   - ☐ Camera equipment
   - ☐ Electronic musical equipment
   - ☐ Exercise machine
   - ☐ Fishing gear
   - ☐ Guns (rifles, pistols, shotguns, muskets)
   - ☐ Hang gliding/parasailing equipment
   - ☐ Model or remote cars or planes
   - ☐ Musical instruments
   - ☐ Scuba diving equipment
   - ☐ Ski or snowboard equipment
   - ☐ Surfboard
   - ☐ Other sports equipment
   - ☐ Other weapons (swords and knives)

10. **Interests in insurance policies**

    - ☐ Credit insurance
    - ☐ Disability insurance

    - ☐ Health insurance
    - ☐ Homeowners' or renters' insurance
    - ☐ Term life insurance
    - ☐ Whole or universal life insurance

11. **Annuities**

12. **Pension or profit-sharing plans**

    - ☐ IRA
    - ☐ Keogh
    - ☐ Pension or retirement plan
    - ☐ 401(k) account
    - ☐ 457 account

13. **Stocks and interests in incorporated and unincorporated companies**

14. **Interests in partnerships**

    - ☐ General partnership interest
    - ☐ Limited partnership interest

15. **Government and corporate bonds and other investment instruments**

    - ☐ Corporate bonds
    - ☐ Deeds of trust
    - ☐ Mortgages you own

Worksheet 3: Property Checklist (continued)

☐ Municipal bonds

☐ Promissory notes

☐ U.S. savings bonds

16. Accounts receivable

☐ Accounts receivable from business

☐ Commissions already earned

17. Family support

☐ Alimony (spousal support, maintenance) due under court order

☐ Child support payments due under court order

☐ Payments due under divorce property settlement

18. Other debts owed you where the amount owed is known and definite

☐ Disability benefits due

☐ Disability insurance due

☐ Judgments obtained against third parties but not yet collected

☐ Sick pay earned

☐ Social Security benefits due

☐ Tax refunds due for returns already filed

☐ Vacation pay earned

☐ Wages due

☐ Workers' compensation due

19. Powers exercisable for your benefit other than those listed under real estate

☐ Right to receive, at some future time, cash, stock, or other personal property placed in an irrevocable trust

☐ Current payments of interest or principal from a trust

☐ General power of appointment over personal property

20. Interests you have because of another person's death

☐ Expected proceeds from a life insurance policy, if the insured has died

☐ Inheritance from an existing estate in probate (the owner has died and the court is overseeing the distribution of the property), even if the final amount is not yet known

☐ Inheritance under a will that is contingent upon one or more events occurring, but only if the will writer has died

☐ Property you are entitled to receive as a beneficiary of a living trust, if the trustor has died

21. All other contingent claims and claims where the amount owed you is not known, including tax refunds, counterclaims, and rights to setoff claims (claims you think you have against a person, government, or corporation but haven't yet sued on)

☐ Claims against a corporation, a government entity, or an individual

☐ Potential tax refund but return not yet filed

22. Patents, copyrights, and other intellectual property

☐ Copyrights

☐ Patents

☐ Trade secrets

☐ Trademarks

☐ Trade names

23. Licenses, franchises, and other general intangibles

☐ Building permits

☐ Cooperative association holdings

Worksheet 3: Property Checklist (continued)

☐ Exclusive licenses

☐ Liquor licenses

☐ Nonexclusive licenses

☐ Patent licenses

☐ Professional licenses

24. Automobiles and other vehicles (not leased)

☐ Car

☐ Minibike or motorscooter

☐ Mobile or motor home if on wheels

☐ Motorcycle

☐ Off-road or all-terrain vehicle

☐ Recreational vehicle (RV)

☐ Trailer

☐ Truck

☐ Van

25. Boats, motors, and accessories

☐ Boat (canoe, kayak, pontoon, rowboat, sailboat, shell, yacht, etc.)

☐ Boat radar, radio, or telephone

☐ Jet ski

☐ Navigation/GPS equipment

☐ Outboard motor

26. Aircraft and accessories

☐ Aircraft

☐ Aircraft radar, radio, GPS, and other accessories

27. Office equipment, furnishings, and supplies

☐ Artwork in your office

☐ Computers, software, modems, printers (for business use)

☐ Copier

☐ Fax machine

☐ Furniture

☐ Rugs

☐ Scanner

☐ Supplies

☐ Telephones, cellphones

28. Machinery, fixtures, equipment, and supplies used in business

☐ Military uniforms and accoutrements

☐ Tools of your trade

29. Business inventory

30. Livestock, poultry, and other animals

☐ Birds

☐ Cats

☐ Dogs

☐ Fish and aquarium equipment

☐ Horses

☐ Livestock and poultry

☐ Other pets

31. Crops—growing or harvested

32. Farming equipment and implements

33. Farm supplies, chemicals, and feed

34. Other personal property of any kind not already listed

☐ Church pew

☐ Country club or golf club membership

☐ Health aids (for example, wheelchair, crutches)

☐ Portable spa or hot tub

☐ Season tickets

Worksheet 4: Property Exemptions

	1	2	3	4	5	6
	Your property	Value of property	Your ownership share (%, $)	Amount of liens	Amount of your equity	Exempt? If not, enter nonexempt amount
1.	Real estate					
2.	Cash on hand (state source of money)					
3.	Deposits of money (indicate sources of money)					
4.	Security deposits					
5.	Household goods, supplies, and furnishings					

	1	2	3	4	5	6
Worksheet 4: Property Exemptions (continued)						
Your property	Value of property	Your ownership share (%, $)	Amount of liens	Amount of your equity	Exempt? If not, enter nonexempt amount
6. Books, pictures, art objects; stamp, coin, and other collections						
7. Apparel						
8. Jewelry						
9. Firearms, sports equipment, and other hobby equipment						
10. Interests in insurance policies						
11. Annuities						

Worksheet 4: Property Exemptions (continued)					
1	2	3	4	5	6
Your property	Value of property	Your ownership share (%, $)	Amount of liens	Amount of your equity	Exempt? If not, enter nonexempt amount
12. Pension or profit-sharing plans					
13. Stocks and interests in incorporated and unincorporated companies					
14. Interests in partnerships					
15. Government and corporate bonds and other investment instruments					
16. Accounts receivable					

Worksheet 4: Property Exemptions (continued)					
1	2	3	4	5	6
Your property	Value of property	Your ownership share (%, $)	Amount of liens	Amount of your equity	Exempt? If not, enter nonexempt amount
17. Family support					
18. Other debts owed you where the amount owed is known and definite					
19. Powers exercisable for your benefit, other than those listed under real estate					
20. Interests you have because of another person's death					
21. All other contingent claims and claims where the amount owed you is not known					
22. Patents, copyrights, and other intellectual property					
23. Licenses, franchises, and other general intangibles					
24. Automobiles and other vehicles					

Worksheet 4: Property Exemptions (continued)					
1	2	3	4	5	6
Your property	Value of property	Your ownership share (%, $)	Amount of liens	Amount of your equity	Exempt? If not, enter nonexempt amount
25. Boats, motors, and accessories					
26. Aircraft and accessories					
27. Office equipment, furnishings, and supplies					
28. Machinery, fixtures, equipment, and supplies used in business					
29. Business inventory					

Worksheet 4: Property Exemptions (continued)

1 Your property	2 Value of property	3 Your ownership share (%, $)	4 Amount of liens	5 Amount of your equity	6 Exempt? If not, enter nonexempt amount
30. Livestock, poultry, and other animals					
31. Crops—growing or harvested					
32. Farming equipment and implements					
33. Farm supplies, chemicals, and feed					
34. Other personal property					
	Subtotal (Column 6):				
	Wildcard Exemption			−	
	Total Value of NONEXEMPT Property				

Worksheet 5: Daily Expenses

Daily Expenses for the Week of _____

Sunday's Expenses	Cost	Monday's Expenses	Cost
Daily Total		Daily Total	

Tuesday's Expenses	Cost	Wednesday's Expenses	Cost
Daily Total		Daily Total	

Worksheet 5 (continued)
Daily Expenses for the Week of _____

Thursday's Expenses	Cost	Friday's Expenses	Cost
Daily Total		**Daily Total**	

Saturday's Expenses	Cost	Other Expenses	Cost
Daily Total		**Daily Total**	

Worksheet 6: Monthly Budget					
Expense Category	Projected				
Home					
Rent/mortgage					
Property tax					
Insurance					
Homeowners' assn. dues					
Telephone					
Gas and electric					
Water and sewer					
Cable					
Garbage and recycling					
Household supplies					
Housewares					
Furniture and appliances					
Cleaning					
Yard/pool care					
Repairs and maintenance					
Food					
Groceries					
Breakfast out					
Lunch out					
Dinner out					
Coffee and tea					
Snacks					
Clothing					
Clothes, shoes, and accessories					
Laundry, dry cleaning					
Tailoring					
Self Care					
Toiletries/cosmetics					
Haircuts					
Gym membership					
Total Expenses Page 1					

Worksheet 6: Monthly Budget (continued)

Expense Category	Projected				
Donations					
Health Care					
Insurance					
Medications					
Vitamins					
Doctor					
Dentist					
Eye care					
Therapy					
Transportation					
Car payments (buy or lease)					
Insurance					
Registration					
Gas					
Maintenance and repairs					
Parking					
Tolls					
Public transit					
Parking tickets					
Road service (such as AAA)					
Entertainment					
Music					
Movies and rentals					
Concerts, theater, ballet, etc.					
Museums					
Sporting events					
Hobbies and lessons					
Club dues or membership					
Books, magazines and newspapers					
Software and games					
Total Expenses Page 2					

Worksheet 6: Monthly Budget (continued)					
Expense Category	Projected				
Dependent Care					
Child care					
Clothing					
School expenses					
Toys and entertainment					
Pets					
Food and supplies					
Veterinarian					
Grooming					
Education					
Tuition					
Loan payments					
Books and supplies					
Travel					
Gifts & Cards					
Personal Business					
Supplies					
Copying					
Postage					
Bank and credit card fees					
Legal fees					
Accounting services					
Taxes					
Insurance					
Savings and Investments					
Other					
Total Expenses Page 3					
Total Expenses Page 1					
Total Expenses Page 2					
Total Expenses (Pages 1, 2, & 3)					
Total Net Income					

Index

E

Earned Income Tax Credit, 44, 57

EBay.com, 42

Education and school expenses, child support and, 32, 39, 184

Electronic Fund Transfers Act, 294, 299

Employee Retirement Income Security Act (ERISA), 190

Employment
  access to your credit report, 260
  child support income withholding, 189–190, 315
  child support wage garnishment, 194
  credit report time limit exceptions for some jobs, 264
  do not disclose where you work, 131, 266
  laws on debt collector contact at debtor's place of, 142
  new hires, child support enforcement and reporting of, 189
  threats to fire you for wage garnishment, 220
  See also Self-employed people/independent contractors; Unemployment; Wage garnishment (attachment)

Equal Credit Opportunity Act, 299

Equifax, 262

Equitable distribution states
  overview, 13
  debts incurred, joint vs. separate, 14
  property acquired, joint vs. separate, 14–16, 249
  property liable for payment of debts, 16, 246
  and tenancy by the entirety, 16, 249
  See also Community property states; Married couples

Eviction
  and bankruptcy, 135
  on credit report, 259
  difficulty renting afterwards, 91
  military servicemember protections, 71
  process of, and time it takes, 90–91
  rent negotiation as alternative to, 69
  resource on, 91

Exempt property (exemptions)
  overview, 242, 246–247, 248
  bank setoffs not allowed on, 102
  bankruptcy exemptions, 236, 251–252, 253
  claiming of, hearing for, 229–230, 255
  collection of judgments stopped by, 218, 229–230
  declaration of, filing, 255
  defined, 314
  domicile and, 253
  exempt funds kept separately from nonexempt funds, 102, 253
  federal laws, 242
  federal nonbankruptcy exemptions, 253
  government assistance as, 99, 252
  homestead exemption, 226, 227, 251, 255
  increasing in value past exemption allowance, 245–246
  judgment proof status and, 99, 242
  lawyer for, 255
  nonexempt property necessary for support of family, 229, 230
  nonexempt property, selling or converting, 243–244, 254–255
  partially exempt property, 245–246
  responsibility of debtor to determine, 248
  second hearing because of changed circumstances, 229
  secured debts as exception to, 75, 242
  specific property, up to specified value, 247
  specified property, regardless of value, 247
  state laws, 242
  substituted for nonexempt property, 247
  types of, 246–248
  waiver of, in credit agreements, 159
  wildcard exemption, 248, 254
  See also Collection of judgments; Exempt property worksheet (Worksheet 4)

Exempt property worksheet (Worksheet 4)
  apply wildcard exemption, 254
  blank form, 334–339
  doubling exemptions for married couples, 253–254

⚖ NOLO

More from Nolo

Nolo.com offers a large library of legal solutions and forms, created by Nolo's in-house legal editors. These reliable documents can be prepared in minutes.

Create a Document Online

Incorporation. Incorporate your business in any state.

LLC Formation. Gain asset protection and pass-through tax status in any state.

Will. Nolo has helped people make over 2 million wills. Is it time to make or revise yours?

Living Trust (avoid probate). Plan now to save your family the cost, delays, and hassle of probate.

Provisional Patent. Preserve your right to obtain a patent by claiming "patent pending" status.

Download Useful Legal Forms

Nolo.com has hundreds of top quality legal forms available for download:

- bill of sale
- promissory note
- nondisclosure agreement
- LLC operating agreement
- corporate minutes
- commercial lease and sublease
- motor vehicle bill of sale
- consignment agreement
- and many more.

More Bestselling Books

Credit Repair
Make a Plan, Improve Your Credit, Avoid Scams
$24.99

How to File for Chapter 7 Bankruptcy
$39.99

Chapter 13 Bankruptcy
Keep Your Property & Repay Debts Over Time
$39.99

The New Bankruptcy
Will It Work For You?
$24.99

The Foreclosure Survival Guide
Keep Your House or Walk Away With Money in Your Pocket
$24.99

Every Nolo title is available in print and for download at Nolo.com.

www.nolo.com